AIDS
AGENDA

AIDS
AGENDA

Emerging Issues in Civil Rights

Edited by

Nan D. Hunter and William B. Rubenstein

THE NEW PRESS

New York

Contents

ACKNOWLEDGMENTS

This book began in 1989 when the Ford Foundation provided funding to the ACLU AIDS Project to undertake an in-depth study of AIDS-related policy issues. The study grew out of a desire to elaborate on a series of briefing papers we had published the previous year.

Many people have been involved in the long process that led to this book. First Shepard Foreman and then Christina Cuevas at the Ford Foundation provided us with guidance, support, and continuing commitment without which we would not have published this book. Other sources also provided financial assistance. The Brooklyn Law School Summer Research Stipend Fund supported Nan Hunter's work in editing the text. The American Foundation for AIDS Research funded a study of AIDS in Puerto Rico, which developed into the chapter on that topic in this volume. David Corkery, who was then AmFAR's Director of Public Affairs, took a special interest in this work. The Skadden Fellowship Foundation has funded Elizabeth B. Cooper's work with the ACLU AIDS Project for two years, thus enabling her to write the chapter of this book on HIV-infected parents. Noel Salinger, the former Development Director of the ACLU, and John Lloyd, the ACLU's Director of Foundation Relations, helped ensure funding support over the years.

Mark Jackson and Don Shacknai became the primary researchers and coordinators on this endeavor. Some of their work is reflected in the chapters they authored; much more of it is not as apparent, although it was certainly as important.

Similar substantive input was provided by a wide variety of experts. In November of 1989, the Project gathered a group of AIDS experts to help identify the subjects for study. After chapters were drafted, they were reviewed by experts in the respective fields, whose feedback was invaluable. Those who generously offered their counsel were Richard Andrias, Peter Arno, Mary Ann Baily, Robert Burgdorf, Alexander Capron, Rick Chamberlin, David Chambers, James Clyne, Marcus Conant, Mark Cunniff, Nancy Dubler, Ruth Eisenberg, Abigail English, Ruth Faden, Maria Favuzzi, Penny Ferrer, Joanne Frankfurt, Mindy Fullilove, William Gold, Larry Gostin, Hunter Handsfield, Karen Hein, Susan Hendricks, Alice Herb, Sandra Hernandez, Susan Jacobs, Kirk Johnson, Ronald Johnson, Patricia King, Helene Knickerbocker, Alan Koral, Peter Kougasian, Frances Kunreuther, Diane LaGamma, Philip Lee, Jeff Levi, Anna Marie Lewis, Malcolm Mackay, Nancy Mahon,

Miguelina Maldonado, Arlene Mayerson, Howard Minkoff, Douglas Morgan, Sondra Nelson, Norman Nickens, Alvin Novick, James Oleske, Catherine O'Neill, David Orentlicher, Andrea Palash, Jude Payne, Millie Pinott, Cathy Potler, Ellen Routenberg, Mark Scherzer, Stephen Schultz, Steven Seiverts, Lauren Shapiro, Gary Stein, Tim Sweeney, Paula Treichler, Leon Warshaw, Susan Waysdord, Deborah Weimer, Virginia Beers Wesloski, Tim Westermoreland, and Leslie Wolffe.

ACLU AIDS Project law student interns — including David Angel, Octavia Melian, and Mary Ellen Tria — have helpfully worked on sections of the study and the book in the past few years. ACLU Staff Assistants Paul D. Hendley, Michael Perelman, and Nancy Tenney provided valuable word processing, copying, proof-reading, and general human support. The ACLU's Director of Media Relations Phil Gutis offered his expertise as well.

Frank Dalton, a student at Columbia University Law School, copy-edited, cite checked, and proof-read the vast bulk of the book. His work was remarkable in both its scope and its quality. *AIDS Agenda* would truly not have been possible without his tireless devotion.

Finally, for countless invaluable discussions and immeasurable personal support, the editors would like to thank their partners, Lisa Duggan and Steven Bromer.

Nan D. Hunter
William B. Rubenstein

Introduction

The AIDS crisis will always be one of the indelible markers of the 1980s. The sudden onset of this fatal disease, part medical mystery and part social tragedy, taxed the capacity of society's institutions: from science, health care, communications, religion, art, social services, and education, to the law. Law was the primary forum in which efforts to exclude persons with this extraordinarily stigmatized disease (from their jobs, their schools, their homes and their families) were attempted and resisted. It was also the forum where society debated the conflict between individual and community interests in the formulation of public policy. *AIDS Agenda: Emerging Issues in Civil Rights* examines how the legal system responded to this challenge and analyzes the increasingly complicated questions related to AIDS which it must face in the future.

From the outset, AIDS law and social policy have been dominated by difficult questions: Should HIV-related medical records be kept confidential? If so, who should have access, and under what circumstances? Should HIV disease (as the full spectrum of AIDS and pre-AIDS symptoms was later named) be classified as a communicable condition and thus trigger laws passed early in the century mandating surveillance and possible isolation? Should people with the disease be considered disabled, and thus included in the scope of handicap discrimination laws? Should the names of all persons with HIV infection be reported to a central registry? Once an antibody test for the virus believed to cause AIDS (HIV) was licensed in 1985, society confronted a seemingly endless stream of new questions: whether testing should be mandated, for whom, under what circumstances, and why.

After a decade of heated debate, most of these questions have now been resolved, although in some instances the answers are different in different states. HIV-related medical records have been made confidential (with a variety of exceptions) by statute in almost all states. Most states do not classify HIV disease as a communicable condition, not because it isn't transmissible, but because the draconian measures associated with older disease laws have been rejected by modern-day public health authorities. HIV disease is, however, now fully recognized as a handicap for purposes of all federal civil rights laws, including an important new law that extends protection for disabled persons (including the HIV-infected) to new levels. While every state has rejected the idea of widespread mandatory HIV testing as ineffective, many states do test particular subpopulations (for example, prisoners and persons arrested for sex offenses), and the federal government continues to test military personnel and immigrants. Often these testing programs are premised on little more than the simple fact that the government has the institutional ability to implement them and the legal authority to compel them. Finally, the states remain divided almost equally between those that require name-reporting of HIV-infected persons and those that do not.

While some of the early issues became more settled in the law, others persisted: Should insurance companies be allowed to exclude persons with this disease (but not other expensive-to-treat conditions) from coverage? How should publicly financed health care, like Medicaid, deal with this new challenge? What policies should be adopted in the workplace? Moreover, the impact of the disease itself shifted. Originally associated almost entirely with gay men, the disease spread to the population of intravenous drug users and their sex partners. This demographic change yielded more new questions for the law and for policy-makers: How does HIV disease impact differently on women, who comprise an increasing proportion of HIV cases? What happens to the children who become orphans when their parents die of AIDS? How are the laws governing medical care for adolescents affected? And in light of limited resources, must HIV care be rationed?

In November 1989, the American Civil Liberties Union's AIDS Project, funded by the Ford Foundation, brought together a group of experts from across the United States to identify the questions that would shape HIV-related law and policy in the decade to come. The primary goal of this group was to highlight those issues that would have the most serious impact on the populations at greatest risk of HIV infection and disease in the years ahead. *AIDS Agenda* presents the results of the study that grew out of that original meeting. Its nine chapters each assess a separate area of HIV-related policy and each contains a set of recommendations for guiding policy-makers through the next wave of the epidemic.

As these studies show, two overarching trends in the dynamics of the disease will have a massive impact on policy. The first is the shift in the population of HIV-infected persons mentioned above: while the rate of new infections has decreased dramatically among gay men, it has surged among intravenous drug users and their sex partners. Consequently, the epidemic has changed, from an almost exclusively male disease, to one affecting an increasing number of women; from an almost exclusively adult disease, to one affecting growing numbers of adolescents and children; from a disease with a majority of white patients, to one in which patients are disproportionately people of color; and from a disease striking the affluent as well as the poor, to one concentrated among the most impoverished and disempowered segments of society.

Second, HIV disease, although still not curable, has become increasingly treatable. This development, too, has multiple consequences. People with HIV disease have the potential to live longer, more productive lives. The disease no longer kills quickly after first diagnosis but, rather, is increasingly a chronic and long-term disability, involving episodes of illness over a period of years. This potential for longer life, however, exists *only* if patients have access to early treatment. Early diagnosis, together with continuity of care and treatment, mark the boundary between years of life and sudden death.

These characteristics alone, however, challenging as they are, do not account for all of the difficulty policy-makers face. HIV has been haunted from the beginning by the intense stigma attached to homosexuality. Now, even though the epidemiology of the disease is shifting, the stigma remains, intensified by attitudes of prejudice toward people of color and those associated with illegal drug use.

As a result, public sentiment to punish people with this disease continues. As the chapters in this book emphasize, the pressure for coercive measures is likely to grow worse as the disease becomes increasingly concentrated among low-income groups, which traditionally have been subject to harsher social control mechanisms. Punitive approaches, however, even if supported by popular opinion, will undercut the willingness of people at risk to make changes in behavior. Such changes must ultimately be voluntary, as high-risk behavior is impossible to police. Thus, the most effective public health programs will be those which succeed in enlisting the cooperation of the persons whose lives are affected.

This conflict, between the need for sound public health strategies and the impulse to punish, will be perhaps most acute in the criminal justice system. As outlined in chapter 8, "The Criminalization of HIV", prosecutors are increasingly seeking convictions of HIV-infected persons for spitting or biting, actions that do not transmit HIV. Our study strongly recommends that individuals not be prosecuted for acts for which there is no significant risk of transmission. Such prosecutions are not only ill-advised and mean-spirited, they also undermine efforts to educate people about the *real* risks of HIV transmission.

Several chapters of *AIDS Agenda* analyze the many aspects of access to health care. To begin with, barriers to health care for people with HIV disease abound. Although limitations in the national Medicaid program create health care access problems for all poor persons, we demonstrate the particular additional problems people with HIV disease have faced in gaining adequate Medicaid coverage. Second, private insurers, especially employers that self-insure, have attempted, quite successfully, to screen out HIV-infected persons through a variety of mechanisms—from HIV-testing individual insurance applicants to creating arbitrary and artificial limitations on HIV-related coverage. Third, health care providers have often simply refused to treat HIV-infected patients. And finally, the national fiscal crisis has created situations in which state Medicaid agencies or public hospitals are essentially rationing their limited resources—often to the detriment of people, such as the HIV-infected, deemed to be "incurable." These factors create an increasing likelihood that any concrete advances in treatment of the disease will be merely hypothetical for many patients. Unless this disparity is narrowed, a brutally stark two-tiered system of care for people with HIV disease will be in place by the end of the decade.

Accordingly, chapter 6, "Wealth = Health: The Public Financing of AIDS Care," recommends specific changes in Medicaid eligibility, coverage, and procedures to better reflect the realities of HIV disease, as well as a reduction or elimination of Medicare's eligibility waiting period. Similarly, chapter 5, "Health Insurance: The Battle over Limits on Coverage," recommends that private insurers, especially entities that self-insure, be prohibited from utilizing practices such as caps and exclusions that arbitrarily limit coverage for HIV disease but not for other comparable conditions. Chapter 4, "'The Very Fabric of Health Care': The Duty of Health Care Providers to Treat People Infected with HIV," calls for better education of health care providers, both about the true risks of treating people with HIV and the methods of preventing transmission and about their legal and ethical obligations to provide care.

Chapter 7, "The HIV Epidemic in Puerto Rico," is a case study that shows how the issues surrounding access to health care become even more critical when financial resources are severely limited. This chapter considers the sociocultural aspects of the epidemic in Puerto Rico, their effect on education and prevention programs, and issues of discrimination and stigma. In conclusion, the study recommends the creation of a comprehensive educational plan to counter the effects of stereotypes and negative attitudes toward persons with HIV disease, increased legal advocacy services to combat discrimination, the prompt removal of the cap on federal Medicaid expenditures on the island, and the mobilization of community leadership to confront the devastating effects of prejudice and discrimination. It also assesses the potential efficacy of civil rights remedies to discriminatory health care rationing programs.

Another theme of the book is the need to refocus and reformulate public policy initiatives in light of the changing patient population. Chapter 1, "Complications of Gender: Women and HIV Disease," observes how most of what has been written about women and HIV has focused on women as mothers, and on the issue of perinatal transmission of HIV from mother to fetus—framing women as *posing* a risk rather than *being* at risk. Viewing women not as vectors of transmission but as persons with concerns about their own care and treatment, the chapter focuses on three critical areas where legal and policy issues for women are specific and gender-linked: prevention, access to health care, and reproductive decision-making. The study recommends the implementation of prevention programs that target women, confront directly the issue of sexual inequality, and are sensitive to the diverse ethnic and cultural backgrounds of women affected by HIV. Access to health care for women requires recognition by the Centers for Disease Control and others of the specific clinical manifestations of the disease in women; testing and counseling programs must be integrated into the locales where women, especially those in the low-income urban neighborhoods hardest hit by HIV disease, actually go for medical and social services; women must also be included in clinical drug trials. Finally, policy regarding reproductive decision-making must start with the assumption that women have the same rights to autonomous determinations of life choices as do men. It is essential to shift the discussion of women and HIV away from debates over the narrow issue of coerced testing, toward a process of developing and implementing innovative policies that guarantee women access to all the components of quality care.

Related chapters on parents and adolescents with HIV disease examine critical gaps in the laws that govern the care of children orphaned by this disease and the ability of minors to consent to testing and treatment. It is crucial that these gaps be corrected and that they be addressed with the same sense of urgency that motivated policy-makers to seek, for example, guarantees of confidentiality for HIV-related medical records in the early years of the epidemic. Thus, chapter 3, "HIV-Infected Parents," urges that HIV infection not be used as a factor in custody and visitation decisions, and that modifications be made in the guardianship system to address the needs of HIV-infected single mothers. These revisions would include the establishment of flexible "springing guardianships" to reflect the intermittent periods of health and incapacity of HIV-infected mothers, as well as streamlined court processes, greater cooperation among social welfare agencies, and increased confidentiality protections.

For adolescents, numerous problems, both legal and social, arise from their dangerous perch between childhood and adulthood. Just as geographic, developmental, psychological, and social factors place them right in the path of the disease, legal constraints undercut attempts to provide adolescents with systematic and effective treatment and prevention programs. For example, the legal authority for adolescents to consent to medical care, including HIV-testing, is often vague, and the legal basis for keeping their medical records confidential (especially from their parents) is similarly murky. What's worse, in many places, adolescents cannot qualify on their own for government benefit programs, including Medicaid. Chapter 2, "Betwixt and Between: Adolescents and HIV," recommends that laws provide clear authority for voluntary adolescent testing and treatment *without* the mandatory parental consent or notification requirements that would deter teenagers from being tested.

Despite the need for so many changes in attitude, policy, and legislation, there is at least one positive note: Congress's 1990 enactment of the Americans with Disabilities Act (ADA). This far-reaching civil rights bill prohibits discrimination based on disability—"disability" being defined to include AIDS and HIV disease. A major priority for advocates and service providers will now be to secure compliance with the new law. Accordingly, chapter 9, "Workplace Issues: HIV and Discrimination," examines the ramifications of the ADA for responding to HIV in the workplace. The chapter recommends that the promise of the ADA be made real for people with HIV disease through intensive implementation programs, including education, adequate administrative oversight, and the provision of legal services.

During the 1980s, U.S. lawmakers played a desperate game of catch-up with what was then a new and terrifying disease. National policy-making, according to the first report of the National Academy of Sciences, reflected an overall "lack of cohesiveness and strategic planning." *AIDS Agenda* is an attempt to help legislators and others concerned with health care policy chart a more coherent and humane course in the coming years. The law's response to HIV disease will forge the contours of fundamental civil rights principles in each of the areas this book addresses. Most importantly, if prompt attention is paid to these issues now, literally thousands of lives may be saved in the coming decade and beyond.

Nan D. Hunter and
William B. Rubenstein

I

EMERGING POPULATIONS

During the 1980s, the public's perception of AIDS was that it was a disease of gay men, and secondarily of male intravenous drug users. With the onset of the 1990s, HIV disease is in fact increasingly a disease of women, of adolescents, of people of color, and of the poor. As the populations most at risk for HIV disease shift, the very concept of civil rights for people with the disease will shift also. The chapters in Part I discuss how this change in the demographics of the disease will be reflected in the law, particularly the ways in which legal issues involving women, adolescents, and parents will shape the new scope of the term "civil rights."

The issues emerging around these new groups present challenges at least as difficult as those raised earlier in the epidemic. They include whether the state or private doctors can skew counseling of pregnant women with HIV in favor of abortion, whether newborns should be tested for HIV without parental consent, whether guardianship for children will have to be revamped to address the problems raised when parents have HIV disease, whether a judge assessing custody or visitation claims can determine and consider the HIV status of the parent, and whether teenagers can secure testing and treatment without notifying parents. All will lead legislators and policymakers to reassess, in many ways, the impact of this disease on a wide range of legal structures.

While HIV-related policy issues during the first decade of the epidemic were often strongly influenced by the biased attitudes of policymakers, particularly by anti-gay prejudice, the emerging civil rights issues are just as likely to be infused by negative attitudes: toward racial minorities, women, indigent persons, and especially those associated with drug use. The major challenges for policymakers will be to transcend their biases, and to consider the critical questions presented with the urgency their context requires.

1

COMPLICATIONS OF GENDER: WOMEN AND HIV DISEASE

By Nan D. Hunter

The popular conception and typical media image of the person with AIDS (PWA) is male — either a gay man or a male intravenous drug user (IVDU). The reality of who is affected by this disease is rapidly shifting, however, as a growing number of PWAs are women. The statistics are dramatic:

- Epidemiologists expect that by 1994 there will be more women than gay men diagnosed with AIDS each year in New York State.[1]

- AIDS is already the leading cause of death for African-American women aged 15 to 44 in New York and New Jersey, and is the third highest cause of death for all women in that age category in those states. Scientists project that AIDS will become one of the five leading causes of death for all women in that age category nationwide.[2]

- HIV disease is spreading at a faster rate among women than among men. During 1990, diagnosed AIDS cases increased 29 percent among women, compared to 18 percent among men.[3]

- Worldwide, the number of AIDS cases among women is expected to equal the number among men by the year 2000.[4]

Media portrayals of women and AIDS early in the epidemic tended to fall into three categories: women were simply absent; women were depicted primarily as vectors of transmission;[5] or women were depicted as the victims of bisexual male partners.[6] Only the last category focused on women as persons at risk of illness and death, and its emphasis on bisexual men was slanted to highlight the risk perceived most threatening to middle-class, primarily white, women.[7]

In fact, the risk to women has been substantial and is rapidly increasing, but it is heavily skewed by race. The rate of death from AIDS is nine times greater among African-American women than among white women.[8] More than 50 percent of American women who were diagnosed during the first decade of the AIDS epidemic were African-American; more than 20 percent were Hispanic.[9] In New York state, by 1990, 52.1 percent of women with AIDS were African-American and 29.8 percent were Hispanic.[10] It is specifically among women of color in the United States that HIV disease has reached epidemic proportions.[11]

The risk is also heavily skewed by economic class. According to data from the U.S. Centers for Disease Control (CDC), half of the cases among women are the result of intravenous drug use, an activity highly correlated to poverty. Another 20 percent of the cases result from sexual contacts with men who are IVDUs. Sexual relations with men who are bisexual account for only 3 percent of the total.[12]

Although more accurate media portrayals of women as PWAs have begun to appear, there is still a tendency to focus on women as *posing* a risk rather than *being* at risk. Most of what has been written about women and AIDS has focused on women as mothers and on the issue of perinatal transmission of HIV from mother to fetus. Many of the epidemiological studies have concerned women who work as prostitutes.[13] This chapter approaches women not as vectors of transmission, but as persons whose lives are at risk and who are entitled to the highest quality of care and treatment.

The impact of HIV disease on women is multifaceted. In many respects, HIV-infected women must fight the same battles as infected men against discrimination and the possibility that states will impose coercive sanctions unrelated to public health effectiveness. As workers, as patients seeking health care providers who will treat them, as persons coping with both public and private health care financing systems, and as defendants charged with criminal offenses, women and men of the same socioeconomic class face many of the same problems. This chapter does not revisit each of those issues, nor does it consider the questions of optimal state policy toward women who work as prostitutes, or men charged with sexual assault, subjects which are treated in other chapters. Instead, the focus here is on three critical areas where the legal and policy issues for women are specific and gender-linked: prevention, access to health care, and reproductive decision-making.

I. Prevention

One of the major achievements in the gay male community during the 1980s was the creation of innovative educational programs encouraging behavior changes to reduce the risk of HIV transmission. As a result, the incidence of new HIV infections among gay men fell sharply. Women face a challenge even more formidable in the 1990s — to develop prevention programs that tackle the issue of negotiating safer sex between women and their partners and that are sensitive to the diverse ethnic and cultural backgrounds of women affected by HIV.

Heterosexually active women approach the issue of negotiating sexual practices with a partner in a context that is fundamentally different in two critical ways from the situation of gay men. First, two male partners more often bring equal social power to what is essentially a bargaining situation. By contrast, women as a group lack the same social power as men. Many heterosexual women, for financial or cultural reasons, do not have equal power to negotiate behavior changes in a partner.[14] Second, two male partners who alternate positions in anal or oral intercourse stand at equal risk of becoming infected unless they use condoms. In heterosexual vaginal intercourse, however, women are more likely than men to become infected. Thus, men engaging in heterosexual intercourse are at less risk than their female partners of becoming infected, and have less of a selfish motivation to use condoms.

Prevention programs that prioritize the goal of stopping male-to-female transmission must be designed to overcome this power differential rather than to ignore it. One approach is to target for women campaigns that confront directly the issue of sexual inequality. Materials geared to promoting women's empowerment, enhancing self-esteem, and teaching sexual negotiation skills — framed in ways sensitive to the particular cultural dynamics of differing racial and ethnic communities[15] — should form the heart of prevention efforts geared to women. As Dr. Mindy Fullilove of the HIV Center for Clinical and Behavioral Studies at Columbia University notes, "a manifestation of policy is carried in [the content of] prevention messages. The messages [currently] directed at women reinforce their 'aloneness' with this problem."[16] Prevention messages should alleviate the sense of isolation many women feel, and reinforce change.

Such programs can draw on the strengths as well as the needs of the communities of the affected women. A study focusing on young African-American women, for example, noted that although the black community has "a vital public dialogue about sex,...the private, intimate conversations between an individual man and an individual woman may be less open and less forthright."[17] Programs should be free to take full advantage of such a "vital public dialogue," using, when appropriate, vernacular language with which community members are familiar and comfortable. Restrictions which limit public funding of AIDS prevention materials to terms and descriptors which are not "offensive" to the general public should be eliminated.[18] The priority of a prevention program should be to develop

> a means of communicating that will empower women to negotiate with men how, and under what circumstances, sexual activity (and relationships) will be conducted.... At the heart of such prevention is the development of explicit communication, free of jargon and ambivalence, set in a context in which black women are again restored to a position of respect.[19]

Specifically, it is the negotiation of condom use that many women report may lead to the risk of physical harm or financial abandonment.[20] Such concerns have led some researchers to seek methods for the prevention of HIV transmission that could be used and controlled by women, without requiring, as condoms do, the cooperation of the male partner.[21] Funding for such research, and the possible development of a cream or jell that would kill the HIV virus, and which women could apply vaginally, should be made a priority.

Nevertheless, not all programs addressing heterosexual transmission should be addressed to women. Policies that assign to women the full responsibility for safer heterosexual practices merely continue and reinforce the assumption of lack of responsibility on the part of men that creates the risk to women. Programs should also be directed to heterosexual men with the same message of the need for changes in sexual practices that is routinely directed toward gay men. In the constellation of safe sex programs, heterosexual men should not be the sole group exempted from responsibility.

For women who have sex with women, the prevention issues are different. Here the primary issue is a false perception of security. Because there have been so few AIDS cases reported among lesbians, there is a widely held view that lesbians have essentially no risk. One early lesson of this disease, however, was that risk depends on behavior, not status. The woman who has sex with a woman who has used intravenous drugs or who has had sexual contacts with an HIV-infected person may be placing herself at risk.[22]

The problem of a false sense of security is compounded by the unwillingness of scientists to conduct research that includes the question of transmission between female partners. The research on the risk of transmission from an HIV-infected woman to a sexual partner has assumed that the partner is male. Basic research needs to be undertaken which would analyze how that risk differs, if it does, when the partner is also female.

II. Access to Care

Meaningful access to care has been an elusive goal for many persons with HIV disease. For women, special barriers have arisen that have led to even greater problems in securing meaningful access to the best of the available treatments at the earliest times. These issues can be divided into three categories: threshold issues of diagnosis, reporting, and study of the disease; insufficient access to testing and treatment; and biased research and development protocols for new drugs.

A. Diagnosis, Reporting, and Study of the Disease

The social invisibility of women in the HIV epidemic begins at the beginning of the care process — with diagnosis and data gathering. A failure to diagnose HIV prevents women from gaining access to medical systems for treating HIV patients; from legal systems that are triggered by an AIDS diagnosis (such as disability benefits); and from resource allocation systems, which allot funding based on the count of AIDS or HIV patients. Even when diagnosed, basic epidemiological counting of PWAs classifies women in somewhat different ways than it does men.

Misdiagnosis of women occurs largely in two situations — one *ad hoc*, and one the result of formal policy. The first kind has occurred because the perception that HIV is a male disease has been widespread among health care providers as well as among the general public. Because physicians do not expect women patients to have HIV disease, they are not alert for its symptoms when treating women. Thus, even well-known signs of AIDS, such as *Pneumocystis carinii* pneumonia, tend to be misdiagnosed in women.[23] Delay in an accurate diagnosis leads to delay in treatment and missed opportunities for medical intervention early enough in the course of the disease to significantly prolong life. The result can be a brutally faster death.

The second kind of misdiagnosis reflects the history of the very definition of AIDS. The official definition of "AIDS" is actually a kind of checklist. HIV disease can be present in forms that range from the early asymptomatic stage to the last stage in which AIDS is fully developed. The definitional criteria for when this final stage is reached — and thus for a formal diagnosis of AIDS — consist of a list of possible symptoms and opportunistic infections. However, this definitional checklist, developed by CDC early in the epidemic when virtually all the people with AIDS in the United States were gay or bisexual men, does not include any gynecological manifestations as possible indicators of AIDS (or of earlier stages of the disease).

There is growing evidence that, for many women, gynecological symptoms are the first manifestations of HIV disease. Chronic pelvic inflammatory disease (PID) and refractory vaginal candidiasis have been identified in the medical literature as signals of underlying immunodeficiency.[24] Researchers have begun to recognize that both may be presenting symptoms of HIV disease. When present in women with HIV disease, PID and vaginal candidiasis are especially resistant to treatment, as well as painful and disabling. Their presence also apparently indicates that rapid onset of other, potentially fatal, infections is likely. Additionally, one study has found a link between cervical cancer and HIV infection, suggesting that abnormalities in cervical cells — as could be detected in a Pap smear test — may also be an early indicator of HIV disease.[25]

The ramifications of being excluded from the CDC definition are both medical and legal. One legal consequence of the noninclusion of gynecological symptoms in the AIDS definition is that women who present with these symptoms are denied presumptive eligibility for disability payments under the Supplemental Security Income (SSI) program, which has been determined by reference to the CDC's official definition of AIDS.[26] Eligibility for SSI often determines eligibility for Medicaid (as discussed in chapter 6, "Wealth = Health"). In response to this situation, civil rights advocates filed a class action complaint asserting that the present noninclusion violates statutory and constitutional protections.[27] In addition, legislation has been introduced that would amend SSI program eligibility to incorporate gynecological symptoms of HIV disease.[28]

The presence or absence of a formal diagnosis of AIDS has legal ramifications in other situations as well. In New York City, for example, the agency responsible for providing shelters for homeless persons adopted a policy of permitting only those with a diagnosis of AIDS to live in shelters with individual rooms and bathrooms.[29]

Because of protests that the exclusion of gynecological symptoms from the definition has led to denials of both health care and disability benefits to women, federal officials modified the definition and are reconsidering whether the disability test should depend on the CDC definition at all.[30] The CDC announced in August 1991 that it would add a new indicator to the official definition of AIDS: if a person's T-cell count is below 200 per cubic millimeters of blood, that person will be formally diagnosed as having AIDS. Advocates for women pointed out, however, that T-cell tests are never done unless a person has tested seropositive for HIV, and the problem remains that doctors often do not recommend HIV testing for women patients. Disputes continue regarding both the medical definition of AIDS and the definition used to determine disability.

Beyond the point of diagnosis, there is the question of how the disease progresses in women. To date, there has been no study of the natural history of HIV disease in women. Women are missing from every aspect of the study of AIDS:

> Fundamental questions about the progression of this disease in women have not been asked or answered. Is cervical cancer more common in HIV-infected women? How does HIV infection affect pregnancy and childbirth? Do the different hormones in women and men affect the course of HIV infection? Do women fall prey to different opportunistic infections than men do? Do women respond differently to treatment regimens established for male patients? Do women suffer different side effects and toxicities from AIDS medications? Do women survive a shorter time after the diagnosis of AIDS has been made? Are the causes of death in women different than in men?[31]

Related to problems with diagnosis and study of the disease is the question of how CDC statistics count women with AIDS. These numbers affect how the issues associated with women and AIDS are addressed, and they significantly shape the allocation of resources. There are multiple ways in which undercounting can harm women. One is simply that if fewer women are recognized as having HIV disease, those locales and institutions that treat large numbers of women will receive less funding, and ultimately the patients' care will be diminished.

Another aspect of the counting issue is the relationship between CDC transmission categories and the formulation of and funding for prevention programs. For example, the relative frequency of transmission by drug use and transmission by sexual contact may be misstated by current statistical procedures because of the CDC's policy of assigning cases to the risk category believed to be most likely. A woman who has used intravenous drugs herself and who also has had sexual relations with a partner who has used drugs is automatically assigned to the transmission category of drug user, even though there is no way to know by which mechanism she became infected.[32] The conflation of risk behaviors which results from this categorization could mask important information, making it more difficult to assess the effectiveness of prevention programs geared to one particular set of behaviors or another. It also erases as a category those women who face double exposure risks.

Recasting the perception of who HIV patients really are will involve revising the fundamental structure for diagnosis, data gathering and other methods of studying the disease. Policymakers can no longer ignore the ways that existing models do not account for the symptoms or situations of women with this disease.

B. Lack of Access to Testing and Treatment

Testing and counseling are the first step to treatment. That essential first step will not be available for women unless testing and counseling programs are much more fully integrated into the locales where women, especially those in the low-income urban neighborhoods hardest hit by HIV disease, actually go for medical and social services.

HIV testing programs are a double-edged sword. There was great resistance to testing in the early stages of the epidemic because of discrimination against HIV-infected persons and the absence of treatments. Now, however, treatment prior to the onset of symptoms has become a reality. In addition to silence, delay and denial equal death. In this context, the absence of convenient access to testing and counseling programs constitutes a denial of care.

By far the biggest access problem for women is poverty. Most women with the disease have low incomes and must rely on inadequate public resources for health care. For many poor people with HIV disease, treatment prior to full-blown illness is only a theoretical possibility, as chapter 6 ("Wealth = Health") outlines. Some issues, however, are particular to women.

Without easy access to testing, early diagnosis will not occur. According to Marie St. Cyr, former director of the Women and AIDS Resource Network of New York, half of the women with HIV disease counseled by her organization first learned that they were infected when a pediatrician diagnosed their child as having the disease.[33] Other advocates report similar experiences with women having little effective access to diagnosis of HIV disease. Even physicians treating women for other conditions, including childbirth, may be reluctant to recommend testing out of an unwillingness to deal with the consequences of learning that the patient has this particular disease.[34] Because of uncertainties about the effects of such HIV treatments as AZT on a fetus, some pregnant women have experienced difficulty in getting prescriptions for these medications. An Institute of Medicine report in 1991 recommended that women not be denied these treatments during pregnancy.[35]

Family planning and prenatal care facilities are among the locations where low-income women are most likely to seek medical care, and thus public health resources have been targeted for the establishment of testing and counseling programs in these facilities. But many more points of intervention are possible and need to be prioritized. Other locales where HIV prevention information could be distributed include social services offices, such as those for the Aid to Families with Dependent Children (AFDC) and the Women, Infants and Children (WIC) programs for nutritional supplements. An Illinois law, for example, requires drug-related information and referrals for treatment to be provided in WIC program offices.[36] Free condoms should be available wherever information is disseminated.

One failure in the provision of services deserves special mention. There is an abysmal shortage of drug abuse treatment programs for women, especially in light of the high correlation between drug use and

HIV infection. Drug treatment programs are scarce to begin with. As of 1987, only 338,365 slots were available for an estimated 4 million addicts.[37] The majority of the programs that do exist serve men only.[38] The situation is especially critical for pregnant women seeking drug treatment.[39] The need for drug treatment programs for women is massive and urgent. To be effective, such programs must provide the kinds of services, such as child care (which is necessary if women are actually to use the facilities), and the kinds of therapeutic models that are geared to the social realities of women's lives.[40]

C. Biased Research Protocols

One of the key demands of AIDS activists during the 1980s was for accelerated development of drugs to treat HIV disease. Significant changes in drug research protocols were adopted by federal agencies in response to these demands. Procedures for the selection of subjects for inclusion in clinical trials, however, have proved extremely resistant to change. The selection bias for participation disfavors women with HIV disease in multiple ways:

> In drug trial recruitment, HIV-infected women suffer quadruple jeopardy: first, they may be excluded because they are women and either potentially or actually pregnant; second, they may be excluded because they are members of minority groups and lack access to the health care system in general, and to research in particular; third, they may be excluded because they are drug users and are presumed to be noncompliant subjects; and fourth, they may be excluded because most of the trials so far have focused on AIDS itself, and many of the women have been infected recently and are not symptomatic or do not have a clinical diagnosis of AIDS. [41]

The current guidelines of the Food and Drug Administration require that selection of subjects for clinical trials be "equitable," but they also categorize all women "of childbearing potential" as excludable from most drug trials.[42] The FDA defines all premenopausal women capable of becoming pregnant, including those using contraception, as falling into the excludible category. Although the FDA guideline does not require exclusion of women, it permits such restrictions, which in fact have been standard practice in the conduct of clinical trials for many years.[43] In 1990, the National Institutes of Health published a revised version of its guide for grants and contracts specifying that the number of women participants in clinical trials should be proportional to the prevalence among women of the condition under study.[44] No reconciliation of the FDA policy (which covers private pharmaceutical company research) and the new and still evolving NIH policy has yet occurred.

Drug manufacturers and investigators justify the exclusion of women by their fear of liability for *in utero* injuries, which could be the basis for claims by children born with congenital anomalies. Although there are no cases directly on point, existing principles of law provide that manufacturers of experimental drugs are protected from strict liability for harm caused by the drug, provided that they have adequately warned and obtained consent from test subjects.[45] Thus, to secure recovery for injuries caused by a new or experimental drug, a plaintiff must prove that the warnings she received prior to taking the drug were inadequate.[46] Although none of these cases has involved reproductive effects on a later born child, there is no case that suggests that the same informed consent standard would not protect against such liability.[47]

In the meantime, drugs for a number of conditions, including HIV disease, are being licensed and marketed without ever having been tested in women. Although another of the reasons cited by drug researchers for excluding women is the desire for homogenous study samples, if gender-based variations in the pharmacological effects of a particular drug do exist, allowing the drug to be licensed without tests that include women amounts to an extraordinary disregard of women's health. In response to this problem, community-based AIDS research groups have developed protocols specifically designed to include women.[48]

Given that the rationale for excluding women most often relates to childbearing, it is not surprising that the greatest reluctance to include women focuses on those who are pregnant.[49] In response to these concerns, a group of experts who convened to recommend a wide range of protocols for clinical research on HIV disease developed a sound approach to the problem of pregnant women in trials. This working group recommended:

> Pregnant women should not be categorically excluded from Phase II/III protocols or from access to drugs under treatment INDs.
>
> If a drug is potentially life saving and no other treatment exists, a pregnant woman must be permitted access either to a Phase II/III trial or to a treatment IND.

> The generalized presumption that pregnant women are eligible for trials can
> be rebutted only by a showing of serious risk to the future child; and either (a)
> the availability of a potentially equally effective alternative treatment for the
> woman; or (b) little expected benefit to her from the particular protocol.[50]

Revision of the FDA's procedures is long overdue. Guidelines should encourage the inclusion, not exclusion, of women as subjects. The classification of women based on childbearing potential should be eliminated. Instead, the FDA should require that drug manufacturers and researchers specify the potential effects of an experimental drug on reproduction, for men as well as women. Research on drugs of possibly great benefit to a woman, such as those which may be lifesaving or constitute a cure, should be open to all women, including pregnant women. Lastly, once revisions are made, it will be essential for the FDA to insist that drug trials not merely be opened to women, but also that previously underrepresented subjects, such as women, be effectively recruited.

III. Reproductive Decision-Making

One of the modes of transmitting HIV is "vertical," i.e., from parent to child.[51] A pregnant woman may transmit HIV *in utero* — through her blood system, which she shares with the fetus. The risk that a baby born to an HIV-infected woman will be HIV-infected is approximately 30 percent.[52] Current testing techniques are imprecise: 70 percent of infants born to HIV-infected mothers are not themselves infected, although all such infants test HIV antibody positive for approximately the first year to 18 months of life because the maternal antibodies are then still circulating in their bloodstreams.[53] Thus, HIV testing of newborns constitutes, in effect, testing of the mothers, all of whom are identified by the seropositivity of the infant, rather than of the seropositive children, only 30 percent of whom are actually infected.

The policy and law issue related to women and AIDS that has garnered by far the most attention has been whether coercion by the state is justified as a mechanism to reduce the number of children with HIV disease or to treat such children.[54] The two most common proposals have been for mandatory HIV testing of pregnant women and mandatory testing of newborn children. A number of "blue ribbon" or expert panels have recommended that such testing be widely available and routinely offered and encouraged, but not required.[55] Nonetheless, calls for coercive testing of these two groups persist.[56]

As scientists develop new treatments and learn more about the disease in infants, there may be new proposals for other kinds of state interventions. One already suggested is that treatment with AZT during pregnancy may benefit the fetus and prolong the life of the child after birth.[57] If this hypothesis proves true, the question will arise of whether to require pregnant women not only to be tested but also, if seropositive, to take certain treatments.

Lastly, although no cases have yet arisen, a number of laws that criminalize HIV transmission could apply to a woman who, knowing that she is infected, decides to become pregnant and to carry her pregnancy to term.[58] In a related area, a number of women who used illegal drugs have been prosecuted for "distribution" of drugs to their children on the basis of perinatal transmission or have been subjected to child-abuse or neglect proceedings as a means of removing the child from their custody. Whether that same kind of prosecutorial strategy will be applied to women with HIV disease, especially those women who may also have used intravenous drugs, is yet to be seen.

Suspicion about the motivation for mandatory testing of either pregnant women or newborns is heightened by the context of such programs. The government has shown no great zeal for insuring the health of babies in the African-American and Hispanic communities, which would be the most affected. Infant mortality rates among those communities in the United States compare to the rates in impoverished nations, and normal prenatal and pediatric care is often unavailable.[59]

Lastly, testing of pregnant women raises issues particular not only to the race and economic status of the persons to be tested, but also as to how medical interventions have been directed against women. To an extraordinary degree, the social role of women — in the family, in the workplace, and in the body politic — has been constructed around the single fact that women, and not men, have the capacity to become pregnant and to give birth.[60] Singling out pregnant women for testing resonates with a history of subordinating women's health to that of others and of using women's reproductive capacity as a mechanism for controlling women. For women of color, it resonates with a history of medical interventions that includes forced sterilizations,[61] as well as the threat of coerced contraception, through such modern devices as implants.[62] Against this background, the eagerness to impose by force of law a testing system which also stigmatizes women raises questions of whether unspoken motives or, at the least, unconsidered consequences, lay beneath the surface of these proposals.

A. Mandatory Prenatal HIV Testing and Directive Counseling

At the outset it is important to identify the different rationales for testing pregnant women and for testing newborns. In the former instance, the only result of testing unique to pregnant women would be to influence the decision whether to continue a pregnancy or to have an abortion. When CDC officials first addressed the issues related to HIV and pregnancy, they reportedly assumed that post-test counseling would always lead to delay of pregnancy or to abortions, presumably since anyone who was "logical" would abort the pregnancy rather than risk HIV transmission.[63] In the second instance, discussed in the next section, the primary rationale for testing is to begin early treatment of the newborn. There is, at least as yet, no treatment that can be administered prior to birth that will cure or substantially ameliorate the disease for the child. This lack of a prenatal treatment distinguishes HIV from syphilis, for which penicillin is a cure for both the mother and the *in utero* child.[64]

Issues related to the testing of pregnant women have been part of AIDS policy discussions since almost the beginning of the epidemic. In December 1985, the CDC first formally recommended that HIV testing and counseling be made available to pregnant women in five groups: those with evidence of HIV infection; intravenous drug users; current or past sexual partners of men "in high risk groups"; women born in countries where heterosexual transmission is thought to be frequent; and prostitutes.[65] In February 1987, the CDC convened a large public conference in Atlanta to discuss the advisability of mandatory HIV testing of several populations, one of which was pregnant women. Conference participants reendorsed the recommendation of offering, but not requiring, testing and counseling at family planning clinics and during pre-natal care.[66] Ultimately, after review by higher-level agency officials, the CDC took no new position on testing of pregnant women and left the 1985 guidelines in place.

Although not adopted at the 1987 conference, proposals for mandatory HIV testing have remained under active discussion. Florida and Delaware have adopted legislation that mandates testing of pregnant women for sexually transmitted diseases, but neither law specifies whether HIV disease is included.[67] Michigan requires HIV testing of pregnant women unless a physician determines that it is inadvisable or unless the woman affirmatively objects and refuses to proceed with the test.[68] Rhode Island allows HIV testing of newborns without maternal consent.[69] New York Health Department officials proposed, then withdrew, a plan to "unblind" the HIV tests of newborns, which would effectively detect seropositive mothers. Two federal health officials predicted in 1989 that the threat posed by perinatal transmission would lead to mandatory testing of all women of reproductive age.[70] A prestigious task force on HIV infection in women and newborns has issued recommendations against policies of forced testing or directive counseling,[71] but clinicians continue to call for their adoption[72] and may be surreptitiously employing such practices, although the extent of this is unknown.[73] Some ethicists have argued that although coercion may not be justified, the state should be permitted to exercise its power to engage in directive counseling, i.e., to urge — or perhaps, as many fear, to pressure — women to be tested and, if positive, to forego pregnancy.[74]

What drives the debate on mandatory prenatal testing is less the set of issues concerning the physical intrusion of the test[75] than the content of the post-test counseling. The demand for such testing is motivated by the desire to prevent HIV transmission by the prevention of the birth of HIV-infected babies, an intervention that depends on persuading pregnant women to have abortions. The opposition to testing is focused on whether directive counseling regarding abortion infringes on the woman's right to make independent, unpressured decisions.

Indeed, to some extent, the content of the counseling is an entirely separate question from the voluntariness of the test. Whether an HIV test is mandated by the state or sought by the woman, post-test counseling could be geared to informing the woman of her options and of the relative risks of each, or designed to influence her more or less strongly to obtain an abortion. The CDC's guidelines discuss only pre-conception decisions and recommend delay or forgoing of pregnancy. Frustrated doctors complained that the antiabortion politics of the Reagan administration had prevented the agency from recommending discussion of abortion for HIV-infected pregnant women.[76] Many doctors endorse not only discussion but advocacy of abortion, at least for this group of women. Survey data found, among clinicians unworried about a party line on abortion, strong support for explicitly directive counseling of HIV-infected pregnant women to obtain abortions. Support for the same kind of directive counseling is weaker when conditions other than HIV are involved.[77]

Biased counseling procedures, if enforced by the state, would violate the principle that reproductive decision-making autonomy is constitutionally protected. Skewing information in such a way as to influence a woman to choose abortion over childbirth, at least if it distorts the interaction between a patient and a private doctor, has been found unconstitutional as an intrusion into the very heart of the decision making process.[78] "Few decisions are more personal and intimate, more properly private, or more basic to individual dignity and autonomy than a woman's decision...whether to end her pregnancy. A woman's right to make that choice freely is fundamental."[79]

The line of cases insulating a women's right to make this choice free of governmental intrusion has been undermined in recent years, however.[80] The Supreme Court has ruled that the government has the authority to restrict access to abortion and even to skew counseling procedures in publicly funded clinics, in order to deter women from choosing abortions.[81]

The same principles of law relied on in the newer cases would permit the government to distort state policies in the opposite direction. Recent court decisions which diminish the autonomy of the woman and enhance the power of the state to achieve the outcome preferred by legislatures could be invoked to justify coercive proabortion counseling as well. The issue whether the state can intervene when a women is HIV-positive to try to end the pregnancy illustrates dramatically that at least one right at issue in the abortion cases really is that of choice — either for or against abortion. Ironically, the outcome of the question whether women will be protected from policies pressuring them to have abortions will probably be determined by how the Supreme Court resolves future cases involving anti-abortion policies.[82]

In addition to the legal issues specific to whether the state may engage in directive counseling, a series of other legal and policy considerations are raised by proposals for prenatal testing that is mandatory or routinized (i.e., performed without a process of informed consent). Courts ruling on the constitutionality of state actions involving bodily intrusion engage in a weighing of the burdens and gains associated with the policy in question, including: the harms or benefits to the coerced individual; any selectivity in the imposition of those harms; the efficacy of the policy in achieving its stated goals; and whether less restrictive alternatives exist by which the same advantages can be secured.[83] Judged by these criteria, a policy of required HIV testing of pregnant women is seriously deficient.

First, the harms associated with testing are significant enough that *forced* testing cannot be justified. In addition to the dignitary harm of involuntary physical intrusion, there is substantial risk of serious social harm to her if she is known to be HIV-infected. Widespread irrational discrimination has been directed against persons with HIV disease, including loss of jobs, health care, custody of children, and housing.[84] Fear of such discrimination could impede prenatal care (which is already often delayed) by causing women to avoid the care as a way of avoiding the test. As discussed above, the benefits of testing include early diagnosis and the possibility of treatments which can slow the progression of the disease. But because there is no guarantee that a woman will actually receive the benefits of such treatment, the possibility of treatment cannot be invoked to take away her right to decide for herself whether to be tested.

Another possible advantage to the woman of being tested could be the greater amount of information available to her to use in her own decision-making process. Although one may oppose a program of directive counseling designed to skew the woman's decision toward abortion, it is also true that the information that one has this disease might be extremely important for the woman who wants to use it to decide whether to seek immediate treatment or to continue a particular pregnancy. There may be a host of other planning decisions as well, for which this information would be crucial. Still, the fundamental question is whether such a rationale is sufficient to *coerce* testing. For the nonreproductive aspects of decision making, it would seem clear that the state has no greater authority to impose this information on a pregnant woman than on anyone else.

The second issue, that of selectivity, varies with the specifics of a proposed testing regime. If mandatory or directive testing programs were adopted for all women, the impact would be selective by gender. The constitutionality of such a program would depend on whether the courts considered males and females to be "similarly situated" with regard to posing a risk of vertical transmission. Although the expectant father might be the original source of HIV infection, testing him will not determine whether the fetus is infected because the father may not have transmitted the virus to the mother. The risk that HIV will be transmitted to the child exists only if the pregnant woman is infected.

Thus, selectivity by gender is likely to be viewed as acceptable under current law.[85]

Many proposals for prenatal testing, however, do not envision that it would be required of all women, but only of women considered at highest risk for HIV infection. As the Working Group on HIV Testing of Pregnant Women and Newborns pointed out, both socio-demographic criteria and geographic seroprevalence rates — the most common bases for proposed targeting — "become merely thinly veiled proxies for ethnicity and poverty."[86] The inevitable effect would be to impose a burden against women in already disadvantaged racial, ethnic, and economic class categories, and to exempt women in socially privileged categories. Even ostensibly universal testing falls prey to this bias. A study of reporting data under a Florida law that required testing pregnant women for illegal drug use found that many positive toxicologies for white women were not reported to the state, while results positive for drugs in African-American and Hispanic women were.[87] HIV testing of pregnant women poses the same risks of unequal enforcement, against the same communities.

Although differential treatment by race or ethnicity is highly suspect in the law, successful challenge would have to show that the discrimination was intentional rather than the mere byproduct of a facially neutral system.[88] Evidence of the disproportionate impact such a policy would be likely to have would suggest a lack of neutrality, but its defenders would argue that its purpose was beneficent, and thus that the differential effect could be justified.

A comparison to other conditions leading to serious health problems for certain groups of children for which tests are not imposed would be more telling of bias. There is no mandatory testing for carriers of traits for Tay-Sachs disease or sickle-cell anemia — serious genetic diseases which can be detected prenatally, but for which, like HIV, there is no prenatal treatment.[89] Additionally, amniocentesis, which tests for chromosomal abnormalities and hereditary diseases such as Down's syndrome, is recommended but not required for all women age 35 and older.[90] Down's syndrome — although not fatal — affects 3,000 to 4,000 newborns each year in the United States,[91] approximately the same number of cases of perinatally acquired AIDS that the CDC projects will occur in 1993.[92] In all these examples, there is no effective prenatal treatment for the fetus, and thus prenatal testing is not required. To treat HIV disease differently suggests that some form of bias is involved.

The third issue to be assessed is whether such testing would actually be effective in reducing vertical transmission of HIV. Any link between testing and reduced transmission depends on an assumption that HIV-infected pregnant women will always decide to terminate their pregnancies, based on an approximately one-in-three chance that their baby would have HIV disease. Several factors render that assumption untenable in many cases. To an outrageous degree, pregnant women in low-income communities do not even have contact with a doctor for prenatal care, at least not before the final trimester of pregnancy.[93] In most states, public funds will not cover the costs of an abortion,[94] and many counties do not have any facility that will perform an abortion.[95] Moreover, abortion providers may discriminate against HIV-infected women.[96] Thus, even if a pregnant woman wanted to have an abortion, she might learn of the HIV infection too late in the pregnancy to do so, she might be unable to afford an abortion, or she might be unable to obtain the abortion.

Even more fundamental, however, is the assumption that she would likely want an abortion or would, if not yet pregnant, decide not to become pregnant. Studies to date have shown that women who learn they are HIV-infected do not elect to have abortions at any higher rate than women who are not infected.[97] For women facing the harshness of life lived in poverty, a 70-percent chance of a healthy baby, coupled with the enhancement of self-esteem associated with motherhood, leads to very different, but no less logical, assessments of what might be the best option.[98] Thus, the very efficacy of mandatory testing in reducing the numbers of HIV-infected babies is open to serious question.

Lastly, constitutional analysis incorporates consideration of whether less restrictive alternatives exist by which the same goals could be as readily achieved. The obvious alternative protocol is to make HIV testing readily available and routinely offered, but voluntary. That policy has received the widest endorsement, but is far from complete implementation.[99]

B. Mandatory Testing of Newborns

Mandatory testing of newborns is a more difficult question than testing of pregnant women. Here, the rationale for testing does not involve the *sub rosa* goal of preventing the birth of an HIV infected child. Coerced reproductive decision-making is not at issue.

As medical technology now stands, however, testing of newborns can identify with certainty *only* the mothers who are HIV-infected, not the children. Because treating the noninfected children of infected mothers (i.e., the great majority) poses the risk that toxic anti-HIV drugs would create harm for those in that 70-percent group even if they helped the 30 percent who were infected, ethicists have found it easy to argue against HIV testing at least until the tests could reliably distinguish infected from uninfected infants (which is possible at about 15 months of age).[100]

But the issue of newborn testing does seem, perhaps more than any other current AIDS issue, the most like a constantly moving target, because future improvements in the sophistication of testing and treatment techniques are likely to complicate it even more. Work has been under way for years on development of a test that could distinguish between the newborn's own HIV infection and the maternal antibodies.[101] Recent research indicates that treatment protocols involving drugs less toxic than AZT may become widely adopted as early interventions for very young children.[102] If, or when, these developments occur, there are likely to be renewed calls for mandatory newborn testing. In such a context, drawing the line at birth appears logical. No direct intrusion on the woman is involved. Although the mothers of infants with HIV disease will be identified by the tests, the 70 percent of infected mothers whose children are born uninfected will not be identified against their will because the children will test negative. The newborn is a fully separate person, and our society accepts the principle that the state may intervene to insist on medical treatment of a minor, at least in an emergency, against the wishes of the parent.[103] Accordingly, while syphilis is the most widespread condition for which states require prenatal tests, there are between six and twelve types of tests automatically performed on every newborn in virtually every state.[104]

There are still, however, several compelling arguments against coerced and automatic testing of newborns. First, unfortunately, one cannot simply assume that identification of the disease will lead only to benefits for the child. Much of the analysis of the newborn testing issue assumes that any reasonable parent would want to have the child tested so that, if she is infected, treatments could begin as soon as possible. Hopefully, this would be true in almost all cases. But there is no vaccination against discrimination, even for the youngest and most helpless of those with HIV disease. A 1989 survey of neonatologists vividly illustrates this point. Half of the doctors who would otherwise have recommended open heart surgery for an infant would not have proceeded with that operation if they had known that the child was HIV-infected.[105] In cases where a parent might be aware of similar upcoming medical decisions to be made about the child, or of other situations in which identification as HIV-infected might prompt a real risk of discrimination, the reasonable parent might well decide to postpone testing. Coerced testing programs take this decision away from the parent.

Second, because there is real risk associated with HIV testing, it is improper to deny authority to the parent to provide consent on behalf of the child, in the same manner as if the child were to undergo surgery. None of the other conditions, mostly metabolic disorders, which are the subject of newborn testing programs, carry comparable, if any, stigma. Thus, the more appropriate analogy is not to routine screening programs but to other procedures with serious risk.

Treating newborns with HIV disease and their parents differently from other family units amounts to another instance of selectivity that masks differentiation based on race and poverty. There is a long history of greater governmental intrusion into the family life decisions of the poor.[106] In the worst-case scenario of a parent withholding consent for reasons not related to the health of the child when testing is indicated, the health care facility could seek a judicial order authorizing forced testing and treatment. In other words, the same procedure could be followed in this situation as would be followed if a parent withheld consent for another serious and risky medical procedure that a child needed.[107]

Third, and perhaps most fundamentally, there is no promise that beneficial treatment will actually be available to the child. Even if the newborn testing techniques existed to pinpoint which infants would be infected with HIV, and even if treatments existed that would prolong their lives, there is no sign that children with this disease will actually receive those expensive treatments. The decade of the 1990s is beginning with cutbacks, not expansions, in access to medical care.[108] Children with HIV disease are likely to be born into families that are African American rather than white, with low incomes, headed by young adults, and living in the urban centers — all characteristics of persons most likely to be without any kind of health care coverage, private or public.[109] Ethically, one could justify *coerced* testing as a form of treatment, on beneficent or communitarian grounds, only if all those who tested positive were in fact assured that they would receive the treatment.[110] There is no program that provides such a guarantee, for either pregnant women or newborns.

Even if it were made potentially available, the actual receipt of the treatment by a very young child would depend on the cooperation of the caretaker parent, likely the mother. If that parent's status to authorize medical testing and treatment had been ignored by the program itself, it seems extremely unlikely that the kind of cooperation necessary to provide maximum care and treatment for the child could be expected.

There are striking similarities between the issues raised by HIV testing and the history of sickle cell testing. In each case, the first response was to mandate testing, first of adults for carrier status, and then of newborns. Widespread discrimination against an already disadvantaged minority followed. Ultimately, a policy of routinely offered voluntary testing has been adopted.

In 1970, a single, inexpensive, and relatively reliable test for sickle-cell hemoglobin became available. Shortly thereafter, a number of states enacted sickle-cell testing programs. Some were compulsory, and none had specific confidentiality provisions. Although well intentioned, these programs and the attention they generated triggered panicked and discriminatory responses. There was confusion over the difference between carrying the trait and having the disease. Some airlines grounded all black employees because of unfounded fears that those with the trait were susceptible to a sickling crisis if a plane depressurized; some insurance companies began charging higher premiums of sickle cell carriers; and the armed forces considered deferring enlistment of all carriers.[111] At the same time incidents of discrimination were erupting, clinicians had nothing to offer sickle-cell carriers except counseling with regard to reproduction. This lack of an effective treatment added to criticism of the testing statutes.[112]

In response to this overreaction, legislatures which had passed mandatory testing laws amended them to make the test voluntary. This process occurred in six states (Georgia, Illinois, Maryland, Massachusetts, New York, and Virginia) and the District of Columbia.[113] Other testing programs were repealed in Kansas, Louisiana, Michigan, New Mexico, North Carolina, and Ohio.[114] When Congress passed the National Sickle Cell Anemia Control Act in 1972, it expressly limited federal funding to voluntary testing programs.[115]

In 1987, a National Institutes of Health consensus conference recommended that states should mandate the offering of sickle-cell disease tests for newborns, based on the preventability of serious episodes of disease, and in some cases of death, by the administration of penicillin. Even in light of this clear and dramatic beneficial treatment, the conference called on states to "mandate the availability of these services while permitting parental refusal."[116] The finding that penicillin is an effective treatment has led to a resurgence of sickle-cell testing for newborns.[117]

The NIH consensus conference can serve as a useful starting point for developing an approach to HIV testing of newborns if improvements in treatment and testing techniques materialize. Basic components of such a program should include the following:

- A full process of informed consent should be afforded the parent, so that she has adequate time to consider the options and gain further information.

- The parent should be informed that no denial of service or assistance or any form of public benefit will result if consent is denied.

- If the parent declines testing, the health care provider would be required to seek a court order to authorize a test before testing could be done. The provider would have the burden of proving that testing is required to provide treatment necessary to prolong the life and health of the child and that this need outweighs the parent's reasons for declining a test.[118]

- Results of such tests shall be disclosed only to the parent(s) or guardian of the child and to the persons providing health care to the child, unless the parent(s) authorizes further disclosure.

- Future follow-up care and treatment should be guaranteed, regardless of ability to pay.

C. Forced Treatment and Penalization for Behavior During Pregnancy

The concern over HIV-infected women becoming mothers is arising in a period when law and medicine are confronting a growing number of issues involving maternal-fetal conflict. The rapid sophistication of perinatal medicine has led to the potential for diagnostic procedures and treatments *in utero* which were impossible two decades ago. A substantial body of legal commentary already has been generated as a result.[119]

To date, there is no treatment or cure for HIV disease *in utero*, although trials of the efficacy of AZT to prevent perinatal transmission are underway. AZT inhibits viral replication and has been demonstrated to be effective in slowing the progression of HIV disease. As such, it is considered a proven treatment (though not a cure) for HIV disease. AZT is also, however, highly toxic to some patients. Moreover, during animal studies, administration of AZT led to the development of vaginal tumors in mice. Thus, its benefits and risks to the fetus are now unknown; and the degree of particularized benefit or risk to women is also uncertain.

Should AZT or some other drug be proven beneficial as an *in utero* treatment, however, the issue will arise whether pregnant women (presumably after being tested) could be forced to undergo such treatments. Law on the question of forced treatment is in development; to date, most of the reported instances concern forced cesarean sections or blood transfusions. Until 1990, the reported cases had generally resulted in judicial authorization being granted for such procedures.[120] The leading case now on point, however, is a ruling from the District of Columbia Court of Appeals holding that it was improper for a hospital, and for the lower court reviewing the hospital's decision, to attempt to balance the woman's interests against those of the state in enhancing fetal health.[121] The case involved the performance of a cesarean on a terminally ill cancer patient in an attempt to save the fetus. Doctors treating the woman knew that the surgery would hasten her death, and had only a small chance of saving the fetus. The patient was too heavily medicated to express her own wishes; her family opposed the surgery. The hospital sought a court order nonetheless, and both the woman and her fetus died.

The appellate court grounded its holding in a constitutionally protected "right of bodily integrity [which] is not extinguished because someone is ill, or even at death's door."[122] Following the court's decision, the hospital adopted a new policy on treatment of severely ill pregnant patients, which provided that "respect for patient autonomy compels us to accede to the treatment decisions of a pregnant patient whenever possible."[123]

This decision is more fully reasoned than earlier cases dealing with forced treatments for purposes of fetal health and so may be considered persuasive by other courts, but it is binding precedent only in the

District of Columbia. It is far from clear how courts in other jurisdictions will rule if confronted with similar situations. Given the sparseness of the law on this question, the strongest support for the same kind of autonomy protective outcome may lie in the policies of professional medical associations.

The American Medical Association,[124] the American College of Obstetricians and Gynecologists,[125] and the American Academy of Pediatrics[126] have all adopted formal positions against forced treatment of pregnant patients. These policies recognize a distinction between an ethical duty on the part of a pregnant patient to maximize fetal health and the general refusal of law to coerce adherence to samaritan principles. In addition, they conclude that use of force destroys the foundation of trust between patient and doctor and that judicial proceedings are an inappropriate mechanism for making treatment decisions.

It is less clear whether physicians will actually follow the ethical advice proffered in these policy statements. A 1987 survey of directors of maternal-fetal medicine fellowship programs found that nearly half believed that women who refused to follow medical advice, to the danger of their fetuses, should be detained for medical supervision. Less than one-quarter consistently agreed that pregnant women had the right to decline medical advice.[127]

A related question which has also engendered sharp debate about maternal-fetal conflict has been whether pregnant women can properly be subjected to criminal prosecution or civil proceedings that allege child abuse or neglect for engaging in behavior during pregnancy which creates a danger to the fetus. This issue has arisen almost entirely with regard to the use of illegal drugs during pregnancy. As the 1990s begin, these cases are just starting to be heard in appellate courts.[128]

As discussed in chapter 8 ("The Criminalization of HIV"), more than twenty states have made it a crime to transmit HIV or to knowingly expose another person to it. Although no woman has yet been prosecuted for transmission *in utero*, a woman who knew that she was HIV-infected, knew the risk of transmission to the fetus, and proceeded nonetheless to continue the pregnancy, could very possibly be held liable for prosecution. Only Texas specifically exempts perinatal transmission from the scope of its criminal law.[129] The potential for criminal prosecution is certainly clear, and the impact it could have on deterring women from seeking HIV testing, prenatal care, or both is substantial.

As direct precedent, these cases seem largely inapposite to the situation of HIV-infected mothers. In the drug-use cases, advocates of legal penalties argue that prosecutions serve as a deterrent that will force pregnant women to avoid behaviors that are known to cause harm to a fetus. Women with HIV disease, by contrast, can do nothing after becoming pregnant to avoid harm to the fetus. For them, as for women who are carriers of genetic anomalies, the only decision is whether to continue a pregnancy. Nothing that occurs during the nine-month gestation alters the risk of transmission.

Nonetheless, these cases are troubling for two reasons. First, some courts have gone beyond illegal behaviors during pregnancy to approve penalization of lawful but hazardous behaviors, such as alcohol use, or even the refusal to follow doctors' directions.[130] Second, the women who are most likely to be subject to prosecution, users of illegal drugs, are also most likely to have HIV disease. Thus, in many instances, the women against whom criminal charges could be filed will be the same women against whom some penalization for HIV status could be directed. Their HIV status, if known, could constitute an additional, even if unacknowledged, basis for prosecutors to decide to bring drug-related charges. Given the much greater likelihood of state intervention in the lives of poor women and women of color, one cannot disentangle these two potential bases for surveillance and penalty in practice, even if they are logically and legally distinct.

IV. Conclusion

Too much of the policy analysis on the subject of women and HIV disease has focused on women solely as mothers. Although the issues associated with reproductive decision-making are critically important, policy development in that area, as in all others, should start with the assumption that women have the same rights to autonomous determinations of life choices as do men. Paradoxically, the most urgent problems have received the least attention: the need for the prevention programs and policies to insure effective access to care, as well as the need for treatments which address the particular impediments faced by women. It is essential to shift the discussion on women and AIDS from a debate over the narrow issue of coerced testing to a process of developing and implementing innovative policies which guarantee women access to all the components of quality care.

NOTES

1. Woodard, *In Future, AIDS Hits Women Worse*, Newsday, Oct. 25, 1990.
2. Chu, Buehler & Berkelman, *Impact of the Human Immunodeficiency Virus Epidemic on Mortality in Women of Reproductive Age, United States*, 264 J. A.M.A. 225 (1990) [hereinafter *Impact of the HIV Epidemic*].
3. U.S. Centers for Disease Control [CDC], *AIDS in Women — United States*, 265 J. A.M.A. 23 (1991).
4. Pearl, *AIDS Spreads More Rapidly Among Women*, Wall St. J., Nov. 30, 1990.
5. One *New York Times* article typified the tendency to describe women in terms of how they might transmit HIV: women who are "drug addicts... are not using condoms that can arrest the spread of AIDS. And they are becoming pregnant despite the knowledge that they could infect a fetus, and bearing children, many of whom will die. But another category of these infected women, the sex partners of men who have injected drugs, are behaving far more responsibly — protecting their mates and avoiding or terminating unwanted pregnancies." Gross, *Bleak Lives: Women Carrying AIDS*, N.Y. Times, Aug. 27, 1987, at A-1.
6. *See, e.g.*, H.S. Kaplan, The Real Truth About Women and AIDS: How to Eliminate the Risks Without Giving Up Love and Sex (1987).
7. For example, an article in the *New York Times* stated that only a tiny number of AIDS cases in women resulted from sexual contact with a bisexual man, but went on to say that "numbers offer little consolation to the individual woman..., especially a middle-class woman" who thinks her chance of involvement with an IVDU is remote. According to this article, "For this kind of woman, experts say, the figure of the male bisexual... has become the bogeyman of the late 1980's." Nordheimer, *AIDS Specter for Women: The Bisexual Man*, N.Y. Times, Apr. 2, 1987, at A-1, col. 2.
8. *Impact of the HIV Epidemic, supra* note 2, at 226.
9. CDC, *HIV/AIDS Surveillance Report* Table 7 at 12 (June 1991) [hereinafter *Surveillance Report*].
10. New York State Dept. of Health, AIDS Institute, *Focus on AIDS in New York State* 1 (Oct. 1990) [hereinafter *Focus on AIDS*].
11. The rate of death from AIDS among African-American women in New York and New Jersey, for example, is comparable to the rate reported among adult women in Abidjan, Ivory Coast, a city where the HIV seroprevalence rate is extremely high. *Impact of the HIV Epidemic, supra* note 2, at 226. These data are at best approximations. It is not possible to identify with certainty how a given person acquired the virus. Reporting methods further confound the problem. *See* text *infra* at note 32.
12. *Surveillance Report, supra* note 9, Table 5 at 10.
13. A chapter on women and AIDS proposed for the National Academy of Sciences book AIDS: The Second Decade (1990) was refocused to become a chapter on AIDS prevention among prostitutes, ostensibly because analysis of that topic could be supported by sufficient data. *See Women and AIDS* (Letters), 251 Science 359 (1991).
14. It is deeply ironic that female prostitutes, often thought of as a pathetically oppressed group of women, have probably been the single subpopulation of

women most able to incorporate safer sexual practices into their relations with men.

15. Women in different ethnic or racial communities will respond best to materials which respect the values of those communities. Mays & Cochran, *Issues in the Perception of AIDS Risk and Risk Reduction Activities by Black and Hispanic/Latina Women*, 43 Amer. Psychologist 949 (1988); Maldonado, *Latinas and HIV/AIDS: Implications for the 90s*, SIECUS Report (Dec. 1990/Jan. 1991) at 10-15; N. Freudenberg, Preventing AIDS: A Guide to Effective Education for the Prevention of HIV Infection 148-50, 171, 175 (1989).

16. Communication with author (Mar. 1991).

17. Fullilove, Fullilove, Haynes & Gross, *Black Women and AIDS Prevention: A View Towards Understanding the Gender Rules*, 27 J. Sex Research 47, 62 (1990) [hereinafter *Black Women and AIDS Prevention*].

18. Federal limitations on the use of funds, which in turn set the limits for how state agencies can structure any programs that utilize federal funds, contain this requirement. 55 Fed. Reg. 23414 (1990). The content restrictions are currently under challenge. Gay Men's Health Crisis v. Sullivan, 733 F. Supp. 619 (S.D.N.Y. 1989).

19. *Black Women and AIDS Prevention, supra* note 17, at 62.

20. Murray, *Report from the First National Women and HIV Conference*, Gay Community News, Jan. 1-13, 1991, at 16 (quoting Dr. Vickie Mays of UCLA); *Focus on AIDS, supra* note 10, at 3.

21. Stein, *HIV Prevention: The Need for Methods Women Can Use*, 80 Am. J. Pub. Health 460 (1990).

22. Chu, Buehler, Fleming & Berkelman, *Epidemiology of Reported Cases of AIDS in Lesbians, United States 1980-89*, 80 Am. J. Pub. Health 1380 (1990).

23. *Focus on AIDS, supra* note 10; *see, e.g.*, Ramos v. Harvard Community Health Plan, No. 86-4114, AIDS Litig. Rep. (Andrews Pub.) 15 (Mass. 1986) (a woman successfully sued her physician for malpractice for failure to diagnose her condition as AIDS).

24. Safrin, Dattel, Hauer & Sweet, *Seroprevalence and Epidemiologic Correlates of Human Immunodeficiency Virus Infection in Women with Acute Pelvic Inflammatory Disease*, 75 Obstetrics & Gynecology 666 (1990); Rhoads, Wright, Redfield & Burke, *Chronic Vaginal Candidiasis in Women With Human Immunodeficiency Virus Infection*, 257 J. A.M.A. 3105 (1987).

25. CDC, *Risk for Cervical Disease in HIV-Infected Women — New York City*, 265 J. A.M.A. 23 (1991).

26. Social Security Ruling 86-20, *Evaluation of Acquired Immunodeficiency Syndrome*.

27. Complaint, S.P. v. Sullivan, No. 90 Civ. 6294 (MGC) (S.D.N.Y. 1990). The case was filed not only on behalf of women presenting with gynecological symptoms, but also children with pediatric symptoms and current and former intravenous drug users who exhibited symptoms related to drug use and poverty.

28. Two such bills were introduced in 1991, one in each chamber of Congress: S. 1188 and H.R. 2299.

29. City of New York, *Continuum of Housing and Services for the Medically Frail and HIV-Ill* (Aug. 3, 1990).

30. Navarro, *Dated AIDS Definition Keeps Benefits from Many Patients*, New York Times, July 8, 1991, at A-1.

31. K. Anastos & C. Marte, *Women — The Missing Persons in the AIDS Epidemic, in*
     The AIDS Reader: Social, Political and Ethical Issues (N. McKenzie ed., 1991).
     Crucial questions about transmission in women also remain unsolved and
     unstudied: whether cervical tissue or vaginal tissue is more likely to become
     infected and whether use of oral contraceptives has an impact on likelihood
     of transmission are two examples. Stein, *The Congressional Biomedical Research
     Caucus Presentation* (1991) (unpublished testimony).

32. *See Surveillance Report, supra* note 9, Table 5 at 11. CDC officials originally
     assigned gay male IVDUs to the category of homosexual transmission. Sub-
     sequently, to correct for the same kind of distortion, a distinct category was
     created for men who had engaged in both kinds of high-risk behaviors.

33. Kolata, *Growing Movement Seeks to Help Women Infected with AIDS Virus*, N.Y.
     Times, May 4, 1989.

34. According to Dr. Janet Mitchell, Director of Obstetrics at Harlem Hospital,
     "We only identify about one-third of potentially HIV-infected women at my
     hospital. I don't know what the prevalence is at Harlem because I can't get
     my ob-gyns to refer women to testing programs and get data. If they don't
     know the woman's HIV status, they don't have to deal with it." Murray,
     Report from the First National Women and HIV Conference, Gay Community
     News, Jan. 7-13, 1991, at 9.

35. HIV Screening of Pregnant Women and Newborns 3708 (L.M. Hardy ed.,
     Institute of Medicine, 1991) [hereinafter Hardy].

36. Ill. Rev. Stat. ch. 127, para, 55.44(b) (1989).

37. Malcolm, *In Making Drug Strategy, No Accord on Treatment*, N.Y. Times, Nov.
     19, 1989, at 1.

38. *Help Is Hard to Find for Addict Mothers*, L.A. Times, Dec. 12, 1986, at J-1.

39. Chavkin, *Drug Addiction and Pregnancy: Policy Crossroads*, 80 Am. J. Pub.
     Health 483 (1990). A challenge to the policy of excluding pregnant women
     from treatment has been filed in New York State court against several alcohol
     and drug treatment facilities. Complaint, Elaine W. v. North Gen., Index No.
     6230/90 (N.Y. Sup. Ct. Nov. 23, 1989).

40. New York State Dept. of Health, Focus on AIDS in New York State 13-14
     (1991).

41. Levine, *Women and HIV/AIDS Research: The Barriers to Equity*, 14 Evaluation
     Rev. 447, 449 (1990).

42. U.S. Dept. of Health, Education, and Welfare, Pub. No. 77-3040, General
     Considerations for the Clinical Evaluation of Drugs 10 (1977).

43. *See* Kinney, *Underrepresentation of Women in New Drug Trials*, 95 Annals
     Internal Med. 495 (1982); Cotton, *Is There Still Too Much Extrapolation from Data
     on Middle-Aged White Men?*, 263 J. A.M.A. 1049 (1990); and Cotton, *Examples
     Abound of Gaps in Medical Knowledge Because of Groups Excluded from Scientific
     Study*, 263 J. A.M.A. 1051 (1990).

44. Kirschstein, *Research on Women's Health*, 81 Am. J. Pub. Health 291, 292 (1991).

45. The Restatement of Torts specifically exempts new and experimental drugs
     from the doctrine of strict liability because there are unavoidably unsafe
     products that are not unreasonably dangerous. Restatement (Second) of Torts,
     § 402a cmt. k.

46. *See, e.g.*, Gaston v. Hunter, 588 P.2d 326 (Ariz. Ct. App. 1976).

47. *Cf.* United Automobile Workers v. Johnson Controls, Inc., 111 S. Ct. 1196
     (1991), in which the Supreme Court ruled that a company's policy of barring
     women of childbearing capacity from certain jobs involved in manufacturing

lead batteries violated the prohibition against sex discrimination in the workplace. As to the company's argument that it was concerned about future litigation if women workers gave birth to children disabled by prenatal exposure to lead, the Court ruled that in light of the unlawfulness of discrimination against women workers, the company's compliance with government safety standards for lead and the explicit warnings to women of the risk, "the basis for holding an employer liable seems remote at best." *Id.* at 1199.

48. Merton, *Community-Based AIDS Research*, 14 Evaluation Rev. 502 (1990).

49. *See id.*

50. Levine, Dubler & Levine, *Building a New Consensus: Ethical Principles and Policies for Clinical Research on HIV/AIDS*, 13 IRB: A Review of Human Subjects Research 1, 16 (1991). Clinical trials of drugs are conducted in three phases. Phase I trials are designed to determine safety. Phases II and III determine efficacy, the final phase of testing involving a larger number of participants. A treatment IND (i.e., treatment investigational new drug) is a separate program established by the Food and Drug Administration through which patients may secure access to a drug from their physicians, without enrollment in a formal clinical trial.

51. All discussions of vertical transmission refer to maternal transmission. Medically, the mother is always the direct source of infection to the fetus or newborn infant, through the blood systems shared during pregnancy, although the father may be the indirect source if he infected the mother.

52. Working Group on HIV Testing of Pregnant Women and Newborns, *HIV Infection, Pregnant Women, and Newborns: A Policy Proposal for Information and Testing*, 264 J. A.M.A. 2416 (1990) [hereinafter Working Group Policy Proposal]; Levine & Bayer, *The Ethics of Screening for Early Intervention in HIV Disease*, 79 Am. J. Pub. Health 1661, 1662 (1989) [hereinafter Levine & Bayer]. For reasons which are not yet understood, recent studies have found that the perinatal transmission rate is lower — only about 13 percent — in Europe than in the United States. *European Study Finds Few Babies Get AIDS*, N.Y. Times, Mar. 5, 1991.

53. Levine & Bayer, *supra* note 52.

54. An article written by three federal health officials, all women, in 1989, outlining federal government efforts to address HIV issues related to women, described the program initiatives at the CDC entirely in terms of preventing perinatal transmission — except for one sentence. The one sentence referred to a study of women prostitutes. Donahue, Danello & Kirschstein, *HIV Infection in Women: An Inventory of Public Health Service Initiatives*, 4 AIDS & Pub. Pol'y J. 120, 122 (1989).

55. Working Group Policy Proposal, *supra* note 52; Hardy, *supra* note 35.

56. M. Angell, *A Dual Approach to the AIDS Epidemic*, 324 New Eng. J. Med. 1498 (1991).

57. Washington Post, July 11, 1989, at A-16. As of late 1990, researchers were planning for a phase III (the final phase) clinical trial of AZT in pregnant women. *CDC Weekly*, Nov. 5, 1990.

58. The possible application of the Illinois statute that criminalizes HIV transmission is discussed in Isaacman, *Are We Outlawing Motherhood for HIV-Infected Women?*, 22 Loyola L. J. 479 (1991).

59. *See* Levine & Dubler, *Uncertain Risks and Bitter Realities: The Reproductive Choices of HIV-Infected Women*, 68 Milbank Q. 321 (1990) [hereinafter Levine & Dubler].

60. The use of women's reproductive capacity to define the entire category of "woman" is notably true in medicine, where the very fields of "obstetrics and gynecology" and "maternal and child health" bespeak both the convergence of the two functions (medical care for childbirth and health care for women) and the prioritization of the first. Amaro, *Women's Reproductive Rights in the Age of AIDS: New Threats to Informed Choice* (1989) [unpublished speech before American Public Health Association].

61. Banks, *Women and AIDS — Racism, Sexism, and Classism,* 17 N.Y.U. Rev. L. & Soc. Change 351, 361-65 (1989-90). One trade newspaper for obstetricians, after conducting a telephone survey in 1987, suggested that a proposal for forced sterilizations of HIV-infected women would have considerable support. Mitchell, *Women, AIDS and Public Policy,* 3 AIDS & Pub. Pol'y J. 50, 51 (1988)[hereinafter Mitchell].

62. The *Philadelphia Inquirer* suggested in an editorial that women on welfare be given incentives to use a contraceptive implant. *Poverty and Norplant: Can Contraception Reduce the Underclass?,* Philadelphia Inquirer, Dec. 12, 1990, at A-18, col. 1.

63. Bayer, *AIDS and the Future of Reproductive Freedom,* 68 Milbank Q. 179, 189-91 (1990) [hereinafter Bayer]. CDC's director of AIDS activities was quoted in 1988 as saying that "[t]here is no reason that the number of [HIV-infected babies] shouldn't decline.... Someone who understands the disease and is logical will not want to be pregnant." *Id.,* at 191.

64. Acuff & Faden, *A History of Prenatal and Newborn Screening Programs: Lessons for the Future, in* AIDS, Women and the Next Generation (R. Faden, G. Geller, & M. Powers eds., 1991) [hereinafter Acuff & Faden]. Syphilis is the only condition for which prenatal testing is widely required by law.

65. 34 Morbidity & Mortality Wkly. Rep. 721 (1985).

66. CDC, Conference on the Role of AIDS Virus Antibody Testing in the Prevention and Control of AIDS, Closing Plenary Session: Reports from the Workshops, Transcript of the Proceedings 3 (February 24-25, 1987).

67. Del. Code Ann. tit. 16, § 708 (Supp. 1990); Fla. Stat. ch. 384.31, 384.23 (Supp. 1991).

68. Mich. Comp. Laws Ann. § 333.5123 (Supp. 1991).

69. R.I. Gen. Laws § 23-6-14(a) (Supp. 1989).

70. Edelman & Haverkos, *The Suitability of HIV-Positive Individuals for Marriage and Pregnancy,* 261 J. A.M.A. 993 (1989).

71. Working Group Policy Proposal, *supra* note 52.

72. Krasinski, Borkowsky, Bebenroth & Moore, *Failure of Voluntary Testing for HIV to Identify Infected Parturient Women in a High- Risk Population,* 318 New Eng. J. Med. 185 (1988).

73. Several studies have found widespread surreptitious HIV testing in hospitals. Henry, Willenbring & Crossley, *Human Immunodeficiency Virus: Analysis of the Use of HIV Antibody Testing,* 259 J. A.M.A. 1819, 1820 (1988); Hilts, *Many Hospitals Found to Ignore Rights of Patients in AIDS Testing,* N.Y. Times, Feb. 17, 1990, at A-1, col. 1.

74. Arras, *AIDS and Reproductive Decisions: Having Children in Fear and Trembling,* 68 Milbank Q. 353 (1990) [hereinafter Arras]; Bayer, *Perinatal Transmission of HIV Infection: The Ethics of Prevention, in* AIDS and the Health Care System (L. Gostin ed., 1990).

75. See chapter 8 ("The Criminalization of HIV") on coerced testing in the criminal justice system for an analysis of the consitutionality of state-mandated blood tests.

76. Grimes, *The CDC and Abortion in HIV-Positive Women (Letter)*, 258 J. A.M.A. 1176 (1987).

77. Bayer, *supra* note 63, at 193. Although 65 percent "agreed" or "strongly agreed" with the statement that "women should not have babies who will be at risk for [AIDS]," there was only 25-percent agreement with that statement when the disease was Tay-Sachs; only 15-percent for cystic fibrosis; and only 9-percent for Downs syndrome. *Id.*

78. *See* Akron Center for Reproductive Health, Inc. v. City of Akron, 462 U.S. 416, 444 (1983) (state cannot require counseling about pregnancy outcome to be conducted in such a way that its goal was less to inform than to influence which option the woman should chose).

79. Thornburgh v. American College of Obstetricians and Gynecologists, 476 U.S. 747, 772 (1986).

80. *Compare* Webster v. Reproductive Health Services, 492 U.S. 490 (1989) *with Akron Center for Reproductive Health*, 462 U.S. 416.

81. Rust v. Sullivan, 111 S. Ct. 1759 (1991).

82. The Court has recognized a broader liberty interest in the right of a competent adult to make medical decisions. Cruzan v. Director, Missouri Dept. of Health, 110 S. Ct. 2841 (1990). In either the abortion context or the context of an HIV-infected pregnant woman, however, that liberty interest would have to be weighed against the asserted interest of the state in preferring childbirth or in preventing the birth of HIV-infected children.

83. *See, e.g.,* Winston v. Lee, 470 U.S. 753 (1985); L. Tribe, American Constitutional Law 1333 -34 (2d ed. 1988).

84. American Civil Liberties Union, AIDS Project, Epidemic of Fear (1990). Data from the New York City Commission on Human Rights indicate that the percentage of complaints of AIDS-related discrimination filed in that office by women increased from 20 percent to 32 percent between 1986 and 1990. Communication with New York City Commission on Human Rights (March 1991).

85. Absent a statute explicitly forbidding discrimination based on pregnancy, the Supreme Court has found that the Constitution imposes no bar to adverse treatment for women based on the capacity to become pregnant since, in the Court's view, men and women are not similarly situated with regard to that capacity. Geduldig v. Aiello, 417 U.S. 484 (1974). A state's constitution could be interpreted by a state supreme court to prohibit pregnancy-based decisions, however, contrary to the interpretation of the federal Constitution in *Geduldig*.

86. Working Group Policy Proposal, *supra* note 52, at 2419.

87. Chasnoff, Landress & Barrett, *The Prevalence of Illicit-Drug or Alcohol Use During Pregnancy and Discrepancies in Mandatory Reporting in Pinellas County, Florida*, 322 New Eng. J. Med. 1202 (1990).

88. Washington v. Davis, 426 U.S. 229 (1976).

89. Tay-Sachs is a genetic disorder prevalent among Jews of East European ancestry. It is a uniformly fatal neurodegenerative disease affecting approximately 1 in 3,600 Jewish children and 1 in 360,000 non-Jewish children. Sickle-cell anemia involves a chemical defect in hemoglobins of red blood cells which is found, in the United States, primarily among African-Americans.

Approximately 2.2 million Americans are carriers of the genetic trait, and about 1 in 600 African-Americans develop sickle-cell anemia. S. Elias & G.J. Annas, Reproductive Genetics and the Law 62-64 (1987).

Although no state currently requires prenatal screening for either condition, the history of Tay-Sachs testing is very different from the history of sickle-cell screening. During the 1970s, several statutes mandating the latter kind of testing were enacted, but have now been repealed. See *infra* notes 105 to 109 and accompanying text.

90. U.S. Dept. of Health, Education, and Welfare, Task Force Report: Predictors of Hereditary Disease or Congential Defects, Consensus Development Conference on Antenatal Diagnosis 35-47 (1979).

91. Nolan, *Protecting Fetuses from Prenatal Hazards: Whose Crimes? What Punishment?*, Crim. Just. Ethics, Winter/Spring 1990, at 13,15.

92. CDC, *HIV Prevalence Estimates and AIDS Case Projections for the United States: Report Based upon a Workshop*, 39 Morbidity & Mortality Wkly. Rep. RR-16 at 13, Table 3 (1990).

93. Levine & Dubler, *supra* note 59, at 340; Arras, *supra* note 74, at 358; Hunter, *Time Limits on Abortion*, *in* Reproductive Laws for the 1990s: A Briefing Handbook 103 (N. Taub & S. Cohen eds., 1988).

94. R. Gold & S. Guardado, *Public Funding of Family Planning, Sterilization and Abortion Services*, 20 Fam. Plan. Persp. 228, 233 (1988).

95. S. Henshaw & J. Van Vort, *Abortion Services in the United States*, 22 Fam. Plan. Persp. 102, 105-06 (1990).

96. City of New York Commission on Human Rights, *HIV-Related Discrimination by Reproductive Health Care Providers in New York City* (Oct. 22, 1990).

97. Selwyn, Schoenbaum, Davenny, Robertson, Feingold, Schulman, Mayers, Klein, Friedland & Rogers, *Prospective Study of Human Immunodeficiency Virus Infection and Pregnancy Outcomes in Intravenous Drug Users*, 261 J. A.M.A. 1289 (1989); Bayer, *supra* note 63, at 180; Gross, *New York's Poorest Women Offered More AIDS Services*, N.Y. Times, Mar. 6, 1988, at A-1.

98. Mitchell, *supra*, note 61. For a richly contextualized discussion of the social realities facing women with HIV disease, see Levine & Dubler, *supra* note 58.

99. Working Group Policy Proposal, *supra* note 52; Hardy, *supra* note 35; Levine & Dubler, *supra* note 59.

100. Hardy, *supra* note 35, at 26-28.

101. Early tests, using polymerase chain reaction techniques, were not sufficiently accurate to merit adoption. Recent research may prove more fruitful. Altman, *Infants' AIDS Test Is Called Reliable*, N.Y. Times, June 19, 1991, at A-13, col. 1.

102. CDC, *Guidelines for Prophylaxis Against Pneumocytis Carinii Pneumonia for Children Infected With Human Immunodeficiency Virus*, 265 J. A.M.A. 1637 (1991).

103. Jehovah's Witnesses v. King County Hosp., 390 U.S. 598 (1968) (per curiam) (upheld statute that permitted children to be declared wards of the court so that court could consent to medical procedures for them when parents opposed blood transfusions on religious grounds). See generally Sher, *Choosing for Children: Adjudicating Medical Care Disputes Between Parents and the State*, 58 N.Y.U. L. Rev. 157 (1983).

104. Acuff, *Prenatal and Newborn Screening: State Legislative Approaches and Current Practice Standards*, *in* AIDS, Women and the Next Generation 121-65 (R. Faden, G. Gelber & M. Powers eds., 1991).

105.   Levin, Driscoll & Fleischman, *Treatment Choice for Infants in the Neonatal Intensive Care Unit at Risk for AIDS*, 265 J. A.M.A. 2976 (1991). Moreover, 20 percent of the doctors surveyed would have changed their recommendation for treating the infant had they known only that the mother was HIV-infected.

106.   Areen, *Intervention Between Parent and Child: A Reappraisal of the State's Role in Child Neglect and Abuse Cases*, 63 Geo. J. L. 887, 894-910 (1975).

107.   Every state has a statute authorizing intervention to override a parent's decisions regarding medical care of a child. C. Jackson, *Severely Disabled Newborns: To Live of Let Die?*, 8 J. Legal Med. 135, 155 n. 143 (1987).

108.   The Ryan White Comprehensive AIDS Resources Emergency Act of 1990 (CARE Act), Pub. L. No. 101-381, authorized much higher levels of funding for AIDS-related care, especially early interventions, than have yet been appropriated.

109.   Ries, *Characteristics of Persons With and Without Health Care Coverage: United States, 1989*, Advance Data from Vital and Health Statistics of the National Center for Health Statistics Table 1, at 2 (June 18, 1991).

110.   Levine & Bayer, *supra* note 52, at 1666.

111.   P. Reilly, Genetics, Law and Social Policy 74 (1977); *see also* Farfel & Holtzman, *Education, Consent and Counseling in Sickle Cell Screening Programs: Report of a Study*, 74 Am. J. Pub. Health 373 (1984).

112.   Acuff & Faden, *supra* note 64.

113.   *Sickle Cell Legislation: Beneficence or 'The New Ghetto Hustle'?*, 13 J. Fam. L. 278, 279 n.6 (1973-74).

114.   *Id.*

115.   42 U.S.C. § 300b(a)(1) (1974); *see* Culliton, *Sickle Cell Anemia: National Program Raises Problems As Well As Hopes*, 178 Science 283 (1972). Congress repealed the legislation in 1981. 95 Stat. 827, Pub L. No. 97-35 tit. XXI, § 2193(b)(1) (1981).

116.   National Institutes of Health, Consensus Conference, *Newborn Screening for Sickle Cell Disease and Other Hemoglobinopathies*, 258 J. A.M.A. 1205, 1209 (1987).

117.   Acuff & Faden, *supra* note 64.

118.   If a parent has "undertaken" reasonable efforts to ensure that acceptable medical treatment is being provided for the [] child," a court should defer to the parent's reasonable choice of how medical care should be provided. *In re* Hofbauer 393 N.E.2d 1009, 1014 (N.Y. 1979)(finding no medical neglect where parents chose nutrition and metabolic therapy for child with Hodgkin's disease and refused to follow medical advice of the majority of the medical profession which recommends radiation and chemotherapy). Where a parent refuses to follow any medical advice or where the medical opinion as to diagnosis and treatment of a life-threatening disease is clear and uncontested, courts will refuse to permit a parent's decision to endanger the child. *In re* Custody of Minor, 434 N.E.2d 601 (Mass. 1982); *In re* Custody of a Minor, 393 N.E.2d 836 (Mass. 1979); *In re* Hamilton, 657 S.W.2d 425 (Tenn.Ct.App. 1983).

119.   *See, e.g.*, Field, *Controlling the Woman to Protect the Fetus*, 17 Law, Med. & Health Care 114 (1989) [hereinafter Field]; Johnsen, *The Creation of Fetal Rights: Conflicts with Women's Constitutional Rights to Liberty, Privacy and Equal Protection*, 95 Yale L.J. 599 (1986); Nelson & Milliken, *Compelled Medical Treatment of Pregnant Women: Life, Liberty and Law in Conflict*, 259 J. A.M.A. 1060 (1988); Nelson, Buggy & Weil, *Forced Medical Treatment of Pregnant Women: "Compelling Each to Live as Seems Good to the Rest,"* 37 Hastings L.J. 703 (1986).

120. Jefferson v. Griffin Spalding County Hosp. Auth., 274 S.E.2d 457 (Ga. 1981) (cesarean section ordered over religious objection); Raleigh Fitkin-Paul Morgan Memorial Hosp. v. Anderson, 201 A.2d 537 (N.J. 1964), *cert. denied* 377 U.S. 985 (1964) (blood transfusion ordered over religious objection); *In re* Jamaica Hospital, 491 N.Y.S.2d 898 (Sup. Ct. 1985) (blood transfusion ordered over religious objection); Crouse Irving Memorial Hosp., Inc. v. Paddock, 485 N.Y.S.2d 443 (Sup. Ct. 1985) (blood transfusion ordered over religious objection). *Contra* Taft v. Taft, 446 N.E.2d 395 (Mass. 1983) (vacating an order requiring vaginal surgery, over religious objection, which would have facilitated delivery).

121. *In re A.C.*, 573 A.2d 1235 (D.C. App. 1990) (en banc).

122. *Id.* at 1247.

123. Greenhouse, *Hospital Sets Policy on Pregnant Patients' Rights*, N.Y. Times, Nov. 29, 1990.

124. Board of Trustees, American Medical Association, *Legal Interventions During Pregnancy*, 264 J. A.M.A. 2663 (1990).

125. American College of Obstetricians and Gynecologists, Committee on Ethics Opinion 55, Patient Choice: Maternal-Fetal Conflict (Oct. 1987).

126. American Academy of Pediatrics, Committee on Substance Abuse, *Drug Exposed Infants*, 86 Pediatrics 639, 642 (1990).

127. Kolder, Gallagher & Parsons, *Court Ordered Obstetrical Interventions*, 316 New Eng. J. Med. 1192 (1987).

128. Johnson v. Florida, 578 So.2d 419 (Fla. Ct. App. 1991) (upholding prosecution for delivery of controlled substances to a minor through umbilical cord); People v. Hardy, 469 N.W.2d 50 (Mich. 1991) (overturning conviction under statute prohibiting drug delivery), *appeal denied*, 471 N.W.2d 619 (Mich. 1991); Ohio v. Gray, No. L-89-239, 1990 WL 125695 (Ohio Ct. App. 1990) (barring prosecution on same grounds); Reves v. Superior Court, 75 Cal.App.3d 214 (1977) (child endangering statute did not include woman's prenatal conduct).

129. Tex. Penal Code Ann. § 22.012(a) (Vernon Supp. 1991).

130. Field, *supra* note 119, at 118.

2

BETWIXT AND BETWEEN: ADOLESCENTS AND HIV

By Phyllis Arnold

I. Introduction

The enormous difficulties that a person with HIV disease encounters in obtaining access to health care are compounded significantly when the infected individual is an adolescent. Adolescents are neither children — whose rights are clearly limited and protectable only by the parent, legal guardian, or the state as *parens patriae* — nor adults. "In many ways, adolescence is a kind of limbo."[1]

Perhaps nowhere is the anomalous status of adolescents more evident than in the area of HIV infection. While children are apt to contract the disease perinatally or through transfusions, adolescents, like adults, are more likely to contract the disease through actions they, in part, control. The corollary logic of permitting adolescents to exercise control over health care decisions made necessary by the consequences of their actions quickly runs into legal roadblocks and difficult planning challenges. General issues of consent and attendant issues of confidentiality are raised routinely in the discussion of the adolescent HIV problem. Beyond the legal questions there is general consensus that HIV testing of adolescents should be undertaken with caution — only after appropriate consideration of its ramifications for this diverse group of subjects for whom effective counseling and treatment are especially critical. With growing evidence that early treatment of

asymptomatic infection is beneficial and that the failure to develop
effective preventive strategies for adolescents poses the risk of massive
morbidity and mortality in the young adult population, it is important
to address the need for HIV testing of teens. However, it is equally
important to do so with an understanding of the need to make integrated HIV testing, treatment, and counseling initiatives available to
adolescents in a culturally and developmentally appropriate manner
that responds to their concerns about autonomy and confidentiality.
This chapter will examine the legal framework surrounding teenagers'
ability to consent to HIV testing and to maintain control over the
dissemination of HIV-related information. It will first address the
nature of the HIV problem in the adolescent community and then touch
briefly on a number of the questions that invariably result from inquiry
into consent and confidentiality issues, including questions of cost,
appropriateness, access to experimental drug therapies, and effectiveness of school-based educational initiatives. Special issues also arise for
adolescents in institutional settings such as foster care and juvenile
detention facilities. Beyond the adolescent-specific difficulties, teenage
youths face the same problems encountered by everyone else with HIV
infection, including, for example, discrimination and refusals to treat.
As the HIV epidemic enters its second decade, one focus of our attention must be the "third wave" of HIV carriers represented by adolescents.[2]

II. Nature of the Problem

The extent of HIV infection in the adolescent community is something
of a mystery. There are only limited direct data available to document
how widespread HIV infection is among adolescents, and few studies
have focused on this population. Until recently, broad HIV testing of
adolescents was thought ill-advised, due, in part, to the limited availability and types of resources with which to treat them and to the fact
that only small numbers of adolescents show symptoms of the virus.[3]

Several screening programs and recent seroprevalence studies have
begun to provide information on HIV infection among adolescents.
Data from studies among some 69,000 Job Corps entrants ages 16 to 21
years revealed a seroprevalence rate of 3.9 per 1,000. Seven percent of
the runaway and homeless youths served by a center in New York City
were HIV-positive. Five out of thirteen college campuses sampled in

different parts of the country revealed evidence of seropositivity among students using health services; serosurveys of close to 14,000 specimens revealed a seropositivity rate of 1 per 500. Finally, surveys of HIV-positive newborns born in New York State between November 30, 1987, and November 30, 1988, which, in turn, reflect the mother's HIV status, revealed that 1 per 1,000 babies born to 15-year-old mothers and 1 per 100 babies born to 19-year-old mothers were HIV-infected. Moreover, while there were only ten HIV-positive babies born to mothers under age 20 up until April 1988, there were eighty-eight such babies born in the thirteen months between April 1988 and May 1989.[4]

The number of fully developed AIDS cases in the adolescent population is relatively small, but the prevalence of HIV disease in its earliest stages may be substantially greater. As of June 1991, the CDC reported a cumulative total of 179,694 cases of diagnosed AIDS in people 13 years of age and older; 699 of these cases were reported in the 13-to-19-year-old age group. That number, however, rises dramatically in the next two age categories: 7,417 cases were reported in the 20-to-24-year-old group and 28,849 cases were reported in the 25-to-29-year-old group.[5] Given the extended latency period before the onset of symptoms, it is clear that young people are becoming infected with the HIV virus in their teens. Indeed, 20 percent of those persons with AIDS who develop the illness between ages 20 and 29 are thought to have acquired the disease during adolescence.[6]

In addition to these direct data, indirect evidence suggests that the risk of HIV infection in adolescents is more widespread. Statistics reflect a high incidence of teenage pregnancy[7] and sexually transmitted disease[8] — both indicators of high-risk sexual activities. Evidence of ongoing intravenous drug use in certain communities[9] is also problematic. In fact, recent evidence suggests that crack cocaine use, which often leads to high-risk sexual behavior, may be a more significant factor in HIV exposure of adolescents than intravenous drug use.[10] Finally, surveys of adolescent attitudes about AIDS further fuel the need to address the peculiar problems that surround HIV testing, prevention, and treatment of this group.[11]

The unique developmental, social, and emotional characteristics of adolescents add to the concern. Indeed, the distinguishing features of teens may make them peculiarly susceptible to infection and potentially difficult to reach with traditional intervention approaches. Adolescent development is characterized by formulation of self-identity and individuation from family processes that often include experimentation and risk-taking behavior with sex and drugs. Adolescents have feelings of invulnerability and tend to deny experiences perceived as overwhelming. Adolescent thinking is concrete, rooted to the present and to current experiences. As noted by one expert, the notion of transmission of an unseen virus and of being an asymptomatic carrier of illness is abstract and conceptually difficult for many adolescents to grasp.[12] Finally, adolescents are subject to intense peer pressure and may thus feel forced to conform to a social norm that encourages dangerous behavior.

Recognizing the distinctive developmental characteristics of adolescents is a critical part of understanding the nature of the HIV problem in this community, for they help explain the high level of risky behavior as well as the widespread denial of the risk of exposure. It is just as important, however, to appreciate that adolescents are a diverse group, and that how we address both teenagers' risky behavior and their own perceptions of the risk of exposure must vary because adolescents do different things at different stages of their lives and in different settings. A 13-year-old is different from and likely to engage in different types of activity than a 17-year-old. Runaway and homeless teens, whose experiences often include physical and sexual abuse, disruptive residential placements, jail, drug use, survival sex, and overall poor health, live different lives from those residing at home. Yet young prostitutes may feel themselves immune if they are not gay men and/or not shooting drugs themselves.[13]

Gay and lesbian youths face peculiar problems of denial, low self-esteem, and lack of social sanction and support at a time when they are struggling with their sexual identity. And yet young lesbians may believe they cannot contract HIV based simply on the low incidence of reported AIDS in lesbians.[14] Young gay men tend to view the virus as a problem faced solely by an older generation of homosexuals, and, indeed, many teenage boys who have had same-sex partners do not identify as gay and may not perceive the risk presented by unprotected sex.[15] For heterosexual teenagers, homophobia may feed the denial generally associated with HIV.[16] Black and Hispanic young people, whose living conditions disproportionately reflect poverty, racism, and alienation, are likely to be directly in the path of the virus, both behaviorally and geographically.

Young people who share needles for drugs (including steroids) or who engage in unprotected sex are at particular risk, especially when these teenagers are in geographic areas with a high incidence of HIV infection. Indeed, many youths engaging in high-risk behaviors appear to be those who also are most likely to be without traditional health, social, and educational support systems.[17] Although it is critical to remember that it is the high-risk behavior rather than his or her geographic group, ethnic group, age, or sexual orientation that puts the youth at risk of infection, the design of effective treatment and prevention strategies must respond to differences in adolescent development, lifestyle, and behavior.

Adolescents need targeted, appropriate, and readily available health care services. Such services are, however, generally unavailable to teenagers, and there is a dearth of trained, skilled adult professionals to accommodate this population.[18] Curtailing risky behavior is the key to arresting the spread of infection in the adolescent community, yet the preventive messages projected may not adequately address the needs of young adults. At a time when a single infected partner may expose one to the virus and when long-term relationships may be measured by weeks or months, telling teenagers to be monogamous is unlikely to be particularly effective. Making condoms available to teenagers is a good idea, but adolescents must also acquire the skills necessary to use them properly and to negotiate their use interpersonally. Finally, lest we spawn a generation of young adults whose understanding of the relationship between HIV and death makes them fearful of intimacy, we should teach teenagers how to be intimate safely. We also should consider presenting teenagers with a picture of people living with HIV and not simply dying of AIDS.

III. The Range of Issues Facing Adolescents with HIV

The law of consent and confidentiality, discussed later in this chapter, is the threshold issue confronting those who would like to facilitate adolescent access to HIV testing and treatment services. Yet it is just the first of many pressing questions.

A. Payment and Adolescent-Friendly Interventions

Counseling, support, and treatment services, whether ambulatory or in-patient, are expensive. Thus, all but independently wealthy teenagers will be unable to absorb these costs themselves, as adolescents generally are uninsured and without other means to pay for health care.

On the other hand, turning to one's parents for payment is hardly an option for one who wants to maintain confidentiality. While federal funds are available for certain medications and Medicaid may cover certain treatments and services,[19] adolescents' independent and confidential eligibility for benefits remains problematic.

The quality and nature of services offered to adolescents is a source of continuing concern. Advocates repeatedly highlight the need to meet adolescents on their own terms through nonjudgmental, directed, and appropriate outreach, counseling, and support services. Informed consent protocols must be crafted in terms that are concrete and meaningful to young adults. Those who work with teenagers must be sensitized to the cultural and developmental factors that make it necessary to reassess intervention strategies and to recast them in adolescent-friendly terms.[20] Perhaps more so than most, adolescents need aggressive advocates to help them navigate the daunting maze of administrative bureaucracy through which so many services are delivered. Even something as seemingly simple as establishing a residence or obtaining necessary documents may prove impossible to an unversed young person.

B. Youths in Special Circumstances

Specialized residential settings, such as foster care and detention, present enormous urgent challenges. For example, the diffusion of responsibility for young people in foster care makes adolescents vulnerable to the erosion of their rights. Natural parents, foster parents, courts, and social workers may become involved in the decision-making process[21] to the point where they may usurp a teenager's otherwise authorized ability to make HIV-related decisions. This extended list of interested parties may threaten to expand the universe of disclosure so as to make confidentiality protections difficult, if not impossible to administer. In New York State, for instance, the law permits the disclosure of HIV-related information to "an authorized agency in connection with foster care or adoption of a child."[22] That agency, in turn, must disclose the medical history of the child to the prospective adoptive or foster parents.[23] Foster parents are expressly authorized to disclose the child's HIV-related information for the purpose of providing care, treatment, or supervision, and prospective adoptive parents are expressly authorized to disclose such information for any purpose so long as the child has been placed with them for adoption.[24] As the universe of permissible recipients expands, it becomes more and more difficult to accord to a youth in foster care the protection that the law generally contemplates.[25]

HIV-positive adolescents in foster care may also confront discriminatory refusals to place them in suitable homes. Finally, the obstacles that teenagers confront in obtaining access to health care and appropriate treatment may, as a practical matter, be compounded significantly when layers of bureaucracy stand between infected youths and emerging medical interventions.[26]

Adolescents who are clients of more than one agency face additional problems. On the one hand, effective treatment requires assurances of confidentiality. On the other hand, those assurances may prevent one agency from knowing what another agency is doing, resulting in fragmented and possibly duplicative or conflicting interventions. It is sound policy to ask adolescents for their permission to disclose HIV-related information to outside agencies. The full development of effective interagency and case management protocols should be on the agenda of service providers.

C. Clinical Trials

Access to experimental drugs and clinical drug trials is a further source of debate. Historically, there have been few if any opportunities for adolescent enrollment into research protocols.[27] Federal law governs this issue and certainly contemplates such participation.[28] However, because of the threshold capacity issue and the need for appropriate psychosocial support, there are especially difficult questions involved in inviting adolescents into the research process predicated on an adult model and designed ultimately for the benefit of third parties.[29] As the medical community advances toward more effective treatment, access to trials may become increasingly an issue.

D. School-Based Initiatives

Recent school-based AIDS-education initiatives are an important part of the prevention effort. Many schools have capitalized on this unique opportunity to reach adolescents by incorporating sex- and HIV education into their curricula,[30] and a number of school teachers believe it appropriate to address, and are addressing, a range of such topics in the classroom.[31] However, it is important to develop techniques and principles for evaluating the effectiveness of these educational programs.

Other school-based programs are also receiving national attention. For example, New York City's Board of Education recently approved a plan to make condoms available on request to its 250,000 high school students.[32] Yet the controversy so often encountered in undertaking such initiatives threatens the ability to communicate potentially lifesaving information to young people.[33]

IV. Consent and Confidentiality

The law of consent and confidentiality appears to be the logical starting point for analysis, for a number of the other issues highlighted turn, in part, on the resolution of consent and confidentiality issues. The permutations of the questions are numerous. In many respects, the model of a willing adolescent who wants to gain independent and confidential access to HIV-related health care is the most straightforward, bringing to bear the interests of the youth, his or her parents, and the state, as the guarantor of the public welfare through its police power. The landscape changes somewhat when a parent seeks testing for an unwilling adolescent, when an adolescent wants to be tested and a parent refuses,[34] or when a residential setting such as detention or foster care, introduces the interests of third parties. These variations of the model pose difficult questions of policy and law. To the extent that these issues may be informed by conclusions drawn from the straightforward model, and to the further extent that consent and confidentiality continue to function as barriers to the delivery of health services to adolescents, it seems appropriate to turn attention first to the legal questions faced by a willing adolescent who wishes to gain independent and confidential access to HIV-related care.

A. Background

The threshold problem confronting adolescents who seek medical care can be stated succinctly. Tort law protects all people against unauthorized intrusions into their bodies. The provision of medical treatment without consent amounts to a tort called "battery" for which a physician may be ordered to pay damages.[35] To be effective, consent must be both informed[36] and given by one with capacity to consent. Minors generally lack legal capacity to consent, thus making parental permission necessary before a health care worker may legally administer treatment to a minor.[37]

Several policies underlie the common law parental consent requirement. Its traditional foundation lies in the assumption that minors lack the cognitive capacity, the experience, and the maturity needed to give meaningful consent to medical procedures.[38] The requirement additionally reflects the acknowledgement that parents have maintenance and support obligations that could be affected materially by an unsuccessful medical procedure.[39] It protects as well the parents' right to exercise control over the upbringing of their children.[40]

There are numerous exceptions to the parental consent requirement that are based broadly either on the minor's particular health need or on his or her status relative to the parents. For example (as discussed below) states have provided minors access, through special legislation, to medical treatment for venereal or other sexually transmitted diseases, alcohol and other substance abuse, and pregnancy. These laws reflect a policy judgment that the benefit of permitting independent minor access to health care outweighs the cost of insisting on parental consent. That policy is especially applicable to conditions for which adolescent reluctance to inform parents may result in deterring teens from seeking appropriate treatment. Alternatively (as also discussed below), minors who demonstrate sufficient maturity to understand fully the implications of and the alternatives to suggested medical procedures, or those whose living arrangements evidence a status inconsistent with the filial relation, frequently may consent to their own medical treatment for any condition. Finally, the authority for health care providers to treat at least older minors for their own benefit appears to have gone unchallenged.[41]

The statutory and common law exceptions to the parental consent rule are often attended by a variety of parental notification provisions that reflect the ongoing tension between and reconciliation of the interests of the minor, the public, and the family. The physician-patient privilege that protects disclosures made in the course of rendering medical diagnoses and treatment also may play a role in resolving issues of confidentiality that arise in providing health care to adolescents.

Indeed, the questions of consent and confidentiality present two distinct problems. A minor's ability to consent independently to medical treatment speaks to the question of one's right to make the decision for oneself. The ability to ensure the confidentiality of that decision speaks to the issue of one's right to control the dissemination of information about that personal choice. These rights are not necessarily coextensive, and confidentiality provisions are not always as protective of the minor's autonomy as are provisions on consent.[42] The result, notwithstanding an adolescent's ability to consent to medical treatment in any given circumstance, is that he or she may confront the prospect of parental notification down the road, with the unfortunate consequence that the fear of disclosure of embarrassing behaviors may ultimately inhibit minors who need health care from seeking it out.

The implications of this divergence between the law of consent and the law of confidentiality are especially troubling in the area of adolescents and HIV disease. Although as a matter of medical and social policy an adolescent who manages to get access to HIV testing and treatment ought to be protected by the overall confidentiality provisions of specific HIV statutes found in many states, regardless of the source of authority for treating the youth, this is not always the obvious result. Moreover, not all states have such HIV confidentiality statutes, leaving open the disturbing prospect that an adolescent who wants to and can be tested and treated for HIV disease will forgo the opportunity out of concern that his or her parents may ultimately learn about the high-risk behaviors that motivated the desire to be tested in the first place.

However strong the reason to facilitate adolescents' access to HIV testing, an effective testing program requires more than a mere test. Adolescents need to be prepared both socially and psychologically to cope effectively with the results of an HIV test. Many in the community of advocates and health care workers believe that before testing is encouraged for adolescents a full range of appropriate and targeted services must be in place for the subject.[43] The absence of age-appropriate support mechanisms may increase adolescents' sense of isolation and fatalism, and thus the risks associated with HIV testing.[44] Adolescents themselves may not fully appreciate the consequences of disclosing their HIV status to others.[45] And while a negative test result may alleviate a young person's anxiety, it may also generate a false sense of security, leading to further high-risk behaviors.

While facilitating a minor's access to HIV testing and treatment is a necessary part of addressing HIV infection in the adolescent population, it is not sufficient. The legal strategies available for overcoming the obstacles presented by the parental consent requirement and by parental notification provisions are only the beginning of the challenge of serving this population. We turn next to an examination of some of those strategies.

B. HIV Statutes Covering Minors

Ten states currently have statutes that authorize minors to consent to HIV testing.[46] The mechanisms vary somewhat. For example, Arizona and New York codify a "mature minor" rule (discussed more fully below) by requiring that a test subject give informed consent to the test and by defining the subject's capacity to consent in terms of his or her ability, "without regard to age," to appreciate and understand the nature and consequences of the proposed procedure and to make an informed decision about it.[47] Several states simply lower the age of consent for purposes of authorizing HIV testing or treatment.[48] California reflects a hybrid of these two schemes, in that it provides that minors 12 years of age and older are capable of giving consent if competent to do so.[49] The remaining states appear to cover minors of any age.[50]

Only four of the states that allow minors access to HIV testing also authorize minor consent to HIV treatment.[51] Most of the HIV statutes impose, for all covered by the law, counseling obligations on the health care provider, either in the form of pre-test counseling through the vehicle of informed consent, or post-test counseling, or both. Counseling provisions generally call for an explanation of the test, including its purposes, uses, and the meaning of its results, an explanation of the nature of the disease and of the procedures to be followed, information about high-risk and preventive behaviors, and efforts to address the emotional and physical consequences.[52] Unique among the statutes is Colorado's, which requires the health care provider to counsel a minor on the importance of involving his or her parents in the treatment.[53]

The laws contain a variety of provisions regarding confidentiality. Several states prohibit those in possession of HIV test-related information from disclosing or being compelled to disclose that information or the identity of the test subject.[54] However, these general confidentiality requirements are typically subject to a host of exceptions permitting disclosure without the subject's consent to those with a medical or administrative "need to know,"[55] including, for example, health care providers, oversight review committees, authorized agencies connected to activities such as foster care or adoption of children, and those permitted access to the information by court order.[56] California imposes penalties on those who negligently or willfully disclose to any third party the results of an HIV test in a way that identifies the subject.[57] And both Delaware and Ohio appear to permit disclosure to the subject's legal guardian,[58] although both statutes are phrased in terms of disclosure to the subject or the subject's legal guardian.

Several states specifically address the issue of parental notification of HIV-related information pertaining to their minor children. Colorado makes absolutely confidential the fact of a minor's consultation, examination, and treatment for HIV infection, but provides for optional notification to the parents or legal guardian if the minor is under 16 years of age or not emancipated.[59] In Michigan, a health care provider may, but is not obligated to, inform the parent or guardian as to the treatment suggested or rendered.[60]

New York's statute reflects a mature minor rule for purposes of authorizing an individual to consent to a proposed disclosure of confidential HIV-related information.[61] But the law permits a physician to disclose such information about a minor to a person known to be authorized by law to consent to health care for the minor if, among other things, the physician reasonably believes that disclosure is medically necessary to provide timely care and treatment. The statute prohibits such disclosure if, in the physician's judgment, either the disclosure would not be in the best interest of the minor or the minor is authorized by law to consent to the particular care and treatment.[62] Washington, whose confidentiality statute generally prohibits the voluntary or compelled disclosure of HIV-related information but authorizes the subject or the subject's legal representative to receive such information, expressly prohibits disclosure to a representative of a "competent" minor over 14 years of age.[63] Iowa appears to be unique in requiring a testing facility to disclose a positive test result to a minor's legal guardian and in prescribing that the minor be so informed before testing.[64]

Although these ten statutes provide some form of explicit authority for adolescents to consent to HIV testing, they are not without their problems. Questions arise over the minor's access to treatment, the right to refuse testing, confidentiality, mandatory parental notification, and financial liability.

First, in terms of facilitating access to HIV-related care, only a handful of these laws expressly authorize a minor to consent to treatment as well as testing. The increasing number and availability of prophylactic treatment interventions makes this an especially unfortunate statutory gap, for while there may have been some benefit initially in testing and counseling minors for purposes of checking the spread of the virus, there is now every reason to authorize minor consent to HIV treatment as well. Absent such express authority in HIV testing statutes, we are left with a senseless regulatory scheme that allows minors to consent to the HIV test but not to the necessary follow-up treatment, forcing advocates and physicians to turn to residual common law or statutory authority, when available, as a basis for the minor's consent to treatment. The importance of allowing minors access to treatment interventions makes this a tortured and tenuous strategy on which to rely.

Second, only Delaware addresses the problem posed by a young person who refuses HIV testing or treatment.[65] Although it may seem obvious that a person who has the right to consent to medical procedures also has the right to refuse them,[66] that is not so clear. There are unarticulated policies underlying the statutes authorizing minors to consent to HIV testing that reflect an accommodation of the interests of the state, in both protecting the public health and promoting parental authority, and of the minor, in exercising autonomy over decisions concerning the integrity of his or her own body. Clearly, when a statute gives a minor the authority to consent to testing or treatment, the legislature has given priority to the converging interests of the minor's autonomy and the state's effort to protect the public health. When the refusal issue arises, these interests diverge and may depend for their readjustment on the initial legislative policy of favoring either minor autonomy or the facilitation of access to health care in the public interest.[67] Delaware appears to be singular to date in having struck the balance in favor of minor autonomy by authorizing minors to consent to and to refuse HIV-related services.

Third, issues arise in the area of confidentiality. In some instances, statutory exceptions are troubling, especially with respect to adolescents who are already a part of a state's foster care or juvenile justice system. Indeed, the state's interest may shift as the state undertakes the role of ensuring public safety in different institutional settings, raising especially thorny questions of access to HIV-related information in situations where private strangers to the parent-child relationship claim an interest in being advised of a subject's HIV status.

In addition, statutes that authorize disclosure of HIV-related information to a subject or to the subject's legal guardian or representative raise questions of interpretation when applied to minors who have exercised their authority under the statute to consent to the test.[68] While both common sense and medical and social policy suggest that a minor who has consented to the test generally ought to be the only permissible recipient of the information, only Arizona and New York appear to sanction that result.[69] Delaware and Ohio do not.[70]

A further confidentiality issue is presented by provisions that give the health care worker the option of parental notification. The absence of guidelines to govern this determination may contribute to the health care worker's hesitancy to treat minors,[71] and leaves this critical element in the delivery of health care to adolescents subject to the fortuitous factors surrounding the selection of a health care provider. Several commentators have suggested that, absent statutory prescription, the general physician-patient privilege should prevail to shield this information from disclosure to parents without the minor's consent, unless there is a substantial reason to breach confidentiality, such as a danger to the patient's life presented by, for example, suicidal ideation.[72]

Fourth, mandatory parental notification is especially troublesome. To the extent that the prospect of such notification deters young people from seeking HIV testing or treatment, it threatens to render meaningless the minor's independent authority to give consent. Although there is some support for the proposition that the Fourteenth Amendment protects one's right of privacy with respect to information about one's HIV status,[73] it is possible that the state's interest in protecting the minor against improvident decision-making and in protecting parental authority will be found sufficiently compelling to sustain the legislative policy of mandatory parental notification.[74] While the serious and long-term consequences of treatment may substantiate the parental interest in playing a role as the minor approaches treatment decisions, there is nothing to suggest that optional parental notification would not sufficiently accommodate such an enhanced concern. Ultimately, this again broaches the question of the policy underlying the HIV testing statute, and it requires decision-makers to focus on the relative importance of facilitating minor access to HIV-related health care that is in the best interest of the minor and of protecting the public health.

Finally, several of the ten states in which adolescents may consent independently to HIV testing or treatment expressly relieve the parents of the obligation to pay for procedures to which they have not consented.[75] More than anything, perhaps, these provisions underscore the practical problem adolescents face in paying for HIV testing and treatment services in a manner that preserves their confidentiality. It seems clear, therefore, that even in states that expressly allow minors to consent to HIV testing or treatment, there may be several barriers to the delivery of appropriate HIV-related health care.

C. Other Sources of Authority for Minor Access to HIV-Related Health Care

Several additional avenues are available through which an adolescent who wants to be tested or treated for HIV infection may be able to do so independently of his or her parents. Based broadly either on the minor's presenting health need or on his or her status relative to the parents, these legislatively and judicially recognized exceptions to the parental consent rule may, depending on the circumstances, provide such authority. These options are important for minors in states without general HIV testing or confidentiality statutes. They also may be helpful in states with such statutes as an alternative means for a minor to receive specific counseling and confidentiality protections.

1. Health Need

Virtually all states have statutes that authorize minors to consent to diagnosis and treatment for venereal or other sexually transmitted disease.[76] These statutes differ as to their minimum eligible age of consent and their provisions regarding parental notification, although the majority of laws leave the notification issue to the discretion of the physician.[77] In those few states where HIV or AIDS is defined by statute, regulation, or case law as a contagious or venereal or sexually transmitted disease, minors thus have the authority to consent to HIV-related services.[78]

Making HIV-related care available to minors through the vehicle of venereal or sexually transmitted disease consent provisions may make some sense. The determination that the benefit of allowing independent minor access to treatment for sexually transmitted disease outweighs the cost of insisting on parental consent applies equally in the area of

HIV infection, where the prospect of parental involvement may deter the youth from seeking treatment. However, while this route of authority for adolescent consent may be unencumbered by risks in some states, it may pose problems in others. Designation of HIV as a sexually transmitted disease may trigger a host of reporting and other regulatory control measures, such as isolation and contact tracing. In light of the limitations of current medical treatment, these measures may be very problematic in the HIV setting where the potential for discrimination is great and where voluntary cooperation and assurances of confidentiality are essential.[79]

Treatment for pregnancy and use of alcohol or other substances is also generally made available to minors without parental consent. Again, eligibility and parental notification provisions vary.[80] The utility of these statutory provisions may depend on the extent to which treatment for HIV disease is a part of the treatment delivered for the specific condition for which the adolescent is statutorily permitted to consent to treatment.

2. Status

The "mature minor" rule provides one of the best sources of authority for minors to consent independently to HIV testing or treatment. A mature minor is generally one who is sufficiently intelligent and mature to understand the risks and benefits of treatment, regardless of his or her financial independence or living situation.[81]

The rule is codified in several states. Arkansas, for example, authorizes the consent to any recommended medical or surgical treatment by "[a]ny unemancipated minor of sufficient intelligence to understand and appreciate the consequences of the proposed surgical or medical treatment or procedure...."[82] Idaho provides that anyone of sufficient intelligence and awareness to generally "comprehend the need for, the nature of and the significant risks ordinarily inherent in any contemplated hospital, medical, dental, or surgical care, treatment or procedure is competent to consent thereto on his own behalf."[83]

Even without statutory recognition, the mature minor rule may be established judicially. In *Younts v. St. Francis Hospital and School of Nursing*,[84] for example, the court dismissed a battery claim asserted by a 17-year-old who, while visiting her mother in the hospital, injured her finger and underwent minor surgery without her mother's consent. The mother was semiconscious at the time and the father was unavailable.

The minor, whose intelligence and capability were acknowledged by the court, was fully conscious throughout the successful procedure and raised no objection. Under these circumstances, the court found the minor mature enough to understand the procedure's nature and consequences and to knowingly consent to such beneficial treatment.[85]

Two recent cases have similarly recognized the mature minor rule. The Illinois Supreme Court permitted a demonstrably mature 17-year-old to refuse blood transfusions on religious grounds.[86] And the Tennessee Supreme Court adopted the rule in sustaining the dismissal after trial of a battery and malpractice claim asserted by a high school student just shy of her eighteenth birthday who obtained osteopathic treatment without parental consent.[87] The minor in that case was a senior in high school who was licensed to drive and who exercised substantial discretion over her access to a parental checking account with which she paid for the challenged services. The court determined that a minor's ability to consent was a question of fact for the jury, to be resolved by examining his or her age, ability, experience, education, training, degree of maturity and judgment, and conduct and demeanor in order to assess whether the total circumstances suggest that the minor has the ability to appreciate the nature of the treatment and its risks and consequences.[88]

Based on both statutory and case law, several commentators have formulated the following criteria for determining the applicability of the mature minor rule: (1) the minor is near majority — generally 15 years of age or older; (2) he or she demonstrates sufficient maturity and intelligence to understand the steps proposed; (3) the treatment is for the benefit of the minor; and (4) the treatment is not overly complex.[89]

The mature minor rule has potential as a source of authority for adolescent consent to HIV testing and treatment. Indeed, the United States Supreme Court has employed the mature minor principle in response to challenges to state-imposed restrictions on minors' access to contraception and abortion.[90] Thus, for example, a statute that conditions a minor's access to abortion on parental notice or consent must provide an alternative mechanism through which she can demonstrate either that she is mature enough to make the decision herself or that, absent a demonstrated maturity, the abortion would be in her best interests.[91] Notwithstanding the ongoing erosion of the federal privacy interest underlying required limitations on abortion restrictions generally,[92] even the most recent of the high Court's decisions in the area of minor access to abortion leave the required bypass mechanism intact, and thus give mature minors some federal constitutional predicate for seeking independent access to abortion.[93] In addition, developing federal constitutional law on the issue of a competent adult's liberty interest in making medical decisions free of governmental interference may provide some basis for urging a comparable interest on behalf of a mature minor.[94]

Emancipation is an additional source of authority for young people to consent to HIV testing and treatment. An "emancipated minor" is generally one who is not subject to parental control.[95] A variety of factors may be recognized either by statute or case law[96] as reflecting a relationship between parent and child that is inconsistent with the filial relationship. Older adolescents who live separately from their parents or who are self-supporting may be found to be emancipated.[97] Marriage, pregnancy, parenthood, and enlistment in the armed forces also may evince a status sufficiently independent of his or her parents to enable a minor to consent to health care.[98] In some states, judicial proceedings are prescribed to declare a minor emancipated.[99] Moreover, in response to the difficulty otherwise encountered of determining whether a minor satisfies mature minor or emancipation requirements, some states have enacted statutes shielding health care workers from liability for erroneous determinations made in good faith.[100]

Of particular relevance when addressing HIV and adolescents is one commentator's view that runaway and homeless youth should be regarded as emancipated to the extent that they refuse to identify or to help locate the parents.[101] This can be an especially helpful source of authority for enabling this segment of the adolescent population to consent to testing and treatment for HIV infection.

D. Parental Notification

Whether based on the presenting health need or on the minor's developmental status or living situation, the alternative sources of authority for minor consent to HIV-related health care leave open the question of what, if any, notification must be made to the parents. The answer to this question may vary considerably, and may, in addition, turn on whether the state has a general HIV confidentiality statute that covers HIV-related information but that does not expressly authorize minors to consent to HIV testing or treatment. In such a case, the minor may have obtained independent access to HIV-related health care through some other statutory or common law mechanism. Thus, it will be necessary to examine the specific parental notification provisions attached to those mechanisms as well as any parental notification provisions attached to the HIV testing or confidentiality statute, with an eye toward applying the more protective of the two.

For example, in Illinois, minors age 12 and over may consent independently to treatment for venereal disease and for drug and alcohol abuse, and parental notification is optional. If the health care provider believes that the family's involvement will not be detrimental to the patient, he or she may, with the minor's consent, make reasonable efforts to involve the family in the treatment. However, in the case of treatment for alcohol abuse, the parent or guardian must be notified following the second treatment unless notification would jeopardize the course of treatment, and must, in any event, be notified if treatment extends beyond a period of three months.[102] The Illinois HIV statute, as here relevant, generally ensures confidentiality of the identity of the test subject and the results of the test, except that disclosure is authorized to the test subject or to his or her legally authorized representative.[103]

Massachusetts authorizes a minor to consent to medical care if he or she is, *inter alia*, married, a parent, a member of the armed forces, pregnant, living apart from the parent or guardian and managing his or her own financial affairs, or if he or she reasonably believes him- or herself to be suffering from or to have had contact with a specified dangerous disease. Records and information pertaining to such care are confidential except that, if the health care worker reasonably believes that the minor's condition threatens his or her life, parental notification is required.[104] The Massachusetts HIV statute absolutely prohibits the disclosure of HIV test results to anyone other than the test subject without the subject's consent.[105]

In New Jersey, minors may consent to medical care for, *inter alia*, venereal disease and sexual assault. In the latter case, parental notification is required unless the physician determines that the best interests of the patient require otherwise.[106] Minors in New Jersey also are authorized to consent to medical care if they are married, pregnant, or parents, in which case, parental notification is optional.[107] By contrast, the New Jersey HIV statute generally permits disclosure of HIV-related information only upon the subject's written, informed consent, and appears to authorize persons 12 years of age or older to give such consent.[108]

V. Conclusion

This patchwork of authority governing minor access to HIV-related health care and parental notification practices is unfortunate, to say the least. Notwithstanding the scramble for legal predicates on which to render treatment based solely on an adolescent's consent, such authority is likely to be available in any of a number of forms. Indeed, several commentators have noted their inability to find a single reported case holding a physician liable for having treated an older minor for his or her own benefit without parental consent.[109]

The search for guidance on the issue of parental notification, where not explicitly prescribed, is equally tortured, but may well lead to the conclusion that notification rests in the discretion of the health care provider. While many statutes expressly direct the consideration of the minor's best interest, health care providers should be aware of both general confidentiality provisions contained in HIV-testing statutes and the indispensability of assurances of confidentiality in the minor's initial decision to seek testing or treatment. Absent statutory direction to the contrary or some evidence that disclosure is necessary to address a danger to the patient, a minor who can consent to his or her own treatment should be afforded the protection that generally surrounds the physician-patient relationship.[110] Although adolescents should be encouraged to enlist the support of a family or surrogate family to help deal with treatment demands and the consequences of illness, they ought not be compelled to do so.

For legislators and advocates, the message seems clear. As the HIV epidemic enters its second decade, it poses an enormous threat to the adolescent population. At the same time that geographic, developmental, psychological, and social factors peculiar to adolescents place them directly in the path of the disease, legal constraints and unknowns undercut the attempt to provide systematic and effective treatment and prevention programs. Laws must provide clear authority for voluntary adolescent testing and treatment without mandatory parental consent or notification requirements that will deter teenagers from being tested. When policy-makers address HIV-related issues, they should evaluate proposals in light of adolescents' needs and the particular issues that adolescents face in growing up at a time when their most secret behaviors may also threaten their lives.

BIBLIOGRAPHIC NOTE

Much of this chapter's discussion of the problems facing adolescents draws liberally from insights developed by Karen Hein, M.D., Associate Professor of Pediatrics and Epidemiology and Social Medicine, Albert Einstein College of Medicine, and Director of the Adolescent AIDS Program at Montefiore Medical Center in New York City. Among those of Dr. Hein's contributions to which the reader is referred are K. Hein, *Fighting AIDS in Adolescents*, Issues in Sci. & Tech., Spring 1991 at 67; K. Hein, *Adolescent Acquired Immunodeficiency Syndrome: A Paradigm for Training in Early Intervention and Care*, 144 Am. J. Diseases Children 46 (1990); K. Hein, *Lessons from New York City on HIV/AIDS in Adolescents*, 90 N.Y. St. J. Med. 143 (1990); K. Hein, *Commentary on Adolescent Acquired Immunodeficiency Syndrome: The Next Wave of the Human Immunodeficiency Virus Epidemic*, 114 J. Pediatrics 144 (1989); K. Hein, *AIDS in Adolescence: Exploring the Challenge*, 10 J. Adolescent Health Care, Supp., 10S (1989).

NOTES

1. J. Paxman & R. Zuckerman, Laws and Policies Affecting Adolescent Health 4 (1987) [hereinafter Paxman & Zuckerman].
2. House Select Comm. on Children, Youth & Families, AIDS and Teenagers: Emerging Issues, House Select Committee on Children, Youth and Families, 100th Cong., 1st Sess. 166 (1987) (Statement of Richard Gordon, Executive Director, Youth Development Branch, Sequoia Young Men's Christian Association) [hereinafter House Select Comm. Hearing]. Gordon characterized teens as the "third wave," after gay and bisexual men and intravenous drug users, of populations likely to be hit hardest by the HIV virus.
3. Larkin Street Youth Center, HIV and Homeless Youth: Meeting the Challenge 1 (1990) [hereinafter Larkin Street Youth Center].
4. K. Hein, *Lessons from New York City on HIV/AIDS in Adolescents*, 90 N.Y. St. J. Med. 143, 143-44 (1990)
5. U.S. Centers for Disease Control [CDC], HIV/AIDS Surveillance Report, July 1991, at 8, 11, 12.
6. V. Anderson, *A Medical Perspective for Residential Service Providers*, in Serving HIV-Infected Children, Youth, and Their Families: A Guide for Residential Group Care Providers 8 (Child Welfare League of America ed., 1989).
7. There are approximately 1 million teenage pregnancies each year, 85 percent of which are unintended. K. Hein, *AIDS in Adolescence: Exploring the Challenge*, 10 J. Adolescent Health Care, Supp., 10S–24S (1989) [hereinafter *AIDS in Adolescence*]. Forty percent of all females become pregnant as adolescents. Prothrow-Stith, *Excerpts from Address*, 10 J. Adolescent Health Care, Supp., at 5S (1989) [hereinafter Prothrow-Stith]. This evidence suggests heterosexual teen activity unaccompanied by safe-sex practices. Indeed, relative to adults, a higher percentage of teenage AIDS cases are acquired through heterosexual

transmission, K. Hein, *Adolescent Acquired Immunodeficiency Syndrome: A Paradigm for Training in Early Intervention and Care*, 144 Am. J. Diseases Children 46, 47 (1990) [hereinafter *Paradigm for Training*]; *AIDS in Adolescence, supra*, at 13S, and there is less use and availability of contraceptives. *AIDS in Adolescence, supra*, at 13S, 23S-24S. It also suggests widespread sexual activity. Studies have shown that seven in ten females and eight in ten males have had intercourse by age 20. Prothrow-Stith at 5S. The years 1985 through 1988 witnessed the greatest proportional increase in reported premarital sexual activity among teenage women since 1970, and the largest relative increase for that eighteen-year period occurred among those 15 years of age. *Premarital Sexual Experience Among Adolescent Women — United States, 1970-1988*, 39 Morbidity & Mortality Wkly. Rep. 929-32 (1991). In 1988, 75 percent of 15-to-24-year-olds who began sexual intercourse before age 18 reported having had two or more partners; 45 percent reported having had four or more partners. *Id.*

8.   Each year, one in seven teenage youths contracts a sexually transmitted disease and between 2.5 and 5 million people under 25 are treated for sexually transmitted diseases. Prothrow-Stith, *supra* note 7, at 5S. Sexually active adolescents have the highest rate of sexually transmitted disease among heterosexuals of all ages. House Select Comm. Hearing, *supra* note 2, at 41 (Statement of Mary-Ann Shafer, M.D., University of California, San Francisco); *see also AIDS in Adolescence, supra* note 7, at 12S. In 1985, those between the ages of 10 and 24 accounted for 40 percent of all syphilis and 62 percent of all gonorrhea cases. Prothrow-Stith, *supra* note 7, at 5S. Moreover, it is estimated that between 125,000 and 200,000 teenagers become involved in prostitution each year. *Id.*

9.   Although the overall incidence of drug use has recently declined in the adolescent population, injectable drug use has been reported as high as 80 percent in certain demographic groups. Larkin Street Youth Center, *supra* note 3, at 2; *AIDS in Adolescence, supra* note 7, at 24S-25S. Drug and alcohol use of any sort poses the additional indirect risk of impairing the judgment necessary to practice safer sex.

10. K. Hein, *Fighting AIDS in Adolescents*, Issues in Sci. & Tech., Spring 1991 at 67, 71 [hereinafter *Fighting AIDS in Adolescents*]; Vermund *et al., Acquired Immunodeficiency Syndrome Surveillance Profiles in New York City and the rest of the United States*, 143 Am. J. Diseases Children 1220, 1224 (1989).

11. Teenage attitudes about HIV are sobering. There is a fair amount of confusion over the modes of transmission. L. Strunin & R. Hingson, *Acquired Immunodeficiency Syndrome and Adolescents: Knowledge, Beliefs, Attitudes, and Behaviors*, 79 Pediatrics 825, 827 (1987) [hereinafter Strunin & Hingson]; *AIDS in Adolescence, supra* note 7, at 26S. Beyond that, only a small percentage of sexually active young people reported changes in their sexual behavior to avoid contracting HIV, and of those who changed their sexual practices, only 20 percent mentioned effective precautions. Strunin and Hingson, *supra*, at 827.

12. *AIDS in Adolescence, supra* note 7, at 25S-26S; *see generally* Larkin Street Youth Center, *supra* note 3, at 2-4; Prothrow-Stith, *supra* note 7, at 5S; H. Huszti & D. Chitwood, *Prevention of Pediatric and Adolescent AIDS, in* Children, Adolescents, & AIDS 147, 162-163 (J. Seibert & R. Olson eds., 1989); House Select Comm. Hearing, *supra* note 2, at 7 (Statement of C. Everett Koop, United States Surgeon General).

13. Larkin Street Youth Center, *supra* note 3, at 4.

14. *Id.*
15. *Cut Down as They Grow Up: AIDS Stalks Gay Teenagers*, N.Y. Times, Dec. 13, 1990, at A1.
16. Larkin Street Youth Center, *supra* note 3, at 4.
17. *Services and Treatment Issues, Recommendations of the Work Group*, 10 J. Adolescent Health Care, Supp., at 48S (1989) [hereinafter *Services and Treatment Issues*]; House Select Comm. Hearing, *supra* note 2, at 167 (Statement of Richard Gordon).
18. *See Fighting AIDS in Adolescents, supra* note 10, at 3, 5-6; *Paradigm for Training, supra* note 7, at 47-48.
19. *See* chapter 6 ("Wealth = Health: The Public Financing of AIDS Care").
20. Larkin Street Youth Center, *supra* note 3, at 27-30; *Services and Treatment Issues, supra* note 17, at 48S-49S.
21. *See* American Bar Association, AIDS/HIV and Confidentiality: Model Policy and Procedures 37-41 (1991).
22. N.Y. Pub. Health Law § 2782(1)(h) (McKinney Supp. 1991).
23. N.Y. Soc. Serv. Law § 373-a (McKinney Supp. 1991).
24. N.Y. Pub. Health Law § 2782(3)(c)-(d) (McKinney Supp. 1991).
25. *See AIDS Testing and Epidemiology for Youth, Recommendations of the Work Group*, 10 J. Adolescent Health Care, Supp., at 55S (1989) [hereinafter *AIDS Testing and Epidemiology*]; A. English, *Adolescents and AIDS: Legal and Ethical Questions Multiply*, 8 Youth L. News 1, 5 (1987) [hereinafter English].
26. *See generally* Child Welfare League of America, Serving HIV-Infected Children, Youth, and Their Families: A Guide for Residential Group Care Providers (1989).
27. *Fighting AIDS in Adolescents, supra* note 10, at 1-2; K. Hein, *Commentary on Adolescent Acquired Immunodeficiency Syndrome: The Next Wave of the Human Immunodeficiency Virus Epidemic*, 114 J. Pediatrics 144, 147 (1989); *AIDS in Adolescence, supra* note 7, at 28S; *see also Services and Treatment Issues, supra* note 17, at 49S; *AIDS Testing and Epidemiology, supra* note 25, at 55S-57S. *But see* "Experimental AIDS Drug Shows Promise in Children," Associated Press, Jan. 16, 1991.
28. *See generally* 45 C.F.R. pt. 46 (1990).
29. *See* Melton, *Ethical and Legal Issues in Research and Intervention*, 10 J. Adolescent Health Care, Supp., at 36S-44S (1989) [hereinafter Melton]; A. Holder, Legal Issues in Pediatrics and Adolescent Medicine 146 - 167 (2d ed. rev. 1985) [hereinafter Holder]; *see also* J. Morrissey, A. Hofmann & J. Thrope, Consent and Confidentiality in the Health Care of Children and Adolescents 87-94 (1986) [hereinafter Morrissey].
30. A. Kenney, S. Guardado & L. Brown, *Sex Education and AIDS Education in the Schools: What States and Large School Districts Are Doing*, 21 Fam. Plan. Persp. 56 (1989).
31. J. Forrest & J. Silverman, *What Public School Teachers Teach About Preventing Pregnancy, AIDS and Sexually Transmitted Diseases*, 21 Fam. Plan. Persp. 65 (1989).
32. *See School Board Approves Plan for Condoms*, N.Y. Times, Feb. 28, 1991, at B1.
33. *See* Ware v. Valley Stream High Sch. Dist., 75 N.Y.2d 114 (1989); House Select Comm. Hearing, *supra* note 2, at 10-14 (Statement of C. Everett Koop); *Condom Plan May Lose Pivotal Vote*, N.Y. Times, Jan. 17, 1991, at B1; *California Woman Fired after AIDS Controversy Loses Supreme Court Appeal*, Associated Press, Jan.

14, 1991; *Plymouth Parents Group Seeks Answers on Sex Education*, Associated Press, Dec. 24, 1990.

34. In such a case, the state may intervene under its *parens patriae* power to protect the interests of the minor. *See generally* Ewald, *Medical Decision Making for Children: An Analysis of Competing Interests*, 25 St. Louis U. L.J. 689, 712-730 (1981-82) [hereinafter Ewald].

35. Schloendorff v. Society of the New York Hosp., 105 N.E. 92 (1914); *see also* Younts v. St. Francis Hosp. and Sch. of Nursing, 469 P.2d 330, 336 (1970).

36. Canterbury v. Spence, 464 F.2d 772 (D.C. Cir. 1972).

37. Bonner v. Moran, 126 F.2d 121, 122 (D.C. Cir. 1941); Zaman v. Schultz, 19 Pa. D. & C. 309, 310 (1933); *see* Wadlington, *Minors and Health Care: The Age of Consent*, 11 Osgoode Hall L.J. 115 (1973) [hereinafter Wadlington].

38. Bonner, 126 F.2d at 122. *See also* Ewald, *supra* note 34, at 692; Pilpel, *Minor's Rights to Medical Care*, 36 Alb. L. Rev. 462, 464 (1971-72) [hereinafter Pilpel].

39. Lacey v. Laird, 139 N.E.2d 25, 30 (1956); Ewald, *supra* note 34, at 692-93; Wilkins, *Children's Rights: Removing the Parental Consent Barrier to Medical Treatment of Minors*, 1975 Ariz. St. L.J. 31, 78 (1975) [hereinafter Wilkins].

40. Morrisey, *supra* note 29, at x. *see also* Wilkins, *supra* note 39, at 59.

41. Morrissey, *supra* note 29, at 15; Holder, *supra* note 29, at 133; Pilpel, *supra* note 38, at 466.

42. *See* Note, *The Constitutional Right of Informational Privacy: Does It Protect Children Suffering from AIDS?*, 14 Fordham Urb. L.J. 927, 929 (1985-86); Morrissey, *supra* note 29, at 18.

43. *See generally* Larkin Street Youth Center, *supra* note 3, at 17-30; *AIDS Testing and Epidemiology*, *supra* note 25, at 52S-57S; English, *supra* note 25, at 2-3.

44. *AIDS Testing and Epidemiology*, *supra* note 25, at 53S. Recent litigation challenging the Job Corps' mandatory testing policy illustrates the problem of screening indiscriminately, with little, if any, follow-up support. *See Dorsey v. Department of Labor*, No. 88-1898 (TFH) (D.D.C. 1988).

45. English, *supra* note 25, at 5.

46. Ariz. Rev. Stat. Ann. §§ 36-661 *et seq.* (1990); Cal. Health & Safety Code § 199.27(a)(1) (West Supp. 1991); Colo. Rev. Stat. § 25-4-1405(6) (1989); Del. Code Ann. tit. 16, § 1202(f) (Supp. 1991); Iowa Code Ann. § 141.22 (West Supp. 1991); Mich. Comp. Laws Ann. § 333.5127(1) (West Supp. 1991); N.Y. Pub. Health Law §§ 2780 *et seq.* (McKinney Supp. 1991); Ohio Rev. Code Ann. § 3701.242(B) (Baldwin 1991); Or. Rev. Stat. § 433.045 (5), § 109.610 (Supp. 1990); Wash Rev. Code Ann. § 70.24.017(13), 70.24.110 (West Supp. 1991). For a helpful and concise discussion and graphic state-by-state display of both HIV and related statutory provisions, see R. North, *Legal Authority for HIV Testing of Adolescents*, 11 J. Adolescent Health Care 176 (1990) [hereinafter North].

47. Ariz. Rev. Stat. Ann. §§ 36-661(2), 36-663(A) (1990); N.Y. Pub. Health Law §§ 2780(5), 2781(1) (McKinney Supp. 1991).

48. Del. Code Ann. tit. 16, § 1202(f) (West Supp. 1990) (minors 12 years of age or older may consent); Wash. Rev. Code Ann. § 70.24.017(13), 70.24.110 (West Supp. 1991) (AIDS and HIV shall be designated as sexually transmitted diseases; minors 14 years of age or older may consent to treatment for sexually transmitted diseases).

49. Cal. Health & Safety Code § 199.27(a)(1) (West Supp. 1991); *cf.* Ballard v. Anderson, 484 P.2d 1345 (1971) (statute authorizing unmarried pregnant minor to consent to pregnancy-related hospital, medical, and surgical care implicitly limited to minors sufficiently mature to give informed consent).

50. Colo. Rev. Stat. § 25-4-1405(6) (1989); Iowa Code Ann. § 141.22 (West Supp. 1991); Mich. Comp. Law Ann. § 333.5127(1) (West Supp. 1991); Ohio Rev. Code Ann. § 3701.242(B) (Baldwin 1991); Or. Rev. Stat. §§ 106.610, 433.045(5) (Supp. 1990) (HIV test considered diagnosis of venereal disease, to which a minor may consent).

51. Colo. Rev. Stat. § 25-4-1405(6) (1989); Iowa Code Ann. § 141.22(6) (West Supp. 1991); Mich. Comp. Laws Ann. § 333.5127(1) (West Supp. 1991); Wash. Rev. Code Ann. § 70.24.017(13), 70.24.110 (West Supp. 1991).

52. *See e.g.,* Del. Code Ann. tit. 16, § 1202(b), (e) (West Supp. 1990); Iowa Code Ann. § 141.22(1), (3) (West Supp. 1991); Mich. Comp. Laws Ann. § 333.5923(2) (West Supp. 1991); N.Y. Pub. Health Law § 2781(2), (3), (5) (McKinney Supp. 1991); Ohio Rev. Code Ann. § 3701.242(A), (C) (Baldwin 1991).

53. Colo. Rev. Stat. § 25-4-1405(6) (1989).

54. Ariz. Rev. Stat. Ann. § 36-664(A) (1990); Del. Code Ann. tit. 16, § 1203(a) (West Supp. 1990); N.Y. Pub. Health Law § 2782(1) (McKinney Supp. 1991); Or. Rev. Stat. § 433.045(3) (Supp. 1990).

55. *See* Morrissey, *supra* note 29, at 119-20.

56. *See, e.g.,* Ariz. Rev. Stat. Ann. § 36-664(A) (1990); Del. Code Ann. tit. 16, § 1203(a) (West Supp. 1990); N.Y. Pub. Health Law § 2782(1) (McKinney Supp. 1991).

57. Cal. Health & Safety Code § 199.21 (West Supp. 1991).

58. *See* Del. Code Ann. tit. 16, § 1203(a)(1) (West Supp. 1990); Ohio Rev. Code Ann. § 3701.243(B)(1)(a) (Baldwin 1991).

59. Colo. Rev. Stat. § 25-4-1405 (6) (1989).

60. Mich. Comp. Laws Ann. § 333.5127(2) (West Supp. 1991).

61. N.Y. Pub. Health Law § 2780(5) (McKinney Supp. 1991).

62. N.Y. Pub. Health Law § 2782 (4)(e) (McKinney Supp. 1991). Because the New York statute is not a treatment statute, if a physician wants to disclose information to a minor's parent or guardian relating to a proposed course of treatment, the minor's ability to block that disclosure will turn on whether other provisions of New York law authorize the particular minor to consent to the type of health care at issue. *See* Legal Action Center, HIV/AIDS: A Legal, Policy and Practical Guide for Human Service Providers in New York 51-54 (1991) [hereinafter Legal Action Center].

63. Wash. Rev. Code Ann. § 70.24.105(2)(a) (West Supp. 1991).

64. Iowa Code Ann. § 141.22(6) (West Supp. 1991).

65. *See* Del. Code Ann. tit. 16, § 1202(f) (West Supp. 1990).

66. *See* Holder, *supra* note 29, at 141; *see also In re* E.G., 549 N.E.2d 322 (Ill. 1989) (accepting mature minor doctrine as basis of minor authority to consent to or to refuse medical treatment); Cruzan v. Director, Missouri Dept. of Health, 110 S. Ct. 2841, 2847 (1990).

67. *See* Melton, *supra* note 29, at 36S-37S.

68. This problem is likely to be encountered more frequently in states with HIV testing statutes that do not explicitly authorize minors to consent to testing. It is not uncommon for the HIV statute to authorize disclosure to the subject or to the subject's legal guardian or representative, leaving open the possibility that a minor whose authority to consent comes from an independent legal source may nonetheless face the prospect of parental notification pursuant to the HIV testing statute.

69. *See* Ariz. Rev. Stat. Ann. §36-664(A)(1) (1990); N.Y. Pub. Health Law § 2782(1)(a) (McKinney Supp. 1991). In New York, mature minors have express

authority to consent to the disclosure of confidential HIV-related information under Public Health Law § 2780(5). The exclusivity of a minor's right to control disclosures may be subject to exceptions that permit disclosure by a physician or pursuant to court order. *See, e.g.,* N.Y. Pub. Health Law §§ 2782(4)(e), § 2785 (McKinney Supp. 1991); *see also* Legal Action Center, *supra* note 62, at 38-41.

70.   *See* Del. Code Ann. tit. 16, § 1203(a)(1) (West Supp.1990); Ohio Rev. Code Ann. §3701.243(B)(1)(a) (Baldwin 1991).

71.   *See* Wilkins, *supra* note 39, at 64.

72.   *See* North, *supra* note 46, at 185; Paxman & Zuckerman, *supra* note 1, at 16; Morrissey, *supra* note 29, at 19, 137; Holder, *supra* note 29, at 143.

73.   *See* Doe v. Borough of Barrington, 729 F. Supp. 376, 382-85 (D.N.J. 1990); Woods v. White, 689 F. Supp. 874, 875-76 (W.D. Wis. 1988), *aff'd,* 899 F.2d 17 (7th Cir. 1990).

74.   *See infra* note 93 and accompanying text pertaining to minor access to abortion.

75.   *See* Mich. Comp. Laws Ann. § 333.5127(3) (West Supp. 1991); Ohio Rev. Code Ann. § 3701.242 (B) (Baldwin 1991); Or. Rev. Stat. § 109.610 (Supp. 1990); Wash. Rev. Code Ann. § 70.24.110 (West Supp. 1991).

76.   *See* North, *supra* note 46, at 177, table 1 at 178-82; Morrissey, *supra* note 29, at 61-62, Appendix at 149-250; Holder, *supra* note 29, at 130.

77.   Morrissey, *supra* note 29, at 62.

78.   *See e.g.,* Idaho Code §§ 39-601, 39-3801 (1985 & Supp. 91); Ky. Rev. Stat. Ann. §§ 214.185, .410 (Michie/Bobbs-Merrill 1991).

79.   *See* New York State Soc'y of Surgeons v. Axelrod, 157 A.D. 2d 54 (N.Y. App. Div. 1990), *aff'd,* N.E.2d (1991) (sustaining Commissioner of Health's refusal to designate HIV as a communicable and sexually transmitted disease).

80.   *See* Morrissey, *supra* note 29, at 63-64, 74-81, Appendix at 149-250; Holder, *supra* note 29, at 131.

81.   *See* Morrissey, *supra* note 29, at 43-48; Holder, *supra* note 29, at 133-35; Ewald, *supra* note 34, at 703-04; Wadlington, *supra* note 37, at 117-20; *see also* Restatement (Second) of Torts § 892A cmt. b.

82.   Ark. Stat. Ann. § 20-9-602(7) (1987).

83.   Idaho Code § 39-4302 (1985).

84.   469 P.2d 330 (1970).

85.   *Id.* at 333-34, 338. Interestingly, the judicial recognition of the mature minor rule may, as in *Younts,* function as a liability-avoidance device for the physician. *Cf.* Bonner v. Moran, 126 F.2d 121 (D.C. Cir. 1941) (where 15 year-old underwent complicated skin graft for benefit of third party, no mature minor rule recognized).

86.   *In re* E.G., 549 N.E.2d 322 (Ill. 1989).

87.   Cardwell v. Bechtol, 724 S.W.2d 739 (Tenn. 1987).

88.   *Id.* at 741-43, 748-49.

89.   *See* Morrissey, *supra* note 29, at 47; Holder, *supra* note 29, at 134; Wadlington, *supra* note 37, at 119.

90.   *See* Bellotti v. Baird, 443 U.S. 622 (1979); Carey v. Population Serv. Int'l, 431 U.S. 678 (1977); Planned Parenthood of Central Mo. v. Danforth, 428 U.S. 52 (1976); *see also* Hodgson v. Minnesota, 110 S. Ct. 2926 (1990); Ohio v. Akron Center for Reproductive Health, 110 S. Ct. 2972 (1990); *see also* Holder, *supra* note 29, at 286-93.

91.   Bellotti, 443 U.S. at 643-44. *See generally,* North, *supra* note 46, at 183-84.

92.   *See* Webster v. Reproductive Health Serv., 109 S. Ct. 3040 (1989).

93. *See* Hodgson v. Minnesota, 110 S.Ct. 2926 (1990). Of course, changes in the calculus of federal interests may still leave state constitutional rights unaffected. Thus, should the United States Supreme Court repudiate doctrine recognizing a woman's privacy right to decide during the first trimester whether to continue or terminate her pregnancy, state constitutions may nevertheless independently guarantee a right to privacy. *See In re* T.W., 551 So.2d 1186 (Fla. 1989) (invalidating bypass and parental consent statute).

94. *See Cruzan*, 110 S. Ct. 2841.

95. *See* Morrissey, *supra* note 29, at 32-39; Holder, *supra* note 29, at 127-29; Ewald, *supra* note 34, at 702-03.

96. *See* Smith v. Seibly, 431 P.2d 719, 723 (Wash. 1967) (emancipation may occur even without statute).

97. *See, e.g.*, Carter v. Cangello, 164 Cal. Rptr. 361 (Ct. App. 1980) (17 year-old living away from home and exercising substantial control over own affairs capable of consenting to treatment under statute notwithstanding parental source of income); Poudre Valley Hosp. Dist. v. Heckart, 491 P.2d 984 (Colo. Ct. App. 1971) (sustaining finding of complete emancipation of self-supporting high school graduate living on his own).

98. *See, e.g.*, Ark. Stat. Ann. § 20-9-602 (1987); Ill. Ann. Stat. ch. 111, paras. 4501-4502 (Smith Hurd 1978); Ind. Code Ann. § 16-8-12-2 (Burns 1990); Mass. Gen. Laws Ann. ch. 112, § 12F (West 1991); Mo. Ann. Stat. § 431.061 (Vernon Supp. 1991); Nev. Rev. Stat. Ann. § 129.030 (Michie 1986); N.J. Stat. Ann. § 9:17A-1 (West Supp. 1991); Tex. Fam. Code Ann. § 35.03 (Vernon Supp. 1991);*see also* Smith, 431 P.2d 719 (Wash. 1967); Swenson v. Swenson, 227 S.W.2d 103 (Mo. Ct. App. 1950).

99. *See, e.g.*, Ill. Ann. Stat. ch. 40, paras. 2201 *et seq.* (Smith-Hurd 1980); Nev. Rev. Stat. Ann. §§ 129.080 *et seq.* (Michie Supp. 1991).

100. *See e.g.*, Mass. Gen. Laws Ann. ch. 112, § 12F (West 1991); Tex. Fam. Code Ann. § 35.03(e)(f) (Vernon Supp. 1991).

101. Holder, *supra* note 29, at 129.

102. Ill. Ann Stat. ch. 111, paras. 4504-4505 (Smith-Hurd 1978).

103. *Id.*, ch. 111 1/2, para. 7309(a) (Smith-Hurd Supp. 1991).

104. Mass. Gen. Laws Ann. ch. 112, § 12F (West 1991).

105. *Id.*, ch. 111 § 70F.

106. N.J. Stat. Ann. § 9:17A-4 (West Supp. 1991).

107. *Id.* § 9:17A-1, :17A-5.

108. *Id.* § 26:5C-6, :5C-8(a), :5C-13.

109. North, *supra* note 46, at 183; Morrissey, *supra* note 29, at 15; Holder, *supra* note 29, at 133; Pilpel, *supra* note 38, at 466.

110. North, *supra* note 46, at 185; Paxman & Zuckerman, *supra* note 1, at 16; Morrissey, *supra* note 29, at 19; Holder, *supra* note 29, at 143.

3

HIV-INFECTED PARENTS AND THE LAW: ISSUES OF CUSTODY, VISITATION AND GUARDIANSHIP

By Elizabeth B. Cooper

When an HIV-infected person is a parent, she[1] is confronted with a wide range of complex decisions. Two pressing concerns involve maintaining custody rights to her children while she is well and arranging for care for them after she has died. These situations involve wrenching decisions with which the legal system has not yet dealt adequately.

The first section of this chapter examines the challenges HIV-infected parents, or those perceived to be HIV-infected, face with respect to their custody and visitation rights in the context of, or following, divorce proceedings. Whether an HIV-infected parent is at risk of having her rights to have custody of or visitation with her children challenged depends on the attitude of that person's former spouse and the community in which they live. When dragged into a contested custody proceeding, most HIV-infected parents have succeeded, but only after arduous and lengthy litigation.

The second part of this chapter examines how a parent, particularly a single parent, attempts to find ways to ensure her child's well-being after her death. Parents are faced with a maze of options, few, if any, of which adequately address the concerns of the parents or the children. This section closes with a number of recommendations that would improve the viable options of these parents.

I. Custody and Visitation

A. Introduction

Custody and visitation decisions are never easy: a family is breaking apart and the children necessarily confront the myriad issues that arise in their post-divorce families. Courts are called upon to intervene in family life and to make sensitive decisions about highly personal matters. Ideally, the parents will make decisions based on "the best interests of the child." Too often, however, the worst characteristics of the litigants emerge, with divorcing parents raising issues based on prejudice rather than on concerns about parenting ability — out of their own biases, anger, or in an attempt to appeal to the anticipated biases of judges. Therefore, it is not surprising that a number of cases have arisen involving claims that a parent's infection, or possible infection, with the human immunodeficiency virus constitutes a reason to deny custody or visitation to that parent.

In these cases, parents[2] have put forward three basic arguments as to why HIV infection ought to limit visitation or custody: first, the infected parent will transmit the virus to the child; second, the parent is rendered physically unfit to parent because of HIV disease; and finally, the child will be unduly harmed emotionally — either by having to deal with a parent who is seriously ill or dying or by societal stigmatization — if raised or visited by a parent with HIV disease. Underlying these arguments are often thinly veiled irrational concerns about allowing a person who is gay or who has had a history of using drugs to raise children.

None of these arguments has merit and each ultimately has been rejected by the courts. This section will analyze each of the three arguments. The first part of this section demonstrates that there is no medical evidence to support concerns of transmission of HIV from parent to child. The second part explains why there is no basis to conclude that a parent's HIV infection renders her *per se* incapable of parenting. The final part considers possible harms to the child based on a parent's HIV infection and shows that these are not a sufficient basis on which to rest custody or visitation decisions.

This discussion will demonstrate that calls for restrictions on custody and visitation rights of HIV-infected parents are grounded in exploitation of irrational reactions to the HIV crisis. In truth, consideration of a parent's HIV status — as with consideration of any illness —

is relevant only to inform the inquiry of "the extent to which the parent remains able to function at a level adequate to the demands of parenting and is capable of helping the child address the psychological and social problems particular to that family's situation."[3] Decisions concerning custody and visitation must focus on the best interests of the child, an analysis that properly does not give credence to the irrational fears and prejudices of others.

Before considering these arguments, we begin with an overview of the child custody system.

B. Custody and Visitation Decisions Generally

The U.S. Supreme Court has held that the rights of parenthood are among the most "basic civil rights" an individual possesses and that a parent's "interest in retaining custody of his children is cognizable and substantial."[4] While state statutory and case law — rather than federal law — guides most custody and visitation determinations, most states have articulated essentially the same standard for determining the placement of a child upon divorce: "the best interests of the child" govern such decisions, and this determination must be made according to the facts presented in each case.[5] While laws in each state may vary, this chapter seeks to explore the effect of the dominant approaches adopted by the states on custody and visitation decisions that involve parents with HIV disease.

The primary approach to custody and visitation decisions in the United States flows from a model law entitled the Uniform Marriage and Divorce Act (UMDA). Many states have either adopted the UMDA or use it as a basis to articulate the factors that a court should consider when faced with making a custody decision.[6] The act identifies five such factors:

1. the wishes of the child's parent or parents as to his custody;

2. the wishes of the child as to his custodian;

3. the interaction and interrelationship of the child with his parent or parents, his siblings, and any other person who may significantly affect the child's best interest;

4. the child's adjustment to his home, school, and community; and

5. the mental and physical health of all individuals involved.[7]

Each state — in fact, each judge — may place different emphasis on which of these, or other, factors are to be considered.

If one parent is granted custody,[8] the other parent likely will have visitation rights.[9] The noncustodial parent may also have child support obligations.[10] The policies of most states mirror those contained in the UMDA's rule on visitation, which says that a court cannot deny a noncustodial parent visitation rights unless "visitation would endanger seriously the child's physical, mental, moral, or emotional health."[11] A court is likely to allow for visitation, even if it has denied custody, based on the principles that: (1) absent extraordinary circumstances, a child has a right to have access to her noncustodial parent;[12] (2) contact with both parents will benefit the child;[13] and, (3) a parent has an inherent right to have access to her children.[14]

Courts considering custody and visitation decisions have a vast amount of discretion. As a result, court decrees often reflect a certain degree of a judge's own orientation, biases, and emotions as well as those of the local community.[15]

C. HIV-Infected Parents

The issue of a parent's antibody status or AIDS diagnosis can be raised either at the time of the original custody or visitation decree, or later, on a motion by one parent to modify that decree. Regardless of when the issue is raised, it often falls upon the HIV-infected litigant to educate the court about HIV disease.[16] The following is an exploration of the three subjects about which courts most often need information.

1. Transmission

A child cannot get HIV from day-to-day household contact with her parent. HIV can be transmitted by sexual contact involving the exchange of bodily fluids; exposure to contaminated blood or blood products through a transfusion, needle sharing, or needle puncture wounds; from a woman to her fetus, either *in utero* or at birth;[17] and through breast feeding.[18] HIV is not transmitted through the air, water, walls, floors or other such surfaces, or insects.[19] Moreover, the virus is killed by household agents such as bleach, alcohol, hydrogen peroxide, paraformaldehyde, Lysol, and heat.[20]

While HIV has been found in saliva and tears, thus creating a theoretical possibility of transmission through these excretions, no cases of HIV infection have been linked to exposure to these fluids. Since the virus has been found in only low concentrations in these fluids,[21] and, further, because a child's exposure to the tears or saliva of a parent is not likely to be extensive,[22] there is no realistic likelihood of transmission of HIV through these sources.[23]

Numerous scientific studies have concluded that HIV cannot be transmitted through normal household contact.[24] In fact, there have simply been no known cases of a parent infecting a child in this context, with the exception of transmission through breast feeding. Courts have a duty to weigh the *actual* risk a parent poses to his or her child in the same manner they would consider any other risk in life:[25] a theoretical possibility of transmission is not the same as a practical possibility of transmission.[26]

Since HIV cannot be transmitted through the day-to-day interactions of parent and child, this fear should have no bearing upon custody and visitation decisions. Relying on such conclusive medical evidence, both the Association of Family and Conciliation Courts and the American Bar Association AIDS Coordinating Committee have adopted policies rejecting theories of casual contagion of HIV as factors to be considered in custody and visitation decisions.[27] Moreover, almost every recent court that has grappled with HIV disease as an element in custody and visitation decisions has found that because HIV cannot be casually transmitted, a parent's HIV infection is relevant only insofar as the court must make an individualized assessment of whether the infected parent (as well as the noninfected parent) is physically and emotionally capable of caring for her child.[28]

2. The Physical Effects of HIV Disease

a. Traditional "Best Interests" Analysis

It is an essential tenet of child custody law that although a parent's physical health is a factor to be considered by a court "to the extent it affects the child's best interest,"[29] a court is not permitted to give disproportionate weight to the existence of a physical disability.[30] Traditionally, courts conduct a highly individualized assessment of whether the parent with a physical disability can provide the level of care necessary to obtain or maintain physical custody of her child. Courts have awarded custody to parents with a range of physical disabilities, including those who are deaf-mute, are paralyzed, or have spina bifida.[31] In addition, in most situations where a parent has had custody of her child and then suffers an accident or medical trauma that results in physical disability, the courts maintain that parent as custodian of the child so long as the parent remains capable of custody.[32] Where there is an indication, however, that a parent suffers from an emotionally disabling condition in conjunction with or as a cause of a physically disabling condition, courts are far less likely to grant custody to that parent. For example, courts have denied or removed custody from parents who have anorexia nervosa,[33] epilepsy complicated by a drinking problem,[34] and viral myocardiopathy complicated by psychological disabilities.[35]

In adjudicating custody and visitation disputes when one parent is physically disabled, one commentator has noted that the court must resolve a conflict between two strong public policies: "the requirement that a custody award serve the best interest of the child, and the moral and legal obligation of society to respect the civil rights of its physically handicapped members, including their right not to be deprived of their children because of their handicap.... [Some courts] have concluded that both policies can be accommodated."[36]

b. "Best Interests" Analysis in Light of Disability Law

Although disability discrimination statutes generally do not apply in the context of custody and visitation determinations, several state courts have found that the principles underlying these laws should apply to a parent with a disability who is seeking to maintain or obtain custody or visitation privileges.[37] The seminal case in this area is *In re Marriage of Carney*, where the court, relying on California law protecting the rights of persons with disabilities, held that a parent's handicap could be considered in a determination of custody "only when there was a sufficient nexus between the handicap and the child's welfare." The court identified four factors that must be considered as part of this analysis: (1) the parent's actual and potential physical capabilities; (2) how the parent has adapted to his or her disability and manages its problems; (3) how other members of the household have adjusted; and (4) any special contributions the parent makes to the family despite, or perhaps because of, his or her disability. The court further explained that a court making a custody decision involving a parent with a physical disability must "[weigh] these and all other relevant factors together [and] then carefully determine whether the parent's condition will in fact have a substantial and lasting adverse effect on the best interests of the child."[38]

At its heart, the *Carney* decision stands for the principle that "if a person has a physical handicap it is impermissible for the court simply to rely on that condition as *prima facie* evidence of the person's unfitness as a parent or of probable detriment to the child; rather, in all cases the court must view the handicapped person as an individual and the family as a whole."[39] The essence of parenting, according to *Carney*, is:

...the ethical, emotional, and intellectual guidance the parent gives to the child throughout his formative years, and often beyond. The source of this guidance is the adult's own experience of life; its motive power is parental love and concern for the child's well-being; and its teachings deal with such fundamental matters as the child's feelings about himself, his relationships with others, his system of values, his standards of conduct, and his goals and priorities in life....[A] handicapped parent is a whole person to the child who needs his affection, sympathy, and wisdom to deal with the problems of growing up. Indeed, in such matters his handicap may well be an asset: few can pass through the crucible of a severe physical disability without learning enduring lessons in patience and tolerance.[40]

The *Carney* approach, reflecting "a growing public policy in favor of giving equal rights to disabled individuals and integrating them into the mainstream of society,"[41] has been adopted by other state courts.[42] For example, a Michigan appeals court, relying on the *Carney* decision, found that it was highly improper for the trial court to rely so heavily on the mother's deafness in awarding custody to their paternal grandparents.[43] A Colorado appeals court affirmed a trial court's decision to remove children from their mother's home and place them with the social services agency, but only after applying *Carney* and finding that the mother's physical and psychological manifestations of Huntington's chorea "contributed to an environment which was injurious to the welfare of each child."[44]

c. Application of the "Best Interests" Standard When a Parent is HIV-Infected

As it is now widely accepted that infection with HIV is legally a disability,[45] a parent with HIV is entitled to the protections extended to other persons with disabilities.[46] Although these statutes do not specifically apply in the family law context, they can be used by courts to help assess the rights of parents with disabilities, as was seen in *Carney*.

Because the variables that arise in HIV disease, as with other disabilities, are numerous, each custody case must be evaluated on an individualized basis. Some general principles are applicable, though. First, a person may be infected with HIV for ten years or more before she begins to show significant symptoms of HIV-related illness. Second, during this extended period, the HIV-infected individual is likely to experience alternating periods of good health and illness. Third, it is likely that most people will not know that the person is HIV-infected unless she chooses to disclose this information. Finally, based on scientific evidence concerning transmission and the typical life-span of an individual who is HIV-infected, there is no logical basis on which to deny an HIV-infected parent custody of her children.

This conclusion was affirmed by a New York court applying disability law principles in the context of HIV infection in the case of *Doe v. Roe*.[47] To resolve a conflict between the child's maternal grandparents and the child's father, the *Doe* court examined the relevance of HIV infection to the custody dispute. After considering the arguments of the parties, and hearing the testimony of a court-appointed psychiatrist, the court concluded that "HIV infection was insufficient grounds for removing the children from the father's custody [and, as such,] there was no compelling need to order the father to undergo an involuntary HIV antibody test."[48] The *Doe* decision, like *Carney* and other similar decisions, stands for the proposition that custody decisions cannot rest solely on a parent's disability. Rather, a fact-based analysis must be conducted to determine whether that disability would appreciably preclude the parent in question from being loving and effective. Specifically, *Doe* held that HIV infection constitutes a disability in the context of a custody determination, and, further, that HIV infection, without more, should not be sufficient grounds on which to base or alter custody arrangements.[49]

The foregoing cases make clear that custody should not be denied to any parent solely on the basis of being HIV-infected if she is able to care for her child. A court may not make leaps of faith based on generalities about HIV disease; rather, it must conduct a detailed, fact-based assessment of the health of that parent.[50] While it is true that in the final stages of full-blown AIDS an individual may require medical attention, frequent hospitalization, and the assistance of others in performing daily activities, the fear that the health of an HIV-infected parent might deteriorate also has no place in custody decisions. Rather, it would be the court's obligation to determine the best interests of the child at the time of the petition; if, indeed, the health of the custodial parent does deteriorate (whether as a result of HIV or not), a new petition may be filed with the court for a modification of the custody award.[51] Courts have adopted this approach when they have addressed parallel situations, such as when the custodian for the child has been over the age of 60,[52] or when she has a potentially deteriorating health condition.[53] If the court finds that a material change in circumstances has occurred, and that it would be in the best interests of the child to do so, the custody order can be modified. As part of this process, the court would have to examine the resources that may be available privately or through government programs that would allow the child to remain with the original custodian.

As compared to *custody* decisions, the granting and maintaining of *visitation* rights are usually not dependent on a parent's ability to provide care for her child, unless significant periods of visitation time are provided for in the visitation order or agreed upon by the parents. As noted above, it is important for the child to maintain contact with a parent who is ill, including a noncustodial parent. For these reasons, the parent's health status should have much less impact on visitation determinations than on custody awards. In any event, the same kind of individualized assessment would have to be conducted, and the strong presumption should be in favor of maximizing parent-child contact.[54]

3. The Impact of HIV-Related Illness on the Child

Thus far this chapter has focused on the effect of HIV-related illness on a parent's ability to care adequately for her child. Any determination of what is in the child's best interests must also incorporate a consideration of the impact of the parent's illness on the child. This section will focus on two ways in which a child might be affected by her parent's HIV-related illness: (1) the emotional difficulties in dealing with an ill (and dying) parent; and, (2) the stigma that may be visited on the child as the offspring of an HIV-infected parent, who may also be gay or have a history of drug use or promiscuity.

a. Emotional Difficulties

The death of one's parent is among the most stressful and disturbing events that a child can face. However, removing the child from the parent solely because the parent's illness may be emotionally disturbing is not supported by either psychological studies or law.

Experts have acknowledged that "a child's need and love for a parent do not disappear simply because the parent becomes handicapped."[55] In fact, despite the arguments of some parents that a child should be shielded from an ill parent, experts state that a child's emotional well-being may be most bolstered by parents who deal with the situation honestly, telling the child in age-appropriate terms about the process the ailing parent is undergoing.[56] This will both satisfy the child's natural curiosity and allay fears that something comparable might happen to him or her.[57] Therefore, basing custody or visitation decisions on a desire to "shield" a child is not likely to be in a child's best interest, and, in fact, may be harmful.

A court does, of course, have the obligation to inquire into the thoughts and desires of the child as part of the "best interests" inquiry.[58] Often this is accomplished through the testimony of the parents. In addition, courts often seek the assistance of an expert psychologist to assess both the child's and the parents' emotional well-being.[59] Moreover, in most states, courts may, and often do, conduct a private examination of the child to learn directly about the child's sentiments, provided she is "of an age and capacity to form an intelligent preference" and it is apparent that the child is not being influenced inappropriately by a parent.[60] Information gleaned from each of these sources will assist the court in its determination of the child's best interests; however, none of these factors, individually, will be controlling of the court's decision.[61] Only if there is "substantial evidence that a child's mental or physical health is being or will be adversely affected by one parent's custody [will custody] not be awarded to that parent."[62]

In reality, it appears that children with stable and loving relationships with their parents adapt well to their parents' disabilities.[63] Thus, courts will not typically deny custody or visitation to the disabled parent based on the argument that the child will have difficulties adjusting to her parent's disability. Rather, courts encourage the development of an environment in which a child is supported in working through any adjustment difficulties she may have.[64] Only when a parent's emotional or physical problems in and of themselves would directly harm the child is it perceived by courts that the child might suffer adverse emotional traumas later in life; only in these extreme situations are courts apt not to award custody to the disabled parent.[65]

b. Stigma

A second argument that parents have raised concerning harm to the child in this context is that the child will be stigmatized or shunned as a result of having a parent with HIV disease. Such an argument has two possible sources: a generalized and panicked response to HIV, or an attempt to use the other parent's HIV infection as a proxy for socially disfavored behavior, such as homosexuality,[66] sexual relations with multiple partners,[67] or drug use. It is true that our society attaches stigma to having HIV, being gay or lesbian, having multiple relationships, or having been a substance abuser; a child with a parent in any of these circumstances may face the opprobrium of her peers. However, such social condemnation should not be tolerated or approved of by the courts.

First, a child in this context may feel stigmatized merely because of the parent's identity, regardless of the child's living situation or to whom legal custody has been awarded. Living with the parent may actually better allow the child to develop a close, nonjudgmental relationship with her parent.[68]

Second, it is inappropriate for a court to give credence to any factors that do not have a direct impact on the parent's ability to provide for the child's best interests. As such, absent a showing of direct harm to a child, societal biases — which in and of themselves do not reflect an individual parent's ability to provide for her child's best interests — should not form the basis for a custody award.[69]

Third, a court may also not assume the role of affirming irrational societal biases. In the critical case in this area, *Palmore v. Sidoti*, the Florida Supreme Court had denied a caucasian woman custody of her own children following her divorce because of her live-in relationship with a black man. While clearly recognizing that the child might be subject to stresses and pressures, the U.S. Supreme Court reversed, holding that, "[t]he Constitution cannot control such prejudices but neither can it tolerate them. Private biases may be outside the reach of the law, but the law cannot, directly or indirectly, give them effect."[70]

According to the principles enunciated in *Palmore* and its progeny, and consistent with proper application of the "best interests" rule, custody and visitation determinations should not be significantly affected by one parent's raising arguments that the child will be stigmatized because the other parent is gay, has had multiple relationships, has a history of having used drugs, or is HIV-infected.[71] While most courts do follow this approach,

> this area is replete with subjective judgments about the desirability of the custodial parent's conforming to social or cultural norms, particularly when sexual behavior is involved. Too often the child's need for stability and continuity becomes secondary to the courts' views on morality, despite the fact that

in this pluralistic society there is widespread disagreement about lifestyle issues.[72]

Nonetheless, many courts refuse to deny custody or visitation based solely on a parent's homosexuality.[73] Courts increasingly have held that an individual's sexual orientation does not indicate whether that person will be a fit parent and have found a parent's homosexuality to be a neutral factor in custody or visitation decisions. At least one court has applied the *Palmore* principle in holding that "it is impermissible to rely on any real or imagined social stigma attaching to [the] Mother's status as a lesbian."[74] Similarly, although courts may change the custodial parent if she is "promiscuous," evidence of a stable home and a solid relationship will avert such a determination.[75] Finally, courts also have held that a parent's past substance abuse "without proof of present abuse or likelihood of future abuse" should not serve as a reason to deny that parent custody.[76]

Palmore and its progeny are equally applicable to HIV-infected parents. As discussed, courts largely have rejected arguments that an HIV-infected parent should not be granted custody or visitation rights.[77] Even if not raised explicitly, as noted above, suggestions of stigma often constitute the subtext of petitions to relieve an HIV-infected parent of custody or visitation rights.

In sum, removing a child from her parent to spare her "the slings and arrows of a disapproving society"[78] does not truly serve her best interest. Acquiescing to such bigotry will not serve the child's needs.[79] Indeed, every such child will have to come to terms with the fact that his or her parent is different from what society has determined is the norm and that the parent will be faced with the scorn of many. For these reasons, courts should refuse to deny child custody to an HIV-infected parent based on speculation about the stigma that the child might suffer. As a New Jersey state court, refusing to remove a child from the home of her lesbian mother, held:

> Taking the children from defendant can be done only at the cost of sacrificing those very qualities they will find most sustaining in meeting the challenges inevitably ahead. Instead of forbearance and feelings of protectiveness, it will foster in them a sense of shame for their mother. Instead of courage and the precept that people of integrity do not shrink from bigots, it counsels the easy option of shirking difficult problems and following the course of expedience. Lastly, it diminishes their regard for the rule of human behavior, everywhere accepted, that we do not forsake those to whom we are indebted for love and nurture merely because they are held in low esteem by others.[80]

D. Conclusion

Cases continue to be brought challenging the custody and visitation rights of HIV-infected parents. The most successful antidote to this type of litigation is education about HIV disease. Whenever courts have given proper credit to experts, they have concluded: (1) HIV cannot be transmitted through day-to-day contacts of parent and child; (2) a mere theoretical possibility of transmission is not a sufficient basis on which to rest a custody or visitation decision; (3) a parent's physical disability is not sufficient, in and of itself, to deprive her of custody or visitation rights, and, in fact, allowing it to be a determining factor, without more, violates legal principles applicable to persons with disabilities; 4) a child does not inherently benefit, and, in fact, may suffer severely, when kept away from a physically ill parent; and (5) possible stigma that a child may face because her parent is HIV-infected, gay, or has used drugs, cannot form the basis of a custody or visitation decision. Because HIV infection is largely irrelevant, court-ordered testing of parents alleged to be HIV-infected is not appropriate.

Each court that has recognized the rights of an HIV-infected parent has done so in the context of acknowledging that it is in the best interest of the child to have regular access to her parent, regardless of the parent's HIV infection. Although there may come a time when an HIV-infected parent may not be able to care for or reasonably interact with her child, the timing and context of that decision varies with each parent and cannot be a reason to alter custody or visitation arrangements earlier than necessary, if at all. Notably, courts that have not reached these conclusions, when appealed, have thus far uniformly been reversed.[81]

The "best interests of the child" standard requires courts to reach no other conclusion.

II. Guardianship

A. Introduction

The first section of this chapter addressed the problems faced by HIV-infected parents struggling to maintain custody of, or visitation with, their children. A different set of problems arises for an HIV-infected parent who needs to make arrangements for the care of her child during her illness or after her death. The legal system provides a variety of mechanisms for parents confronting this issue.

For a number of reasons, the traditional legal means for arranging care of a child after a parent's death inadequately address the situation confronting parents with HIV disease generally, much less the specific situation of most HIV-infected parents, who are single women of color caring for their children in a context fraught with racism and poverty.[82] These inadequacies are particularly troublesome because of the nature of HIV disease. Contrary to popular belief, people with HIV disease do not contract the illness and then die shortly thereafter. In fact, people can live with HIV infection for long periods of time, often more than ten years. Throughout the period of HIV infection, they can be alternately quite healthy and able to care for themselves and their children and then quite sick and unable to offer such care. For example, a person might be infected with HIV for five years without encountering any opportunistic infections, but might then come down with *Pneumocystis carinii* pneumonia (PCP), a debilitating form of pneumonia which may require extended hospitalization. After recovering, the individual might be fully able to care for herself and her children again for a year, or several years.

As will be shown below, the laws in those states with the greatest number of HIV-infected parents do not incorporate sufficient mechanisms to allow a child to be cared for by another adult for the limited period her parent may be incapacitated. Moreover, society's stigmatization of people with HIV disease further complicates access to the avenues that technically are available for HIV-infected parents.

A second set of issues faced by parents with HIV disease is that the existing legal mechanisms are designed for a family situation that does not comport with the socioeconomic reality of most HIV-infected parents. The existing legal structures that are supposed to establish care for surviving children were designed largely to accommodate the needs of middle-class nuclear families; they are not structured to meet the needs of families that do not fit this model. When one parent falls ill or dies, there is a traditional assumption that the other parent is available and will care for the child. In the context of HIV, there may not be another parent available to assume child-rearing responsibilities. The lack of an available second parent may occur because the other parent may already have died from HIV disease. Alternatively, as HIV-infection is often prevalent in areas where poverty and drug use are extensive, other social, economic, and health problems may result in the other parent's not being present, capable of, or interested in assuming child-rearing responsibilities.

Finally, courts, particularly in large cities, are not prepared to deal with the large number of cases that have been, and will continue to be, filed to arrange for the long-term care of orphaned children. The legal system is designed to handle, at best, the occasional situation in which a child is without either parent to care for her and where one or both of the parents have left instructions for her care. HIV disease challenges not only the assumptions of this system, but also its very capacity. In major urban areas today, thousands of HIV-infected mothers will require the assistance of the courts. Yet, already many are backlogged with matters relating to guardianship and other aspects of family law and family life. The problems of uncertainty and delay that will be highlighted below are only exacerbated by the large number of parents with HIV disease.[83]

These failures of the legal system are particularly pernicious in that parents with HIV disease have identified the future care of their children to be one of the most central concerns in their lives.[84] After a brief introduction to the legal system, this section considers the pivotal obstacles faced by parents with HIV disease. The section concludes with recommendations for ameliorating these problems.

B. Existing Mechanisms For Care of Children after the Death of a Parent

Traditionally, we presume that when one parent dies, the surviving parent assumes care and custody of the children; such an arrangement — when it actually occurs — is automatic and does not require legal intervention. However, many situations arise that do not fit this model: for examples, both parents might die simultaneously; or, when one parent dies, there may be no other parent present to assume care of the child; or, the dying parent might not want the surviving parent to care for the child. The legal system has developed certain mechanisms to allow a parent to attempt to ensure care as she sees fit for the surviving child, ranging from the appointment of a guardian to the placement of the child in the care of the state.[85] The option, or combination of options, a parent chooses will depend on her individual circumstances.

1. Guardianship

Most parents choose an individual whom they wish to be appointed guardian by a court as a means of arranging for the care of their children.[86] In most states the parent can execute a will in which a proposed guardian is named to create a legal relationship between the nominee and the child.[87] Jurisdiction over such matters lies in specialized courts, generally referred to as surrogate, or probate, courts,[88] which deal with the distribution of a decedent's property as well as with the appointment of guardians and conservators. Some states also, or solely, allow the parent to identify the proposed guardian through the filing of a petition for guardianship (by either the parent or the proposed guardian) in a family court or its equivalent.[89] In either case, the proper court must approve and officially appoint the proposed guardian.[90]

Although guardianship laws vary from state to state, consistent principles underlie the notion of a guardianship.[91] For example, once appointed, a guardian is the individual who is responsible for the child's care and well-being; she can receive benefits for the child, enroll her in school, and consent to medical care for her, if necessary.[92] In other words, she will be recognized, by government entities and the general public, as having the legal right to make decisions and take actions for the benefit of the child. While the guardian, once appointed, is recognized as the legal caretaker of the child, in many states the parent retains some parental rights, including those of visitation, and certain liabilities, including providing financial support for the care of the child unless other arrangements have been approved by the court.[93] The letters of guardianship, issued by the court, will contain any limitations the court has placed on the guardian's authority.[94]

Guardianships in this context generally are regarded as permanent arrangements and customarily remain in effect until the child reaches the age of majority or marries, whichever comes first.[95] However, they are not recognized as being permanent in a legal sense and are subject to change, especially if circumstances change, the child is harmed, or if the biological parent chooses to challenge the arrangement.[96]

2. Adoption

By contrast, rather than establishing a more limited relationship by the appointment of a guardian, some parents choose to initiate the legal mechanisms necessary to arrange for a permanent transfer of parental rights and responsibilities: adoption. This process results in the termination of all rights and obligations of the birth parent and vests these rights with the adoptive parent.[97] As such, a court is not likely to allow a third party to adopt a child absent the other parent's consent, death, or clear and convincing evidence that the other parent has abandoned the child, is unfit, or is incompetent.[98]

The distinctive aspect of adoption is its permanency.[99] As discussed above, guardianships may be subject to change if the arrangement proves unsatisfactory; moreover, they terminate when the ward reaches majority or marries. Foster care arrangements, discussed below, are designed with the intent of being temporary or transitional.

3. Foster Care

Some parents may choose, or be forced, to place their children in foster care; however, this is rarely a desired option. When a child is placed in foster care, even if she is living with another family member, she is officially a ward of the state.[100] As discussed below, parents lose a significant amount of control over their children's future when the state becomes the custodian of the children.[101]

If a parent chooses to place her child in foster care, in some jurisdictions she may have the option of requesting that the child be placed with a relative before the agency attempts to place the child with a stranger; placement with a relative is referred to as "kinship foster care."[102] However, in some states, while that request is being processed and the relative is being investigated to determine whether she will be approved as a fit foster parent (a period that may extend for many months) the child may be placed with a stranger or remain with the agency. In some circumstances the investigation may be conducted prior to the child's being removed from the home of her biological parents; in emergencies, the child may be placed with the relative while the investigation is occurring.[103]

4. Informal Arrangements

It is not always feasible to make formal arrangements for the child of a parent with HIV disease: the parent may not have informed her family of her HIV status; the parent's denial of her situation may result in her denying that future care must be arranged for her child; there may exist conflicting family pressures to appoint certain people as guardian; the parent may not want to subject the putative guardian to the scrutiny of the courts; or the parent may die suddenly, before any legal action has been commenced. Thus, parents often arrange for the care of their child without seeking judicial approval.

Some parents arrange for a temporary guardian[104] or custodian for the time they are hospitalized or are otherwise unable to care for their children through the use of a power of attorney, a temporary care agreement, or a similar written document. Such documents allow the parent to identify who she would like to "make the necessary arrangements for the care, education, and well-being" of the child, without the necessity of going to court.[105] While these papers do not necessarily constitute legal documents and therefore are not always recognized by courts, health care providers, or schools, they provide a record of a parent's wishes and may assist the designated person in caring for the child of the ill parent.[106]

Other parents die without even these minimal written directions. However, often they have expressed their wishes to family members, close friends, or health professionals. In most of these situations, the child is already being cared for by a family member within the parent's household and that person is likely to remain the child's custodian after the parent dies.

C. Problems with the Existing Mechanisms for HIV-Infected Parents

As noted above, the needs of low-income, single parents with HIV disease often are not met by these legal mechanisms. This section will explore the range of obstacles faced by HIV-infected parents in attempting to secure care for their children.

1. The Need for Flexible Mechanism

Existing legal mechanisms fail HIV-infected parents for many reasons. Chief among these failures are: first, the system's inability to allow a parent to plan, while still well, for periods of future illness without being forced to relinquish her rights immediately; and, second, the system's failure to provide a mechanism whereby a parent could relinquish control of her children for the discrete periods of time when she is incapacitated but then resume care for them when she is fully able and desires to do so. The legal mechanisms discussed above — guardianship, foster care, and adoption — are not well-suited to deal with HIV disease.

Guardianships do not adequately address the needs of a parent with HIV disease primarily because a parent must relinquish legal control of her children from the point at which the court appoints the guardian. While there are practical benefits to establishing a guardianship early in one's illness, the vast majority of parents do not want to yield care and control of their children while they are alive and able to take care of them.[107] In addition to the basic fact that they can still care for their children and have no need to relinquish control, HIV-infected parents often regard their children as a sign of the future — an indication that maybe everything will work out and that AIDS will not "win." It is not surprising, then, that parents resist the appointment of a guardian while they are conscious and alive.

There are several alternative procedures by which a person can arrange for the appointment of a guardian; each option, however, is largely unsatisfactory. A parent who delays before filing a petition risks becoming ill unexpectedly and being unable to complete and file the appropriate papers.[108] If she arranges for the proposed guardian to complete and file the necessary papers after her incapacity or death,[109] the system may not honor her wishes and she will be unavailable to testify to them. Moreover, there is often a significant time lag between the mother's incapacity or death and court approval of the guardianship, a time period during which the state may place the children in foster care.[110]

The third imperfect option is for the mother to nominate a guardian in her will.[111] By writing a will, a parent can make her wishes known without having to yield custody of her child.[112] The disadvantages arise because custody does not change until the named person obtains an order of legal guardianship from the court. This necessarily creates a period of uncertainty and means that there is no guarantee that the nominated guardian will be appointed by the court. The will, therefore, itself does not create the guardianship; rather, upon the death of the parent it becomes a catalyst for a court to begin the process that should lead to the appointment of the proposed guardian.[113] Nonetheless, most advocates find that using a will provides the best balance between the parent's interest in maintaining custody and control over the child and her interest in ensuring that her child is cared for by the person selected by the parent.[114]

The other formal legal mechanisms discussed above — foster care and adoption — do no better at addressing the specific issues raised by HIV disease. While adoption may provide the birth parent with peace of mind concerning her child's future and is the most secure arrangement, it is difficult to set up,[115] and, more importantly, is permanent, and thus cannot allow for the varying periods of illness and health an HIV-infected parent might have. Therefore, this drastic move is not one that appeals to many parents.[116]

Foster care ideally should be able to accommodate alternating periods of health and illness; in reality, however, it does not. While foster care policy varies from state to state, parents who have placed their children in foster care, and kinship foster care, may be confronted with myriad problems primarily involving the foster care agency's intrusion into and oversight of the family's situation. For example, the agency may determine how often and when the parent and children may visit, and may remove the children from the home of the relative and place them in a stranger's home if the agency is not satisfied with the level of care being provided. The parent may also encounter difficulty in getting her children back from foster care, such that a parent may be charged with abuse and neglect when she attempts to retrieve her children if she has not had regular contact with them or if the agency believes the parent is using drugs and is not in a drug rehabilitation program.[117] In addition, because even kinship foster care is viewed as only a temporary arrangement, and because it is not uncommon for relatives to feel awkward about adopting a niece or grandchild, it is likely that ultimately — consistent with principles of permanent planning — the child will have to be placed elsewhere.[118] Thus, even though financial remuneration and additional support services may be available through kinship foster care, thereby making it an option potentially preferred over informal care arrangements and other more formal arrangements, advocates generally find that the risks inherent in the foster care system outweigh these possible benefits.[119] Essentially, the bureaucracy involved in the foster care system works strongly against using this mechanism as a means of providing care for the child of a parent with HIV.

The available informal mechanisms also do not meet the needs of HIV-infected parents attempting to plan for the care of their children. Informal arrangements can break down for a variety of reasons, including: that a long-absent, surviving biological parent may present himself and seek custody of the child, contrary to the deceased parent's wishes; that unexpected medical, school-based, or other emergencies may arise in which the child's caretaker will not have the legally-recognized authority to act on the child's behalf; and, that without a familial relationship or a legal agreement, it may be significantly more difficult for the caretaker, if she is receiving government benefits, to obtain additional support to help care for the child.[120] Using either foster care or informal arrangements, there is significant danger that the undocumented intent of the deceased parent will not be acknowledged, either by institutions, such as schools and medical clinics, which must be negotiated by the adult caretaker, or by the courts if a guardian is ultimately to be appointed.

In sum, the limited legal mechanisms available to parents do not adequately accommodate the unique demands of parents living with HIV disease. Such parents are put to an all-or-nothing choice and are constantly gambling about when to make the choice; such a system benefits neither them nor their children.

2. Socioeconomic Status of Parents with HIV Disease

The socioeconomic status of most single, HIV-infected parents exacerbates the issues discussed above and creates additional problems as well. These additional problems include: the uncertainty and delay of making arrangements for the child's care created by the absence of the child's other parent; issues concerning the availability of public benefits for the family; and issues that arise from the mother's general lack of access to health care and legal services.

a. Absence of the Surviving Parent

When establishing a guardianship (either through a will or a petition), HIV-infected single mothers often attempt to leave the surviving children in the care of another female relative[121] rather than with the child's father.[122] However, the basic premise in the law is that a surviving biological parent has a *prima facie* right to be guardian of his or her child.[123] Therefore, if the surviving parent wants custody of the child, a conflict may arise between the dying parent's perspective on what is best and the surviving parent's rights.[124] The law is clear, however, that a surviving parent's rights cannot be displaced by a court's appointment of a third party as guardian unless it can be established[125] that the surviving parent has been given proper notice[126] and has consented,[127] died,[128] has waived his rights or been found to have abandoned the child,[129] or has been adjudicated unfit or incompetent.[130]

Without these findings, and absent extraordinary circumstances, the surviving parent is likely to succeed in a challenge to the appointment of another as guardian.[131] In fact, it may be that the father was unable to assume custody of his child at the time of the mother's death but that at a later time he becomes interested and able to do so.[132] The law correctly protects the father from being deprived of custody of his child without due process of law; however, these protections are not without their costs in terms of uncertainty and delay to the HIV-infected parent and to the child. Thus, there exists an element of uncertainty to the legal mechanisms that are supposed to provide certainty for care of the surviving children.

b. Public Benefits

A second set of issues implicated by the socioeconomic status of HIV-infected mothers concerns the impact her decision will have on the distribution of government benefits to her, her child, and to the guardian. Two immediate concerns arise: first, how the mother can physically continue to receive her benefits during periods of extreme illness; and second, the detrimental impact any change in custody may have on the mother's benefit package.

A single mother caring for children may qualify for a number of public benefits; the exact nature of these benefits varies from state to state. However, the benefit check(s) for the mother and child are typically made payable to the mother herself. Often an HIV-infected mother will make an informal arrangement for another person to care for her child during times of severe illness. In such situations, the caretaker may not be able to get and cash the mother's benefit check and will thus be left to care for the child on her own income. This problem can be addressed by the mother's execution of a power-of-attorney document to the caretaker, but many mothers in this situation would not be aware that this recourse is readily available.[133]

A second problem arises when the mother relinquishes control of the child when a guardianship is granted. If the child moves in with the guardian, it is likely that the child will be removed from the parent's entitlement budget and placed on the guardian's budget.[134] If this occurs, public benefits would then flow to the guardian, as caretaker of the child, leaving the mother with a sudden diminution in income and possibly an inability to maintain her own household.[135] Benefits that both the child and parent receive will also change if the child is adopted.[136]

c. Lack of Access to Health Care and Legal Services

The various legal options available to HIV-infected parents often do not reflect the reality of their lives: specifically, the legal system envisions a relatively healthy individual making rational decisions with the advice of a trained legal professional. For most HIV-infected women, however, these decisions are made without the privilege of adequate health care services, and thus often occur late in illness, and without the benefit of an attorney.

Discussions of future care for one's children are not easy under the best of circumstances. To resolve such matters, a parent must first come to terms with the fact that she is dying and that she will not be present to guide her child's life. "Often the children are all [the parents] have, and the thought of planning for others to raise them is more than they can handle."[137] For these reasons, what may appear to be a straightforward solution may be unacceptable to a particular parent. Furthermore, these decisions may be complicated by the possibility that the surviving child is, herself, HIV-infected.[138]

The parent who has to make these decisions may need time to think about the available options, may desire counseling services, and likely will need to consult with close friends and family members. Unfortunately, for HIV-infected mothers, the time available to weigh the relevant considerations may be cut short. Because of her lack of access to health care, a woman's health already may be declining when she first considers these issues; moreover, sudden illness and rapid decline are not unusual with HIV disease.[139] Further, "[w]omen with children frequently delay meeting their own needs, and so are in an advanced stage of the disease process before seeking health care and legal assistance."[140]

As a result of these often contradictory stresses, an apparently straightforward plan may be quite protracted in its creation, and, despite the serious nature of the conflicts involved, they may have to be settled hastily. Making such arrangements may be complicated by a lack of access to the legal assistance and guidance that often is necessary to make essential decisions and to arrange proper future care for children.

3. Discrimination and Lack of Confidentiality

An additional factor unique to HIV disease flows from society's stigmatization of people with this illness. People with HIV disease can face hostile societal reactions and discrimination in nearly every aspect of their lives.[141] Utilizing the legal system — through any of the aforementioned mechanisms — enhances the possibilities for such stigmatization and discrimination, of the parent and the child, and even of those who associate with them.

While lawyers filing guardianship petitions and wills typically do not include in such documents the nature of the parent's illness, the mere filing of such papers opens up the possibility that the illness will come to light. For example, a guardianship must be approved by a judge, who might ask the nature of the mother's illness. Additionally, the court in many states has the authority to order a social worker to visit and assess the proposed guardian's home and/or to undertake other intrusive examinations of the family situation.[142] In each of these instances, adverse but irrelevant information about the mother's illness can be revealed and can then be used as a basis for discriminating against her or the child. While confidentiality should be the norm for the legal system, and indeed in many places laws exist to protect the confidentiality of HIV-related information, too often this information is revealed to the detriment of the parent and child.

D. Proposals for the Future

The plethora of psychosocial and legal issues that arise when the parent of a young child develops AIDS can be overwhelming. The priorities of our legal and social systems should be to maintain a semblance of normalcy for the children while their parent is ill and hospitalized and to devise custody arrangements that both satisfy the parent's concerns about care for her child and meet the needs of the child. Unfortunately, as discussed above, these needs and priorities too often have not been addressed by those vested with the power and authority to implement and enforce them. The following modifications to the guardianship procedures and to other programs concerned with providing care to surviving children should be enacted.

First, in response to the inadequacies of the existing legal mechanisms to accommodate the needs of HIV-infected parents, each state should consider establishing a mechanism to create a "springing guardianship." Such a provision would allow a petition for guardianship to be filed and processed while the child's parent is still well; however, the proposed guardian would not assume her responsibilities until the death or incapacity of the parent.[143] This program would obviate the need for a parent to relinquish legal custody of her child before she needed to or was ready to do so, would provide the parent with the much-sought peace of mind that her child would be well cared for after the parent's death or incapacity, and would afford the child a smoother transition at an extraordinarily stressful and trying time. Some also suggest that the springing guardianship should be capable of "un-springing," permitting a parent who regains capacity to once again become the guardian of her child. In this circumstance, there would exist a legal presumption that the guardianship would "unspring" at the request of the mother.[144]

Some commentators have expressed concerns about "springing guardianships," including: difficulties with providing proper and timely notice to the father; the discovery that the guardian approved by a court at the time the petition was filed may no longer be suitable, able, or interested at the time she is to take on her responsibilities; and difficulties identifying the point at which the guardianship should "spring" into effect. Moreover, disagreements may arise between the guardian and the relinquishing parent as to whether and when it is appropriate for the guardianship to "unspring."[145]

The Florida legislature has developed a mechanism that may provide the basis for a model springing guardianship law, thereby establishing a viable means by which an HIV-infected parent could arrange for care for her child. The relevant statute provides that a parent may seek the appointment of a "standby guardian" who "shall be empowered to assume the duties of his office immediately on the death or adjudication of incapacity of the last surviving natural parent or adoptive parent of a minor...."[146] The nominated guardian must petition for confirmation of appointment within twenty days of her assumption of duties as guardian; moreover, if the court finds the standby guardian to be statutorily "qualified," she must be appointed "unless the court determines that appointing such person is contrary to the best interests of the ward."[147]

This approach is the most promising of existing statutes[148] because it provides for an expedited process in the surrogate's court that does not first require a will to be probated. Moreover, there is a statutory presumption that the nominated guardian is to be appointed by the court. For these reasons it contains basic provisions that should be included in a statute that would authorize the creation of a springing guardianship. However, for the springing guardianship statute to be

truly effective, it would have to provide for all aspects of the appointment process to be completed upon the filing of the nomination and
petition, with the exception of the issuance of the letters of guardianship. These letters could be issued only upon a brief hearing that would
confirm the suitability and availability of the proposed guardian and
the incapacity or death of the parent.

While springing guardianships may not work in all circumstances,
there is great worth in having available an additional, flexible tool
which parents can use to make care arrangements for their children.[149]
Moreover, statutory innovations like the Florida law make clear that it
is possible for legislative reforms to address the needs of HIV-infected
parents and their children.

A second helpful modification would be the development of a
mechanism whereby kinship foster parents are not asked to choose
between adopting the child or making her available for others to adopt
when it is apparent that the mother will not recover or has died. Some
have suggested the creation of a category called "relative guardianship," whereby kinship foster parents could obtain "letters of guardianship so that they will have all of the rights and responsibilities over
the child, including, but not limited to, educational and medical control
over the child."[150]

Third, in response to the hesitation of courts to appoint guardians
in the absence of biological fathers, the standard for showing that a
parent has abandoned a child could be relaxed and still provide sufficient protection of that parent's rights. As has already occurred in some
courts, the filing parent should be required to show that she has made
reasonable efforts to reach the absent parent. Upon such a showing, a
court could approve the guardianship, but without prejudice to the
rights of the absent parent. This modification would remove a tremen-
dously difficult and time-consuming obstacle from the filing parent's
efforts to ensure future care for her child without compromising the
absent parent's constitutional rights.

Fourth, in response to the problems of access to government benefits, significantly greater interagency cooperation is needed. When
custody and guardianship arrangements are implemented, it is not
surprising that housing, welfare benefits, and social security payments
may also be affected. Yet advocates report an absence of cooperation,
and, in fact, outright hostility, among agencies. Parents cannot make
the best decisions concerning the future care of their children if the
agencies charged with protecting families on a financial precipice make

arbitrary decisions and work at cross-purposes. A system must be developed that will allow agencies to accommodate the needs of the mother during her illnesses and to further accommodate the needs of children struggling to adjust to the illness, and ultimately, to the loss of a parent.

Fifth, women must be given access to a more reliable health care system that truly responds to their needs. If provided with the proper care and services, women likely would live longer, and thus remain with their children longer. They would also have more time to prepare for their children's care upon their own incapacity or death.

Sixth, in response to the extraordinary burdens on the court system, a means to expedite the process of appointing a guardian, whether through a petition or a will, must be developed. The current procedures force both the parent and child to languish at a time they are most vulnerable and most in need of support from family members and close friends. Additional court clerks and attorneys must be made available to facilitate the guardianship procedures. Further, it may be appropriate to develop a "fast track" within existing structures for people in acute stages of HIV disease and other life-threatening illnesses.

One of the most efficient models of linking parents with HIV disease with legal assistance is that found at Montefiore Hospital, located in the Bronx, in New York City. The Montefiore model connects Legal Aid attorneys with patients directly in the hospital by integrating the attorneys into the regular service-provision aspects of patient care. Legal Aid is working in conjunction with Montefiore to replicate this model throughout New York City and is serving as a guide for hospitals and legal services clinics throughout the country.[151]

Finally, in response to the particularly stigmatizing nature of HIV disease, greater efforts must be made to protect the confidentiality of both parent and child and to enforce statutory penalties that may exist for any breach that does occur.

Essentially, our legal systems do not envision young adults dying in large numbers and thus needing ways to obtain care for their surviving children. As they stand today, the laws of our states do not establish mechanisms that provide sufficiently for children who lose a parent or parents to HIV disease. Reform of the laws, regulations, and procedures governing guardianship must be our priority if we are to ensure that children of HIV-infected parents receive the kind of care one would expect to find as an integral part of a just society.

Bibliographical Note

The author would like to express her sincere gratitude to several people for their assistance in the development of this chapter. Without their contributions, this chapter would never have come to be; responsibility, however, for any flaws that may exist in the final draft is soley my own. First, Nancy Mahon's insightful note, *Public Hysteria, Private Conflict: Child Custody and Visitation Disputes Involving and HIV Infected Parent*, 63 N.Y.U. L. Rev. 1092 (1988), provided both conceptual guidance and a wealth of information for the part of the chapter addressing custody issues in the context of divorce and separation.

There currently exists very little written analysis concerning the impact of HIV disease on future planning for surviving children. As a result, I have relied significantly on the insight and experience of a select number of practitioners who must be considered the preeminent experts in the field. I am indebted to the following people for their assistance: Alice Herb and Diane LaGamma, attorneys at Montefiore Medical Center, Division of Legal and Ethical Issues in Health Care, Department of Epidemiology and Social Medicine, 111 E. 210th St., Bronx, New York; Susan Jacobs, Staff Counsel, Legal Action Center, 153 Waverly Place, New York, New York; Helene Knickerbocker, Staff Counsel, Gay Men's Health Crisis, 129 W. 20th St., New York, New York; Mildred Pinott, Staff Counsel, Community Legal Services, 230 E. 106th St., New York, New York; Lauren Shapiro, Director, HIV Project, Brooklyn Legal Services, Corp. B, 105 Court Street, Brooklyn, New York. In addition, I would like to thank the following people for their very helpful editing suggestions and substantive guidance: Rick Chamberlin, ABA Family Law Section, attorney in private practice, San Francisco, California; David L. Chambers, Wade H. McCree, Jr., Collegiate Professor of Law, University of Michigan Law School; Ruth Eisenberg, Esq., Former Staff Attorney, Whitman-Walker Clinic, Washington, D.C.; Susan L. Waysdorf, Staff Attorney/Skadden Fellow, Whitman-Walker Clinic; Andrea Palash, Former Staff Attorney, National Gay Rights Advocates, San Francisco, California; and Deborah Weimer, University of Maryland Law School, AIDS Legal Clinic.

NOTES

1. Throughout this chapter the feminine pronoun is used to describe the HIV-infected parent. This is a stylistic accommodation used for convenience; unless otherwise stated, the facts and conclusions articulated herein apply to both men and women.
2. In addition to parents, other persons with a relationship to the child often seek visitation and/or custody rights. *See, e.g.*, Doe v. Roe, 526 N.Y.S.2d 718 (Sup. Ct. 1988) (maternal grandparents seeking custody); *In re* Brian Todd Batey, No. 134-752, slip. op. (Cal. San Diego Super. Ct. 1988) (custody granted to life partner of biological father who had custody of son prior to his death from AIDS); *In re* Alison D., 572 N.E.2d 27 (N.Y. 1991) (nonbiological lesbian

coparent denied visitation rights); *see also* M. Marzano-Lesnevich, *Grandparents' Rights*, N.J. Law., Jan./Feb. 1991, at 46.

Generally, a third party will not succeed against the rights or wishes of living natural parents of the child. H. Davidson & K. Gerlach, *Child Custody Disputes: The Child's Perspective, in* Legal Rights of Children § 6.12 (R. Horowitz & H. Davidson eds., 1984) [hereinafter Davidson & Gerlach]; 1 S. Schlissel, Separation Agreements and Marital Contracts § 14.07 (1986) [hereinafter Schlissel].

3. R. Achtenberg, *AIDS and Child Custody: A Guide to Advocacy* 1-2 (National Center for Lesbian Rights, 1989) [hereinafter Achtenberg].

4. Stanley v. Illinois, 405 U.S. 645, 651-52 (1972).

5. 1 J. McCahey, M. Kaufman, C. Kraut & J. Zett, Child Custody Visitation: Law and Practice § 1.01 (1983) [hereinafter McCahey]; Schlissel, *supra* note 2, § 12.04; Davidson & Gerlach, *supra* note 2, § 6.01.

6. Issues of visitation and custody arise even when parents were never married or when they have been married but never legally separated. The marital status of the parents should not serve as the basis for an award of custody or visitation, so long as a parent can establish his or her relationship to the child.

7. Unif. Marriage and Divorce Act § 402 (1979) [hereinafter UMDA].

8. The parent awarded custody is responsible for determining "the child's upbringing, including his education, health care, and religious training...." *Id.* § 408. A court may award joint custody of the child to both parents. This means either that one parent will have sole physical custody but that both parents have control and responsibility for the child's upbringing, or, that both parents share physical custody and decision-making responsibility. Schlissel, *supra* note 2, § 12.01; Davidson & Gerlach, *supra* note 2, § 6.10; McCahey, *supra* note 5, § 1.03[5].

9. "[V]isitation is concerned with the issue of maintaining associational ties between a child and a party not having custody. Rights of visitation, then, necessarily act as a limitation on the power of the custodian." Davidson & Gerlach, *supra* note 2, § 6.10 (*citing* Comment, *Post-Divorce Visitation: A Study in the Deprivation of Rights*, 27 De Paul L. Rev. 113, 113-14 (1977)).

10. *See generally* Schlissel, *supra* note 2, ch. 14.

11. UMDA § 407 (a) (1979). Even when a parent has engaged in what might be characterized as violations of acceptable behavior, visitation often is granted, but with certain provisions — such as the presence of a chaperone or another form of supervision — to protect the child's well-being. Davidson & Gerlach, *supra* note 2, § 6.11; 2 McCahey, *supra* note 5, § 10.09[1].

12. UMDA § 407 & cmt. ("visitation rights should be arranged to an extent and in a fashion which suits the child's interest rather than the interest of either the custodial or noncustodial parent"); McCahey, *supra* note 5, § 1.03[4][a] (when broadly considering a child's psychological best interest, "visitation is seen as a right belonging to the child as well as important to the child's development").

13. McCahey, *supra* note 5, § 1.03[4][a] (*citing* Bishop, "Child Custody: An Overview," 53 Conn. B.J. 269 (1979)) (according to some commentators, "[p]reventing a child from getting to know the noncustodial parent interferes with the child's opportunity to know himself in a whole way...."); Davidson & Gerlach, *supra* note 2, § 6.10 (*citing* Comment, *Post-Divorce Visitation: A Study in the Deprivation of Rights*, 27 De Paul L. Rev. 113, 114 ("[j]udges recognize that a child's emotional and psychological well-being requires that he or she

not be estranged from [the non-custodial] parent"); *see also* Stewart v. Stewart, 521 N.E.2d 956 (Ind. Ct. App. 1988); Jane W. v. John W., 519 N.Y.S.2d 603 (Sup. Ct. 1987).

14. *See* Stanley v. Illinois, 405 U.S. 645; *see also* UMDA § 407 cmt. (the strong presumption in favor of visitation, and the high burden that must be reached to deny it, were deliberately chosen to prevent the "denial of visitation to [a] noncustodial parent on the basis of moral judgments about parental behavior which have no relevance to the parent's interest in or capacity to maintain a close and benign relationship to the child"). However, one commentator has noted that "the recent trend in visitation cases suggests that the traditional parental right to visitation has been relegated to the status of a claim or privilege because it is subject to a determination that visitation is in the child's best interests." Davidson & Gerlach, *supra* note 2, § 6.11 (*citing* Henszey, *Visitation By a Non-Custodial Parent: What Is The "Best Interest" Doctrine?*, 15 J. Fam. L. 213, 214 (1976-77)).

15. 1 J. Atkinson, Modern Child Custody Practice, § 4.01 (1986) [hereinafter Atkinson]; Schlissel, *supra* note 2, § 12.04.

16. Achtenberg, *supra* note 3, at 17-18.

17. A. Lifson, *Do Alternative Modes for Transmission of Human Immunodeficiency Virus Exist?*, 259 J. A.M.A. 1353 (1988).

18. G. Friedland & R. Klein, *Transmission of the Human Immunodeficiency Virus*, 317 New Eng. J. Med. 1125, 1132 (1987) [hereinafter Friedland & Klein]; P. Van de Perre *et al.*, *Postnatal Transmission of Human Immunodeficiency Virus Type 1 from Mother to Infant-A Prospective Cohort Study in Kigali, Rwanda*, 325 New Eng. J. Med. 593 (1991).

19. Friedland & Klein, *supra* note 18, at 1132; Bayer, Levine & Wolf, *HIV Antibody Screening*, 256 J. A.M.A. 1768, 1769 (1986); *Recommendations for Prevention of HIV Transmission in Health-Care Settings*, 258 J. A.M.A. 1441, 1445 (1987).

20. Friedland & Klein, *supra* note 18, at 1132.

21. Centers for Disease Control (CDC), *Recommendations for Preventing Transmission of Infection with Human T-Lymphotropic Virus Type III/Lymphadenopathy-Associated Virus in the Workplace*, 34 Morbidity & Mortality Wkly. Rep. 681 (1985).

22. Friedland & Klein, *supra* note 18, at 1127.

23. Achtenberg, *supra* note 3, at 10 (*citing* M. Somde & P. Volberding, Medical Management of AIDS 19 (1988)).

24. Most noted among these surveys was the one conducted by the Montefiore Medical Center. This study followed fifty families in which one member had AIDS; there had been no transmissions within any of these families (except one child born to a woman with AIDS) even though family or household members generally shared "household facilities, including beds, toilets, bathing facilities, and kitchens, as well as items likely to be soiled by patient's saliva or body fluids (e.g., eating utensils, plates, drinking glasses, and towels)." Further, no specific precautions were taken and the household members helped those with HIV disease to bathe, dress, and eat. In addition, normal familial affection was shared in the forms of hugging and kissing on the cheeks and lips. Friedland & Klein, *supra* note 18, at 1132.

25. Such an approach could be contrasted with the improper analysis undertaken by the trial court in *Stewart*, 521 N.E.2d at 959, which held that "even if there [is] a one percent chance that this child is going to contract [AIDS] from him, I'm not going to expose her to it."

26. An AIDS expert, testifying in a case in California, explained the difference as follows: "When I use the term 'theoretically possible'.....I do not mean that the possibility of transmission is in any way real or significant. Because it is impossible to prove or conclusively establish negative findings unless the finding in question violated established principles of science, scientists will always say a theoretical possibility exists, even if the possibility is so extremely remote as to be without real value." Johnetta J. v. Municipal Court of Cal., 267 Cal. Rptr. 666, 674 (1990); *see also* Bailey v. Bailey, 677 S.W.2d 874 (Ark. Ct. App. 1984) (court denied father's petition to change custody based on mother's having herpes, finding that as herpes is not easily transmissible there was no reasonable likelihood that the children would be harmed; as such, there was not a sufficient change in circumstances to warrant a change of custody).

27. Achtenberg, *supra* note 3, at 10.

28. *See Stewart,* 521 N.E.2d at 964 (reversing denial of visitation to HIV-infected father that had been entered by trial court at least in part because, "[a]n examination of the evidence leads to but one conclusion: the medical evidence and studies available at the time of trial showed that AIDS is not transmitted through everyday household contact"); Doe v. Roe, 526 N.Y.S.2d 718, 725 (Sup. Ct. 1988) (denying maternal grandparents' request to test father for HIV antibodies, stating, "[t]here is no claim, nor could there be on the available medical evidence, that the children would be in danger from living with their fathers if he were seropositive"); Conkel v. Conkel, 509 N.E.2d 983, 987 (Ohio Ct. App. 1987) (denying mother's appeal of visitation grant to father, at least in part because "AIDS or other HIV-associated diseases are not contracted by casual household contact"); *see also* Steven L. v. Dawn J., 561 N.Y.S.2d 322 (Fam. Ct. 1990); Jane W. v. John W., 519 N.Y.S.2d 603 (Sup. Ct. 1987).

    Courts have not always been so enlightened. *See* A. Zarembke, *Child Custody and AIDS, in* AIDS Practice Manual, at 16-3 to 16-4 (3d ed. 1991), *citing* Jordan v. Jordan, No. FV12-1357-84, slip op. (N.J. Super. Ct. 1986) (court ordered the temporary custody rights of a father with AIDS limited to supervised visitation under the direction of the Probation Department); G.R.M. v. J.R.A., No. RF-84-0000 (P.R. Super. Ct. 1986) (court accepted evidence that HIV is not casually transmitted, but granted mother's motion limiting visitation rights of infected father on the grounds that there was a possibility that there might be routes of transmission other than those already known).

29. 2 McCahey, *supra* note 5, § 10.08; UMDA § 402(5) (courts should consider "the mental and physical health of all individuals involved").

30. *See, e.g.,* Moye v. Moye, 627 P.2d 799 (Idaho 1981) (reversal of award of custody to father on the grounds that the lower court had placed too much emphasis on the mother's epilepsy and had not paid sufficient attention to the father's parenting ability); *In re* Marriage of R.R. and R.R., 575 S.W.2d 766 (Mo. Ct. App. 1978) (reversal of trial court's award of custody to the mother on grounds that court below had placed disproportionate impact on fact that father was in wheelchair due to multiple sclerosis and had failed to give adequate consideration to mother's history of forgery and dishonesty).

31. *See, e.g.,* Warnick v. Couey, 359 So.2d 801 (Ala. Civ. App. 1978) (custody remains with partially paralyzed father); Harper v. Harper, 559 So.2d 9 (La. Ct. App. 1990) (court granted custody to mother with spina bifida); Bier v. Sherrard, 623 P.2d 550, 552 (Mont. 1981) (best interests of the children met by placement with deaf-mute father who was employed and had a stable home

and with whom children had "a better interaction" and who was found to be a more stable person than the mother); Perry v. Perry, 234 S.E.2d 449 (N.C. Ct. App. 1977), *cert. denied*, 235 S.E.2d 784 (N.C. 1977) (child remained in custody of mother who had suffered from a stroke and remained partially paralyzed).

Courts do not always provide a clear analysis of the parent's disability and its impact on her ability to have custody of her child. *See, e.g., In re* Marriage of Ford, 415 N.E.2d 546 (Ill. App. 1981) (in upholding trial court's award of custody of children to mother, the appeals court held that the court below did not give undue consideration to the father's inability to jump, run, hop, or play certain sports, among other factors); O'Neal v. O'Neal, 394 So.2d 681, 682 (La. Ct. App. 1981) (without identifying the nature of the mother's medical problems, court held that "it is evident... that she has had and continues to have medical problems that both prevent her working full time and contraindicate her having the responsibility of her child at this time"); *In re* Mihalovich, 659 S.W.2d 798, 801 (Mo. Ct. App. 1983) (appeals court reversed trial court's award of oldest child to father and youngest two to mother; instead, mother was to have custody of all three children, at least in part because of the accident which left the father disabled and "effectively precludes him from any physical assistance in the care and upbringing of a child").

32. This conclusion is based on three interdependent factors: (1) the child has thrived with the parent prior to the occurrence of the disabling condition; (2) the parent is still able to provide for the care of the child; and (3) there is a strong presumption against moving children from one residential custodian to another. *See, e.g., Warnick*, 359 So.2d 801 (where child had been in father's physical custody for four years and was doing well with him and the grandparents, who lived in the same household, there was no basis for changing custody to the mother even though the father became partially paralyzed from a job-related injury after the custody determination and the mother's living situation had improved in the same period); *Perry*, 234 S.E.2d 449 (court refused to transfer custody from mother who had suffered from a stroke and remained partially paralyzed where testimony was presented concerning the mother's physical condition, her living arrangements, and her ability to care for the child; court instead ordered father to pay additional child support, as mother no longer could work).

33. Spohrer v. Spohrer, 428 So.2d 1350 (La. Ct. App. 1983) (mother found to be in an unstable emotional condition and to be suffering from life-threatening physical symptoms of severe anorexia nervosa).

34. Hardman v. Hardman, 214 S.W.2d 391 (Ky. Ct. App. 1948) (mother found to be unable to care for children either because of over indulgence in alcohol or as a result of severe epileptic attacks that occurred at least once every two weeks).

35. Staudacher v. Staudacher, 246 N.W.2d 34 (Minn. 1976); *see also* M.A.B. v. R.B., 510 N.Y.S.2d 960 (Sup. Ct. 1986) (gay father granted custody of one of his three children — the eldest, who had behavior problems; mother was unable to control or assist child, at least in part due to severe health problems — peritonitis, endometriosis, and colitis — that caused her to be hospitalized as an inpatient about eighty times in the past ten years).

36. 2 McCahey, *supra* note 5, § 10.08[1].

37. *See, e.g., In re* Marriage of Carney, 598 P.2d 36 (Cal. 1979); Hatz v. Hatz, 455 N.Y.S.2d 535 (Fam. Ct. 1982), *aff'd* 468 N.Y.S.2d 943 (1983); Moye v. Moye, 627 P.2d 799 (Idaho 1981).

38. *Carney,* 598 P.2d at 42. Based on its analysis of the father's rights under the existing "best interests" standard and the principles underlying California disability law, the *Carney* court did not need to reach the father's constitutional due process and equal protection arguments. The father had argued that individuals with disabilities constituted a suspect class within the fourteenth amendment and therefore could not be discriminated against in the context of custody determinations.

39. *Id.*

40. *Id.* at 44.

41. 1 Atkinson, *supra* note 15, § 4.30.

42. At least one other California court has applied *Carney*. In the case of *In re* Levin, 162 Cal. Rptr. 757 (Ct. App. 1980), the Court of Appeals found that the trial court had placed inappropriate weight on the mother's having had a debilitating stroke. The decision is based on the *Carney* holding that it is impermissible to premise a child custody award solely on the basis of a parent's physical handicap. The court remanded the matter for a reevaluation of the facts under the appropriate law.

43. Bednarski v. Bednarski, 366 N.W.2d 69 (Mich. Ct. App. 1985). The court remanded the matter to the trial court because that court had inappropriately weighed the mother's deafness against her, because it did not consider the statutory presumption "that the best interests of the child are served by awarding custody to the parent, unless there is clear and convincing evidence to the contrary," and because it did not adequately consider the effect of changing the custodial environment of the child who had been living with the mother. *Id.* at 72-73.

44. *Ex rel.* B.W., 626 P.2d 742 (Colo. Ct. App. 1981) (mother had violent confrontations with her children and in the course of one argument threw hot coffee on a child, causing him first- and second-degree burns).

45. Interpreting the Federal Rehabilitation Act of 1973, the Supreme Court, in School Bd. of Nassau County v. Arline, 480 U.S. 273, 287 (1987), stressed that a person with a contagious disease is otherwise qualified unless she poses a "significant health and safety risk[]" to others; such an analysis is highly dependent on an individual's circumstances. As HIV infection alone does not cause one to be a threat to the health or safety of others, this should not be the basis for denying custody. However, if a person with AIDS were unable to care for her children, even without "reasonable accommodation" provided by government or private support services, one reasonably would not expect a court to find her "otherwise qualified." It is for these reasons that under the principles of disability law, HIV infection alone cannot be the basis for denial of custody.

46. Discrimination based on handicap in numerous contexts is prohibited by federal legislation and by numerous state and local statutes. The relevant federal statutes include the Rehabilitation Act of 1973, 29 U.S.C. § 794 (1988), the Americans with Disabilities Act, 42 U.S.C.A. § 12101 (Supp. 1991), passed by Congress in July 1990, and the Fair Housing Act, 42 U.S.C. §§ 3601-3619 (1988). A survey of relevant state and local antidiscrimination measures can be found in American Civil Liberties Union AIDS Project, Epidemic of Fear, Appendix A (1990) [hereinafter Epidemic of Fear].

47. 526 N.Y.S.2d 718 (Sup. Ct. 1988). The principles in *Carney* were explicitly
     adopted by the New York State courts for the first time in *Hatz*, 455 N.Y.S.2d
     535. The *Hatz* court held that it was in the child's best interest to remain in the
     custody of her mother, notwithstanding the mother's having been involved
     in a car accident in which she sustained permanent injuries resulting in
     paraplegia. In reaching this decision, the court stated that "adopting the
     standard of the California Supreme Court [in *Carney*] is appropriate and keeps
     in mind the fact that we are dealing with a *person* with a physical condition
     which must be adjusted to and not a nonfunctioning being." *Id.* at 537
     (emphasis in original).

48. *Doe*, 526 N.Y.S.2d at 726.

49. *See also Steven L.*, 561 N.Y.S.2d 322 (court denied father's petition for a change
     of custody based on mother's being seropositive, and, relying on *Doe*, held
     that the mere fact that a person is seropositive, without more, does not
     constitute a "material change of circumstances" warranting change in cus-
     tody); Doe v. Roe, Civ. No. 29094 (Md. Cir. Ct. May 1988) (despite allegations
     of father's weakness and dementia related to AIDS, court found no substan-
     tiated reason to terminate joint physical custody arrangement).

50. Achtenberg, *supra* note 3, at 7. The court also should consider the health of the
     ostensibly noninfected parent.

51. UMDA § 409.

52. Glover v. McRipley, 406 N.W.2d 246 (Ct. App. Mich. 1987) (age of the
     grandparents — 60 and 56 — not a basis on which to order a change in
     custody, because it does not outweigh the bonds developed between them
     and the child over the past five years); Collins v. Collins, 115 A.D.2d 979 (1985)
     (age of the father, who was more than 65 years old, was not a relevant basis
     on which to order a change in custody; speculation about a parent's possible
     illness or death in the foreseeable future is *not* a basis for determining physical
     residence).

53. *Harper*, 559 So.2d at 10 (court appointed mother who had spina bifida as
     custodian for the minor child and further held that "[i]f the health of either
     parent deteriorated to the extent that the child could not be properly cared
     for, a modification could be requested").

54. *See, e.g., Stewart*, 521 N.E.2d 956 (appeals court reversed trial court's termina-
     tion of HIV-infected father's visitation rights); *Jane W.*, 519 N.Y.S.2d 603 (court
     held that father would not be precluded from visitation *pendente lite* on the
     basis of his AIDS diagnosis); *Conkel*, 509 N.E.2d 983 (court refused to terminate
     gay father's visitation rights, a request made by the mother on the grounds,
     inter alia, that because the father is gay he might have AIDS); Tubb v. Tubb,
     No. 3306 slip op. (Tenn. Ch. Ct. June 22, 1990) (court, holding that an HIV-in-
     fected father is entitled to visit his two children, stated, "It is clear that the
     father loves the two children...has been a good father to them, and it is critical
     that he be able to be with his children at the present time because of his bleak
     future....").

55. Note, *Public Hysteria, Private Conflict: Child Custody and Visitation Disputes
     Involving an HIV Infected Parent*, 63 N.Y.U. L. Rev. 1092, 1108 (1988) (authored
     by Nancy B. Mahon) [hereinafter Mahon].

56. Achtenberg, *supra* note 3, at 20-22.

57. Mahon, *supra* note 55, at 1108; *see also* Doe v. Roe, Civ. No. 28094 (Md. Cir. Ct.
     May 1988) (maintaining joint physical custody, with mother and HIV-infected
     father, should allow the child "to continue to receive the obvious benefits he

has enjoyed thus far by spending substantial time with both parents in a normal day-to-day setting....This is particularly important now...[because] at some point in the future it may no longer be possible because of his father's health").

58.   The UMDA provides that the court shall consider "the wishes of the child as to his custodian." UMDA § 402(2); *see, e.g., Bednarski,* 366 N.W.2d at 73 ("The evidence introduced indicated that three-year-old Rebecca looked to her mother for guidance, discipline, the necessities of life, and parental comfort"); *Marriage of R.R.,* 575 S.W.2d at 768-69 ("There was no evidence whatever concerning potential emotional damage to children resulting from living with a parent confined permanently or partially to a wheelchair"); *Bier,* 523 P.2d at 552 ("The testimony... shows that the children have a good relationship with their father and that he can provide a stable home").

59.   UMDA § 403(b) ("The court may seek the advice of professional personnel"); 1 McCahey, *supra* note 5, § 1.03[4][b]; *see also Carney,* 598 P.2d 36; *Harper,* 559 So.2d 9; *Spohrer,* 428 So.2d 1350.

60.   UMDA § 403 ("The court may interview the child in chambers to ascertain the child's wishes as to his custodian and as to visitation"); Schlissel, *supra* note 2, § 12.07; Davidson & Gerlach, *supra* note 2, § 6.07; 1 McCahey, *supra* note 5, § 1.03[4][d] ("Although courts will consider the custodial preference expressed by a child who is of sufficient age and intelligence, in some instances it may be harmful to place the child in the position of choosing one parent over the other"); *see also Marriage of Ford,* 415 N.E.2d 546; *Glover,* 406 N.W.2d 246. Note that some courts appoint counsel or a *guardian ad litem* to represent the child's interests. Davidson & Gerlach, *supra* note 2, § 6.09.

61.   Schlissel, *supra* note 2, § 12.07.

62.   2 McCahey, *supra* note 5, § 10.08[2].

63.   *See, e.g., Warnick,* 359 So.2d at 803 (custody awarded to partially paralyzed father, at least in part because "[t]he evidence indicates [that the child] is well adjusted and loves her father and grandparents"); *Carney,* 598 P.2d at 40 (children adapted well to father following accident that left him paralyzed); *Levin,* 162 Cal. Rptr. at 759 (child has "no aversion to her mother's wheelchair"); *Marriage of R.R.,* 575 S.W.2d at 768-69 ("There was no evidence whatever concerning potential emotional damage to children resulting from living with a parent confined permanently or partially to a wheelchair"); *Moye,* 627 P.2d 799; *Bier,* 623 P.2d 550. *See also Glover,* 406 N.W.2d at 249, 251 (even though court had reservations about maintaining custody of child with grandparents because of the age difference, court refused to award custody to father because of the importance of maintaining the established custodial environment and because this extended family provided tremendous love and affection to the child).

64.   "Presumption of harm to the child based on bias or mere speculation should not be indulged by the courts." 2 McCahey, *supra* note 5, § 10.09[1]; *see Hatz,* 455 N.Y.S.2d at 537. The *Hatz* court, summarizing the comments of a psychologist testifying as an expert witness, noted that the child "...needed to come to grips with her mother's handicapping condition. He did not think it fair to take her away from the situation and possibly miss the opportunity to adjust to this painful event in her life. This adjustment would be more likely to occur were the child to live through the situation rather than be taken away from it." In *M.A.B.,* 510 N.Y.S.2d 960, the court granted custody of unruly son to gay father despite the son's "discomfort" with his father's homosexuality, on

the grounds that the father was in a better position to act in the child's best interest than the mother, who was often physically ill and had attendant emotional difficulties.

65. *B.W.*, 626 P.2d 742; *Hardman*, 214 S.W.2d 391; *Spohrer*, 428 So.2d 1350.

66. In *Conkel*, 509 N.E. 2d 983, the mother argued that because the father was *gay* and *possibly* had AIDS, the children would be subject to "the slings and arrows of a disapproving society," which they would not receive if they were raised in the "normal," "healthy" home that she could provide. The court rejected these arguments and affirmed the lower court's decision to grant the father overnight visitation with his sons. *See also Stewart*, 521 N.E.2d 956 (father's homosexuality, as well as allegations that he was HIV-infected, were raised by mother in failed attempt to limit father's visitation of children).

67. In Anne D. v. Raymond D., 528 N.Y.S.2d 775 (Sup. Ct. 1988), the estranged husband sought a court order to mandate his wife to submit to a test for HIV antibodies because she had engaged in extramarital affairs. The court denied the husband's motion on the grounds that his mere allegations did not prove a sufficient predicate for such intrusive action in connection with a custody determination. By so holding, the court also rejected the husband's assertions that the results of the test would be a "determinative factor" in deciding whether she would be a fit custodial parent.

68. In M.P. v. S.P., 404 A.2d 1256, 1262-63 (N.J. Super. Ct. App. Div. 1979), the court held that the children's

> ...discomforture, if any, [with their mother] comes about....because she is a lesbian and because the community will not accept her. Neither prejudice of the small community in which they live nor the curiosity of their peers...will be abated by a change of custody....These are matters which courts cannot control, and there is little to gain by creating an artificial world where the children may deem that life is different than it is.... [We must not] forsake those to whom we are indebted for love and nurture merely because they are held in low esteem by others.

See also M.A.B., 510 N.Y.S.2d at 963 ("Given the realities of reactions that may be anticipated from B.'s peers, the taunting, teasing and ostracism, B. will have genuine social pressure to grapple with and will require strength to integrate the fact of his father's homosexuality into his own life. To accept that these problems are inevitable is, however, a long distance from saying that the father's homosexual *conduct* has had an adverse affect upon B.") (emphasis in original); *Hatz*, 455 N.Y.S.2d at 537.

69. The UMDA provides that a "court shall not consider conduct of a proposed custodian that does not affect his relationship to the child." UMDA § 402. However, courts do not always agree "on what evidence is needed to establish the required nexus between the parent's conduct and the harm to the child." 2 McCahey, *supra* note 5, § 10.09[1] at 10-96. Although the primary purpose of this provision is to focus the courts on making a custody award in the *child's* best interest, it also "is designed to exclude irrelevant evidence which might also adversely affect the child." Davidson & Gerlach, *supra* note 2, § 6.06.

70. Palmore v. Sidoti, 466 U.S. 429, 433 (1989); *see also* S.N.E. v. R.L.B., 699 P.2d 875, 879 (Alaska 1985) (applying *Palmore*); *M.A.B.*, 510 N.Y.S.2d at 964 (same); 2 McCahey, *supra* note 5, § 10.09[1].

71. 2 McCahey, *supra* note 5, § 10.08[1]; Schlissel, *supra* note 2, § 12.05.

72. 4 McCahey, *supra* note 5, § 25.04.

73. Court decisions in which a parent's homosexuality has not affected the custody or visitation determination include: *S.N.E.*, 699 P.2d 875; *M.P.*, 404 A.2d 1256; *M.A.B.*, 510 N.Y.S.2d 960; *Conkel*, 509 N.E.2d 983. *See generally* Hammer, *Family Law II: The Role of Sexual Preference in Child Custody Disputes*, 1986 Ann. Surv. Am. L. 685, 698. However, some courts persist in finding that a parent's homosexuality disqualifies the parent from being the child's primary custodian. *See, e.g.*, Thigpen v. Carpenter, 730 S.W.2d 510 (Ark. 1987); S.E.G. v. R.A.G., 735 S.W.2d 164 (Mo. Ct. App. 1987); Constant A. v. Paul A., 496 A.2d 1 (Pa. 1985); Roe v. Roe, 324 S.E.2d 691 (Va. 1985).

74. *S.N.E.*, 699 P.2d 875.

75. *See, e.g.*, Armstrong v. Armstrong, 515 So.2d 27 (Ala. Ct. App. 1987) (mother's cohabitation with a man while her daughter was in the house was insufficient to justify a change in custody, as there was no evidence of a substantial detrimental effect on the daughter); Barton v. Minton, 484 So.2d 317 (La. Ct. App. 1986) (trial court erred when it ordered a transfer of custody from the mother to the father on the grounds that the mother had committed continuous acts of adultery, as mother married her partner shortly after the divorce); Feldman v. Feldman, 358 N.Y.S.2d 507 (App. Div. 1974) (mother's private sexual activities, as an alleged "swinger," should not affect award of custody to her; trial court erred when it granted father's request for a change in custody).

76. 2 McCahey, *supra* note 5, § 10.08[1].

77. *See, e.g.*, *Conkel*, 509 N.E.2d 983 (court, relying in part on *Palmore*, denied mother's appeal of granting of overnight visitation to gay father); *Stewart*, 521 N.E.2d 956; *Doe*, 526 N.Y.S.2d 718; *Jane W.*, 519 N.Y.S.2d 603.

78. *Conkel*, 509 N.E.2d at 984.

79. Mahon, *supra* note 55, at 1137 (*citing* Commonwealth *ex rel.* Lucas v. Kreischer, 299 A.2d 243, 246 (Pa. 1973) ("[I]f a child is raised in a happy home, she can conquer prejudice or any other adversity she encounters")).

80. *M.P.*, 404 A.2d at 1263.

81. It is unfortunate, however, that some parents may not have the time, energy, good health, or resources to challenge an adverse ruling from the trial court; further, some parents may resist going to court at all, and may yield to the demands of the uninfected parent, forgoing an attempt to maintain custody or visitation over her child. The risk that a parent faces by relying on a court to determine the boundaries of her relationship with her child cannot be underestimated. As such, nonlitigatory approaches to resolving custody and visitation disputes in this context are important avenues to be explored.

82. This is not to say that middle-class people, gay men, and others, do not also face equally painful dilemmas in arranging for the care of their children.

83. Teltsch, *Mothers Dying of AIDS Get Child Custody Help*, N.Y. Times, August 27, 1991, at B 1, col. 2.

84. A. Herb, D. LaGamma, C. Zuckerman & N.N. Dubler, Legal Services for a Parent with AIDS 2 (Montefiore Medical Center, 1990) [hereinafter Legal Services].

85. *See generally* M. Soler, A. Shotton, J. Bell, E. Jameson, C. Shauffer & L. Warboys, Representing the Child Client, ¶ 3.06 (1991) [hereinafter Soler]; Haralambie, Handling Child Custody Cases § 14.01 (1983 & Supp. 1991) [hereinafter Haralambie].

86. It is possible to establish a guardianship for both the minor and the minor's estate in almost every state. The latter must be created when a minor child's property is of a certain nature or exceeds a certain amount, as determined by each state. Soler, *supra* note 85, ¶ 3.06[1], [2][b]. In some states a parent may nominate coguardians to provide care for her child or her child's estate. *See, e.g.,* Cal. Prob. Code § 2105 (West 1981); Fla. Stat. Ann. § 744.361 (West Supp. 1991).

87. Some states, however, will not allow for a testamentary nomination of a guardian unless the other parent of the surviving child is already deceased. *See, e.g.,* Md. Code Ann. Est. & Trusts § 7 (1991).

88. Soler, *supra* note 85, ¶ 3.06; Haralambie, *supra* note 85, § 14.01 (1983 & Supp. 1991); *see also* N.J. Stat. Ann. §§ 3B:12-12 (jurisdiction of surrogate to appoint guardians for minors), 3B:12-13 (power to designate testamentary guardian) (West 1983); N.Y. Surr. Ct. Proc. Act §§ 1701 (power of court), 1707 (decree appointing guardian) (Supp. 1991). The Uniform Probate Act, a model law in effect in fifteen states, similarly empowers probate courts to appoint guardians for surviving children. *See* Uniform Probate Act, §§ 5-201 *et seq.*

89. Haralambie, *supra* note 85, § 14.01; *see also* N.Y. Dom. Rel. Law § 81 (McKinney 1988) (appointment of guardians by parent).

90. In appointing a guardian, the court will examine what arrangement would further the best interests of the child. *See, e.g.,* N.J. Stat. Ann. § 3B:12-17 (West 1983) (The court may "make an order...as may be for the best interest and welfare of the minor"); N.Y. Surr. Ct. Act § 1707 (McKinney Supp. 1991) ("If the court be satisfied that the interests of the infant will be promoted by the appointment of a guardian...it must make a decree accordingly"). This necessarily means that "the custodial parent has no absolute right to determine the child's future custody by will;" Haralambie, *supra* note 85, §14.08.

91. Haralambie, *supra* note 85, § 14.02; Soler, *supra* note 85, ¶ 3.06[2].

92. Soler, *supra* note 85, ¶3.06[2][1]; Haralambie, *supra* note 85, § 14.02; *see also* Cal. Prob. Code § 2107 (powers granted guardian nominated by will) (West 1981); N.J. Stat. Ann. §§ 3B:12-51 ("A guardian of the person of a minor has the powers and responsibilities of a parent who has not been deprived of custody of his minor and unemancipated child, except that a guardian is not legally obligated to provide for the ward from his own funds"); 3B:12-52 (powers and duties of a guardian of the person of a minor, including, to take reasonable care of the ward's personal effects and "to facilitate the ward's education, social, or other activities and to authorize medical or other professional care, treatment, or advice") (West 1983); N.Y. Surr. Ct. Proc. Act § 2108 (McKinney 1967) ("Except to the extent the court for good cause determines otherwise...the guardian shall be granted in the order of appointment, to the extent provided in the nomination, the same authority with respect to the person of the ward as a parent having legal custody of a child"); *id.* § 2353 (unless the ward is age 14 or older, when she also must consent, "the guardian has the same right as a parent having legal custody of a child to give consent to medical treatment performed upon the ward and to require the ward to receive medical treatment").

Because the guardian is given such authority, the child's wishes are often considered by the court in reaching its determination, particularly as the child nears the age of majority; most states provide that from age 14 a child may object to the appointment of a guardian. Cal. Prob. Code § 1513 (West 1981) (court considers a "statement of the proposed ward's attitude concerning the proposed guardianship, unless the statement of the attitude is affected by the proposed ward's developmental, physical, or emotional condition"); Haralambie, *supra* note 85, § 14.06; *see also* N.Y. Surr. Ct. Proc. Act § 1706(a) (McKinney Supp. 1991) ("If the infant is over the age of 14 years the court shall ascertain his preference for a suitable guardian"). Moreover, most states allow a child of age 14 or older to nominate her own guardian. *See* Soler, *supra* note 85, ¶ 3.06[5][c]; N.Y. Surr. Ct. Act § 1703 (McKinney 1967).

93. *See* Soler, *supra* note 85, ¶ 3.06[2][a] ("While the guardianship does not terminate the parent-child relationship, it transfers the primary duties and privileges of parenting to the guardian"); *see also id.* ¶ 3.06[5][d][iv]; Haralambie, *supra* note 85, § 14.02 ("While guardianship, in and of itself, does not terminate parental rights, it may terminate the parent's authority over the child for the duration of the guardianship"); Cal. Civil Code § 204 (West 1982).

94. "The 'letter of guardianship' is the official court document that vests legal custody of the minor in the guardian. The document also serves as proof that the guardian has taken an oath and filed a bond if required to do so. The letters of guardianship list all the powers, restrictions, conditions, and limitations of the guardianship." Soler, *supra* note 85, ¶ 3.06[5][d][viii]; *see also id.* ¶ 3.06[2][a]; Haralambie, *supra* note 85, § 14.02; Cal. Prob. Code § 2310 (West 1981); Fla. Stat. Ann. §§ 744.345, 744.347, 744.351 (West Supp. 1991); N.J. Stat. Ann. § 3B:12-37 (West 1983). Although most states provide for exceptions in the guardian's authority, in some states, a guardian assumes control over all aspects of the child's life. Cal. Civil Code § 204(1) (West 1982); D. LaGamma & A. Herb, *Providing for the Future Care of Children, in* AIDS Practice Manual 5-5 (National Lawyers Guild AIDS Network 1991) [hereinafter LaGamma].

95. *See* Soler, *supra* note 85, ¶ 3.06[3][a]; Cal. Prob. Code § 1600 (West 1981); N.J. Stat. Ann. § 3B:12-55 (West 1983); N.Y. Dom. Rel. Law § 84 (McKinney 1988); N.Y. Surr. Ct. Proc. Act § 1600 (McKinney 1967).

96. *See* Fla. Stat. Ann. §§ 744.467 (resignation of guardian), 744.474 (reasons for removal of guardian) (West Supp. 1991); N.Y. Surr. Ct. Proc. Act § 1707(2) ("The term of office of a guardian...expires when the infant attains majority, or after such other shorter period as the court establishes upon good cause shown") (West Supp. 1991). When a biological parent challenges an appointment of a guardian that occurred at a prior date, the court considers what is in the best interest of the child to determine which adult should be the child's guardian. LaGamma, *supra* note 94, at 5-4.

97. *See, e.g.,* N.Y. Dom. Rel. Law § 117 (McKinney 1988); Fla. Stat. Ann. § 63.172 (West 1985); N.J. Stat. Ann. § 9:3-50 (West Supp. 1991). Adoption is similar to the other forms of arranging care for children in that the court in this context also applies the "best interests of the child" standard. *See, e.g.,* Fla. Stat. Ann. § 63.022(2)(l) (West Supp. 1991); N.J. Stat. Ann. § 9:3-40 (West Supp. 1991).

98. *See* Santosky v. Kramer, 455 U.S. 745 (1982) (termination of parental rights at state-initiated proceedings cannot be accomplished absent clear and convincing evidence of parental neglect or unfitness). For example, New Jersey law states that:

> Any parent who has not executed a surrender...and whose parental rights have not been terminated by court order shall have the right to object to the adoption of his child. No judgment of adoption shall be entered over an objection of such parent...unless the court finds that such parent has substantially failed to perform the regular and

expected parental functions of care and support of the child, which shall include maintenance of an emotional relationship with the child.

N.J. Stat. Ann. §§ 9:3-45 (West Supp. 1991), 9:3-46 (West Supp. 1991); *see also* Cal. Civil Code § 221.20 (West Supp. 1991) (birth parents; consent); N.Y. Dom. Rel. Law § 111 (McKinney 1988) (consent must be provided by the parents of children conceived or born in wedlock, a mother of a child born out of wedlock, and certain fathers of children born out of wedlock).

Most states also provide that the child to be adopted must give her consent if she is over a certain age. *See, e.g.*, Cal. Civil Code § 221.12 (West Supp. 1991) (age 12); Fla. Stat. Ann. § 63.062 (West 1985) (age 12); N.J. Stat. Ann. § 9:3-49 (West Supp. 1991) (age 10); N.Y. Dom. Rel. Law § 111 (McKinney 1988) (age 14).

99. *See supra* n. 97 and accompanying text.

100. *See, e.g.*, N.Y. Soc. Serv. Law §§ 371, 383 (McKinney 1983). *See generally* M. Hardin, A. Shalleck, *Children Living Apart from Their Parents, in* Legal Rights of Children § 9 (R. Horowitz & H. Davidson eds., 1984) [hereinafter Hardin & Shalleck].

101. A parent may wish to visit her child, but because of her illness or hospitalization she may be unable to keep her visitation appointments. Even though it is the goal of the foster care agency to unite families (N.Y. Soc. Serv. Law §§ 384-a-b (McKinney 1983 & Supp. 1991)), such incidents may result in the permanent removal of the child from her parent. *Id.*; Interview with Susan Jacobs, Staff Attorney at the Legal Action Center, New York, New York. If it is determined that the child and parent cannot or should not be reunited, the goal of the foster care system becomes "permanency planning," i.e., adoption. Hardin & Shalleck, *supra* note 100, § 9.09; *see also* N.Y. Soc. Serv. Law § 384-b. As a result, if the foster parents, including family members caring for the child under kinship foster care (see *infra* notes 102-103, 117-119 and accompanying text), do not want to adopt the child, the foster care system may remove the child from the family in order to facilitate the adoption of the child. Interview with Mildred Pinott, Staff Attorney at the Legal Aid Society, Volunteer Division, in New York, New York.

102. *See, e.g.*, N.Y. Soc. Serv. Law § 384(a)(1-a) (McKinney 1983); South Brooklyn Legal Services, Corp. B & Gay Men's Health Crisis, Facing the Future: A Legal Handbook for Parents with HIV Disease 131 (1991) (available from Lauren Shapiro, Esq., Brooklyn Legal Services, Corp. B, 105 Court Street, Brooklyn, New York 11201) [hereinafter Facing the Future].

103. Placement of the child occurs much more quickly in the case of an emergency (e.g., the filing of charges of abuse and neglect against the biological parent). As a practical matter, kinship foster care is used most often in the context of such proceedings. Interview with Lauren Shapiro, Director of the HIV Unit of South Brooklyn Legal Services, Brooklyn, New York; Interview with Sue Jacobs, Staff Counsel at the Legal Action Center, in New York, New York.

104. *See* Soler, *supra* note 85, ¶ 3.06[3][f]. "Some states provide an intermediate step between formal and informal guardianship. For example, California provides for the appointment of a 'temporary' guardian....This procedure may offer an appropriate means to provide minors with the authority needed for a specific purpose, especially where the guardian would be unwilling to take on a long term commitment." *Id.* ¶ 3.06[3][f] (*citing* Cal. Prob. Code § 2250 (West Supp.

1991)). The powers and duties of a temporary guardian may be limited to those that are "necessary to provide for the temporary care, maintenance, and support of the ward." Cal. Prob. Code § 2252 (West 1981).

105. Facing the Future, *supra* note 102, at 15; Haralambie, *supra* note 85, § 14.04. This usually can be accomplished with a letter signed by the client and acknowledged by a notary public. LaGamma, *supra* note 94, at 5-7.

106. Soler, *supra* note 85, ¶ 3.06[4][f] ("Informal guardianships are subject to instant termination by parents and most likely will not enable the informal guardian to qualify for benefits for the child or to enroll the child in school"). However, durable powers of attorney increasingly are being recognized by courts. Unif. Probate Code § 5-102 provides that "[a] parent or guardian of a minor or incapacitated person by a properly executed power of attorney, may delegate to another person, for a period not exceeding 6 months, any power regarding care, custody or property of the minor child or ward, except the power to consent to marriage or adoption of a minor ward." The person granted the power of attorney is likely to have greater success in attempting to exercise the granted powers if she is also the proposed guardian. Telephone Interview with Rick Chamberlin, Family Law Specialist, San Francisco, California; *see also* Soler, *supra* note 85, ¶3.06[4][f] ("Generally, the informal guardian should be someone with whom the child already has a fairly strong relationship").

107. A. Herb, D. LaGamma & N.N. Dubler, Legal Services for Persons with AIDS (PWAs) of Predominantly Heterosexual, Poor Minority Background, Presented at the Fifth International Conference on AIDS (June 8, 1989) [hereinafter Montreal Paper]; LaGamma, *supra* note 94, at 5-5. Moreover, judges often express discomfort at appointing a guardian when a mother appears well and capable of caring for her child. Interview with Diane LaGamma, attorney at Montefiore Medical Center, in Bronx, New York.

108. Unfiled papers may, nevertheless, be used as evidence of the parent's intention of how care should be provided for her child. Interview with Helene Knickerbocker, Staff Counsel at Gay Men's Health Crisis, in New York, New York. When weighing whether to seek to have a guardian appointed prior to her incapacity or death, a parent must also balance the benefits of being able to resolve some of the court's questions about her proposed guardian with the stress of having to face potentially difficult and trying questions posed by the court that may seem — and be — unacceptably intrusive. *Id.*

109. As is discussed in greater detail at note 113 and accompanying text, some surrogate's courts allow a petition to be filed without benefit of the filing of a will. *See, e.g.,* Cal. Prob. Code § 1500 *et seq.* (West 1981 & Supp. 1991); Fla. Stat. Ann. § 744.101 *et seq.* (West 1985 & Supp. 1991). The petition for guardianship should be consistent with the content of the deceased parent's will, if one exists. In fact, it usually is the proposed guardian who files the petition for guardianship with the court. Soler, *supra* note 85, ¶ 3.06[5][d][i].

110. If a guardian has not been appointed at the time of the parent's death or incapacity, most jurisdictions appoint a temporary guardian so that there will be an adult officially empowered to make important decisions on behalf of the children — such as obtain benefits for them, enroll them in a new school, consent to medical care — until the petition is processed. Haralambie, *supra* note 85, § 14.04; Soler, *supra* note 85, ¶ 3.06[4][f]; Cal. Prob. Code § 2250 (West 1981). Depending on the process used, it may take many months for the appointment to be made. If a surviving parent challenges the proposed appointment, a final appointment may take even longer.

111. Haralambie, *supra* note 85, § 14.08; Soler, *supra* note 85, ¶ 3.06[5][c]; *see also*
      N.Y. Surr. Ct. Proc. Act §§ 1710-1711 (McKinney 1967); N.J. Stat. Ann. §
      3B:12-13 (West 1983).

112. Advocates report that a court is particularly likely to appoint the proposed
      guardian noted in the parent's will where: (1) the parent who is dying is the
      primary caretaker for the child; (2) it can be established that the parent has a
      good relationship with the child; (3) the surviving parent does not raise a
      challenge; (4) the child is very young; and (5) the investigation yields no bar
      to the appointment. Interview with Rick Chamberlin, Family Law Specialist,
      in San Francisco, California; Interview with Mildred Pinott, Staff Counsel at
      Community Legal Services, in New York, New York. For a further exploration
      of some of the advantages and disadvantages of using a will to appoint a
      guardian for a child, see Legal Services, *supra* note 84, at 37-39.

113. This process includes the filing of the petition for guardianship by the pro-
      posed guardian. *See, e.g.*, Cal. Prob. Code § 1500 (West 1981); Fla. Stat. Ann. §
      744.3125 (West Supp. 1991). Some surrogate's courts will not consider the
      petition for guardianship until the will has been probated. *See, e.g.*, N.Y. Dom.
      Rel. Law § 81 (McKinney 1988); N.Y. Surr. Ct. Proc. Act § 1710 (McKinney
      1967) ("A person shall not exercise within the state any power or authority as
      guardian...unless the will has been duly admitted to probate and recorded in
      the proper court and letters of guardianship have been issued thereon").
      Other courts allow the proposed guardian to petition directly following the
      parent's death and do not even require the will to be filed (although it may
      be used as evidence of the mother's intent, if necessary). Some attorneys may
      choose to petition the family court immediately after the parent's death and
      use the will as evidence of the mother's intent for the future care of her child.
      Interview with Helene Knickerbocker, Staff Counsel at Gay Men's Health
      Crisis, in New York, New York. Clearly, these latter routes avoid a great deal
      of delay in the appointment of a legal guardian for the child.

      Prior to the appointment, the court will order an investigation to deter-
      mine the fitness of the proposed guardian. The investigation may include: a
      search of the child abuse records of the state to ensure that the proposed
      guardian is not listed therein, Cal. Prob. Code § 1516 (West 1981); N.Y. Surr.
      Ct. Proc. Act §§ 1706-1707 (McKinney Supp. 1991); a probe of the information
      provided by the proposed guardian to the court, Cal. Prob. Code § 1513 (West
      1981); N.Y. Surr. Ct. Proc. Act § 1704(6) (McKinney 1967); and a review of the
      prospective guardian's credit history and the existence of any criminal his-
      tory. Fla. Stat. Ann. § 744.3145 (West Supp. 1991). *See generally* Soler, *supra*
      note 85, ¶ 3.06[5][d][v].

      Some states also require certain education and training of the guardian
      to help ensure that she will be able to protect the interests of the ward, Fla.
      Stat. Ann. § 744.3145 (West Supp. 1991), as well as the filing of a guardian
      report and plan. *Id.* §§ 744.362, 744.363.

114. Interview with Helene Knickerbocker, Staff Counsel at Gay Men's Health
      Crisis, in New York, New York. Although there are no guarantees when one
      uses a will, advocates find that it can be a powerful tool for the parent to help
      ensure that her child will be cared for by the person the parent has concluded
      will best protect the interests of her child. *Id.*

115. "[T]he process of adoption is lengthy; the necessary consents may be impossi-
      ble to obtain; and the proposed adoptive parents may not meet the standards
      of the court." LaGamma, *supra* note 94, at 5-7; *see also* Haralambie, *supra* note

85, § 15.01 ("Adoption is a creature of statute, and the controlling statues are strictly construed").

116. The finality of this decision is something that is understandably difficult for a parent with HIV disease to accept. Some advocates support the movement toward open adoption, in which both the birth parent(s) and adoptive parent(s) maintain a relationship with the child. Interview with Deborah Weimer, Assistant Professor of Law, University of Maryland School of Law, Clinical Law Office, AIDS Law Clinic.

117. Facing the Future, *supra* note 102, at 14. Yet, it may be obstacles established by state bureaucracy that prevent a woman from visiting her child (e.g., being forced to wait many hours for a medical appointment in a health clinic) or from gaining entry to a drug rehabilitation program (e.g., due to a drastic shortage of treatment centers, especially for women).

118. Carrieri, *Foster Care — Placement with Relatives*, N.Y. L.J., June 20, 1991, at 1, col. 1 [hereinafter Carrieri].

119. In some jurisdictions, such as New York City, kinship foster care parents receive the same governmental payments as other foster parents — a sum that is substantially greater than would be available through welfare if she were to apply for it and qualify. Interview with Lauren Shapiro, Director of the HIV Unit of South Brooklyn Legal Services, Brooklyn, New York. In addition, there are a greater range of support services available to foster parents, including kinship foster parents, than to those who otherwise have custody or guardianship of the child. *See* N.Y. Soc. Serv. Law §§ 384-a-b (McKinney 1983 & Supp. 1991). In jurisdictions where these forms of assistance are not available, there is even less incentive to elect the option of foster care. Facing the Future, *supra* note 102, at 13-14; interview with Lauren Shapiro, Director of the HIV Project at Brooklyn Legal Services, Corp. B, in Brooklyn, New York. *See generally* Hardin & Shalleck, *supra* note 100, §§ 9.02-9.15.

120. *See, e.g.*, Soler, *supra* note 85, ¶ 3.06[4][f]; Facing the Future, *supra* note 102, at 14.

121. Legal Services, *supra* note 84, at 32; Montreal Paper, *supra* note 107, at 7. Oftentimes, culturally specific patterns of family arrangements, not as prevalent in white, middle-class families, produce strong support systems; unfortunately, the strength of these supports are not always recognized by the courts charged with making guardianship determinations.

122. There is no requirement that parents be married for either parent to assert a desire to be custodian of the child. *See, e.g.*, Fla. Stat. Ann. § 744.3021 (West Supp. 1991) ("Upon petition of a parent, brother, sister, next of kin, or other person interested in the welfare of a minor, a guardian for a minor may be appointed by the court"). Further, it is not uncommon for the children of one mother to have different fathers. Legal Services, *supra* note 84, at 6, 32.

123. Moss v. Vest, 262 P.2d 116, 1919 (Idaho 1953); Lawson v. Lawson, 94 S.E.2d 215, 218-19 (Va. 1956). The Constitution similarly protects a parent from being deprived of custody of her children without due process of law in state-initiated proceedings. *See* Lehr v. Robertson, 463 U.S. 248, 262 (1983) ("When an unwed father demonstrates a full commitment to the responsibilities of parenthood by 'com[ing] forward to participate in the rearing of his child,' his interest in personal contact with his child acquires substantial protection under the Due Process Clause") (*quoting* Caban v. Mohammed, 441 U.S. 380, 392 (1979)); *Stanley*, 405 U.S. 645.

124. Many states create "statutory priorities for court appointment, favoring the closest relative...." Haralambie, *supra* note 85, § 14.05. "However, courts are not bound by this preference if it would be contrary to the child's best interest to appoint such [a] person as guardian." Soler, *supra* note 85, ¶¶ 3.06[5][c], [5][d][vii]; *see also* N.J. Stat. Ann. § 3B:12-21 (West 1983) (the court "may appoint the parents or either of them or the survivor of them as the guardian....If neither parent or the survivor of them will accept the guardianship, then the heirs, or some of them, may be appointed as guardian. If none of the heirs will accept the guardianship, then some other person shall be appointed as the guardian....This section shall not be construed to restrict the power of the court to appoint a substitute guardian on the application of the minor or otherwise"); LaGamma, *supra* note 94, at 5-4; Legal Services, *supra* note 84, at 34.

125. It is the burden of the party seeking to have the guardian appointed to establish that the other parent is not available, for any of the reasons discussed in the text (immediately below); this is not a process that typically would involve the state or any other government agency.

126. State law tends to contain extensive requirements concerning notice in the context of a guardianship, especially if the nominating parent wishes to have the court appoint a third party rather than the surviving parent. Soler, *supra* note 85, ¶ 3.06[5][d][iv]. However, some courts dispense with the notice requirement as to a particular person if the petitioner can show that she used "reasonable diligence" to locate the person. *Id.* (*citing* Cal. Prob. Code § 1511(g)(1)); *see, e.g.*, Fla. Stat. Ann. § 744.3371 (West Supp. 1991) ("When a petition for appointment of a guardian for a minor is filed, formal notice must be served on the minor's parents. If the petitioner has custody of the minor and the petition alleges that, after diligent search, the parents cannot be found, the parents may be served by informal notice, delivered to their last known address or addresses. When a parent petitions for appointment as guardian for his minor child, no notice is necessary unless the other parent is living and does not consent to the appointment").

127. *See, e.g.*, Cal. Prob. Code § 1500 (b)(1) (West 1981) (A parent may nominate a guardian...of a minor child, *inter alia*, "(a) Where the other parent nominates, or consents in writing to the nomination of, the same guardian for the same child...."); N.J. Stat. Ann. § 3B:12-14 (West 1983); N.Y. Dom. Rel. Law § 81 (McKinney 1988).

128. *See, e.g.*, Cal. Prob. Code § 1500(b)(1) (West 1981) (A parent may nominate a guardian of a minor child, when, *inter alia*, "at the time the petition for appointment of the guardian is filed, (b)... the other parent is dead or lacks legal capacity to consent to the nomination...."); N.Y. Dom. Rel. Law § 81 (McKinney 1988).

129. A parent who has abandoned her child is not entitled to receive notice; however, in reality, the determination of abandonment generally is not resolved until notice of the nonmoving parent has been attempted. *See, e.g.*, Cal. Civil Code § 221.20 (West Supp. 1991); Cal. Prob. Code § 1500 (West 1981); *id.* § 1511 (consent not necessary when, *inter alia*, "the birth father or mother has been judicially deprived of the custody and control of the child...[,] has deserted the child without provision for identification of the child [or]...has relinquished the child for adoption.... ") (West 1981); N.Y. Surr. Ct. Act § 1705 (McKinney 1967 & Supp. 1991) ("No process shall be necessary to a parent

who has abandoned the infant or is deprived of civil rights or divorced from the parent having legal custody of the infant…..").

According to many advocates, in practice it is very difficult for one parent to establish that the other parent has abandoned the child. The filing parent must prove that she made diligent efforts to find the other parent. For example, she may have to establish that she has searched the death certificate records, motor vehicle records, and many other available public records in a broad geographic area. It is particularly draining and arduous for a parent of fragile health and limited time to show such due diligence in making a good faith effort to find the father — or fathers — of her children. Legal Services, *supra* note 84, at 45; Interview with Mildred Pinott, Staff Counsel at Community Legal Services, in New York, New York.

Courts within New York City often apply varying standards before they will appoint a guardian other than the biological father. For example, some courts provide that parents need only sign an affidavit that the other parent has abandoned the child; this allows the proceedings to be conclusive to all but the other parent thereby preserving that parent's due process rights, arranging care for the child, and serving the needs of the parent with HIV disease. Other courts apply more stringent requirements, such as those discussed above. Interview with Diane LaGamma, attorney at Montefiore Medical Center, in Bronx, New York. In Maryland, it is most important to prove that the biological father received notice, or that notice diligently was attempted, of the guardianship proceedings. Md. Fam. Law Code Ann. § 5-322 (1989). The procedures a court demands are often highly dependent on the particular judge and the particular court.

130.   *See, e.g.,* Cal. Civil Code § 221.29 (West Supp. 1991) (a parent may nominate a guardian…of a minor child without the consent of the surviving parent when, *inter alia,* "the birth father or mother has been judicially deprived of the custody and control of the child…."); Cal. Prob. Code § 1500 (West 1981); N.Y. Soc. Serv. Law § 384-b (4)-(b)(7) (McKinney 1983 & Supp. 1991) (custody may be taken from a biological parent if she is shown to be unfit or to have been persistently neglectful); N.Y. Surr. Ct. Proc. Act § 1705 (McKinney 1967 & Supp. 1991) (no notice of guardianship proceedings need be provided to a parent who is "incompetent or who is otherwise judicially deprived of custody of the infant…..").

131.   In most jurisdictions, if the court finds that "extraordinary circumstances" do exist, the court may apply the "best interests of the child" standard to determine custody. *See, e.g.,* Bennett v. Jeffreys, 387 N.Y.S.2d 821, 823, 826 (N.Y. 1976). In California, if the surviving parent appears after the guardianship has been awarded to a third party, the guardian must establish that the child will suffer a detriment if custody is awarded to the surviving parent in order to maintain custody. Cal. Civil Code § 4600(c) (West Supp. 1991).

132.   A father may be unavailable for any number of reasons that make it impossible or impractical for him to assume parenting responsibilities at the time a guardian is first appointed. For example, he may be absent because of his use of drugs; however, in the time between the appointment and the father's challenge thereof, he may have successfully completed rehabilitation from drug use. It would be inappropriate at that time to deny the father a relationship with his child. In fact, this points out another failure of our system: there is no clear legal mechanism to allow a parent who has been denied custody or guardianship of his child on the merits to have a legal relationship — or

perhaps even visitation with — his child. Interview with Susan Jacobs, Staff Counsel at the Legal Action Center, in New York, New York.

133. A power of attorney is a simple document that states the executor's intent and is notarized; it does not need to be prepared by a lawyer. *See supra* note 105 and accompanying text. Alternatively, the mother can arrange to have the caretaker appointed as the representative payee of her government benefits.

134. Generally, the benefits follow the living arrangements of the people involved rather than their legal relationships. For example, the "crucial criterion" for eligibility for Aid to Families with Dependent Children (AFDC) "is the presence in the home of a needy, dependent child who has been deprived of parental support.... Deprivation of parental support can occur only because one parent has died, left the home, or is in the home and is incapacitated. The dependency requirement is satisfied if the child lives with a relative of specified degree," J. Weill & N. Ebb, *Public Benefits Programs for Children and Their Families, in* Legal Rights of Children § 5.04 (R. Horowitz & H. Davidson eds., 1984) (*citing* 42 U.S.C.A. § 602 *et seq.* (1984 & Supp. 1991)) [hereinafter Weill & Ebb]; So long as the legal guardian of the child also is a relative of specified degree, the household may be eligible to receive AFDC. If the guardian does not fall within this category, however, the household cannot qualify for AFDC but could be eligible for state-funded general assistance programs.

135. If the mother has been found eligible to receive Supplemental Security Income (SSI), 42 U.S.C. § 1381 *et seq.* (1988), the benefits she receives under this program might increase, but they are not likely to decrease if her child were to move to the home of the guardian; such determinations are highly dependent on the circumstances presented. *Id.; see also* Weill & Ebb, *supra* note 134, § 5.07 (SSI benefits are the one form of parental benefits income that is not officially deemed available to the child). Under these circumstances, the loss of other benefits may not create as much disruption for the mother and her care.

136. This occurs because the relationship with the biological parent is being severed and a new relationship is being created with the adoptive parents. *See supra* note 97-99 and accompanying text.

137. LaGamma, *supra* note 94, at 5-2.

138. Almost all children born from HIV-infected mothers will test positive for HIV antibodies at birth because they will have received their mother's antibodies; however, the age of 12 to 18 months that the infant loses her mother's antibodies and it becomes possible to determine whether she is actually HIV-infected and has developed her own antibodies. Approximately 30 percent of children born of HIV-infected women will themselves actually be HIV-infected. M. Gwinn *et al., Prevalence of HIV Infection in Childbearing Women in the United States,* 265 J. A.M.A. 1704, 1705 (1991).

139. HIV-infected women often suffer from gynecological and other symptoms that are related to their HIV infection but not so recognized by their health care providers. As a result, even if a women seeks medical attention for these illnesses, it is very possible that she will not receive medical attention for the HIV infection, thereby losing an opportunity to obtain early intervention and prophylactic treatments. *See* chapter 1,Complications of Gender: Women and HIV Disease.

140. LaGamma, *supra* note 94, at 5-3. In a world of poverty, a mother's concern for her own health often follows the more immediate concerns of shelter, food,

and her children's health and well-being. Interview with Mildred Pinott, Staff Counsel at Community Legal Services, in New York, New York.

141. Epidemic of Fear, *supra* note 46.

142. Courts — and social service agencies — have rather extensive ability to investigate and monitor whether the proposed guardian is indeed the person best able to pursue the child's best interest. *See, e.g.,* Cal. Prob. Code § 1513 (West 1981); Fla. Stat. Ann. § 744.107 (West Supp. 1991); N.Y. Soc. Serv. Law §§ 384-a -b (McKinney 1983 & Supp. 1991); *see also*, Montreal Paper, *supra* note 107, at 7 (All care arrangements — whether they take effect before of after the parents's death — "are subject to reversal by social service agencies and courts interpreting the child's 'best interest'"); *see also* Adoption Assistance and Child Welfare Act of 1980, 42 U.S.C.A. § 670 *et seq.* (1984 & Supp 1991).

143. The only bar to the guardianships going into effect at the time of the parent's incapacity or death would be the showing of changed circumstances establishing that the proposed guardian could or should not assume her anticipated responsibilities. However, a confirmatory and expedited court hearing could be held to ensure that the prior approval of the guardian should result in her appointment. Such hearings are provided for in other contexts. See *infra* notes 146-48 and accompanying text for a discussion of standby guardians and preneed guardians and the attendant appointment processes.

144. Two commentators have suggested comparable proposals: "A Minor's Custodian Law," which would permit a "person to designate a temporary custodian for the minor children whenever the parent lacks the capacity to make such decisions;" and, "A Guardian upon Death Law," which would permit "a person to designate the person or persons to serve as guardians of the minor children upon the person's death, without the necessity for further legal proceedings." Zarembka & Franke, *Women in the AIDS Epidemic: A Portrait of Unmet Needs*, 9 St. Louis U. Pub. L. Rev. 519, 541 (1990).

145. Interviews with Susan Jacobs, Staff Counsel at the Legal Action Center, in New York, New York, and with Lauren Shapiro, Director of the HIV Project at Brooklyn Legal Services, Corp. B., in Brooklyn, New York, discussing potential problems with, but supporting, the concept of a springing guardianship.

146. Fla. Stat. Ann. § 744.304(1), (3) (West Supp. 1991).

147. *Id.* §§ 744.304(4), 744.312(4). Florida law also provides for a "preneed guardian." To arrange for the appointment of a preneed guardian, a competent adult would have to write a "declaration that names such guardian to serve in the event of the declarant's incapacity." *Id.* § 744.304(1). The declarant then may file the declaration with the clerk of the court; the declaration is then produced when a petition for incapacity is filed. Under this law,

> ...[p]roduction of the declaration in a proceeding for incapacity shall constitute a rebuttable presumption that the preneed guardian is entitled to serve as guardian. The court shall not be bound to appoint the preneed guardian if the preneed guardian is found to be unqualified to serve as guardian.
>
> The preneed guardian shall assume the duties of guardian immediately upon an adjudication of incapacity.

Id. § 744.3045(4), (5). As is provided with the standby guardian, the preneed guardian must petition for confirmation of appointment within twenty days of assuming her duties as guardian. In addition, so long as "the court finds the preneed guardian to be qualified...appointment of the guardian must be confirmed," *Id.* § 744.3045(7), so long as the appointment would not be "contrary to the best interests of the ward." *Id.* § 744.312(4). The principle behind providing for a preneed guardian is to create a smoother transition than might otherwise be possible in the event a previously competent adult is found incompetent. This principle is also integral to the establishment of a springing guardianship.

148. New York State has a provision concerning standby guardians, but it is more limited than the Florida law insofar as it allows for the appointment of a standby guardian only in the case of a mentally retarded or developmentally disabled person. N.Y. Surr. Ct. Proc. Act § 1757(1) (McKinney Supp. 1991). Its procedural appointment provisions, however, closely mirror those provided under Florida law. *Id.* § 1757(2):

> Such standby guardian, or alternate..., shall without further proceedings be empowered to assume the duties of his or her office immediately upon death, renunciation or adjudication of incompetency of the guardian or standby guardian appointed pursuant to this article, subject only to confirmation of his or her appointment by the court within sixty days following assumption of his or her duties of such office. Before confirming the appointment of the standby guardian or alternate guardian, the court may conduct a hearing... upon petition by anyone on behalf of the mentally retarded or developmentally disabled person if such person is eighteen years of age or older, or upon its discretion.

Id.

California law provides that although the nomination of a guardian is normally effective when made, it is possible to arrange the nomination such that it "becomes effective only upon the occurrence of such specified condition or conditions as are stated in the writing, including but not limited to such conditions as the subsequent legal incapacity or death of the person making the nomination." Cal. Prob. Code § 1502(b) (West 1981). This provision allows a parent to draw up papers to nominate a guardian with the assurances that the document will not lose its validity if the parent dies or loses capacity. The parent can create an admissible document that duly records her wishes without having to rely on a will or on a document that might lose its effectiveness upon her incapacity or death. In that sense, it is similar to a power of attorney. It does not, however, allow a court to conduct its inquiry into the background of the proposed guardian or the child's best interests at any time prior to the parent's incapacity or death, and thus is not as effective as the "springing guardianship" proposed here.

149. Some advocates note that, ideally, the local child welfare agency should be able to provide a temporary placement for the child while his or her mother is ill or incapacitated. Indeed, some statutory provisions seem to require this. *See, e.g.*, N.Y. Soc. Serv. Law § 384(a) (McKinney 1983). However, the almost uniform report of experience with such agencies makes clear that they are not capable of providing this highly specific, time-sensitive duty. Interview with Lauren Shapiro, Director of the HIV Project at Brooklyn Legal Services, Corp. B., in Brooklyn, New York.

150. Carrieri, *supra* note 118, at 4, col. 6.

151. Further information concerning the Montefiore/Legal Aid project is available from Alice Herb, Esq., Montefiore Medical Center, Division of Legal and Ethical Issues in Health Care, Department of Epidemiology and Social Medicine, 111 E. 210th St., Bronx, New York, or from Mildred Pinott, Esq., Staff Counsel, Community Law Offices, Legal Aid Society, 230 E. 106th St., New York, New York. The clinical law program at the University of Maryland has established a similar program, training second- and third-year law students to provide direct legal services for the patients in the university's hospital, located across the street from the legal clinic. Further information about this program is available from Deborah Weimer, Esq., Assistant Professor of Law, University of Maryland School of Law, Clinical Law Office, 510 W. Baltimore St., Baltimore, Maryland, 21201.

II

RIGHTS IN THE CONTEXT OF
HEALTH CARE

Health care appears poised to become one of the major domestic political issues of the next decade. Two events in 1991 signaled enormous growth in public concern over this issue. The prestigious Journal of the American Medical Association drew wide attention when it endorsed major changes in the nation's health care system and published a special issue exploring possible reforms. Later in the year, voter dissatisfaction with the status quo determined the outcome of a closely watched Senate race in Pennsylvania.

Debates about AIDS-related issues prefigured many of the questions now surfacing about all health care. The chapters comprising Part II address three critical components of this discussion: financing health care, access to care, and quality of care.

Many Americans, for example, are apprehensive about shortcomings in the private insurance system, worrying that they could be wiped out financially or face the denial of adequate care, in the event of catastrophic illness. That nightmare has been all too real for thousands of Americans with HIV disease, as Chapters 4 (on denial of care) and 5 (on insurance) describe. Indeed, HIV disease has become almost the model of ways in which the private insurance system can avoid health care costs, typically shifting the responsibility onto the already over-burdened publicly financed system (either Medicaid or Medicare). Those public systems, as Chapter 6 details, are in crisis. One result, born of desperation, has been increasing calls for rationing health care. Chapter 7 describes the dynamics of HIV disease in Puerto Rico, where Island officials face one of the highest infection rates in the United States and are forced to respond without even the inadequate level of Medicaid funding available throughout the rest of the country. Rationing is, essentially, already a reality there.

Juxtaposed against the tightening belt of the health care system is an important legal development: the increasing application of civil rights principles to the issues surrounding access to care. Several of the chapters in Part II discuss the ramifications for AIDS issues of the laws against discrimination based on disability, as well as the possible application of other legal principles to these problems. Indeed, in future years, the arguments developed on behalf of people with HIV disease may form the foundation for a broader demand for health care as a human right.

4

"THE VERY FABRIC OF HEALTH CARE": THE DUTY OF HEALTH CARE PROVIDERS TO TREAT PEOPLE INFECTED WITH HIV*

By Mark Jackson and Nan D. Hunter

I. Discrimination in Health Care

HIV disease is fundamentally a medical crisis. Persons with HIV-related conditions need high-quality comprehensive health care. Although HIV can be transmitted by certain kinds of direct contact with infected blood or blood products, health care workers are in the best position to know and apply appropriate precautions. Therefore, it is especially disappointing to find that people infected with HIV encounter discrimination even when seeking health care. A nationwide survey of HIV-related discrimination found that 5 percent of the more than 13,000 reported complaints were related to health care.[1] Numerous other studies have documented that large numbers of health care professionals assert that they would refuse to provide care for patients with HIV disease.[2] Although many health care workers have been heroic in their dedication to providing HIV care, there are, unfortunately, numerous counterexamples.

---

* Then U.S. Surgeon General C. Everett Koop stated in 1987 that refusals to treat HIV-infected patients "threaten the very fabric of health care." Boffey, *Doctors Who Shun AIDS Patients Are Assailed by Surgeon General*, N.Y. Times, Sept. 10, 1987, at A-1.

The problem of health care providers refusing to treat HIV-infected patients arises in two distinct contexts. First, some providers have refused to treat patients for their *HIV-related* illnesses. Second, certain providers have refused to treat HIV-infected patients who have consulted them in connection with a medical problem that is *unrelated* to HIV. Although both situations create serious problems for HIV-infected people, each raises different issues.

In addition to the blatant refusals to treat that can be readily identified, more subtle instances of refusal, such as providers claiming they have no expertise in treating AIDS patients or accepting patients only by referral, may occur more frequently.[3] There are certainly situations in which a doctor could justifiably refer an HIV-infected patient for specialized treatment of an HIV-related condition. Unfortunately, many doctors have abused the practice and have referred HIV-infected patients in cases where they were capable of treating the patient or could easily have learned how to treat the patient.

Moreover, refusal to treat is not the only problem. Health care workers have also provided their HIV-infected patients with negligent or substandard care, breached their duties of confidentiality, and ordered HIV tests without the patient's consent. These practices exacerbate the fact that people infected with HIV are often members of stigmatized groups who are more likely to receive substandard medical care in the first place.

A sample of the charges of discrimination filed around the country against health care providers gives a sense of the kinds of situations and the geographical diversity involved:

- A hospital in Dallas was sued for failure to provide AZT to more than an arbitrary number of patients, despite the need of other HIV-infected patients for the drug.[4]

- An alcohol and drug rehabilitation program forced an HIV-infected patient out of the program, after his test results became known.[5]

- A hospital in the District of Columbia allegedly refused to perform a medically necessary hysterectomy on a patient because she was HIV-infected and then refused to house her in the psychiatric ward where she was to receive other treatment, because of a policy against placing persons with AIDS in double-occupancy rooms.[6]

- A North Carolina hospital allegedly denied dialysis treatment to a patient with end-stage renal disease because he was HIV-infected.[7]

- A physician at a Pennsylvania hospital was sued for refusing to continue treating a patient for allergies until she had an HIV test, and then refusing to treat her because she was HIV-positive.[8]

- A California hospital allegedly dumped a patient who needed a hernia operation after performing an HIV test without consent and learning that the patient was seropositive.[9]

- Hospitals in Massachusetts and New York have been accused of forcing psychiatric patients who are HIV-infected into isolation.[10]

- An orthopedist in upstate New York and a chiropractor in California allegedly refused to see patients with HIV disease, claiming that they were not equipped to do so.[11]

- Dentists in California, Hawaii, Illinois, New York and Virginia have allegedly refused to provide dental care to patients with HIV disease, including patients of long standing.[12]

- Nursing homes have been notorious for their failure to provide services to people with HIV disease. Nearly half of the nursing home administrators surveyed by the University of Illinois (Chicago) said they would refuse to accept a person with AIDS as a patient even if assured full reimbursement for any additional costs.[13] The refusal to accept HIV patients has especially affected persons without strong family or support networks, who may be forced to remain in the hospital unnecessarily because there is no residential facility willing to admit them. Nursing homes have been sued for surreptitious HIV testing and for denying admission to persons with HIV disease.[14]

The incidence of health care discrimination is likely to be substantially greater than the number of reported cases. People seeking health care are less likely than others to pursue a discrimination claim because their immediate and overwhelming priority is to obtain medical services and maximize their physical health.[15] Some people may not recognize that they have been discriminated against because doctors can disguise their refusals to treat HIV-infected patients with medical justifications. Finally, as with other forms of HIV-related discrimination, a person may not want to be identified as HIV-positive, or potentially so, given the extensive prejudice against persons with this disease.

II. Reasons for Denial of Care

Although health care providers offer a variety of reasons for refusing to treat people infected with HIV, the reason most commonly stated is that providers fear that they might contract the disease themselves. Providers frequently point to the fact that there is a proven risk that they can be exposed to the virus through needle-sticks and other occupational exposures. As of August 1990, there had been thirty-seven reported cases in which health care personnel were believed to have contracted HIV in the workplace, mostly through accidental needle-sticks.[16]

Every study of health care workers and HIV has concluded that the risk of a health care worker contracting HIV from an occupational exposure is extremely low. These studies monitored health care workers who had sustained parenteral exposures to HIV (such as needle-sticks, cuts with sharp objects, and puncture wounds from contaminated instruments) and found that even among those workers, an exceedingly small number seroconverted as a result of such exposure. For example, one study of 963 subjects found that four seroconverted, for a seroconversion rate of 0.47 percent.[17] In another study of 1,309 subjects, only one seroconverted, excluding those with other risk factors, for an observed risk of 0.004 percent.[18] Of 292 health care workers at UCLA (102 of whom were designated to be "high--exposure," and 101 as "low-exposure"), none had seroconverted.[19] Several other studies have reached similar conclusions.[20] Moreover, a significant portion of those exposures could have been avoided if the workers had employed the precautionary measures recommended by the U.S. Centers for Disease Control (CDC).[21]

The studies that find a minuscule risk of seroconversion after an accidental needle-stick or other exposure[22] must be adjusted, however, to account for the fact that, typically, health care workers experience not one, but many such accidents in the course of a life's work. The cumulative risk will not be much altered if only a small number of those lifetime needle-sticks involve HIV-infected blood. But for the health care workers who treat significant numbers of HIV-infected patients, the risk of transmission is multiplied because of the greater likelihood of repeated exposures to HIV-infected patient blood. Even for these workers, however, the overall risk is still extremely low, especially when compared to other risks (such as hepatitis, which is transmitted much more easily than HIV and has been fatal to far more health care workers) that have not led health care workers to refuse to treat patients.[23]

The full set of reasons underlying widespread reluctance to treat persons with HIV is probably complex. Several studies have concluded that such discriminatory behavior is caused not by fear of HIV, but by underlying biases against the people who are most likely to be infected.[24] Workers' fears of contracting HIV are no doubt fueled by the tremendous publicity that has accompanied those few cases in which health care job-related exposures have occurred.[25] Other reasons may be economic, such as the fear that non — HIV-infected patients will stop seeing a physician whom they know to be treating HIV patients, or that HIV patients in a nursing home will drive away others, typically elderly persons, often from different backgrounds. Albert Jonsen identifies "at least four salient components: the perception of serious risk, the influence of prejudice, the burden of caring for AIDS patients, and the presumption of professional freedom of choice."[26]

The problem of physicians and other care providers refusing to treat patients with HIV disease is likely to grow worse if hysteria about HIV-infected doctors and dentists persists. After five dental patients in Florida were infected with HIV apparently as a result of failures in infection control practices in one dental office, public demand for forced HIV testing of physicians mushroomed. These issues are discussed in more detail in chapter 9 ("Workplace Issues: HIV and Discrimination") which includes a discussion of HIV testing of health care workers. If such testing programs are established, one probable by-product will be demands by physicians that patients be tested. Physicians who face the loss or suspension of their profession if they are suspected or discovered to be HIV-positive will be all the more likely to want to remove patients from their practices who might be the source of an HIV infection. Although the American Medical Association, among others, has soundly condemned as unethical the refusal of doctors to provide treatment to persons with HIV disease, the tension between legal requirement, ethical duty, and practice is likely to continue.

III. Legal Remedies

Legal remedies are one important mechanism to force the provision of health care services to HIV-infected people. In examining this issue, we recognize that an HIV-infected person may not want to force an unwilling provider to treat him or her for HIV or any other illness. Litigation can, however, serve many important functions. A successful claim against an individual physician would send a clear message to medical providers that they cannot refuse to treat people simply because they are HIV-infected and that they can no longer defer learning about how to treat HIV-related illnesses. Such a message might also encourage providers to educate themselves about the actual risks related to HIV and the appropriate precautions to take to avoid contracting the virus. In turn, doctors who have been educated about HIV are likely to be more willing to provide treatment to HIV-infected individuals.

Litigation can also play the critical role of increasing the availability of institutional care for HIV-infected individuals. As discussed below, certain medical facilities that formerly have denied treatment to people with HIV-related illnesses might be obligated to provide care to these people. Successful litigation against institutions may also encourage other institutions to establish facilities for the treatment of HIV-infected patients.

There are two general categories of laws that can provide a remedy against discrimination in the provision of health care: civil rights statutes and statutes that mandate a duty to treat in certain specific contexts. The former category consists of laws that prohibit discrimination based on disability in general or on AIDS or HIV disease in particular. The second category consists of laws that, usually as a condition of the receipt of some kind of funding, impose an obligation on care providers to offer treatment that they would not otherwise be compelled to offer.

A. Civil Rights Laws

1. Section 504 of the Rehabilitation Act of 1973

Section 504 of the Rehabilitation Act of 1973 prohibits discrimination against "otherwise qualified" handicapped persons by those receiving federal funds.[27] Under the Act, health care providers who receive federal financial assistance may not discriminate against the handicapped.[28] For example, they may not: deny services to the handicapped or provide lesser services; provide a less effective benefit; provide different or separate aid unless such differences are necessary to provide equal benefit; aid discrimination by providing assistance to a program that discriminates; deny handicapped people participation as planning or advisory board members; or otherwise limit the participation of the handicapped.[29] While facilities cannot be expected to guarantee that they will obtain identical results for all their patients, they must provide disabled patients with an equal *opportunity* to obtain the same results or benefits as other patients.[30]

According to the Act, a "handicapped individual" is one who has a physical or mental impairment that substantially limits a major life activity, or has a record of such an impairment, or is regarded as having such an impairment.[31] Under section 504, the term "handicap" includes HIV-infected individuals — ranging from a person who is asymptomatic to a person with full-blown AIDS — as well as those who are perceived to be HIV-positive.[32]

A person who is "handicapped" pursuant to the act cannot be discriminated against if he or she is "otherwise qualified" for a particular benefit.[33] Courts have interpreted "otherwise qualified" to refer to a person who is qualified *in spite of* a handicap.[34] Typically, this provision has been used by handicapped people who have been discriminated against in activities such as education and employment. Plaintiffs have argued that in spite of their handicaps they are qualified to attend classes or perform jobs; or if they are not qualified, that the defendants could make reasonable accommodations to allow them to be included.[35]

Consistent with this definition, the Code of Federal Regulations (CFR) defines "otherwise qualified" in the health care context to mean that the handicapped person meets the program's eligibility requirements for receipt of services.[36] In the typical case, this would mean that a person suffering from a disability (such as blindness) could not be denied treatment by a hospital for an illness (such as cancer) because he is blind, because in spite of his blindness he "otherwise qualifies" for the program.

The Rehabilitation Act applies to cases in which a provider who receives federal funds fails to provide treatment to an HIV-infected individual. First, a provider who refuses to treat an HIV-infected person for a condition *unrelated* to HIV is clearly discriminating against an "otherwise qualified" patient because of a handicap. An HIV-infected individual is "otherwise qualified," for example, to undergo root canal work in spite of his or her HIV infection. The need to treat a dental condition is unaffected by HIV disease. Second, if a person with HIV disease seeks treatment for an opportunistic disease *related* to HIV, such as *Pneumocystis carinii* pneumonia, and the hospital typically treats patients with pneumonia, that hospital would similarly be discriminating against an otherwise qualified patient because he or she has HIV if it refuses to provide treatment.

2. Americans with Disabilites Act

The Americans with Disabilities Act (ADA) provides HIV-infected people with an even broader remedy in the event they are unfairly denied treatment by health care providers. Section 302 of Title III provides that

No individual shall be discriminated against on the basis of disability in the full and equal enjoyment of the goods, services, facilities, privileges, advantages, or accommodations of any place of public accommodations by any person who owns, leases (or leases to), or operates a place of public accommodation.[37]

The Act specifically includes in its definition of public accommodations, the "professional office of a health care provider, hospital, or other service establishment."[38] Thus, this law prohibits discrimination by *any* health care provider, not just those who receive federal funds and are already covered by section 504.

When the ADA takes effect, it will constitute the single most comprehensive protection in the law against discrimination in health care services. Persons alleging discrimination will be able to file lawsuits in federal courts to obtain a court order (injunction) directing the defendant to stop discriminatory conduct and to provide services. Attorneys' fees are also available under the act, although monetary damages are not. Individuals may also file complaints with the Department of Justice, which is authorized by the ADA to conduct investigations and to bring lawsuits when there is a pattern of repeated discrimination.

The public-accommodations provision of the ADA will take effect in stages; in general, suits could be filed against public accommodations that discriminate as of January 26, 1992. For providers with twenty-five or fewer employees and gross receipts of $1 million or less, suits may be filed beginning July 26, 1992; and for providers with ten or fewer employees and gross receipts of $500,000 or less, suits may be filed beginning January 26, 1993.

3. State Antidiscrimination Laws

In addition to the two federal statutes just described, almost all states have some law that prohibits discrimination based on disability. These laws vary enormously, however, in scope and coverage. In some states, it is not clear that HIV-related illnesses, especially asymptomatic HIV disease, fall within that state's definition of handicap or disability.[39] Additionally, only one state (California) has a statute that clearly defines "public accommodation" to include the offices of health care providers. Other states' laws typically list several examples of the kinds of entities that are public accommodations and then provide that other "similar services" are also covered. As a result, in many of the HIV discrimination cases filed against doctors or dentists under state laws, most of the litigation has concerned the threshold question of whether a physician's office falls within the scope of the statute.[40] When the ADA has fully taken effect, plaintiffs are likely to rely on the clarity of that federal law, rather than continue to use the state disability laws.

Because of the weaknesses in state laws against disability discrimination, and because of the crisis in refusals to treat directed against HIV patients, four states have enacted laws that are geared to curtailing such abuses without having to redefine "public accommodations" in the more general statute.

Wisconsin has adopted the strongest measure to combat HIV-related discrimination in the health care industry. That state has passed legislation that expressly prohibits health care providers from refusing to treat people infected with HIV or from providing them with substandard care, isolating them, or abusing them in any way.[41] The statute provides for actual and punitive damages for an intentional violation of the statute and authorizes licensing boards to enforce the prohibitions.

Iowa has enacted a statute that provides that a person cannot be denied admission to a health care facility based upon that patient's particular disease or condition.[42] It further provides that the decision to accept or deny admission of a patient with a specific disease shall be based solely on the ability of the health care facility to provide the level of care required for that patient.

Maryland law prohibits people engaged in various professions, including health care providers, from refusing, withholding, denying, or discriminating against an individual with respect to providing services for which the licensee is licensed and qualified to render because the individual is HIV-positive.[43]

Ohio law prohibits a health care provider from requesting proof of a person's HIV status for the purpose of refusing to treat that individual if he or she is HIV-positive.[44] The law provides, however, that a provider is not refusing to treat an individual under the law, if he or she refers an HIV-infected person to another facility or provider based on "reasonable professional judgment."[45]

4. Issues in Future Litigation

Although the ADA now furnishes a dramatic and comprehensive new legal mechanism for challenging instances of refusal to treat and other discrimination against HIV patients, it — like any other law — raises questions even as it provides answers. Cases involving discrimination in the provision of health care services are likely to be contested by defendants on two primary grounds.

One likely ground for a refusal to treat is that the HIV virus is contagious and thus the danger associated with an HIV-infected patient renders that person not eligible or otherwise qualified for treatment.[46] Under either the ADA or section 504, in order to justify a decision not to treat a patient on that ground, a provider would have to demonstrate that there was a significant risk that the virus would be transmitted to others (either providers or other patients) even if the provider made reasonable accommodations to prevent such transmission.[47]

Under a significant risk standard, there is no justification for such a refusal to treat. With the use of the universal precautions outlined by the CDC, the risk that the patient will transmit the virus to the provider or to other patients does not rise to the level of significant. Moreover, because health care institutions are in the business of treating people with diseases, infectious and otherwise, such institutions should be able and expected to safely handle a greater degree of risk than other entities, such as a school or an employer. To allow a hospital or particular physicians to refuse treatment to HIV patients, when the probability of a patient-to-doctor infection is lower than for other infections that can cause death, would completely eviscerate the anti-discrimination principles behind the law.

The second likely ground for a defense is a claim that the particular doctor or other care provider is not qualified or equipped to treat persons with HIV disease. This kind of evasion of the duty to treat is more subtle, and is often accompanied by a referral to another provider, often a doctor who, through a willingness to care for HIV patients, has acquired the reputation of being "an AIDS doctor." Such abuse of patient referrals is one of the most insidious forms of HIV-related discrimination.

One issue that the courts interpreting the ADA will have to face in cases involving a physician who insists on referring out a patient with HIV disease is whether the patient's condition requires treatment that the doctor reasonably believes is outside her own experience and expertise or whether the referral is simply a ruse to avoid treating patients to whom the doctor feels an aversion or who, the doctor fears, might give her a reputation as "an AIDS doctor." Physicians should be held to a standard of treating HIV disease to the same extent that they would treat any other comparable disease (cancer, for example, or, to use the example of a disease that can be contagious, tuberculosis).[48] Thus if a general practitioner had always referred patients to a surgeon for any kind of surgery, referral of an HIV patient for surgery would be reasonable. If only HIV patients were referred, however, by a physician who otherwise routinely performed the kind of surgery needed, those referrals should be found to be violative of the antidiscrimination law.

B. Duty to Treat Provisions

1. The Legal Duty to Treat

The law does not impose on physicians a general duty to treat. This rule is based on the principle that there is no affirmative duty on the part of any person to provide assistance to another.[49] There are exceptions to the rule, however. A physician can refuse to treat a patient for any reason or for no reason, but not for a prohibited reason. Most of the prohibited reasons are the categories established by civil rights laws: usually race, sex, and religion, as well as disability. Under the civil rights approach, enumerated classes of people are protected from discrimination based on a particular characteristic.

There are a variety of other provisions of law that, taken together, substantially alleviate the general no-duty principle. Most of these other exceptions (discussed below) are legislatively created and embodied in statutes. Two, however, derive primarily from the case law (i.e., judge-made law) of torts or personal injury cases. They are that a hospital emergency room has a duty to treat a patient with an unmistakable emergency,[50] and that all providers have a duty to continue to care for a patient once they have agreed to treat him or her.

The emergency room exception is limited. Although a hospital has a duty to provide emergency care, that duty applies only to emergency room settings.[51] It is unlikely that the emergency room exception will apply in most HIV-related cases. Although a person with HIV can potentially have a medical complication that requires emergency attention, most HIV-related treatments occur on a nonemergency basis.

A doctor also has a duty to provide "continued care." If a provider-patient relationship has been established, the provider cannot simply terminate or abandon that relationship.[52] Once established, the relationship generally may be terminated in only four situations: where both parties consent to termination; where the patient decides to terminate the treatment; where services are no longer needed; or where the physician gives reasonable notice to the patient.[53] The purpose of the notice requirement is to give the patient an opportunity to secure an alternative source of care.[54]

It is unclear how helpful this exception to the "no-duty" rule will be to a person with an HIV-related illness. If a doctor or institution has begun to provide HIV-related treatment, the patient can probably compel that provider to continue treatment. If a quick referral is made, however, a provider can probably avoid an obligation for further treatment. Because physicians cannot terminate their relationships with patients without ensuring that the patients are able to obtain alternative care, the duty to provide continued care may at least protect a patient from being left without any care giver.

2. The Hill-Burton Act

The Hill-Burton Act[55] was enacted by Congress in 1946 to provide funding for the construction and modernization of public and non-profit medical facilities. In addition to encouraging construction, Congress sought to expand the availability of those facilities to people who had limited access to health care. Accordingly, Congress built into the Act a requirement that facilities that received funding had to provide a "reasonable volume" of care to people who could not afford to pay for medical services ("uncompensated care") and had to provide care without discrimination to persons residing in the facilities' "service area" who could otherwise pay for the services ("community service assurance").[56]

The community service obligation constitutes a sweeping and unequivocal command that Hill-Burton facilities provide care to any resident of the area who can pay for such care.[57] Unlike the uncompensated care requirement, which lapses after twenty years from the completion of the construction or until the amount of the grant or loan is repaid, the community service obligation is permanent.[58]

The language of this regulation, on its face, prohibits affected facilities from refusing to treat a person on the basis of his or her illness, provided the facility generally provides that type of care.[59] The regulation would allow a Hill-Burton facility to deny services on only four grounds: (1) if they are not medically necessary; (2) if they are not available at the particular institution;[60] (3) if the patient cannot pay for nonemergency care and the facility is not required to provide uncompensated care; and (4) if the person does not reside in the facility's service area. Accordingly, unless one of the above conditions is present, a person with HIV who has been denied treatment by a Hill-Burton hospital should be able to compel that institution to provide treatment.[61]

Despite the fact that the community service obligation would appear to be a powerful tool for a person who has been denied treatment, there has been very little litigation under this section of the statute. In fact, there is not a single reported case in which a party has successfully sued a Hill-Burton facility, under the community service obligation, on the basis that it wrongfully refused to treat that party.[62] This should not be particularly surprising. It would be unusual for a health care facility to refuse to treat a person for an illness the facility is equipped to treat when the person is able to pay for such care. HIV may constitute the first illness for which health care facilities have denied treatment on the basis of the illness itself.

3. Medicaid and Medicare

The Medicaid and Medicare programs[63] also contain provisions that can be used to prohibit participating facilities from discriminating against people infected with HIV.[64]

Hospitals and nursing homes participating in the Medicaid and Medicare programs cannot discriminate in admitting or accepting patients, treating patients, providing accommodations or services, accessing equipment and facilities, or in assigning personnel. Medicaid programs cannot discriminate by illness or disorder; they *can* discriminate, however, on the basis of medical necessity.[65] Medical assistance must be made available to a medically needy person "equal in amount, duration, and scope" to that made available to all other medically needy persons in his or her particular category.[66]

Further, a Medicare participating hospital with an emergency department must provide an appropriate medical screening examination to any individual requesting treatment, even if that individual is not a Medicare beneficiary. If an examination reveals a medical emergency or active labor, the hospital must treat that person or make an appropriate transfer. A patient whose condition is not stabilized may not be transferred unless the patient requests the transfer or the benefits of the transfer outweigh the risks and the transfer is appropriate. An appropriate transfer is one in which the receiving facility has space and has agreed to accept the patient. An individual who was illegally dumped by a facility may bring a civil action for personal injury damages and/or equitable relief. The antidumping statute has rarely been used, however, either for purposes of agency enforcement or in private actions.[67]

4. State Licensing Laws

State licensing of health care providers and facilities can also be a potential tool in increasing HIV-infected people's access to health care. Every state has enacted licensing statutes and regulations that both set forth the qualifications for a license holder and establish a standard of conduct by which licensed practitioners must abide. Each state's licensing statute provides for a licensing board to ensure that licensees comply with the standards contained in the statutes or regulations. Licensing boards are empowered to issue regulations defining what constitutes "unprofessional" or "immoral" conduct and are further empowered to suspend or revoke the licenses of those licensees who violate those standards.

For example, New York State Education Law section 6509, which governs health care professionals, includes in its definition of professional misconduct "committing unprofessional conduct, as defined by the board of regents in its rules or by the commissioner in regulations approved by the board of regents."[68] The New York Board of Regents has, in turn, promulgated regulations which prohibit, among other things, "abandoning or neglecting a patient or client under and in need of immediate professional care, without making reasonable arrangements for the continuation of such care."[69]

Several states, concerned about the overall quality of health care, have strengthened their physician licensure and quality assurance regulations. Florida, for instance, has established a Division of Medical Quality Assurance within the Department of Professional Regulation, which is empowered to use whatever resources and make whatever efforts are necessary to investigate and discipline physicians guilty of unprofessional conduct "in order to take forceful corrective measures to assure quality medical care throughout the state." The state has created eleven professional boards to conduct investigations of reported breaches of the state's standards.[70]

A health care provider who refuses to treat a person infected with HIV could be subject to disciplinary action by his or her state's licensing board for engaging in unprofessional conduct. A complaint against such a person would be much more plausible if the state's medical association had adopted a policy stating that a health care provider has an obligation to treat persons with HIV disease. A provider who refuses to provide treatment based on a claim that he or she is not qualified to treat HIV could also be subject to disciplinary action on the basis that such lack of knowledge is not commensurate with the standard that prevails in his or her specialty.[71]

Surprisingly, only a few state medical boards have specifically addressed the issue of HIV in their regulations. New Jersey's medical licensing board has issued the following directive:

> A licensee of this Board may not categorically refuse to treat a patient who has AIDS or AIDS-related complex, or an HIV-positive blood test, when he or she possesses the skill and experience to treat the condition presented.[72]

The regulation further provides that if the physician is unable to render care, "the licensee retains the responsibility to make alternative arrangements for the proper care of a patient." Under the New Jersey regulation, a provider who refuses to treat an HIV-infected person, or does not make a proper referral in those cases in which the provider is not qualified, would be subject to disciplinary proceedings, including possible suspension or revocation of his or her license. As discussed above, Maryland expressly prohibits licensed health care professionals from refusing to treat HIV-infected individuals if such treatment is within the scope of that person's license, and the person is qualified to render treatment.[73]

In order to ensure that health care providers in a given state are providing people infected with HIV the same level of care that other patients receive, states should affirmatively require licensees to provide treatment to HIV-infected people when they are qualified to do so.

Conclusion

As the number of HIV-infected persons increases, there will be a concomitant growing need for doctors and other health care workers to treat them. It is critical, therefore, that health care providers do not wrongfully refuse to treat these patients or provide them with inferior care. One step toward ensuring adequate and equal care is to better educate health care workers and institutions about how to treat this disease, the true risks of patient-doctor contact, and the methods of preventing transmission.

We also recommend an intensive and targeted effort to educate practitioners, hospital staffs and students in medical, dental, and nursing schools about their ethical and legal duties to provide care. To succeed, such programs must encourage workers to acknowledge and confront their attitudes toward injection drug users, gay men, people of color, and others likely to need HIV care. Even if such attitudes persist, however, knowledge that significant legal penalties will result can deter discriminatory behavior.[74] Cumulatively, the legal remedies discussed in this chapter establish a duty of care to all patients regardless of illness.

NOTES

1. American Civil Liberties Union, AIDS Project, Epidemic of Fear 31 (1990) [hereinafter Epidemic of Fear].
2. *Id.* at 78-80. Epidemic of Fear described several other studies, including (1) a survey of more than 500 dentists in which 63 percent of the respondents did not want to treat persons considered to be at risk for AIDS; (2) a survey of nursing home administrators in which 47 percent said they would refuse to accept a person with AIDS as a patient; (3) a Virginia study of paramedics in which 40 percent of the respondents said they were unwilling to administer treatment to HIV-infected persons; (4) another study that reported that more than 90 percent of 1,000 surgeons surveyed endorsed a policy of refusing to operate on HIV-infected persons; (5) a recent study in which 20 percent of the hospitals surveyed reported at least one instance of a staff member refusing to care for an HIV-infected patient, and in which at least 25 percent of the

hospitals had a policy of immediately transferring any such patient. The 1988 report of the San Francisco AIDS Legal Referral Panel found that health care discrimination cases represented 4.9 percent of all referrals. These complaints involved breach of confidentiality, erroneous test results, inappropriate ordering of HIV tests, testing without a patient's consent, refusal to treat, and abandonment. L. Gostin, U.S. Public Health Service, AIDS Litigation Project, (National AIDS Program Office 1990).

3. *See* Note, *AIDS Discrimination by Medical Care Providers: Is Washington Law an Adequate Remedy?*, 63 Wash. L. Rev. 701, 708 (1988) [hereinafter *AIDS Discrimination*].

4. Dallas Gay Alliance, Inc. v. Dallas County Hosp. Dist., 719 F. Supp. 1380 (N.D. Tex. 1989).

5. Doe v. Centinela Hosp., 57 U.S.L.W. 2034 (C.D. Cal. 1988).

6. Doe v. Howard Univ., No. 88-3412[SS], AIDS Litig. Rep. (Andrews Pub.) 2111 (D.D.C. Mar. 24, 1989).

7. Complaint, Roe v. Cumberland County Hosp. Sys., Inc., No. 88-62-CIV-3 (E.D.N.C. June 10, 1988).

8. Doe v. Lankenau Hosp., No. 88-8007, AIDS Litig. Rep. (Andrews Pub.) 1803 (E.D. Pa. Nov. 29, 1988).

9. Doe v. Shasta Gen. Hosp., No. 92336 (Cal. Shasta City Super. Ct. 1987) (case on file with American Civil Liberties Union).

10. Rhodes v. Charter Hosp., 730 F. Supp. 1383 (S.D. Mass 1989); Complaint, Doe v. Saint Francis Hosp., No. 3-P-D-87-123301 1987 (N.Y. State Div. Human Rights 1987).

11. Elstein v. State Div. of Human Rights, 555 N.Y.S.2d 516 (1990), *appeal denied*, 564 N.E.2d 671 (N.Y. 1990); Walsh v. Cimanec, No. 608500, AIDS Litig. Rep. (Andrews Pub.) 2957 (Cal. San Diego County Super. Ct. July 14, 1989).

12. Bearden v. Sutter Place Dental Clinic, No. 899907, AIDS Litig. Rep. (Andrews Pub.) 2274 (Cal. San Francisco County Super Ct. Feb. 24, 1989); Doe v. Kahala Dental Group, 808 P.2d 1276 (Haw. 1991); Robertson v. Chen, No. 1989SP0061, AIDS Litig. Rep. (Andrews Pub.) 3042 (Ill. Dept. Human Relations July 28, 1989); G.S. v. Baksh, No. 1987 CPO 113 (Ill. Human Rights Comm'n Sept. 26, 1988); Sattler v. New York City Comm'n on Human Rights, 354 N.Y.S.2d 763 (Sup. Ct. 1990); Hurwitz v. New York City Comm'n on Human Rights, 535 N.Y.S.2d 1007 (Sup. Ct. 1988), *aff'd* 553 N.Y.S.2d 323 (App. Div. 1990); Complaint, B. v. A Dentist (New York City Comm'n on Human Rights 1989); Complaint, Whittacre & Whitemore v. Northern Dispensary, Nos. AU-00015021387, GA-00023030687-DN 1988 (N.Y. City Comm'n on Human Rights 1988); Patient v. Ellenborgen, No. 89-848, AIDS Litig. Rep. (Andrews Pub.) 3369 (Va. Arlington County Cir. Ct. Sept. 22, 1989).

13. Seigel, *Nursing Homes Shun AIDS Patients*, Chicago Sun-Times, July 19, 1989, at C-2.

14. Doe v. American Nursing Home, No. 89-45979, AIDS Litig. Rep. (Andrews Pub.) 3637 (N.Y. Sup. Ct. 1989); Complaint, Frazier v. Marcus Garvey Nursing Home, No. 9K-P-D-88-132002 1988 (N.Y. State Div. Human Rights 1988); Complaint, McEnany v. Four Seasons Nursing Centers, Inc., No. 409241 (Tex. Dist. Ct. Dec. 2, 1986).

15. *AIDS Discrimination*, *supra* note 3, at 720.

16. M. Barnes, N. Rango, G. Burke & L. Chiarello, *The HIV-Infected Health Care Professional: Employment Policies and Public Health*, 18 Law Med. & Health Care 311, 312 (1990).

17. R. Marcus, *Surveillance of Health Care Workers Exposed to Blood from Patients Infected with the Human Immunodeficiency Virus*, 319 N. Eng. J. Med. 1118 (1988) [hereinafter Marcus].

18. R. Klein, *Low Occupational Risk of Human Immunodeficiency Virus Infection Among Dental Professionals*, 318 N. Eng. J. Med. 86 (1988).

19. T. Kuhl, *Occupational Risk of HIV, HBV and HSV-2 Infections in Health Care Personnel Caring for AIDS Patients*, 77 Am. J. Pub. Health 1306 (1987).

20. *See Health Recommendations for Prevention of HIV Transmission in Health Care Settings*, 36 Morbidity & Mortality Wkly. Rep. 53 (1987).

21. Marcus, *supra* note 17, at 1119 (of the 1,201 exposures, 37 percent might have been prevented by using recommended infection-control procedures); D. Cotton, *The Impact of AIDS on the Medical Care System*, 260 J. A.M.A. 519, 520 1988 [hereinafter Cotton].

22. The most reliable estimate of the risk of HIV infection after a single needle-stick (or comparable) exposure to HIV- contaminated blood is 0.4 percent. Bell, *HIV Infection in Health Care Workers: Occupational Risk and Prevention*, in AIDS and the Health Care System 115, 119-20 (L. Gostin ed. 1990).

23. *AIDS Discrimination*, *supra* note 3, at 704.

24. Kelly, St. Lawrence, Smith, Hood & Cook, *Medical Students' Attitudes Toward AIDS and Homosexual Patients*, 62 J. Med. Educ. 549 (1987); Pleck, O'Donnell & Snarey, *AIDS-Phobia, Contact with AIDS and AIDS-Related Job Stress in Hospital Workers*, 15 J. Homosexuality 41 (1988); *see also*, Simross, *The Unwanted Challenge*, L.A. Times, July 27, 1988, at 1.

25. Cotton, *supra* note 21, at 520-21.

26. A. Jonsen, *The Duty to Treat Patients with AIDS and HIV Infection*, in AIDS and the Health Care System 155, 157 (L. Gostin ed., 1990).

27. Section 504 of the Rehabilitation Act of 1973, as amended, provides in relevant part:

> No otherwise qualified individual with handicaps in the United States...shall, solely by reason of her or his handicap, be excluded from the participation in, be denied the benefits of, or be subjected to discrimination under any program or activity receiving Federal financial assistance.

29. U.S.C. § 794(a) (1988).

28. A "provider" may be an institution, such as a hospital, or an individual physician.The Civil Rights Restoration Act of 1987 amended section 504 so that it applies specifically to "an entire corporation, partnership, or other proprietorship...which is principally engaged in the business of providing... health care...." 42 U.S.C. § 6107(4)(C) (1988). Therefore, section 504 prohibits health care organizations from discriminating if any component receives federal funding, not just the particular program receiving federal funds. "Federal financial assistance" includes any grant, loan, contract (other than procurement, insurance, or guaranty), or any other arrangement by which a federal agency provides or otherwise makes available assistance such as funds, property, or personnel services. 45 C.F.R. § 84.3(h) (1990).

Several cases discuss what constitutes federal financial assistance. Gen-erally, receipt of Medicaid or Medicare funds by an institution does constitute federal financial assistance for purposes of section 504. United States v. Baylor Univ. Medical Center, 736 F.2d 1039, 1048-49 (5th Cir. 1984), *cert. denied*, 469 U.S. 1189 (1984); *see also* United States v. University Hosp. of the State of New

York at Stony Brook, 575 F. Supp. 607, 612-13 (E.D.N.Y. 1983) (hospital's receipt of Medicare and Medicaid funds constitutes federal financial assistance despite defendant's argument that they are procurement or insurance contracts); Bernard v. Blue Cross, 528 F. Supp. 125, 132 (S.D.N.Y. 1981) (court implies in dicta that since Blue Cross is a conduit for Medicare funds and receives payment for administrative expenses, it could be deemed to receive federal financial assistance).

29. 45 C.F.R. §§ 84.4(b)(1), 84.52(a) (1990).

30. *Id.* § 84.4(b)(2).

31. 29 U.S.C. § 706(7)(B) (1988)

32. *See, e.g.*, School Bd. of Nassau County v. Arline, 480 U.S. 273 (1987) ("handicap" includes contagious diseases); United Stated Dept. of Justice, Memorandum on Application of Rehabilitation Act's § 504 to HIV-Infected Persons (Dec. 27, 1988).

33. *Arline*, 480 U.S. at 286.

34. Doe v. New York Univ., 666 F.2d 761, 775 (2d Cir. 1981). The court in *Doe* wrote:

> ...it is now clear that [the phrase "otherwise qualified handicapped individual"] refers to a person who is qualified *in spite of* her handicap and that an institution is not required to disregard disabilities of a handicapped applicant, provided the handicap is relevant to reasonable qualifications for acceptance, or to make substantial modifications in its reasonable standards or program to accommodate handicapped individuals but may take an applicant's handicap into consideration, along with all other relevant factors in determining whether she is qualified for admission.

Id.; accord Southeastern Community College v. Davis, 442 U.S. 397, 406 (1979).

35. In connection with HIV, courts have ruled that employers cannot fire infected employees when they are "otherwise qualified" to perform their responsibilities in spite of their illness. Chalk v. United States Dist. Court, 840 F.2d 701, 705 (9th Cir. 1988). Similarly, courts have universally held that otherwise qualified children cannot be denied access to school because of their HIV infection. *See* Thomas v. Atascadero Unified Sch. Dist., 662 F. Supp. 376 (C.D. Cal. 1987); Ray v. School Dist. of DeSoto County, 666 F. Supp. 1524 (M.D. Fla. 1987).

36. 45 C.F.R. § 84.3(k)(4) (1990).

37. 42 U.S.C.A. § 12182 (Supp. 1991).

38. 42 U.S.C.A. § 12181(7)(F) (Supp. 1991). In fact, the Act sets forth the following in its "Findings and Purposes" section:

> discrimination against individuals with disabilities persists in such critical areas as employment, housing, public accommodations, education, transportation, communication, recreation, institutionalization, *health services*, voting, and access to public services[.]

Id. § 12101(a)(3) (emphasis added).

39. For a description of each state's law, see Epidemic of Fear, *supra* note 1, Appendix A at 83.

40. *See, e.g., Kahala Dental Group*, 808 P.2d 1276; *Elstein*, 555 N.Y.S.2d 516; Campanella v. Hurwitz, No. GA-00021030487-DN (N.Y. Comm'n Human Rights Dec. 9, 1988).

41.   Wisconsin Act 201 provides as follows:

> No health care provider, home health agency or inpatient health care
> facility may do any of the following with respect to an individual
> who has acquired immunodeficiency syndrome or has a positive test
> for the presence of HIV, antigen or nonantigenic products of HIV or
> an antibody to HIV, solely because the individual has HIV infection
> or an illness or medical condition that is caused by, arises from or is
> related to HIV infection:
> (a) Refuse to treat the individual, if his or her condition is within the
> scope of licensure or certification of the health care provider, home
> health agency or inpatient health care facility.
> (b) Provide care to the individual at a standard that is lower than that
> provided other individuals with like medical needs.
> (c) Isolate the individual unless medically necessary.
> (d) Subject the individual to indignity, including humiliating, de-
> grading or abusive treatment.

Wis. Stat. Ann. § 146.024 (West Supp. 1991).

42.   Iowa Code Ann. § 135C.23 (West Supp. 1991).
43.   Md. S.B. 719 ch. 789 (1989) (codified in various section of Md. Health Occ.
      Code (Supp. 1991)).
44.   Ohio S.B. 2 (1989).
45.   *Id*.
46.   The section of the ADA that covers public accommodations, Title III, does not
      have an "otherwise qualified" requirement. Instead, it provides that "eligibil-
      ity criteria that screen out or tend to screen out" persons with a disability are
      prohibited unless they "can be shown to be necessary" for the provision of
      the goods or services in question. ADA § 302(2).
47.   *Arline*, 480 U.S. at 287 n.16, 288-89. In *Arline*, a teacher with tuberculosis
      brought an action under the Rehabilitation Act claiming that the school in
      which she was employed improperly dismissed her based on her handicap.
      The U.S. Supreme Court ruled that the teacher's contagious condition consti-
      tuted a handicap and that in order to dismiss her, the school needed to find
      that there was a "significant risk" that she would transmit the virus to her
      students. The Court held that in cases involving contagious diseases, courts
      must base their determinations as to whether a person is "otherwise qualified"
      on reasonable medical judgments about the nature of the risk, the duration of
      the risk, the severity of the risk, and the probability that the disease will be
      transmitted and cause harm. *Id*. at 289.

> The *Arline* court wrote:

> The fact that *some* persons who have contagious diseases may pose
> a serious health threat to others under certain circumstances does
> not justify excluding from the coverage of the Act *all* person with
> actual or perceived contagious diseases. Such exclusion would mean
> that those accused of being contagious would never have the oppor-
> tunity to have their condition evaluated in light of medical evidence
> and a determination made as to whether they were "otherwise
> qualified." Rather, they would be vulnerable to discrimination on

the basis of mythology — precisely the type of injury Congress sought to prevent.

Id. at 286.

48. 45 C.F.R. § 84 at para. 36 (1990).

49. Restatement (Second) of Torts, § 314 (1965); *see also* Agnew v. Parks, 343 P.2d 118 (Cal. Dist. Ct. App. 1959); Childs v. Weis, 440 S.W.2d 104 (Tex. Civ. App. 1969) (duty to treat dependent on physician-patient relationship; if no such relationship is developed, there can be no liability for failing to treat).

50. If a hospital has an emergency room with a custom of accepting those who present themselves with a medical emergency, that hospital has a duty to treat any person who appears with a bona fide emergency. Wilmington Gen. Hosp. v. Manlove, 174 A.2d 135 (Del. 1961) (although a private hospital has no duty to provide care, by maintaining an emergency room the hospital 'undertook' to provide emergency medical care and was therefore liable for not providing that care in an unmistakable emergency); Stanturf v. Sipes, 447 S.W.2d 558 (Mo. 1969) (hospital potentially liable for failure to provide emergency rooms treatment to a man with frostbite who could not pay a twenty-five dollar deposit, even though a third party was willing to pay the deposit, because the plaintiff had reasonably relied on the hospital's practice of accepting anyone who could pay the deposit); *see also* Mercy Medical Center, Inc. v. Winnebago County, 206 N.W.2d 198 (Wis. 1973) (court stated in dicta that private hospitals with emergency rooms and facilities have a duty to treat); Richard v. Adair Hosp. Found. Corp., 566 S.W.2d 791 (Ky. App. 1978) (a hospital may be held liable for failure to admit a patient with an unmistakable emergency).

Several jurisdictions have either not adopted *Manlove* or have applied it narrowly. For example, in Guerrerro v. Copper Queen Hosp., 537 P.2d 1329 (Ariz. 1975), a hospital refused to provide emergency treatment for two children with severe burns. The court held that a private hospital has no duty to accept a patient or to serve everyone unless a different policy has been established by statute. The court found that Arizona had a policy requiring hospitals to provide emergency room care and that statutory duty to treat was violated when the emergency room turned the patients away without treatment. Other courts have defined "unmistakable emergency" narrowly, thereby limiting the duty to treat. *See, e.g.*, Hill v. Ohio County, 468 S.W.2d 306 (Ky. 1971); Campbell v. Mincey, 413 F. Supp. 16 (N.D. Miss. 1975) (both courts finding it permissible for hospitals to turn away women in labor if they were not referred by a local physician).

The federal tax laws also contain provisions which impose obligations on certain health care facilities with emergency rooms. In order to qualify for section 501 (c) (3) federal tax exempt status as a charitable institution, a hospital must operate an emergency room open to all and provide care to all members of the community able to pay. Rev. Rul. 83-157, 1983-42 I.R.B. 9. However, tax exemption is of limited usefulness in fighting HIV-related discrimination since most persons subject to discrimination will not have standing to challenge the tax exempt status of a hospital. *See* Eastern Ky. Welfare Rights Org. v. Simon, 426 U.S. 26 (1976).

51. Because of this limitation, a person with a medical emergency who appears at a hospital that does have an emergency room may not have a legal right to receive treatment. Conversely, if a person needs treatment but not for an emergency, the hospital has no duty to provide services.

This duty also varies from jurisdiction to jurisdiction. For example, in Massachusetts, license regulations require all *physicians* to give emergency care in any medical emergency. Mass. Bd. of Registration in Med., Mass. Regs. Code tit. 243, § 2.06 (1990).

52. Determining when a provider-patient relationship has been established is a difficult process. Emergency room treatment in and of itself, for example, does not establish a provider-patient relationship. *See* Birmingham Baptist Hosp. v. Crews, 159 So. 224 (1934) (private hospital emergency room physician diagnosed and treated a 2-year-old child for diphtheria but denied the child admission to the hospital because of a policy prohibiting admission of patients with contagious diseases. The court held the hospital had no continuing duty to treat the child since the hospital had not accepted the child as a patient); Le Jeune Road Hosp. v. Watson, 171 So. 2d 202 (Fla. Dist. Ct. App. 1965) (private hospital had a duty to treat an 11-year-old appendectomy patient since he was dressed in a hospital gown, examined, and given medication); *see also* Joyner v. Alton Ochsner Medical Found., 230 So.2d 913 (La. App. 1970); Harper v. Baptist Medical Center, 341 So. 133 (Ala. 1976).

   A provider-patient relationship is generally considered to be established when a physician agrees to *treat* a patient. An examination prior to an agreement to treat may not establish a physician-patient relationship. However, at least one court has held that such a relationship may be created when a physician accepts an appointment with a patient for a specific condition. Lyons v. Grether, 239 S.E.2d 103 (Va. 1977) (patient scheduled an appointment specifically for treatment of a vaginal infection; the physician refused to treat her when she arrived with a seeing-eye dog).

53. 61 Am. Jur. 2d §§ 234-35.

54. *See, e.g.,* Capps v. Valk, 369 P.2d 238 (Kan. 1962) (failure to follow up after surgery constituted abandonment since doctor did not provide patient with necessary notice to enable him to obtain alternative care).

55. The Hospital Survey and Construction Act, 60 Stat. 1040, Pub. L. No. 79-725 (1946).

56. In 1975, Congress enacted a new federal program (Title XVI), replacing Hill-Burton for hospital construction and modernization. Title XVI of the Public Health Services Act requires recipients of federal funds to provide essentially the same assurances as those set forth under Hill-Burton. *See* American Hosp. Ass'n v. Schweiker, 721 F.2d 170 (7th Cir. 1983). Unfortunately, however, Congress has not authorized any new funding under this section of Title XVI. K. Wing, *The Community Service Obligation of Hill-Burton Health Facilities*, 23 Boston Coll. L. Rev. 577, 588 [hereinafter Wing].

57. The current regulations setting forth the community service obligation provides, in part:

> In order to comply with its community service assurance, a facility shall make the services provided in the facility or portion thereof constructed, modernized, or converted with Federal assistance under Title VI or XVI of the Act available to all persons residing (and, in the case of facilities assisted under Title XVI of the Act, employed) in the facility's service area without discrimination on the ground of race, color, national origin, creed, *or any other ground unrelated to an*

*individual's need for the service or the availability of the needed service in
the facility.*

42 C.F.R. § 124.603 (1990) (emphasis added); *see also* Wyoming Hosp. Ass'n v.
Harris, 727 F.2d 936 (10th Cir. 1984) (upholding both the uncompensated care
and community service obligations under the Hill-Burton Act and noting that
the language of the community service obligation was "unambiguous").

58. 42 C.F.R. § 124.501 (b)(1) (1990). Obligations under the new Title XVI, however, are not limited to any period of time. 42 U.S.C. § 300s-1(b)(1)(K) (1988);
42 C.F.R. 124.501(b)(2) (1990); *see also* Lugo v. Simon, 426 F. Supp. 28 (N.D.
Ohio 1976) (upholding reasonableness of twenty-year limitation on uncompensated care obligation, but rejecting such a limitation on community service
obligation).

59. The regulations provide examples of actions that would be prohibited under
the act. For example, the regulations prohibit facilities from refusing to
participate in the Medicare and Medicaid programs, from discriminating
against individual recipients, and from following certain admissions policies,
such as accepting only patients with private physicians who have staff privileges at the hospital. 42 C.F.R. § 124.603(c)-(d) (1990).

60. Hill-Burton facilities do not have to add categories of services not currently
provided. The regulations indicate, for example, that institutions that serve
specific age groups, such as geriatric or children's hospitals, and institutions
specializing in particular disorders, such as orthopedic or mental health
facilities, are not required to provide a broad spectrum of care. 43 Fed. Reg.
at 49,962 (1978). This exception, however, should not be interpreted to mean
that a general hospital can claim that it is not required to treat people with
HIV because such care would constitute a new category of service.

61. At least one court has found that an individual has a private right of action
under Hill-Burton even though the act does not expressly provide for one.
Cook v. Ochsner, 319 F. Supp. 603 (E.D. La. 1970). A party cannot, however,
institute an action against an individual physician employed by a Hill-Burton
facility because he or she would not be considered a "participant" under the
act. Walker v. Pierce, 560 F.2d 609 (4th Cir. 1977). Certain commentators have
argued that the Hill-Burton Act was not intended, and cannot therefore be
used to compel institutions to provide services. They argue that the Act was
intended to provide *facilities* to certain areas and not to mandate *services*. Wing,
supra note 56, at 589. This position is refuted not only by the language of the
statute, but by the applicable legislative history. Note, *Due Process for Hill-Burton Assisted Facilities*, 32 Vand. L. Rev. 1469, 1475-76 n.30 (1979). Other commentators take the position that the community service obligation was intended merely to ban *racial* discrimination and was not intended to require
medical institutions to make their facilities generally available. Wing, *supra*
note 56, at 599-600. As Wing points out, however, the language of the statute
belies such an interpretation. *Id.* at 601-02. Moreover, Congress expressly
rejected attempts to limit the obligation to racial discrimination. *Id.* at 607; *see
also* Wyoming Hosp. Ass'n, 727 F.2d at 940 ("The community service obligation is not limited to traditional antidiscrimination concerns").

62. Practically all the litigation under Hill-Burton has been brought pursuant to
the uncompensated care portion of the statute. Courts in those cases have
consistently upheld the validity of the access requirements of Hill-Burton. *See
Wyoming Hosp. Ass'n*, 727 F.2d at 936 (upholding HHS's 1979 regulations as

rationally based and upholding the constitutionality of applying regulations to recipients of Hill-Burton funds prior to the adoption of the new regulations); *American Hosp. Ass'n*, 721 F.2d 170 (upholding the statutory authority of the Secretary of HHS to issue regulations regarding the uncompensated care requirement and the constitutionality of such regulations); Metropolitan Medical Center & Extended Care Facility v. Harris, 693 F.2d 775 (8th Cir. 1982) (reaffirming the purpose behind the uncompensated care requirement and rejecting a facility's claim for Medicare reimbursement for its uncompensated care under Hill-Burton); Cook v. Ochsner Found. Hosp., 559 F.2d 968 (5th Cir. 1977) (upholding HEW regulations providing for a twenty-year limitation on uncompensated care requirement and the percentage levels set as presumptive compliance with the "reasonable volume of services" rule); *Lugo*, 426 F. Supp. 28 (rejecting claim that the compliance guidelines issued by HEW were not reasonably related to the ends of the statute and that the twenty-year limitation on uncompensated care was not arbitrary and capricious).

63. The operations of these programs are described in chapter 6 ("Wealth = Health").

64. The programs themselves, of course, may not discriminate in determining which individuals can qualify for their program. Doe v. Colautti, 454 F. Supp. 621 (E.D. Pa. 1978), *aff'd* 592 F.2d 704 (3d Cir. 1978).

65. 42 U.S.C. §§ 440.220-.230 (1988).

66. *Id.* § 1396a(a)(10)(C)(ii).

67. 42 U.S.C. § 1395dd (1988) (COBRA antidumping statute). From August 1986 to January 1988, only 129 allegations of such violations were filed.

68. N.Y. Educ. Law § 6509 (McKinney 1985).

69. N.Y. Comp. Codes R. & Regs. tit. 8, § 29.2(1) (1989); *see also* Pennsylvania Medical Practices Act, 63 Pa. Cons. Stat. § 422.1 (Supp. 1991); 49 Pa. Code § 16.61 (1987).

70. *Physician Discipline Emerges as a State Priority*, Intergovernmental Health Pol'y Project St. Health Notes, July/Aug. 1988.

71. One commentator has argued that as HIV disease becomes more prevalent, general practitioners, including dentists, will have an obligation to be trained in the diagnosis and treatment of HIV disease. L. Gostin, A National Review of Court and Human Rights Commission Decisions, Part II: Discrimination, AIDS Reference Guide para. 1514, at 14 (AIDS Litig. Project, June 1990). Certain specialists will also need to be able to provide services to people with HIV. *Id.* Gostin concludes that: "Failure to maintain basic skills in relation to one disease may be grounds for revocation of a physician's license." *Id.*

72. *Id.*

73. Md. S.B. 719 ch. 789 (1989).

74. R. Blendon & K. Donelan, *Discrimination Against People with AIDS: The Public's Perspective*, 319 New Eng. J. Med. 1022, 1026 (1988).

5

HEALTH INSURANCE: THE BATTLE OVER LIMITS ON COVERAGE

By Mark H. Jackson

I. Introduction

Access to health insurance determines access to health care for millions of Americans.[1] For those Americans with HIV disease, obstacles to insurance coverage exist which do not threaten the health of other citizens, including others who also have serious, fatal, and expensive-to-treat conditions. This chapter examines insurance practices that limit coverage for HIV disease but not for other diseases of similar expense. It outlines both the remedies already available in the law and the gaps in the law which permit such practices to continue. Ultimately, all Americans will pay for the impact of discriminatory practices, because the inevitable cost of providing even lesser quality care will be substantial and will come from taxpayer-supported funds such as Medicaid.

Although private insurance still constitutes an important mode of access to health care for many people infected with HIV,[2] there is a serious risk that, absent reform, people with HIV disease will be increasingly shut out of the insurance market.

Current underwriting practices have already served to limit the role of private insurance in financing the cost of HIV care.[3] Insurers now routinely test people who apply for individual health insurance coverage for HIV infection.[4] Although some states have established "risk pools" to provide insurance to people who are otherwise unable to qualify for insurance, these programs have not provided significant help to people with HIV.[5] Even for those who are covered, private insurance tends not to reimburse, or reimburses at insufficient levels for treatments that predate HIV but are becoming increasingly important for treating people infected with HIV, including home health care, experimental drug treatments, extended nursing care, mental health services, personal service care, and dental care.[6] In addition, many people who are employed and covered by insurance when they first test positive for the virus ultimately lose their coverage when they become so ill that they are forced to terminate the employment.[7] This phenomenon may increase as the use of AZT and other new therapies enables people who are disabled by HIV to live longer.

It is important at the outset to distinguish between two categories of health insurance providers: commercial insurance companies and companies that are self-insured. Traditional health insurance companies receive premiums from their members and, in turn, become liable for paying the claims of their group members. These companies "pool" the people covered so as to spread the risk of health care costs among a greater number of people. Self-insured companies, on the other hand, create their own reserve and bear the risk of paying the claims of their employees.[8]

The number of employees covered by self-insured plans has been growing steadily since the passage of the 1974 Employee Retirement and Income Security Act (ERISA). More than 50 percent of those employees who receive health insurance through their employment work for companies that are self-insured.[9]

One of the critical differences between commercial insurers and self-insured plans is that only commercial insurers are subject to state regulations, which cover a wide range of insurance practices. State regulations typically mandate, among other things, that insurers provide certain benefits to those they insure. Self-insured plans, which are governed by ERISA, are largely exempt from state regulation.

This chapter will examine four principal ways in which certain employers and insurers have attempted to reduce their share of HIV costs. With respect to each of these four forms of discrimination, it will first describe the reported instances in which employers and insurers have taken the particular action. It will then evaluate the legal remedies currently available to combat each form of discrimination. It will discuss regulations which have been enacted by certain states to prevent insurers from engaging in such acts in the future. Finally, this chapter will recommend specific reforms intended to prevent all types of HIV-related discrimination in the insurance industry and to make certain that insurers continue to play a significant role in funding HIV care.

II. Discriminatory Exclusions and Caps on HIV-Related Costs

In some respects, the concept of "discrimination" is, in a generic sense, inherent in the insurance industry. Insurance companies, in order to maximize profits, seek to exclude from their policies persons at greatest risk of incurring expenses. But even given that operating principle, insurers are obligated to apply the same standards and procedures for ascertaining risk to all who apply and for determining which medical procedures are covered under a given policy. Unfortunately, that has not always been true in situations involving HIV disease.

Employers and insurers have reportedly attempted to exclude arbitrarily classes of people they consider to be more at risk of HIV infection than others, to exclude entirely or limit coverage for certain types of treatment for persons infected with HIV, and to engage in "post-claim underwriting," which denies coverage to people who are already covered under a policy. Although these examples do not demonstrate a universal problem — many employers and insurers clearly are covering HIV-related illnesses just as they cover other diseases — they indicate that without stricter regulation other providers may take steps to decrease what would otherwise be their share of the cost of the treatment of HIV-related illnesses.[10]

Attempts by employers and insurers to restrict or eliminate coverage for HIV-related illnesses have occurred at a time when employers and insurers have been attempting to reduce their overall health care costs. Insurers and employers have announced plans to eliminate certain treatments from their coverage and have placed limits on the coverage they will offer for given treatments.

It is also important to note that small businesses are experiencing particular difficulties in providing health insurance to their employees. Most small businesses cannot self-insure because their employee pool is not large enough. Often when an employee of a small business incurs significant health care bills — as a result of HIV disease or any other illness that is expensive to treat — its commercial insurer increases the company's rates dramatically the following year. Small companies have had to choose between discontinuing health care coverage (or severely restricting its scope) and going out of business.[11]

To a certain extent, therefore, the problems relating to insurance which face people with HIV-related illnesses are part of a larger problem. It would be wrong, however, to ignore the fact that people with HIV-related illnesses have faced even greater hurdles than others. There is strong evidence that many employers and insurers have singled out HIV as a disease to be excluded from coverage or to be drastically limited. Such policies can only be explained as acts of prejudice against those populations most likely to become infected with HIV.

A. Instances of Discriminatory Treatment

1. Exclusions

First, some employers and insurers have attempted to exclude HIV-related costs entirely from their coverage. Although their policies cover procedures and treatments as costly as, or more costly than, the treatment for HIV, these insurers have singled out HIV disease for exclusion.[12]

a. In a well-publicized case, Circle K, the nation's second largest convenience store chain, which is self-insured, announced that it would not cover medical costs of new employees who became sick or injured as a result of AIDS, alcohol, drug abuse, or self-inflicted wounds.[13] Company spokespersons explained the policy by stating that the company was no longer going to insure certain "personal life style decisions."[14] The company ultimately withdrew its proposed change after intense public pressure.

b. In late December 1985 or early January 1986, a Beaverton, Oregon, Datsun dealer, another self-insured company, revised its insurance plan specifically to exclude the reimbursement of costs associated with the treatment of AIDS. An employee who had been with the company, and covered by its insurance policy since 1982, brought a complaint against the company with the Oregon Civil Rights Division of the Bureau of Labor and Industries. The Civil Rights Division found for the employee.[15]

c. The Laborer's Health and Welfare Fund for Southern California, a self-insured plan that insures 20,000 construction workers and their families, excluded all AIDS claims except from people under age 13 and those who contracted the disease through blood transfusions.[16]

d. Gottschalk Industries, a self-insured department store chain based in Fresno, California, refused to pay for any AIDS-related treatments prior to 1988.[17] According to a company representative, it amended its policy in 1988 to cover AIDS costs for those employees who have been with the company for at least ten years.[18]

e. In July 1987, G.I.C. Insurance Company of San Antonio modified its plan to exclude "any charges for care and treatment arising out of or resulting from [AIDS]."[19] A company memorandum read that "[t]his exclusion is in accordance with the Texas Insurance Code, and approved by the State Board of Insurance."[20]

f. The Associated Press reported that Wisconsin insurance regulators granted two insurance companies — Rural Securities Inc., of Madison, and Employers Health Insurance Co., of Green Bay — permission to market policies that limit or deny payments to in-state clients who suffer from AIDS or AIDS-related illnesses.[21] A representative of the Wisconsin Insurance Department denied that the department permitted any company to market such policies, although he reported that fifteen companies had attempted to do so.[22]

g. The Arizona Insurance Department reported that it had received a complaint from the mother of a person with AIDS claiming that her son's health insurer was denying coverage of her son's medical treatment. After the Insurance Department intervened, the insurer paid over $60,000 in medical bills.[23]

h. Regis Corporation, a chain of unisex hair chains, amended its group health plan, which was written through Blue Cross/Blue Shield of Minnesota, to exclude reimbursement for "any charges for supplies and services needed for disorders or complications due to [AIDS]."[24]

Many insurers have attempted to exclude HIV-related costs from their policies but have been prohibited from doing so by state insurance departments. In California, for example, a state that prohibits HIV-related exclusions, the Insurance Department by early 1988 reportedly had denied more than forty AIDS-related policy amendments that would have reduced coverage.[25] The Florida Department of Insurance also received complaints about insurers placing discriminatory exclusions and caps on their policies. The Department resolved the problems with insurance companies as part of their policy review process.[26]

2. Caps

In addition to their attempts to exclude, employers and insurers have placed discriminatory limits on the amount of coverage they will provide for HIV-related treatments.

a. The National Gay Rights Advocates charged both Reserve Life Insurance Company of Dallas and Providers Fidelity Life Insurance Company of Pennsylvania with placing a $10,000 lifetime limit on medical claims for AIDS, compared to limits of $250,000 or more for other diseases.[27]

b. Preston Trucking Company, a self-insured company in Maryland imposed a $50,000 lifetime maximum for medical expenses related to AIDS.[28] According to a representative of the company, the restriction was removed as of January 1990.[29]

c. In Texas, a person diagnosed with AIDS filed suit in federal court charging that H & H Music Company, after learning that one of its employees was diagnosed with AIDS, canceled its group plan (which provided benefits of up to $1,000,000 in medical costs) and became self-insured, offering a policy which limited benefits payable for AIDS treatments to $5,000.[30] The court dismissed plaintiff's complaint on the basis that he had no cause of action under ERISA, and the dismissal was affirmed on appeal.

d. In a similar Georgia case, a retail furniture firm was sued by a person with HIV disease after it modified its health insurance plan to limit coverage of AIDS and AIDS-related conditions from $1 million to $25,000; again, the federal district court denied relief under ERISA.[31]

e. In Florida, a person with AIDS filed a complaint with the Florida Commission on Human Relations claiming that his employer, Arvida JMB Corporation, changed insurance companies when it was notified that he had AIDS. Whereas the former plan guaranteed $1 million in coverage, the new plan limited AIDS-related medical expenses to $5,000 and a lifetime cap of $15,000.[32] Ultimately, the employer changed the policy back to a plan that did not contain an AIDS-related cap.[33]

f. Central Parking System of Oklahoma has a self-insured benefit plan which contains a $10,000 lifetime maximum benefit for PWAs.[34]

g. Galaxy Carpet Mills of Chatsworth, Georgia modified its self-insured plan to include a provision limiting lifetime medical reimbursements for people with AIDS or other sexually transmitted diseases to $10,000.[35] The company dropped the clause after receiving more than 500 calls objecting to the provision.[36]

h. The Kansas Department of Insurance approved riders on individual insurance products marketed by Security General Life, Pyramid Life, and American Republic Life that would limit a company's exposure for people treated for AIDS. The riders generally allow $75,000 lifetime maximums for the treatment of AIDS or ARC.[37]

i. Provident Indemnity Life Insurance Co., in Norristown, Pennsylvania, instituted a $5,000-per-year, $20,000-per-lifetime cap on medical coverage for AIDS on small group policies.[38] Provident eventually eliminated the yearly cap when it discovered that AIDS claims constituted a smaller part of the total claims than it had anticipated.[39]

j. Allied Benefits Systems, of Chicago, administered an insurance policy for one of its clients that set a lifetime cap of $10,000 on AIDS-related medical costs unless the policyholder could prove that the virus was contracted "involuntarily."[40] According to a representative of Allied, the company ultimately eliminated that cap.[41]

k. ITI modified its health coverage to impose a $50,000 lifetime cap on AIDS-related treatments for employees and dependents diagnosed with AIDS after October 1, 1989.[42]

l. The West Virginia Insurance Department has received complaints about Multiple Employer Trusts (METS) and Multiple Employer Welfare Associations (MEWAS), insurers that are licensed in other states but provide policies to various employers within West Virginia. These trusts have reportedly amended their policies to place lifetime caps (of as low as $25,000) on HIV-related treatments after learning that someone covered by the plan had been infected with HIV.[43]

m. The New York City based Tollman-Hundley Hotels company is reported to have reduced its lifetime coverage for HIV-related claims from $1 million to $10,000 in 1991.[44]

n. Indiana-based Lincoln Foodservice Products, Inc., has been sued by an employee with AIDS for placing a $50,000 lifetime, and $25,000 yearly, cap on AIDS-related coverage just before he became ill.[45]

3. Restrictions on Prescription Coverage

In addition to placing overall "caps" on coverage of HIV-related treatments, certain employers and insurers have refused to reimburse policy holders — or have placed limits on reimbursements — for drug therapies that have been prescribed for people infected with HIV.[46]

a. The George Washington University Health Plan HMO introduced a $3,000 annual limit on reimbursement for prescription drugs for all enrollees.[47] Since AZT treatments have cost up to $10,000 a year,[48] a person infected with HIV who requires the drug would be forced to pay most of the cost himself.

b. PCS, an Arizona-based company which administers prescription drug programs covering 18.3 million people, offers a plan to its clients which exclude AIDS drugs from coverage. The company told *New York Newsday* that although the company offers such plans, it "doesn't currently recommend those plans."[49]

c. Some of the nation's largest insurance companies have refused to cover drug treatments if they were prescribed for conditions other than those explicitly listed by the FDA (off-label uses).[50] For example, in 1989 Prudential was willing to pay for AZT only for patients who had a far-below normal T-cell count, and not for patients who were prescribed AZT as a prophylaxis against opportunistic diseases.[51] Similarly, although many insurers were willing to pay for the use of intravenous pentamidine, a drug used to treat *Pneumocystis* pneumonia, they were not willing to pay for the aerosolized version of the drug, which is widely used to prevent the pneumonia.[52] As new drug treatments are developed, we can continue to expect insurance companies to refuse to cover them for significant periods of time on the basis that they constitute "experimental" treatments.[53]

B. Legal Remedies

1. Statutory Protections

It is well-established that insurers have the right to exclude certain risks from the coverage they offer, or to limit the amount of the risk they assume — so long as the exclusion or limitation does not violate an applicable statute or is not contrary to public policy.[54] This principle is predicated on the fact that an insurance policy is considered a contract, and as such, parties to it are free to incorporate such terms as they wish provided they are legally valid.[55] Accordingly, unless there are statutes or regulations that are interpreted as prohibiting HIV-related exclusions and limitations, insurers are free to impose restrictions on HIV-related expenses.

The most logical remedy for a person seeking to challenge an HIV-related cap or exclusion in his or her insurance would be one of the several federal or state antidiscrimination statutes.[56] Insurers who place caps or exclusions on HIV-related treatments and do not impose such limitations on similar diseases are obviously engaging in a form of discrimination. News stories reporting on such practices indicate that at least some employers and insurers are treating HIV differently than other diseases because they have determined that HIV is a disease that primarily affects gay men and insurers do not approve of the gay lifestyle.[57] Other providers have limited HIV coverage simply because of the perceived costs of providing such coverage.

Unfortunately, it would be difficult for a person seeking to challenge a discriminatory cap or exclusion to prevail in an action pursuant to traditional antidiscrimination statutes. It is not enough to demonstrate that an insurer is treating one disease (HIV) differently than other similar diseases; absent a specific restriction, insurers are permitted to do that. A plaintiff must show that he or she is part of protected class of people who are being treated differently than similarly situated people. As set forth below, because discrimination statutes provide incomplete protection, the federal and state governments should enact specific statutes or regulations requiring employers and insurers to treat HIV-related illnesses as they treat other illnesses.

Title VII. A person alleging HIV-related discrimination against an insurance provider might succeed under Title VII of the Civil Rights Act of 1964[58] or the section of practically every state's discrimination statute prohibiting discrimination on the basis of gender. Section 703 (a)(1) of Title VII provides, in relevant part, that it shall be an unlawful employment practice for an employer

> to discriminate against any individual with respect to his compensation, terms, conditions, or privileges of employment because of such individual's race, color religion, sex or national origin.[59]

A person alleging HIV-related discrimination can succeed in a Title VII claim if he or she can demonstrate that an insurance company policy treats a class protected by the statute differently than other classes of people ("disparate treatment") or that a facially neutral policy impacts on a protected class in a discriminatory manner ("disparate impact").[60]

There are two possible bases for a disparate impact claim under Title VII by a worker denied coverage of an HIV-related condition.[61] The first argument is that such discrimination constitutes sex discrimination against male workers because the large majority of HIV-infected patients are male.[62] The second argument would assert a claim of race discrimination, if the plaintiff were a person of color, based on the disproportionate number of HIV patients who are persons of color.

Once a plaintiff has made such a showing, an insurer would have to demonstrate that the practice "serves, in a significant way, the legitimate goals of the employer."[63] Since financial considerations alone are insufficient justifications for discrimination, an insurance provider might have a difficult time meeting this standard.

A 1974 decision by the Supreme Court, however, established an obstacle to a successful discrimination claim against insurers. In *General*

Electric v. Gilbert,[64] female employees of General Electric were denied disability benefits under their employer's disability plan while they were absent from work as a result of pregnancy. They brought an action against their employer claiming that the exclusion of pregnancy-related benefits constituted sex discrimination in violation of Title VII. The Supreme Court dismissed the plaintiffs' claims on the basis that statistics demonstrating discriminatory impact, by themselves, were insufficient to make out a claim under Title VII. The Court ruled that the plaintiffs failed to show that the distinctions involving pregnancy were "mere pretexts designed to effect an invidious discrimination against the members of one sex or the other...."[65] In fact, the Court in *Gilbert* cited its opinion in *Geduldig v. Aiello,*[66] upholding a similar practice, which read:

> The lack of identity between the excluded disability and gender as such under this insurance program becomes clear upon the most cursory analysis. The program divides potential recipients into two groups — pregnant women and nonpregnant persons. While the first group is exclusively female, the second includes members of both sexes.[67]

The Court in *Gilbert* also appeared to make a distinction between insurers discriminating against a class of *people* and insurers deciding not to include a particular *condition* in their policies. The Court again cited language from *Geduldig* to emphasize that the latter did not violate Title VII:

> The California insurance program does not exclude anyone from benefit eligibility because of gender but merely removes one physical condition — pregnancy — from the list of compensable disabilities.[68]

In light of *Gilbert,* a plaintiff would have to show (in addition to providing statistics demonstrating that HIV-related caps and exclusions had a disparate impact on males or on persons of color) that an insurer instituted HIV-related caps and exclusions in order to "effect an invidious discrimination" against those groups. Because women and whites are also infected with HIV, a court might rule that insurers were not attempting to discriminate based on sex or race. In addition, a plaintiff would have to convince a court that the insurer was seeking to discriminate against a class of people, rather than merely to exclude a particular condition (HIV) from its coverage.

The *Gilbert* Court, however, does provide an opening for a plaintiff alleging HIV-related discrimination. The Court, in part, based its finding that there was no invidious discrimination on its conclusion that pregnancy is "significantly different from the typical covered disease or disability."[69] The Court suggested that it might hold otherwise if it were confronted with "a disease or disability comparable in all other respects to covered diseases or disabilities and yet confined to the members of one race or sex."[70]

The Americans with Disabilities Act. The Americans with Disabilities Act (ADA) prohibits covered entities from discriminating against people with physical or mental disabilities in such areas as employment, housing, public accommodations, education, transportation, communication, recreation, institutionalization, health services, voting, and access to public services. The legislative history of the act clearly indicates that people infected with HIV are considered "disabled" under the bill.[71]

With respect to employment, Section 102 of the ADA provides:

> No covered entity shall discriminate against a qualified individual with a disability because of the disability of such individual in regard to job application procedures, the hiring, advancement, or discharge of employees, employee compensation, job training, and other terms, conditions, and privileges of employment.

The ADA defines "discrimination," in part, as:

> excluding or otherwise denying equal jobs or benefits to a qualified individual because of the known disability of an individual with whom the qualified individual is known to have a relationship or association.[72]

Since insurance is clearly a "condition" or "benefit" of employment, these sections appear to prohibit employers from offering insurance, whether through self-insurance or through the purchase of a group plan, that treats people infected with HIV differently than other employees.

Unfortunately, Title V of the ADA contains a provision that appears to exempt insurance companies and employee benefit plans from certain provisions of the act. Section 501(c) reads as follows:

> INSURANCE. — Titles I through IV of this Act shall not be construed to prohibit or restrict —
>
> (1) an insurer, hospital or medical service company, health maintenance organization, or any agent, or entity that administers benefit plans, or similar organizations from underwriting risks, classifying risks, or administering such risks that are based on or not inconsistent with state law;
>
> (2) a person or organization covered by this Act from establishing, sponsoring, observing or administering the terms of a bona fide benefit plan that are based

on underwriting risks, classifying risks, or administering such risks that are based on or not inconsistent with State law; or

(3) a person or organization covered by this Act from establishing, sponsoring, observing or administering the terms of a bona fide benefit plan that is not subject to State laws that regulate insurance.

Paragraphs (1), (2), and (3) shall not be used as a subterfuge to evade the purposes of title I and II.

In view of these exemptions, it remains to be seen how useful the ADA will be to a person infected with HIV who wishes to challenge a discriminatory act by his or her insurer.[73]

Rehabilitation Act of 1973. Although the *Rehabilitation Act of 1973* prohibits certain parties from discriminating against a person because of a disability, and in fact, has been interpreted by courts to include HIV within its definition of "disability,"[74] the act probably would not apply to actions by insurance companies. In order to succeed in a claim under the Rehabilitation Act, a party must show that the defendant receives federal funds. Since insurance companies are not recipients of federal funds, they are outside the purview of the act.

State Unfair Trade Statutes. HIV-related caps and exclusions may violate the provisions contained in every state's insurance code banning unfair trade practices. Those provisions typically prohibit "unfair discrimination between individuals of the same class and of essentially the same hazard."[75] For example, section 26.1-04-03 of North Dakota's insurance code defines "unfair discrimination," in pertinent part, as follows:

Making or permitting any unfair discrimination between individuals of the same class and of essentially the same hazard in the amount of premium, policy fees, or rates charged for any policy or contract of accident or health insurance or in the benefits payable thereunder, or in any of the terms or conditions of such contract or in any other manner whatever.

It would appear that under this provision an insurer could not offer less coverage to an insured who becomes infected with HIV than an insured who requires treatment for another serious illness. Such an action on behalf of an insurer may constitute unfair discrimination because it treats people of "essentially the same hazard" differently. In fact, the Commissioner of Insurance for North Dakota has interpreted the above-quoted section to preclude insurers from imposing HIV-related caps and exclusions.[76]

Unfortunately, the language of the unfair trade statutes, such as the one quoted above, is ambiguous. These statutes can be read to mean that insurers cannot offer people with essentially the same health risk different coverage but that they can offer everyone with the same health risk identical policies — all of which exclude or limit the coverage for HIV-related illnesses.[77]

State Handicap Discrimination Statutes. A potential remedy for a person claiming HIV-related discrimination in the insurance context is state discrimination statutes that prohibit discrimination against, *inter alia,* people with physical disabilities. For example, section 46a-58(a) of the General Statutes of Connecticut provides:

> It shall be a discriminatory practice in violation of this section for any person to subject, or cause to be subjected, any other person to the deprivation of any rights, privileges or immunities, secured or protected by the constitution or laws of this state or of the United States, on account of religion, national origin, alienage, color, race, sex, blindness or physical disability.

The statute defines "physically disabled" to include:

> any individual who has any chronic physical handicap, infirmity or impairment, whether congenital or resulting from illness, including, but not limited to, epilepsy, deafness or hearing impairment or reliance on a wheelchair or other remedial appliance or device.[78]

Pursuant to such a provision, a plaintiff can allege that his or her HIV status constitutes a disability (using the cases under the Rehabilitation Act as support) and that because of that disability, he or she is being discriminated against unfairly by an insurance company.

There are no reported cases involving challenges to an insurer under a state statute barring discrimination on the basis of a disability. One explanation for this is that state handicap discrimination laws are widely believed not to apply to self-insured companies; these laws are thought to be pre-empted by ERISA, the federal law that governs self-insureds. Nevertheless, one state's civil rights commission ruled in 1990 (in an AIDS-related cap case) that ERISA did not preempt the application of its handicap discrimination law.[79] If this ruling is upheld on appeal, it could increase the use of state handicap discrimination laws in the fight against exclusions and caps. Yet, a major conceptual problem with this approach is that it is difficult to apply a statute which relates to disabilities to insurance companies that are *in the business* of insuring against the risk of medical expenses. Insurers treat people with disabilities differently than they treat people without disabilities. The justification for applying these statutes in cases of HIV-related discrimination is that although insurance companies can conceivably be permitted to exclude certain *treatments* from their coverage (regardless of a person's condition), they should not be permitted to exclude coverage based solely on a person's *condition*. For example, although an insurer may be permitted to exclude organ transplants resulting from any illness from coverage, it should not be permitted to deny coverage for a particular disease, such as kidney failure, that might have necessitated a transplant.[80]

Although the above analysis suggests that a plaintiff would have a difficult time prevailing in a discrimination case against an insurer on the basis of an AIDS-related cap or exclusion, the cases do leave enough of an opening to justify bringing the suit. On the other hand, it is clear that federal and state antidiscrimination statutes may not adequately protect people infected with HIV from insurance discrimination. For that reason, it is critical that states enact specific statutes or regulations prohibiting such discrimination.

2. Regulatory Protections

a. State Regulation

Whatever the gaps in existing law, a state legislature, or, through delegation, a state insurance commissioner, is fully empowered to require insurers doing business in that state to cover HIV-related diseases in all their health and sickness policies. Under their police powers, states have broad authority to regulate insurance companies to assure that state residents have adequate health care coverage. Courts will readily uphold such regulations so long as they are rationally related to their stated goal.[81] State legislatures typically delegate to insurance commissioners the power to grant, renew, or revoke licenses, fix the minimum surpluses an insurer must maintain, and approve or disapprove of the forms of insurance policies.[82]

In fact, courts have specifically upheld state regulations requiring insurers to provide coverage for certain conditions in their health and sickness policies. In *Metropolitan Life Insurance Co. v. Massachusetts Travelers Insurance Co.*,[83] the Supreme Court upheld a Massachusetts statute that mandated that insurers cover certain mental health services in their basic health policies. In so doing, the Court noted that twenty-six states had promulgated sixty-nine "mandated benefit laws," including alcoholism coverage, birth defect coverage, outpatient kidney dialysis coverage, and restrictive surgery for insured mastectomies.[84]

Although insurers have challenged these actions on various grounds, including violations of the due process and contracts clauses of the U.S. Constitution, such challenges have been uniformly rejected.[85]

In virtually ever state, the Commissioner of Insurance would have the power to issue regulations prohibiting insurers from treating HIV disease differently than other sicknesses or illnesses. In those states where the commissioner cannot point to general statutory authority for such action, the legislature can certainly grant him or her such authority, or enact a statutory prohibition against such discrimination. As the above discussion makes clear, it is critical that states pass statutes or regulations that specifically prohibit such HIV-related discrimination. Such measures are needed so that insurers are put on notice that states will not tolerate this form of discrimination and so that potential insureds are aware of their rights and are encouraged to bring complaints to the attention of the insurance department in their state.

Our research[86] indicates that fourteen states have enacted rules (either through statute, regulation, or department guidelines) expressly prohibiting insurance companies from either excluding coverage for AIDS and/or HIV-related illnesses or limiting benefits solely for treatment of that disease.[87] Typically, these regulations prohibit insurers from treating HIV-related coverage or benefits differently than other sicknesses or illnesses.[88] Some states that require the insurance commissioner to approve forms of insurance contracts provide that the state shall not approve any form that contains a discriminatory cap or exclusion.[89]

Certain other states, while not enacting measures specifically prohibiting caps and exclusions, apparently take the position that such practices are prohibited under their general insurance laws.[90] Finally, several state insurance commissioners, without referring to a particular statute or regulation, take the position that HIV-related caps and exclusions are not permitted in their states.[91]

b. Federal Regulation

Unfortunately, even the most comprehensive state regulations banning discriminatory underwriting practices will have only a limited impact on insurance providers since those regulations control only insurance companies and HMOs in a given state. State regulations do not directly cover the substantial number of companies that are self-insured. In 1984, more than half of the employed labor force worked for self-insured firms, and the number of self-insured firms has been growing since then.[92] As the examples cited earlier in this section illustrate, most of the companies that placed discriminatory caps and exclusions on their policies were self-insured. In more than one instance, in fact, a company *switched* to a self-insured plan for the apparent purpose of imposing AIDS-related restrictions.[93]

Self-insured plans, while not subject to state regulation, are governed by ERISA. The U.S. Supreme Court has determined that ERISA preempts state laws which purport to regulate employee benefit plans.[94] Although ERISA itself does not contain a prohibition against discrimination, section 1144(d) of the statute provides that ERISA shall not "alter, amend, modify, invalidate, impair, or supersede any law of the United States." Courts have interpreted this provision to mean that individuals can bring discrimination claims against self-insured companies under Title VII of the Civil Rights Act of 1964, or a parallel state discrimination statute, so long as they are members of a protected class under the federal statute. When the ADA fully takes effect, workers will also be able to sue self-insured employers alleging discrimination based on disability. However, as discussed above, the extent to which disability discrimination principles can be applied to insurance is unclear.[95]

A decision by a federal court in Texas indicates that unless ERISA is amended, that statute may not protect HIV-infected people from attempts by employers to restrict or exclude coverage for HIV-related illnesses.[96] McGann began working for defendant company in 1982. At that time, the company's policy, which was provided by a commercial insurer, provided that employers diagnosed with AIDS were entitled to maximum benefits of $1 million during their lifetimes. After McGann advised the company in December 1987 that he was diagnosed as having AIDS, the company, in July 1988, changed its medical coverage to a self-insured plan and decreased benefits for AIDS to a maximum of $3,000. McGann commenced an action in federal court alleging that the company's actions violated ERISA.

In granting the company's motion to dismiss plaintiff's claim, the Texas court ruled that ERISA did not require self-insured companies to provide medical coverage. In sweeping language that would protect companies from any conceivable discriminatory conduct, the court wrote:

> The purpose of the changes in the medical plan made by Defendants jibe with the ultimate purpose of ERISA: protection of the plan. Defendants made changes in the plan because in past years the plan suffered various financial losses. Defendants were faced with either dropping the plan altogether or making changes. The alterations were not made to discriminate against McGann or anyone who was diagnosed with A.I.D.S.[97]

On the other hand, ERISA has been used successfully to prevent self-insured companies from arbitrarily denying coverage to employees infected with HIV when the plan does not contain an HIV-related cap or exclusion. In *John Doe v. Cooper Investments*,[98] for example, a Colorado District Court judge issued a temporary restraining order requiring a company to continue providing health insurance coverage to an employee who was terminated two weeks after the employee revealed that he was infected with HIV.[99] The plaintiff alleged that the company violated his "protected rights... to obtain and utilize the benefits provided by the [health care] plan" in violation of §§ 502(a) and 510 of ERISA.

Similarly, in *Warn v. Agip Petroleum Company*,[100] a Texas employer fired plaintiff who had been diagnosed with AIDS, along with five other employees who had incurred significant medical expenses. The company took this action after its insurance carrier increased the company's monthly premium from $35,000 to $62,000. The employee commenced a lawsuit alleging that the employer violated ERISA's prohibition against discharging or discriminating against employees for exercising rights granted under an employee benefit plan. The company ultimately settled the case by reinstating plaintiff to his former position and to participation in the company's group health insurance plan.[101]

There is no principled justification for permitting self-insured companies to avoid paying for HIV-related care (or any other illness) when many commercial insurers are required to pay for such treatments. An individual with HIV disease who is employed by a self-insured company should not be denied adequate health care merely because he happens to work for an employer that is self-insured. As long as our national custom links insurance to employment, our laws should require that all insurance providers provide certain levels of protection. ERISA should be amended so that it clearly prohibits employers from arbitrarily eliminating coverage for certain diseases or illnesses such as HIV disease.

III. Redlining: Attempts by Insurers to Screen Out Gay Male Applicants

A. Instances of Discrimination

Although it is extremely difficult to identify examples of insurers engaging in redlining, it is widely believed that certain insurance companies do seek to screen out certain portions of the population based on personal characteristics deemed to be associated with a higher risk of contracting HIV disease.[102] Specifically, insurers are attempting to avoid issuing policies to men who have characteristics associated with being gay. It has been reported in the press that insurance companies are increasingly relying on factors such as occupations, marital status, and place of residence to make coverage decisions when issuing individual insurance policies.[103] In response to a survey conducted by the Congressional Office of Technology Assessment, eighteen of sixty-one commercial insurance companies surveyed indicated "occasional reliance on sexual orientation as a factor in underwriting."[104]

Insurers clearly have declined to provide insurance — or have offered coverage at excessive rates — to people in certain localities or engaged in certain occupations which are believed to attract a disproportionate number of gay men:

a. On November 15, 1988, HealthAmerica Corp. and the State of California settled a lawsuit commenced by the state which alleged that the HMO had falsely advertised a health insurance plan in San Francisco insofar as it had refused to issue policies there in order to avoid insuring AIDS carriers. The HMO agreed to pay $250,000 to the state and to certain individuals.[105]

b. A Washington, D.C. lawyer filed a lawsuit in U.S. District Court for the District of Columbia charging that Mutual Insurance Co. denied him coverage in 1987 because they believed he was gay (the plaintiff had performed legal work for people with AIDS).[106]

c. A Houston-area company was ordered by the Texas Board of Insurance to discontinue its use of zip codes in making underwriting decisions. The department determined that the practice appeared to discriminate on the basis of sexual orientation.[107]

d. American Salon, a trade magazine for the hair care industry, has reported that certain insurers have increased premiums as much as 40 percent.[108]

e. Hartford Life Insurance, of Hartford, Connecticut, and Times Insurance Co., of Milwaukee, list entertainment groups as ineligible for insurance.[109]

f. United States Life Insurance Co., of New York, lists artists, authors, composers, entertainers, and theater employees as ineligible for insurance.[110]

g. The Great Republic Insurance Company, of California, issued an internal memorandum in 1985 citing concern about AIDS and requiring a special questionnaire for single men without dependents whose jobs entailed no physical exertion. The memorandum gave as examples, florists, interior decorators, antiques dealers, jewelers, fashion workers, hairdressers, and restaurant employees.[111]

h. Guardian Life Insurance Co. does not cover hairdressers and restaurant workers nationwide.[112]

Although self-insured companies are not in a position to redline their employees with respect to insurance coverage, employers may attempt to screen out gay men from employment in order to avoid the possibility of hugh medical costs down the road.[113]

B. Legal Remedies

Insurers who engage in redlining in order to screen out gay men would violate the unfair trade practices provisions referred to above. Although the language of these statutes does not expressly prohibit discrimination on the basis of sexual orientation, certain states take the position that using sexual orientation as a factor in determining coverage would constitute an unfair business practice.

An insurer who rejects the application of a person based solely on that person's occupation, zip code, or marital status is discriminating between individuals "of the same hazard." Obviously, there is no basis for an insurer to determine that simply because a man is a florist, for instance, that he is gay. Moreover, even if an insurer were able to determine that a particular applicant was gay, the fact that he is gay, in and of itself, does not make that man more of a health risk than a heterosexual man. Such a distinction would ignore the fact that the particular gay man who applied for insurance may not engage in any activity that can transmit the virus, or that the straight man may be engaging in truly risky behavior.

Several states have avoided any ambiguity and have specifically made it an unfair business practice for an insurer to ask applicants questions that would seek to learn his or her sexual orientation. According to a 1988 survey, twenty-three states also claim to prohibit discrimination based on sexual orientation.[114] Sixteen states expressly prohibit insurance companies from asking questions which seek to learn a person's sexual orientation.[115] These statutes prohibit insurers from using martial status, living arrangements, occupation, gender, beneficiary designation, zip code, or other territorial classification to determine insurability. In fact, although not binding on states, the National Association of Insurance Commissioners issued guidelines that prohibit insurers from inquiring into an applicant's sexual orientation. Every state, at a minimum, should adopt the NAIC's guidelines.

IV. Discrimination in the Administration of Insurance Plans

A. Instances of Discrimination

Insurance companies have attempted unfairly to use the "preexisting condition" and "material misrepresentation" clauses in insurance contracts to avoid having to pay legitimate medical expenses for the treatment of HIV-related illnesses.[116] Although those clauses exist in practically every health insurance plan, it is believed that insurers are aggressively using those clauses against people with HIV in bad faith. Some insurers have attempted to take advantage of the fact that a person who ultimately tests positive for HIV may have experienced certain symptoms prior to becoming covered under a given policy by singling out those claimants for exceptionally detailed examinations. In some instances, a person with AIDS may die before an insurer completes its investigations.

B. Legal Remedies

A person who believes that his or her insurer has abused a preexisting condition clause in order to avoid paying for HIV-related care should find relief under the unfair business practices provisions discussed above. Most states' statutes consider an unreasonable refusal to cover a claim, or an unreasonable delay in affirming coverage, to constitute an unfair business practice.[117] California has enacted a specific regulation dealing with insurer abuse of preexisting condition clauses.[118] That statute defines as an unfair act a delay of more than sixty days in the payment of hospital, medical, or surgical benefits for AIDS or ARC, even if the delay is allegedly for the purpose of investigating whether the condition arose prior to commencement of coverage. Certain states require that in order for an insurer to claim that a diagnosis of AIDS was a preexisting condition, it must point to a previous clinical diagnosis of AIDS.[119] Virginia enacted a regulation that prohibits insurers from issuing policies in which a "preexisting condition" relevant to HIV infection is "based on the sole existence of a positive HIV-related test result...without the manifestation of symptoms of actual diagnosis of AIDS.[120]

Additionally, a person whose insurer has wrongfully withheld payment for an HIV-related claim on the basis of a preexisting condition clause may pursue a common law cause of action against that insurer on a breach of contract theory.[121]

V. Conclusion

There is substantial evidence that certain employers and insurers have attempted to exclude or limit their coverage for HIV-related illnesses. The problem is particularly apparent among self-insured companies. In order to provide people with HIV disease with access to adequate health care, it is critical that the federal and state governments enact measures prohibiting health insurance providers from treating HIV disease differently than other illnesses. States should enact specific statutes or regulations banning such discriminatory practices. Similarly, the federal government must amend ERISA to provide similar prohibitions, so that companies are not encouraged to self-insure in order to avoid such prohibitions and to ensure that people are provided with access to adequate health care regardless of how their employer chooses to provide health insurance.

Insurers have also sought to exclude from their policies people with characteristics believed to be associated with being gay, as well as refusing unfairly to reimburse bona fide claims on the basis of a preexisting condition clause. States should enact strong measures to outlaw such blatantly discriminatory acts.

NOTES

1. Employment is practically a precondition to acquiring health insurance. Almost two-thirds of the population receives its' insurance coverage through the workplace — half as workers, half as dependents of workers. M. Baily, *Private Insurance and the HIV Epidemic*, HCFA Cooperative Agreement No. 18-C-99141/3-01 at 23 [hereinafter Baily].

2. One commentator projected that in 1991 AIDS-related costs would be shared among the different payors as follows:

Payor	Percentage of AIDS Patients Covered
Insurers	
Insurance Companies	24%
Self-Insureds	12%
Plans	
HMOs	4%
Medicaid	40%
Medicare	3%
No Coverage	17%

H.T. Greely, *AIDS and the American Health Care Financing System*, 51 U. Pitt. L. Rev. 73, 96 (1989). A study by the Health Resources and Services Administration (HRSA) of 1988 data on 75,000 HIV-infected patients found that there were no categories of care for which private insurance paid the majority of patient service. Atlantic Information Services, Aug. 1990, at 1.

3. Aside from these underwriting practices, the demographics of HIV disease are also rendering private insurance less relevant to the care of people with HIV. Those populations with the largest percentage increase in HIV cases — intravenous drug users, their sexual partners, and their children — are likely to be unemployed, and thus without insurance.

4. California is the only state that completely prohibits insurance carriers from requiring HIV tests from applicants for health insurance. M.D. Casey, *The Status of State Regulation of Insurance Practices Regarding HIV Disease in the United States* 16 (1989) [hereinafter Casey]. A report of the Congressional Office of Technology Assessment (OTA) indicated that 86 percent of commercial insurers attempt to identify individual health insurance applicants infected with HIV. L.M. Tonery, *AIDS: A Crisis in Health Care Financing*, Fed'n Ins. & Corp. Couns. Q., Winter 1990, at 139 [hereinafter Tonery].

   The overall effect of mandatory testing for HIV in the health insurance context is not as significant as it might be, since the overwhelming majority of those insured are covered under group policies obtained through their employment. These group plans do not test members for HIV and thus place no medical requirements on prospective insured people (although the policies typically include preexisting condition clauses). *See* Baily, *supra* note 1, at 11.

Only about 10 to 15 percent of the insurance market is comprised of individually underwritten policies. *Id.*

5. The theory behind risk pools is that a person can acquire insurance regardless of his or her current health status because the insurance would be available through the group. Communicating for Agriculture, Inc., *Comprehensive Health Insurance for High-Risk Individuals: A State-by-State Analysis* (3d ed. 1988).

    Risk pools, which are created by state law, are an association of all health insurance companies doing business in a state. An individual who participates in the plan must pay a premium well in excess of a premium for an individual policy in that state. (Risk pool coverage is about 25 percent to 50 percent above the premium for an individual policy.) Baily, *supra* note 1, at 321. States typically impose a cap on such premiums of between 125 to 150 percent of standard individual premiums in the state. *Comprehensive Health Insurance* at 3. Because participants in the plan tend to have large health care bills, individual premiums do not cover the full cost of the claims. To make up the deficit, most states assess the participating members of the pooling association in proportion to their share of the state health insurance market. *Id.* at 4. Several states subsidize their assessment through some form of tax credit against premiums or other state taxes. Presently, self-insured companies are exempt from risk pool assessments, although federal legislation has been introduced to include self-insurers as well. *Id.*

6. Baily, *supra* note 1, at 29. Baily reports that private insurance is geared toward acute care rather than the chronic, long-term care that HIV-related illnesses require. *Id.*

7. M.A. Baily, *Private Insurance and a Source of Financing for HIV-Related Care*, Testimony Before the National Commission on AIDS, at 3 (Nov. 3, 1989) [hereinafter Baily Testimony]; J. Green & P. Arno, *The 'Medicaidization' of AIDS — Trends in the Financing of HIV-Related Medical Care*, 264 J. A.M.A. 1261, 1265 (1990). Although a federal statute, the Comprehensive Omnibus Budget Reconciliation Act of 1986 (COBRA), provides employees with the opportunity to continue their group insurance by paying the premiums themselves at statutory levels, many people with AIDS cannot afford to take advantage of this statute. Some states have instituted programs whereby Medicaid will pay the COBRA premium in order to keep individuals on private insurance — and off Medicaid. *See, e.g.,* Cal. A.B. 532, ch. 1055 (1989); Colo. S.B. I-X (1989); Conn. Pub. Act No. 90-318 (1990); Wis. Act 336 (1989). Initial reports have demonstrated that these programs have provided HIV-infected people with continued access to health care while saving the states money. Colorado Dept. Soc. Serv., *Economic Feasibility of Medicaid Paying Private Insurance Premiums for Persons Living with AIDS* 21 (Feb. 15, 1990).

8. There are two types of self-insured plans: one in which the employer bears the entire risk of paying claims, and one in which the employer assumes the risk up to a certain limit, beyond which an insurer bears, or shares with the employer, the risk of additional claims. *See* A. Jensen & J. Gabel, *The Erosion of Purchased Health Insurance*, Inquiry, Fall 1988, at 328-29.

    Commercial insurers and self-insured plans are not entirely unrelated. A significant portion of the business of many commercial insurers consists of *administering* self-insured plans. Telephone Interview with Jade C. Payne,

Senior Policy Analyst, Health Insurance Association of America (Aug. 22, 1990).

9. Tolchin, *More Companies Choosing to Self-Insure Benefits*, N.Y. Times, Aug. 3, 1990, at D-10.

10. G. Oppenheimer & R. Padgug, *AIDS: The Risks to Insurers, the Threat to Equity*, Hastings Center Rep., Oct. 1986, at 21. Some commentators have noted that many insurers have not yet developed their approach to HIV-related claims, and that it is likely that a growing number of employers and insurers will take steps to reduce their share of HIV-related costs. In testimony before the National Commission on AIDS, Mary Ann Baily stated that although her research had indicated only "scattered" attempts by providers to exclude AIDS-related conditions,

> Employers and insurers are... only just beginning to react. Most have had only limited claim experience. Their responses to surveys indicate that if and when they find that HIV-related care is a significant factor in health costs, they are likely to take action by restructuring benefits, increasing cost-sharing, and so on.

Baily Testimony, *supra* note 7. Bailey believes that restrictions on HIV coverage will be part of an overall attempt by insurers to reduce their costs. Telephone Interview with Mary Ann Baily (Aug. 20, 1990).

11. A system that relies largely on employers to provide health insurance coverage should not allow such a situation to continue. It is unclear why rates should increase so dramatically for a small company with an employee suffering from a serious illness. Insurers should not be permitted to force a small employer to bear the full cost of its employees' health care needs. A commercial insurer that provides coverage to a large number of employers — small or otherwise — should be required to spread that cost among other insureds. There has been some progress in this regard. Certain groups have begun to investigate the possibility of pooling small businesses together for the purposes of sharing the risk of health care. These efforts should be encouraged so that small employers, and their employees, are not forced to shoulder an inordinate share of the health care bill.

12. The treatment costs of AIDS are not as high as the costs for treatment of some cancers and other diseases. *More Workplaces Dealing with AIDS Cases, New Treatments Increase*, Bureau of Nat'l Affairs Daily Labor Rep. (Mar. 7, 1990).

13. *Company Halting Health Plan On Some "Life Style" Illnesses*, N.Y. Times, Aug. 6, 1988, at A-1.

14. *Id.*

15. Doe v. Beaverton Nissan, No. ST-EM-HP-870108-1353 (Or. Bur. Labor & Indus. 1986).

16. R. Cohen & L. Wiseberg, *Double Jeopardy — Threat to Life and Human Rights: Discrimination Against Persons with AIDS*, Human Rights Internet, Mar. 1990, at 39 [hereinafter Cohen & Wiseberg].

17. J. Hamilton & S. Garland, *Insurers Pass the Buck on AIDS Patients*, Business Week, Mar. 28, 1988, at 27 [hereinafter Hamilton & Garland]; Personal Conversation with Peter Groom, Esq., California Insurance Department Legal Department.

18. Telephone Interview with the Corporate Benefits Administrator of Gottschalk Industries.

19. Memorandum to "All Group Policyholders" of G.I.C. Insurance Company (July 15, 1987).

20. *Id.* G.I.C. was subsequently fined $7,000 by the State Insurance Commissioner for attempting to impose such an exclusion. Letter from A.W. Pogue, Commissioner of Texas State Board of Insurance, to Mark Jackson (Apr. 19, 1990). The company is currently in receivership.

21. *Wisconsin Office Admits Giving Legally Questionable AIDS Exclusions,* The Associated Press, Nov. 22, 1987. The Associated Press quoted officials at the Insurance Department as stating that the department had been assured by the companies that the exclusions would not be exercised. *Id.*

22. Telephone Interview with Representative of the Wisconsin Insurance Department.

23. Letter from Susan Gallinger, Director of Insurance for the State of Arizona, to Mark Jackson (Apr. 24, 1990).

24. Memorandum of the Regis Corporation (May 27, 1987).

25. Hamilton & Garland, *supra* note 17, at 27. Blue Cross of California, at the insistence of an employer, requested permission to exclude coverage of treatment for AIDS and other sexually transmitted diseases. The California Insurance Commissioner denied the request. Baily, *supra* note 1, at 58-59.

26. Letter from Thomas D. Terfinko, Administrative Assistant, Florida Department of Insurance, to Mark Jackson (Apr. 11, 1990).

27. Baily, *supra* note 1, at 54. Reserve is no longer selling insurance policies. Telephone Interview with Representative of Reserve Life Insurance Company.

28. Cohen & Wiseberg, *supra* note 16, at 39.

29. Telephone Interview with Representative of Preston Trucking.

30. McGann v. H & H Music Company, 742 F. Supp. 392 (S.D. Tex. 1990) (See *infra*, p.198, for a discussion of this decision.), *aff'd,* 946 F.2d 401 (5th Cir. 1991).

31. Beavers v. Storehouse, Inc., 18 Pens. Rep. (BNA) 1427, 60 U.S.L.W. 2140 (Aug. 27, 1991) (D. Ga. 1991).

32. *A Case of AIDS Insurance Discrimination in Boca Raton,* The Weekly News, Dec. 16, 1987, at 3.

33. Telephone Conversation with Jill Hansen, Esq., Plaintiff's Counsel (Mar. 30, 1990). Subsequently, the company announced that it would discontinue its prescription benefits that allowed employees to fill any prescription for five dollars. After the plaintiff registered complaints, the company discontinued that restriction as well. *AIDS Patient Says He's Victimized by Employer Changing Health Plans,* Sun Sentinel, Mar. 20, 1989, at B-1; *AIDS Patient Almost Pays Price of Bureaucracy,* South Florida News, Apr. 3, 1989, at 5-A.

34. Central Parking System Group Benefit and Summary Plan Description, (Mar. 1, 1986, as amended Apr. 1, 1988).

35. *The No-Fault Health Policy; Insurers Turn Up the Heat,* Village Voice, Jan. 9, 1990, at 15.

36. M. Bradford, *Cap on AIDS Claims Dropped; Firm Revises Benefit Policy,* Crains, Feb. 19, 1990, at 2.

37. Telephone Interview with Larry Gill, Kansas Department of Insurance.

38. Hamilton & Garland, *supra* note 17, at 27.

39. Telephone Interview with Representative of Provident.

40. D. Barr, Letter to the Editor, N.Y. Times, Mar. 20, 1989, at A-18 [hereinafter Barr].

41. Telephone Interview with Ben Schenker, Representative of Allied Benefit Systems.

42. Internal ITI Memorandum (Sept. 21, 1989).

43. Telephone Interview with John Davidson, Director of Consumer Services, West Virginia Insurance Department. Davidson explained that although such amendments would be illegal under West Virginia law, these trusts claim to have ERISA exemptions.

44. *See* S. Henry, *Redlining People With AIDS*, 253 Nation 582 (1991). According to the article, the company "would neither confirm nor deny this policy."

45. *See id.* at 583, *reporting on*, Westhoven v. Lincoln Foodservice Products, Inc. No. EMha 89030350 (Ind. Civ. Rights Comm'n Dec. 3, 1990).

46. *AIDS in the Workplace*, New York Newsday, Nov. 5, 1989, at 94 [hereinafter *AIDS in the Workplace*]; Barr, *supra* note 40.

47. Cohen & Wiseberg, *supra* note 16, at 39; Baily, *supra* note 1, at 50. A representative of the HMO stated that the $3,000 cap on prescription drugs was not AIDS-specific but was initiated in response to the rising costs of all drugs. Telephone Interview with Representative of The George Washington University HMO.

48. Tonery, *supra* note 4, at 143.

49. *AIDS in the Workplace, supra* note 46. A representative of the company reported that PCS will not accept business from companies that seek to exclude AIDS costs from both its Major Medical and its overall health policy. Telephone Interview with Representative of PCS. The State of New York Insurance Department, in response to an inquiry, was unable to identify any insurers doing business in New York State that maintained contracts with PCS containing such limitations. Letter from James W. Clyne, Deputy Superintendent to Honorable Manfred Orenstein, Minority Leader, New York State Senate (Feb. 21, 1989).

50. Boodman, *Insurers Balk at 'Experimental' Drugs*, Washington Post, Mar. 28, 1989, at 17.

51. *Id.*

52. *Id.*

53. *See* M. Scherzer, *Insurance, in* AIDS and the Law 185, 190 (Harlon L. Dalton et al. eds., 1987) [hereinafter Scherzer].

54. General Ins. Co. of America v. City of Belvedere, 562 F. Supp. 88 (N.D. Cal. 1984); Bates v. State Farm Mutual Automoblie Ins. Co., 719 P.2d 171 (Wash. App. 1986). Recognizing that insurers have greater bargaining power than prospective insureds, courts only enforce caps and exclusions if they are set forth in language that is "conspicuous, plain and clear." *General Ins.*, 562 F. Supp. at 90. Provisions that purport to limit liability are construed strictly against the insurer. *Id.*

55. Couch on Insurance (1984) [hereinafter Couch]. Of course, society has already chosen to intervene in insurance contracts to protect the interests of consumers. Insurance companies are heavily regulated by states through state statute and insurance department regulation. As set forth in greater detail later in the text, states have the authority, among other things, to determine what entities may sell insurance in its state; to set the amount of assets such a company must maintain to cover claims; to approve the form and content of its policies; and to require that certain provisions be included within a given policy.

56. Although an insurer's discriminatory treatment of HIV-related illnesses would appear to be a clear violation of the principle of equal protection

(pursuant to the U.S. Constitution and most state constitutions), such a claim would have little chance of succeeding against an insurance company. Constitutional protections exist only as against the government. Therefore, a basic element of an equal protection claim is that the state must have enough connection with the allegedly discriminatory act as to constitute "state action." Jackson v. Metropolitan Edison Co., 419 U.S. 345 (1974); Moose Lodge No. 107 v. Irvis, 407 U.S. 163 (1972). Most courts have ruled that acts of insurance companies do not constitute "state action" even though states closely regulate the insurance industry, and in most cases they approve insurance forms that contain the allegedly discriminatory provision. Broderick v. Associated Hosp. Serv. of Philadelphia, 536 F.2d 1 (3d Cir. 1976) (statutory requirement that state approve Blue Cross and Blue Shield contracts and rates insufficient to constitute "state action" under federal and state discrimination statutes); Jackson v. Associate Hosp. Serv. of Philadelphia, 414 F. Supp. 315 (E.D. Pa. 1976) (fact that state-regulated Blue Cross and Blue Shield did not make policy of providing less extensive coverage of maternity leave, as compared with other disabilities, "state action"); Schreiner v. McKenzie Tank Lines & Risk Management Serv., Inc., 408 So.2d 712 (Fla. App. 1982) (Florida's equal protection clause contains a state action requirement that is not met simply by virtue of the state's regulation of insurance companies.)

57. Some insurers have attempted to justify HIV-related caps and exclusions on the ground that HIV is "self-inflicted," because a person who contracts HIV has purposely engaged in an activity that may transmit the virus. This rationale is a transparent attempt to hide an obvious prejudice. After all, insurers, as a matter of course, cover people who engage in voluntary activities that could potentially cause an illness (such as smoking or overeating).

58. 42 U.S.C. § 2000e-2(a)(1) (1988).

59. *Id.*

60. Wards Cove Packing Co. v. Atonio, 490 U.S. 642 (1989); General Electric Co. v. Gilbert, 429 U.S. 125, 136-37 (1976); Griggs v. Duke Power Co., 401 U.S. 424, 431 (1971).

61. A plaintiff would need to argue disparate impact rather than disparate treatment because HIV-related exclusions are facially neutral as to gender or race — expressing exclusion by way of disease.

62. The plaintiff in the Beaverton Nissan case, *supra* note 15, successfully used this theory in his complaint before the Civil Rights Division.

63. *Wards Cove*, 490 U.S. at 658.

64. 429 U.S. 125 (1976).

65. *Id.* at 134. Congress ultimately overcame the *Gilbert* ruling by enacting section 1 of the Pregnancy Discrimination Act of 1978, 42 U.S.C. § 2000(e)(k) (1988), which provides that discrimination on the basis of sex includes discrimination on the basis of pregnancy and related medical conditions.

66. 417 U.S. 484 (1974).

67. *Id.* at 135; *see also Wards Cove*, 490 U.S. at 657 (statistics showing a high percentage of non-white workers in low-skilled cannery jobs and a low percentage of non-white workers in the skilled non-cannery positions were insufficient to make out a disparate impact claim; plaintiff must also demonstrate that the "application of a specific or particular employment practice...created the disparate impact under attack").

68. 417 U.S. at 497.

69. 429 U.S. at 125.
70. *Id.* at 136.
71. For a discussion of the ADA's legislative history, see chapter 9 ("Workplace Issues: HIV and Discrimination").
72. Section 102 (b) (4).
73. For a further discussion of this issue, see chapter 9 ("Workplace Issues: HIV and Discrimination").
74. Chalk v. United States Dist. Court Central Dist. Colo., 840 F.2d 701 (9th Cir. 1988); Glover v. Eastern Neb. Community Office of Retardation, 867 F.2d 461 (8th Cir. 1989), *cert. den.* 110 S. Ct. 321 (1989).
75. *See, e.g.,* 40 Pa. Cons. Stat. § 1171.5; Mich. Comp. Laws §§ 500.2002 *et seq.;* Tex. Rev. Civ. Stat. Ann. art. 21.21.
76. Letter from Vance Magnuson, Life, Health, Accident Forms and Rate Analyst, North Dakota Insurance Department (undated).
77. It should be noted that in the majority of states, these unfair trade practices provisions do not establish a private right of action. J. Appleman, Insurance Law and Practice, (West 1981 & Supp.); *see also* Bell v. League Life Ins. Co., 387 N.W.2d 154 (Mich. App. 1986). This means that a person who believes that he or she is the victim of HIV-related discrimination must bring a complaint to the state's insurance commissioner, who has the responsibility of investigating the claim and, if there is merit, of taking action against the insurer.
78. Conn. Gen. Stat. § 46a-51(15); *see also* Mass. Gen. Laws ch. 175, § 193 T; N.J. Rev. Stat. § 10:5-5q; N.Y. Exec. Law § 292(21). For a more comprehensive description of state antidiscrimination statutes, see ACLU AIDS Project, Epidemic of Fear, Appendix A (1990).
79. *Westhoven,* No. EMha89030350. The employer has appealed that ruling in state court. *See* Henry, *supra* note 44, at 583.
80. *But see* Bernard B. v. Blue Cross & Blue Shield of Greater New York, 528 F. Supp. 125 (S.D.N.Y. 1981). In *Bernard B.,* plaintiffs brought an action against Blue Cross/Blue Shield (BCBS), the Superintendent of the State of New York Insurance Department, and the New York City Health and Hospitals Corporation (NYCHHC) alleging that BCBS's exclusion from insurance coverage of psychiatric inpatient care in NYCHHC hospitals violated, *inter alia,* section 504 of the Rehabilitation Act of 1973 and the equal protection clause of the Fourteenth Amendment. Plaintiff claimed that the failure of BCBS to cover such care constituted discrimination solely because of handicap. *Id.*

The court's opinion dismissing plaintiff's claims demonstrated the difficulty of alleging discrimination based on handicap against insurers. The court wrote:

> It is one thing to argue that a disabled person is protected against discrimination solely because of his disability with regard to employment, education, or other activities covered by the Rehabilitation Act. It is quite another thing to say, in the context of medical insurance, that all forms of medical care must be covered because any exclusion is a discrimination based upon disability.

Id. at 133 n.9.

Although *Bernard B.* appears to support the right of an insurer to exclude a *condition* from coverage (mental illness), rather than a generic treatment, it is unclear whether cases related to mental illness, which is unlike most other illnesses, would control cases related to physical illnesses. It would be more difficult for a court to uphold a limitation on a particular physical illness when the company fully covers a very similar physical illness.

81. Insurers' Action Council Inc. v. Markman, 490 F. Supp. 921 (D. Minn. 1980); American Family Life Assurance Co. v. Commissioner of Ins., 446 N.E.2d 1061 (Mass. 1983); Blue Cross of Va. v. Virginia, 269 S.E.2d 827 (Va. 1980).

82. Couch, *supra* note 55, §§ 21:1 *et seq.*

83. 471 U.S. 724 (1985).

84. *Id.* at 730 n.10; *see also Markman,* 490 F. Supp. at 921 (upholding Minnesota statute requiring insurers to offer certain basic levels of coverage, including major medical); *Blue Cross of Va.,* 269 S.E.2d at 827 (affirming state corporation commissioner's order requiring insurers to include in their prepaid medical and surgical plans services rendered by optometrists, opticians, and psychologists); Metropolitan Life Ins. Co. v. Whaland, 410 A.D.2d 635 (N.Y. App. Div. 1979) (upholding state statute requiring that group insurance contracts provide that expenses for treatment of mental disorders be reimbursed on a level at least as favorable as physical ailments); Blue Cross & Blue Shield of Kansas City v. Bell, 596 F. Supp. 1053 (D. Kan. 1984) (upholding state statute requiring Blue Cross and Blue Shield to cover services performed by optometrists, dentists, or podiatrists).

85. *Markman,* 490 F. Supp. at 924, 930; *Bell,* 596 F. Supp. at 1059. In Health Ins. Ass'n of America v. Harnett, 405 N.Y.S.2d 634 (1978), the New York Court of Appeals affirmed a statute requiring insurers to provide maternity care coverage in all health insurance policies. The court rejected the claim by the plaintiff, a trade association of insurance carriers, that the requirement violated its members' due process rights. The court based its ruling on its view that there was "some fair, just and reasonable connection between [the statute] and the promotion of the health, comfort, safety and welfare of society." *Id.* at 639.

There are, of course, limits on a state's power to regulate insurers. For example, a state cannot impair the existing contract rights between an insurer and an insured. In *Harnett,* for example, the New York Court of Appeals, while upholding a state statute mandating insurers to provide maternity care coverage in its health insurance policies, ruled that the application of the statute to existing policies would constitute an impairment of the obligation of contract. 405 N.Y.S.2d at 641; *see also Markman,* 490 F. Supp. at 921 (distinguishing the statute in that case from the statute in *Harnett* on the basis that the subject statute did not apply retroactively); *Bell,* 596 F. Supp. 1053 (upholding statute requiring that insurers reimburse services performed by optometrists, dentists, and podiatrists to all persons who reside or are employed in Kansas on the basis that the impairment was inconsequential).

86. The information contained in this section was gleaned from responses to a survey conducted by the ACLU AIDS Project. The survey was sent to each of the fifty state insurance commissioners. Additional information was acquired from responses to a second survey conducted by the Office of the President Pro Tempore California State Senate. The authors are grateful to the President Pro Tempore's office for providing them with the responses to its survey.

87. Ariz. AIDS Guidelines R4-14-802; Colo. S.B. 167 (1989); D.C. Code 35-223 (1987); Fla. Stat. Ann. § 627.411; Ga. Ins. Dept. Rule 120-2-43-05; Ind. Ins. Dept. Rule 39, 1-139-7; Kan. H.B. 425 § 54; Me. Pub. L. ch. (1989); Mo. Code Regs, tit. 4 CSR § 190-1411452(A); Ohio Rev. Code Ann. § 3901.45; Or. Admin. R. 836-50-210; Tex. H.B. 2608 § 11; Utah Proposed Rule R 540-132; Va. Ins. Reg.

34, § 7. According to Baily, the following additional states prohibit such exclusions: New York, California, Pennsylvania, Maryland, Michigan, Minnesota, Tennessee, Delaware, and South Dakota. Baily, *supra* note 1.

88. The AIDS Guidelines of the State of Arizona Department of Insurance provide:

> Insurers shall not issue for delivery in Arizona any contracts which exclude AIDS or AIDS related conditions from coverage. Benefits for AIDS or AIDS related conditions shall be provided for in the same manner as are provided for all other diseases.

89. State of Colorado Division of Insurance Regulation No. 87-2 § L reads:

> Policies or certificates which exclude or limit coverage for expenses related to the treatment of AIDS and HIV resulting from AIDS, will not be approved for use in Colorado except to the extent that such exclusions or limitations are consistent with the exclusions or limitations applicable to other illnesses or conditions covered by the policy or certificate.

90. The insurance departments of Maryland, North Dakota, and Washington take the position that the imposition of caps and exclusions on AIDS-related treatments would violate their nondiscrimination regulations. Letter from Vance Magnuson, Life, Health and Accident Forms and Rate Analyst (Apr. 30, 1990).

Other states permit insurance companies to exclude or limit only the coverage for treatments specifically delineated in their regulations. Since the listed treatments do not include those for HIV disease, the companies cannot impose discriminatory caps and exclusions on HIV-related care. Letter from Jim Long, Commissioner of Insurance of North Carolina (Apr. 11, 1990); Telephone Interview with Sue Sullivan, Assistant Commissioner, Oklahoma Insurance Department.

91. California, Connecticut, Iowa, Massachusetts, Michigan, Minnesota, Nevada, New Hampshire, South Dakota, and Tennessee.

92. Baily, *supra* note 1, at 13.

93. *McGann*, 742 F. Supp. 392, *aff'd*, 946 F.2d 401 (5th Cir. 1991); *Beavers*, 18 Pen. Rep. (BNA) 1427, 60 U.S.L.W. 2140. The Health Insurance Association of America has suggested that 51 percent of the firms that converted to self-insurance between 1981 and 1984 did so to avoid state regulations mandating certain benefits. H.I.A.A., Research Bulletin: "The Rise of State Mandated Benefits," 2 (H.I.A.A. 1989).

94. Shaw v. Delta Airlines, Inc., 463 U.S. 85 (1983).

95. It is important to note, however, that although self-insured plans are largely exempt from state regulation, employee benefit plans that *purchase* group policies for their members are not so exempt. *Metropolitan Life*, 471 U.S. at 724 (ruling that a state statute requiring insurers to cover certain mental health care benefits in general health insurance policies was not preempted by ERISA insofar as it determined the content of the group policies certain employee benefit plans purchase). Similarly, in Wadsworth v. Whaland, 562 F.2d 70 (1st Cir. 1977), administrators of various health and welfare funds challenged a New Hampshire law that required "issuers" of group health insurance policies to provide coverage for the treatment of mental illnesses and emotional disorders. *Id*. at 72. The First Circuit ruled that although ERISA precluded the

state from "deeming" the funds to be "insurance companies," and thus subject to the statute, ERISA did not preclude the state from indirectly regulating the funds by determining the content of the group plans purchased by the funds. *Id.* at 78.

96. *McGann*, 742 F. Supp. 392. As this book went to press, the *McGann* decision was affirmed by the Fifth Circuit, 946 F.2d 401 (5th Cir. 1991).

97. *Id.*

98. No. 89-B-597, 16 Pens. Rep. (BNA) 766 (C.D. Colo. April 18, 1989).

99. *Id.*

100. No. H89-1594, slip. op. (S.D. Tex. June 30, 1989).

101. *Id.*

102. B. Schatz, *The AIDS Insurance Crisis: Underwriting or Overreaching?*, 100 Harv. L. Rev. 1782, 1787 (1987); Scherzer, *supra* note 53, at 197. Ray Merrick of the Texas Insurance Department stated that his department has identified "two or three" companies that had attempted to deny coverage to individuals in certain zip codes. The companies discontinued the practice after intervention by the department. Interview with Ray Merrick.

103. M. Freudenheim, *Health Insurers, to Reduce Losses, Blacklist Dozens of Occupations*, N.Y. Times, Feb. 5, 1990, at A-1.

104. Baily, *supra* note 1, at 139.

105. AIDS Litig. Rep. (Andrews Pub.) 1801 (Nov. 29, 1988).

106. *AIDS Case Lawyer Sues over Insurance Denial*, Washington Post, Mar. 2, 1988, at B5.

107. Letter from A.W. Pogue, Commissioner of Texas State Board of Insurance (Apr. 19, 1990).

108. Bonfield, *'High Risk' Businesses Face Hunt For Insurance*, Cincinnati Business Courier, Nov. 13, 1989, at 1.

109. *Insurers Avoid Arts Groups as AIDS Risks*, United Press Int'l (UPI), Oct. 29, 1989.

110. *Id.*

111. Lambert, *AIDS Insurance Coverage Is Increasingly Hard to Get*, N.Y. Times, Aug. 7, 1989, at A-1. *See also* T. Jacoby, *Who Will Pay the AIDS Bill?*, Newsweek, Apr. 11, 1988, at 71.

112. *AIDS in the Workplace, supra* note 46.

113. Baily, *supra* note 1, at 51.

114. Faden & Kass (1988). Baily reports that eight states have formally adopted the model guidelines of the National Association of Insurance Commissioners, which prohibits such discrimination. Six states have enacted their own versions of those prohibitions. Baily, *supra* note 1, at 19. Texas has a prohibition against using factors related to sexual orientation to determine who will be required or requested to take an HIV test.

115. Arizona, Colorado, District of Columbia, Florida, Georgia, Indiana, Iowa, Maryland, Massachusetts, Missouri, Ohio, Oregon, South Dakota, Vermont, Virginia, and Wisconsin.

116. Scherzer has noted that the large number of material misrepresentation cases involving AIDS-related claims may demonstrate that the insurance industry "is overly suspicious about AIDS claims or is trying to send the public a message about AIDS." Scherzer, *supra* note 53, at 198-99. *See also* Baily, *supra* note 1, at 58.

117. Vail v. Texas Farm Bureau Mutual Ins. Co., 754 S.W.2d 129 (Tex. 1988) (affirming trial court's award to insured under Deceptive Trade Practices Act

based on insured's failure to pay under policy). Section 1171.5 of Pennsylvania Statutes Annotated defines the following as unfair business practices:

(i) Misrepresenting pertinent facts of policy or contract provisions relating to coverage at issue.

(ii) Failing to acknowledge and act promptly upon written or oral communication with respect to claims arising under insurance policies.

(iii) Failing to adopt and implement reasonable standards for the prompt investigation of claims arising under insurance policies.

(iv) Refusing to pay claims without conducting a reasonable investigation based upon all available information.

(v) Failing to affirm or deny coverage of claims within a reasonable time after proof of loss statements have been completed....

118. California S.B. 1328 (1989).
119. Casey, *supra* note 4, at 35. Other states, including Wyoming, require a showing that "symptoms exist[ed] prior to the issuance of a policy that would cause an ordinarily prudent person to seek medical advice. *Id*.
120. Va. Ins. Reg. 34, § 6.
121. For a discussion of the elements of proof for such a claim, see Scherzer, *supra* note 53, at 5-5 to 5-8.

6

WEALTH = HEALTH: THE PUBLIC FINANCING OF AIDS CARE

By Daniel Shacknai

I. Introduction

People with HIV disease rely far more on the public health care financing system, composed mainly of Medicaid and Medicare, than individuals with other illnesses. Researchers estimate that 25 percent of AIDS costs are funded through Medicaid — more than double the estimated 11 percent share of health care costs Medicaid expends generally.[1]

Trends indicate that the American public health care system will be called on to provide an even greater share of HIV care in the 1990s.[2] A growing proportion of HIV-infected people will be poor, uninsured, or underinsured. Although recently enacted legislation may improve some people's ability to retain private coverage,[3] and certain states have increased their regulation of private insurers,[4] the same basic set of impoverishing circumstances still surrounds those affected by HIV. HIV-related medical care remains expensive.[5] Many HIV-infected individuals continue to lack private insurance coverage.[6] And the virus, while increasingly treatable, remains highly debilitating over time, forcing many infected people to quit their jobs and turn to marginal government benefits for their income. Those benefits, comprised of Supplemental Security Income (SSI) and Social Security Disability Income (SSDI), are insufficient to enable a recipient to pay for his or her medical expenses.[7]

Medicaid (and to a lesser extent Medicare), general assistance, and other state and federal programs will be forced to assume the medical costs of an increasingly indigent HIV-infected population. The public policy tug-of-war pitting coverage against cost will intensify during the 1990s. How that battle is played out will have a tremendous impact on low-income HIV-infected patients, as well as those with other illnesses.

It is becoming increasingly clear that HIV disease shares many characteristics with other illnesses. In terms of Medicaid's approach to people with HIV, the system appears, at least superficially, to function as it does for any other group: financial eligibility and disability requirements are not HIV-specific nor are the reimbursement rates that are paid to doctors and hospitals. Likewise, the cost of treating HIV illness is not radically different from the cost of treating other serious conditions, such as heart disease and cancer. Federal spending on HIV, which partially supports the Medicaid program and fully funds the Medicare program, now accounts for only 1 percent of the amount the government spends on health care annually.[8]

While HIV has certain features common to other serious medical conditions, it is very different from those conditions in many important respects. Its uniqueness presents some special challenges to the public health care system. HIV is a complex virus that leads to a course of illness varying widely from patient to patient. Thus, HIV disease requires a flexible continuum of care to match the highly variable nature of the illness. The public health care system does not even approach this desired level of care. Like most bureaucracies, Medicaid and Medicare do not function with a great deal of flexibility and have not adapted well to the special problems associated with HIV.

Even when people with HIV have succeeded in gaining access to treatment through Medicaid, they have accessed only the lower level of our nation's "two-tiered" health care system. Persons relying on Medicaid continue to "lag behind the privately insured on a number of important dimensions of [health care] access."[9] In even worse straits, of course, are persons without private insurance, who are not Medicaid-eligible; they may well obtain no outpatient care at all.

This chapter will examine the American public health care financing system through the lens of HIV. It demonstrates how eligibility, coverage, and procedural obstacles which affect all Medicaid recipients often have a particularly harsh impact on persons with HIV disease. Its analysis is based in part on a survey of staff members at AIDS service organizations in ten states, who reported, from the front lines and from the perspective of people with HIV disease, how the ramifications of the overall system impede access to health care. These problems occur in a context in which sweeping changes in our national health care provision system, although necessary, do not appear to be imminent. Thus, it is important to consider policy options that will improve the present system, and thereby improve the lives of thousands of people.

II. Barriers to Health Care for Persons with HIV Disease

People with HIV disease do not choose the public health care system for medical treatment — the system chooses them. The system is intended to function as a last resort or medical "safety net."[10] It is composed mainly of two relatively independent programs — Medicaid, which is funded jointly by the federal and local governments and which is designed to provide care for poor persons, and Medicare, which is funded wholly by the federal government and which is designed to provide care for the disabled or elderly. The two programs are often confused by the public, but in addition to several important distinctions separating them, there is a tremendous disparity in the amount each contributes to the nation's HIV-related costs. Recent projections indicate that by 1992 Medicaid will pay 26 percent of the total national AIDS bill as compared with 2.5 percent to be paid by Medicare.[11]

The public burden of paying for HIV care thus falls largely to Medicaid. But for various reasons, among them its eligibility requirements, coverage limitations, and procedural hassles, this crucial program often fails to provide comprehensive access to health care for people with HIV disease. Further, because Medicaid tends to reimburse hospitals and physicians at grossly inadequate levels, providers are discouraged from caring for the ill poor — and particularly, from caring for the HIV-infected poor.

A. Eligibility

1. Description of the Systems

There are two related sets of requirements, "financial" and "categorical," that people with HIV disease must meet to be eligible for Medicaid in most states. This means that individuals and families must prove that they are part of one or more covered categories of persons, and that they are sufficiently poor.

In most states, Medicaid's financial guidelines include both income and assets and are linked to limits set by the SSI program. The 1990 monthly income limit for SSI (that is to say, if you make more, you do not qualify) is $386, although in some states the amount is higher; assets of $2,000 are allowed, exclusive of a car and the home in which one lives. In some states, persons whose assets are in excess of this limit can "spend down" to the ordinary Medicaid limit by incurring certain medical expenses; one can also spend down monthly income to the Medicaid limit in these states.[12]

In order to meet Medicaid's categorical requirements, one must be a member of a family receiving Aid to Families with Dependent Children (AFDC), a blind or disabled person (as determined by the Social Security Administration (SSA), a pregnant woman, a child under the age of 7, or an adult over 65. Some states also deem people between the ages of 7 and 21 categorically eligible for Medicaid. Although in most states automatic Medicaid eligibility is extended to those on SSI, more than ten states have Medicaid requirements even *stricter* than the SSI rules.[13]

Medicare, at least for those under 65, requires an on-the-books work history sufficient to establish Social Security Disability Insurance (SSDI) payments. Even then, the disabled person must receive SSDI checks for two years before becoming eligible for Medicare. This twenty-nine-month gap (which includes a five-month determination period — from the time of disability to the time one becomes eligible for Medicare) has meant that people with full-blown AIDS often do not live long enough after they are classified as totally disabled to take advantage of the program. Several commentators have recommended that Congress "federalize" the cost of AIDS care by eliminating this two-year waiting period, as it has done for end-stage renal disease. The cost of such reform is the major obstacle to its adoption.[14]

2. Effects of Eligibility on People with HIV and AIDS

These categorical and financial eligibility requirements significantly limit health care access for people with HIV disease. The harshest impact falls on three groups: those not yet diagnosed with full-blown AIDS, women, and people without access to health care.

Categorical guidelines provide that a person with a documented diagnosis of AIDS is automatically considered "disabled" by SSI, and therefore eligible for Medicaid, provided that the person has met the financial guidelines. However, seropositive persons with mild or no symptoms, and persons who have more serious symptoms but are still largely ambulatory, have great difficulty qualifying for Medicaid. Even though seropositive persons with non-AIDS-defining symptoms may at times be sicker than those diagnosed with AIDS, their disability claims are analyzed by the SSA on a highly subjective case-by-case basis. The situation is compounded by the fact that the agencies that make disability determinations function differently in each state.

An unfortunate consequence of this system is that people without an AIDS diagnosis must engage in the humiliating and time-consuming practice of proving on paper that they are disabled. Advocates in several states report that applicants are forced to paint as pathetic a picture of their daily lives as possible in order to be designated "disabled."[15] These efforts are critical, since Medicaid coverage hinges on this disability determination and otherwise eligible patients who do not demonstrate total disability to SSA are effectively denied medical care.

SSA's utilization of an AIDS diagnosis for automatic SSI eligibility also harms those who have the most difficulty getting such a diagnosis — women and those without access to health care.[16] As is more fully discussed in chapter 1 ("Complications of Gender"), women are often not diagnosed with AIDS because the definition of what constitutes AIDS does not adequately include the manifestations of HIV disease in women. The definition was developed through surveillance of the disease in men, particularly in gay men, and has not yet been officially updated to reflect the different course of the virus in other populations.

Moreover, all persons who do not have adequate health care may have difficulty obtaining an official AIDS diagnosis. This is because the diagnosis of opportunistic infections often requires expensive testing which may not be routinely undertaken in public hospitals. If, for example, *Pneumocystis carinii* pneumonia (PCP) is not properly diagnosed, an individual may not be able to get an AIDS diagnosis. What's worse, in some instances there are incentives for hospitals not to render an official AIDS diagnosis. In New York City, for example, a homeless person with AIDS cannot be discharged from a city hospital to a homeless shelter; he or she must be kept in the hospital until adequate housing can be found. However, an HIV-infected individual without an AIDS diagnosis can be discharged. In addition, the hospital may be wary of administering expensive tests where the liklihood of timely payment appears doubtful. Given the overcrowding in the city's hospitals, a hospital may be particularly inclined not to make the AIDS diagnosis.

Advocates in various states report several additional complications with Medicaid's categorical eligibility requirements: first, SSA disability determinations take much longer for those without bona fide AIDS diagnoses. This means that a person with symptomatic HIV disease must go through an extended waiting period — even if he or she will ultimately qualify for the program. Second, some SSA offices make "presumptive" decisions which allow applicants SSI benefits (and therefore Medicaid) while the agency makes its final determination. This presumptive determination process, however, is conducted in a manner that appears to advocates and applicants to be inconsistent, if not random. Third, although doctors are increasingly diagnosing AIDS without employing the invasive confirmatory tests that are no longer considered essential for an AIDS diagnosis (such as the bronchoscopy for PCP), a physician's diagnosis of AIDS without such tests may be rejected (or questioned at length) by SSA. An applicant may have a highly debilitating CDC-defined opportunistic infection and yet not be considered disabled by SSA. Fourth, in combination with financial requirements, categorical guidelines create a situation in which a person with AIDS who is experiencing a period of good health cannot work without losing Medicaid coverage, even when that person is permitted to work under an SSA "trial work period."[17]

The increasing use of early intervention through prophylactic drug therapy for treating asymptomatic persons with HIV has raised another important issue. Because asymptomatic people may not qualify as "disabled" under Medicaid, they are effectively denied access to drugs that may prolong their lives.[18] Recently proposed legislation would allow states the option of extending Medicaid coverage to asymptomatic seropositive persons for purposes of receiving preventive drug therapies and limited outpatient care.[19] The principal debate over this reform centers on its cost. Although early use of AZT and pentamidine has been shown to postpone hospitalization and acute care by delaying the onset of severe AIDS-related symptoms, the resulting savings have not yet been fully documented. Whether the absence of clear economic proof that early intervention saves money would delay a state's eventual acceptance of this option is unknown.

The inequities in the categorical eligibility requirements have led certain commentators to recommend abolishing them entirely. Medicaid eligibility would then depend solely on one's financial situation, permitting people who are uninsured and poor to qualify for Medicaid before becoming totally disabled.[20] Obviously, because this plan would add vast numbers of people to the Medicaid rolls, it would be very expensive to implement.

For persons with HIV disease, financial requirements make Medicaid coverage hard to qualify for but easy to lose. Although several states have Medicaid programs that allow income somewhere above the SSI guidelines, none permits monthly income above the federal poverty line.[21] Disabled people with assets, but without private insurance, are thus forced to spend almost all of their savings before being "insured" by Medicaid. Many states allow persons to "spend down" excess income and assets by incurring (and sometimes paying for) medical expenditures: if a person can show that he has incurred medical costs in an amount that, if paid, would make him financially eligible for Medicaid, he would qualify. Thirteen states, however, have no spend-down provision at all. Advocates from Texas and Colorado, two states that do not have spend-down programs, report that people with HIV disease with "too much" money have no alternative but to pay health care expenses out-of-pocket until they become poor enough to qualify for Medicaid. People with monthly incomes above the SSI limit (including those on SSD) who do not reside near a public hospital may have no access to health care whatsoever.

Once a person obtains Medicaid coverage, she must battle to maintain it. Many people with HIV disease who become too ill to work apply for both SSI and SSDI. If they meet the stringent financial and categorical eligibility requirements, they will receive SSI and Medicaid (in most states) automatically.[22] Medicaid may become the secondary insurer or a payor of continuation premiums for people who leave the workplace *with* private insurance coverage.[23] However, many people leave work uninsured or quickly lose their private coverage by failing to pay premiums during a period of illness. For these people, Medicaid coverage acquired through SSI is vital because it is the only remaining means of paying for health care services. Ironically, when SSD payments supplant SSI benefits five months after the submission of an application, the amount of the new checks often negatively affects Medicaid coverage. The average SSD benefit of $550 per month (in 1989) is well above the Medicaid/SSI income limit. In thirty-seven states, receiving the average SSD benefit requires that the Medicaid spend-down amount be increased; in thirteen states this means that a person's coverage will be terminated.

A second difficulty is caused by the unpredictability of HIV illness. A person diagnosed with AIDS may experience several bouts of acute illness alongside periods of relatively good health. Thus, a person who is deemed disabled by the SSA at the time he or she applies may at a later point become healthy enough to work. For many people with HIV, work can play a very positive role: it can reduce a person's stress as well as limit his or her dependence on the welfare system and other support persons. The SSDI program has implemented a "trial work period" which allows those receiving disability payments to continue receiving monthly benefits while working for a period of nine months. This program was designed to give individuals an opportunity to assess the possibility of their returning to work permanently. Unfortunately, people with HIV who wish to take advantage of this program risk losing their Medicaid eligibility, or simply end up spending down the entire amount of their pay check. This burden is similarly harmful to other persons with disabling conditions that can go into periodic remission. Medicaid thus *discourages* employment, ensuring that those impoverished by its financial and categorical eligibility requirements stay poor.

In addition, people with HIV must frequently "recertify" that they are still financially eligible. Although this requirement is in no way limited to HIV-infected persons, securing the necessary paperwork (while complying with requests for "face-to-face" appointments) may at times be too physically taxing on people with HIV. This is particularly true for those without friends, family, and other advocates.

If a person with AIDS survives the twenty-nine-month waiting period, Medicare presents no additional eligibility obstacles. Mercifully, Medicare recertifies its recipients approximately every seven years.

B. Coverage of HIV-Related Health Care Costs

1. Description of the Systems

Medicaid and Medicare function essentially as charge plans for those eligible. Medicare, although largely irrelevant to people with HIV, provides two different plans, both of which require substantial copayments for many services. Medicare "Part A" (hospital insurance) covers inpatient hospital care, skilled nursing facilities, hospice care, and visits by approved health care professionals. "Part B" coverage (medical insurance), which one may elect not to accept, carries a monthly fee and covers varying degrees of physician services, outpatient hospital care, and some home health and mental health care.[24] Among the more crucial health care options *excluded* from Medicare coverage are prescription drugs and long-term care facilities.

Medicaid coverage varies according to state; while some services are mandated by federal rules, others are optional. Among the important optional services for people with HIV disease are prescription drugs (although every state has elected to cover this service), community mental health services, and personal care.[25] Many states that purport to offer these services, however, place serious restrictions on their coverage.[26] Virtually all states cover inpatient and outpatient hospital care, skilled and intermediate nursing facilities, and physician services. Other kinds of care, especially treatment in long-term care facilities, are less broadly covered. While there is no deductible or copayment for Medicaid services, spend-down programs compel recipients with excess income to pay for certain medical costs in order to retain coverage.

On the surface, the range of medical services covered by Medicaid and Medicare (both individually and together)[27] appears to be quite broad. Nevertheless, health care coverage through the public system has frequently proven inadequate for people with HIV disease.

2. Effects of Coverage Limitations on People with HIV Disease

People with HIV disease require a high degree of flexibility in accessing health care resources over time. Different kinds of treatment are neccessary at different stages of the disease. The public health care system's extremely low reimbursement rates for various health care services limit the range of treatments and services available. Because HIV patients typically need such a variety of treatments, the coverage limitations have a disparately harmful impact on people with HIV disease.

It is true that Medicaid/Medicare coverage can be fairly comprehensive for a given HIV-infected person at a given time. A person with HIV disease whose only medical needs are AZT and an occasional visit to the doctor may have these costs completely covered by Medicaid. Yet this same person at a later stage illness may face coverage conditions that severely restrict access to appropriate care.

Researchers have documented a shift away from the use of traditional acute care settings and an increase in the use of outpatient AIDS care.[28] Health care providers are increasingly prescribing long-term care, hospice care, nursing care, and home- and community-based care for their patients with HIV disease as alternatives to inpatient hospital care.[29] In addition to providing patients with quality care, these health care options cost less than traditional in-hospital care; they also offer the additional benefit of freeing up beds at often crowded public hospitals.[30]

It is therefore critical to people with HIV disease that long-term health care options are available. Yet, the public health care system is inconsistent in funding these options. Home- and community-based services, which include home health care, personal care attendants, chore aid, and other homemaker services, are covered by Medicaid in only ten states.[31] Medicaid covers hospice services in only about half the states. Advocates further report that Medicaid inadequately covers inpatient and outpatient mental health services, rehabilitative care, and detox-therapeutic communities for intravenous drug users (IVDUs) with HIV. The Watkins Commission found that people with HIV do not have access to community-based or dual treatment facilities because these care settings are not covered by Medicaid.[32] Custodial care in any setting, and intermediate nursing home care are excluded from both parts A and B of Medicare coverage.

Medicaid's low reimbursement rates present another kind of barrier to health care. As the Watkins Commission Report documented, Medicaid reimbursements are far below inpatient costs for people with HIV, contributing to the reluctance of health care providers to treat this population. While the average national inpatient cost of caring for a patient with AIDS is approximately $630 per day, the average Medicaid reimbursement rate in southern states is $282 per day and in other regions of the country about $500 per day.[33] Advocates in California report that many private hospitals have simply canceled their contracts with Medi-Cal (California Medicaid). The reimbursement shortfall is even more dramatic for long-term care facilities, which cost an estimated $200 per day but are reimbursed by Medicaid at only $50 per day.[34] Outpatient physician visits, which cost about $80, are reimbursed at $8 in New York City.[35] Some physicians who treat people with AIDS reportedly do not even bother to submit claims for Medicaid reimbursements.[36] The response of other physicians, hospitals, and long-term care facilities, however, is to attempt to exclude Medicaid patients outright. Medicaid's low reimbursement rates, coupled with the high degree of stigmatization associated with AIDS, make people with AIDS who are insured by the public system particularly vulnerable to exclusion by health care providers.[37]

Issues of coverage and reimbursement are thus intimately connected: while Medicaid may ostensibly "cover" a particular service, if it does not reimburse providers sufficiently for that service, the coverage is of no use to those who need medical care. Providers are more willing to serve Medicare patients, for whom reimbursement levels are higher.

Finally, Medicaid provides inadequate coverage for prescribed drugs. While all states cover prescription drugs, some limit the number of refills, the total quantity of each prescription, or the total cost of the drug for which it will reimburse.[38] Presently every state reimburses for AZT, yet fourteen states do not cover aerosolized pentamidine. Other drugs, including fansidar, dapsone, and ganciclovir, are restricted in many states.[39]

Moreover, low-income people continue to have trouble accessing experimental treatments. Under significant pressure to speed up development of new pharmaceuticals to treat HIV disease, the Food and Drug Administration adopted new regulations to broaden the use of investigational new drugs (treatment INDs), which were to be made available to persons with HIV disease with the understanding that there was some increased risk involved due to a lack of complete testing. Low-income persons, however, have effectively been denied drugs granted treatment IND status, because state Medicaid programs require that all covered drugs have *full* approval from the FDA.[40]

The administration of reimbursed drugs presents yet another problem for people covered by Medicaid. Some states, for example, reimburse for pentamidine, an FDA-approved drug, only in intravenous form, even though the drug has been shown to be safer and more effective when given in aerosolized form. Some commentators predict that the growing disparity among the states in Medicaid drug coverage may cause people with HIV disease to migrate to states with more liberal coverage policies.[41]

C. Procedural and Administrative Aspects of Public Health Programs

Medicare and Medicaid are two separate and distinct bureaucratic entities. The federal Medicare program has a single set of application and recertification guidelines that govern people in every state. Procedures for Medicaid, conversely, vary from state to state. Nationwide, the Medicare program is far more standardized than Medicaid, which is a means-tested benefit administered by local welfare offices, and has been described by advocates as often mismanaged and disorganized.

Further, Medicaid requires applicants to complete substantial amounts of paperwork to obtain and maintain coverage. An HIV-infected person may be too ill to complete the mounds of paperwork, assemble the extensive documents, and spend hours in a crowded office — all of which are necessary to apply for coverage.[42] Baily writes that the "consequence of this complexity must be to discourage persons from applying, especially persons who are already very sick."[43]

Once certified, a person with HIV disease may also have difficulty maintaining his or her Medicaid coverage. Without assistance from an advocate or social worker, a physically weakened person may be unable to complete the lengthy recertification forms. Although Medicaid is often delinquent in processing its forms and producing its cards, clients are required to adhere to strict deadlines.

The performance of Medicaid programs varies by state. However, the survey of advocates revealed serious problems in virtually all programs. An advocate from California reported that regardless of their health status, people with HIV in the Los Angeles area must go in person to the Medicaid office to complete certain parts of the application process. Once there, they confront long lines and workers who express fears of infection, having received little or no AIDS education. The agency accepts telephone inquiries on the status of applications only four hours per week. Advocates in Florida reported that computer and technical errors have compounded bureaucratic delays in that state. One advocate reported that obtaining and maintaining Medicaid can be "especially difficult for those lacking education, lacking English language skills, and lacking knowledge of how to work the system."

A widespread problem with Medicaid seems to be the agency's inability to disseminate the information it collects. Clients in many states have difficulty simply finding out the status of their applications or the name of the worker to whom their case has been assigned. Further, clients are often not informed about new programs that have been established to improve office efficiency. A New York advocate called that state's spend-down program "complicated and misunderstood." Procedural intricacies have reportedly caused the spend-down program in Washington, D.C., to be underutilized.

Some states have implemented programs designed to eliminate some of the procedural hurdles facing HIV-infected individuals. In New York City, a special unit at Medicaid has been assigned to handle all applications by people with HIV disease. While major problems remain, advocates report that this unit has improved communication between clients and the Medicaid office by providing a central point of information, at least for those clients who reside in the vicinity.

III. Improving The System

The foregoing review of some of the barriers facing people with HIV disease in accessing appropriate health care demonstrates that the public health care system is not sufficiently inclusive, comprehensive, or flexible. This chapter has not even addressed the very serious problems regarding the *quality* of care provided to Medicaid recipients. Stated simply, when judged by the principle that all persons should have access to treatment that encompasses the current standard of care for their medical condition, the public health care system in the United States is a failure.

The recommendations that follow address those aspects of the eligibility, coverage, and procedural problems outlined above.

A. Eligibility

- *States should extend limited Medicaid coverage to financially eligible persons with HIV who require early intervention treatment.*

Categorical requirements currently prevent states from granting Medicaid eligibility to persons who are infected with HIV but largely asymptomatic. The result is that indigent seropositive persons often go without preventive therapies and services. Asymptomatic persons infected with HIV should be provided with outpatient services, including prescribed drugs (among them, AZT and aerosolized pentamidine), physician services, lab and X-ray services, clinical services, and case management. In addition to providing crucial services to a medically needy population, early intervention would be a far more effective way to sustain life. The cost of PCP prophylaxis for an HIV-infected person is estimated at $1,100 per year, while the cost of a single hospital stay to treat PCP is estimated at $17,000.[44]

- *Medicaid's categorical and financial requirements should be relaxed so that people with HIV can more easily access the system.*

Allowable income and asset levels should, at minimum, be increased to the federal poverty line. Spend-down programs should be made available in all states. Categorical guidelines should be amended to include symptomatic persons without an AIDS diagnosis, at least (as some have proposed) in an optional category or "buy-in" system. There is no good reason to deny people at that stage of HIV disease important prophylaxis treatments that may save or prolong their lives. Moreover, because of the acknowledged episodic nature of the disease, the disability status of such a person should not be withdrawn with each period of remission. If the SSA guidelines defining who is "disabled" remain too rigid, Medicaid should create its own, more inclusive, standard for determining disability.

- *Alternatively, Medicaid should eliminate its categorical requirements and expand to include all medically needy persons regardless of "category" or level of disability.*

This reform would greatly expand the number of persons eligible for Medicaid nationwide. The increased cost, however, would be offset by a vast reduction in the social, and ultimately financial, cost of denying sick members of society access to medical treatment other than public hospital emergency rooms and "charity" care from willing providers.

B. Coverage

- *Coverage alternatives, particularly residential and out-of-hospital care options, should be made available so that people with HIV disease are provided an appropriate continuum of care.*

State Medicaid restrictions on nursing home, hospice, and home-based care merely serve to *increase* the cost of treatment to states because patients are forced to remain, unnecessarily, in hospitals — the most expensive care facility. Government should also enhance coverage for dual treatment facilities, detox centers, and therapeutic communities. The spread of HIV infection among intravenous drug users, their sexual partners, and children demands that HIV care be made available along with drug treatment. Although few facilities presently offer such services, Medicaid should not erect yet another obstacle to the development of these critical programs.

All states should apply for home- and community-based care waivers. Administrative problems in the waiver application process, which have been widely reported, should also be addressed.[45] Some commentators have proposed eliminating the waiver requirement for states that wish to provide home- and community-based services to certain Medicaid-eligible individuals.[46] Case management services, personal care, and respite care are among the important benefits available under the banner of home- and community-based care. If the waiver process cannot be sufficiently streamlined, it is essential that the government eliminate the need for such waivers.

- *States should pay COBRA continuation premiums for eligible seropositive persons wishing to retain their private insurance coverage.*

Allowing an individual to extend his or her insurance coverage provides that person with the opportunity to receive more comprehensive coverage and access to a wider choice of physicians and hospitals. Medicaid would save money by this reform since it would act as a "secondary" payor. Although Medicaid would be forced to finance an average monthly premium of between $80 and $150 per individual, it would avoid the more sizable costs of drugs, physicians, and hospital care for the twenty-nine months before Medicare coverage takes effect. This would slow the "Medicaidization" of AIDS by stopping the dramatic decline in recent years of the share of HIV-related costs borne by the private insurance sector.[47] Several states, including Michigan, Washington, Maryland, Virginia, and the District of Columbia, have already adopted the idea of picking up COBRA payments.

- *States should increase the level of Medicaid reimbursements for health care services important to people with HIV disease.*

As one commentator has pointed out, AIDS medical care has been "distorted to match reimbursement patterns, rather than the needs of the sick."[48] Inadequate Medicaid reimbursement for drugs, physicians, nursing homes, and hospital care has diminished people's access to such care. States should institute reforms that will enhance reimbursement rates, which in turn will open up certain care options to people with AIDS.

One method would be for states to utilize diagnosis-related groups (DRGs) in determining reimbursement levels for inpatient hospital care.[49] Disease-specific DRGs allow facilities the flexibility to enhance reimbursement for relatively expensive conditions such as PCP. In states that do not allow a specific diagnosis to be singled out for greater reimbursement, other innovative approaches may be possible.[50] In addition, those hospitals that provide a disproportionate share of HIV care should receive enhanced reimbursement.[51] This would reduce the losses suffered by those hospitals that accept Medicaid patients and would reduce their reluctance to treat persons with HIV.

Innovative approaches to nursing home reimbursements have also been adopted in some states and should be extended to others. Flexible per diem payments in New York are ideal for HIV-infected persons since they "allow for the variability of patient needs that occur from day to day."[52] Other financing options include the introduction of home- and community-based waivers, modified hospice payments, and the use of case management services. The federal government can encourage states to adopt these approaches by increasing its share of financing when states introduce such programs.[53]

C. Procedure

- *States should improve the management of their programs to facilitate communications with clients and the processing of information.*

Clients and applicants should have access to the information they provide to Medicaid. Clients should be able to determine quickly the status of their applications or cases, and whether any documentation is missing from their files.

- *Workers at Medicaid offices should receive training about HIV disease.*

- *Application and recertification deadlines should be relaxed to compensate for applicants who may be temporarily unable to submit material due to illness.*

To facilitate a more flexible approach, states with large numbers of HIV-infected applicants should consider implementing HIV-specific programs, such as HIV-dedicated units.

D. Financing

* *Government must direct more money to the development of comprehensive, cost-effective medical services for low-income persons with HIV.*

The Comprehensive AIDS Resources Emergency Act of 1990 (the CARE bill) authorized emergency relief grants for five years to metropolitan areas reporting more than 2,000 AIDS cases to the Centers for Disease Control and created federal programs for early intervention. Funds were authorized for nursing homes, subacute care facilities, and community health centers, as well as public or not-for-profit hospitals. Monies were also to be available for renovating and rehabilitating buildings into congregate care facilities. Such facilities, almost nonexistent at present, are vitally important to the growing intersection of the homeless (individuals and families) and IVDUs.

Unfortunately, the actual appropriations budgeted by Congress for CARE programs fell far short of what was authorized and what is needed.

* *The government should either reduce Medicare's waiting period or eliminate it entirely.*

If the current twenty-nine-month waiting period remains in place, Medicare will continue to have little significance to people with HIV disease. Modifying Medicare's waiting period would make the program more relevant to people with HIV and ensure that the federal government bears an appropriate share of HIV-related costs. (This type of change would not necessarily alter the main eligibility criteria of Medicare, which for those under 65 is eligibility for SSDI payments). If such a plan were adopted, the substantial copayments now required under Medicare, as well as certain coverage limitations, should be modified.

At present, the main advantage of Medicare is that it reimburses at higher levels than Medicaid, thus giving patients a greater choice of physicians and hospitals. Medicare reimbursements also allow hospitals to decrease the losses inherent in serving publicly insured patients. It is clear that changes in Medicare could have a dramatic impact on state Medicaid programs. If Medicare were to reduce its waiting requirements, for example, certain reforms in Medicaid would no longer be necessary. Reforms to each system should be coordinated so that the two bureaucracies could function more cooperatively; linking of Medicaid and Medicare eligibility and coverage rules would result in better, more consistent care for clients.

One obstacle to cooperation between the two systems is that Medicaid is run largely on the state level, while Medicare is administered federally through SSA. If Medicaid rules and guidelines were standardized, it would be easier for the two programs to work together, and it would ensure that states offer roughly equal levels of coverage. Some reformers have recommended that Medicaid and Medicare be folded into one large program, eliminating the cost of running separate bureaucracies while improving overall system efficiency.[54]

IV. Conclusion

The HIV crisis has highlighted enormous flaws in the public health care financing system. Most of the changes recommended in this chapter would benefit not only people with HIV disease, but all low-income Americans, with any disease. The crisis in HIV-care has dramatically illustrated the cost to all of society of failing to provide needed services to indigent persons who are ill.

NOTES

1. J. Green & P. Arno, The "Medicaidization" of AIDS: Trends in the Financing of HIV-Related Medical Care, 264 J. A.M.A. 1261, 1261 (1990) [hereinafter Green & Arno].
2. Id.
3. The Consolidated Omnibus Budget Reconciliation Act (COBRA) of 1985 requires most employers to offer departing employees "continuation" of their health insurance policies, and insurance companies to offer "conversion" from group to individual coverage when the continuation period expires. COBRA was amended in 1989 to extend the continuation period to 29 months if the employee resigned because of a disability, long enough to satisfy the waiting period required for persons with disabilities to qualify for Medicare. See text infra at page 195.
4. Some states prohibit commercial insurers from selling policies that exclude or cap AIDS-related coverage. See chapter 5 ("Health Insurance") on HIV disease and insurance.
5. Lifetime AIDS costs are now estimated to be between $53,500 and $100,580 per case, although it is unclear how the trend toward early intervention will affect those numbers. Spolar, Footing the Bill, Washington Post, June 19, 1990, at Z-9 [hereinafter Spolar].
6. M.A. Baily, The Economic Consequences of HIV Infection for the Medicaid and Medicare Programs: An Exploratory Study 8 (1989) [hereinafter HIV and Medicaid]. See generally chapter 5 ("Health Insurance").

7.   SSI pays about $386 per month, while the average SSDI benefit in 1989 was about $550 per month. T.P. McCormack, The AIDS Benefits Handbook 12-22 (1990) [hereinafter McCormack]. The annual cost of low-dose AZT alone is, at a minimum, about $3,000. Spolar, *supra* note 5.

8.   Spolar, *supra* note 5.

9.   Green & Arno, *supra* note 1, at 1265.

10. Baily maintains that the true payors of last resort are public hospitals and health care providers who render partially or totally unreimbursed care, the cost of which is ultimately passed on to the public through higher fees or taxes. HIV and Medicaid, *supra* note 6, at 17.

11. H.T. Greely, *AIDS and the American Health Care Financing System*, 51 U. Pitt. L. Rev. 73, 96 (1989) [hereinafter Greely].

12. McCormack, *supra* note 7, at 57.

13. *Id.* at 60.

14. Greely indicates that because of the pressure on the federal government to reduce the deficit, it is unlikely that Congress will shift AIDS costs from the states to the federal government. Also, payouts for end-stage renal disease have been higher than expected, making it a politically weak model upon which to base AIDS financing reform. Greely, *supra* note 11, at 145-46.

15. Advocates also point to the use of interminable questionnaires containing inappropriate personal questions about hygienic habits and other daily activities. Others who know the system well recommend that people include a psychological dimension to their applications to strengthen their claims. One commentator stresses that the opinions of mental health therapists and others "can be crucial in getting approval for a non-AIDS diagnosed" patient. He recommends securing a written psychological evaluation, whether the applicant is presently receiving therapy or not. McCormack, *supra* note 7, at 13.

16. Indeed, litigation has been filed against the Social Security Administration on this basis. *See* Complaint, S.P. v. Sullivan, No. 90 Civ. 6294 (MGC) (S.D.N.Y. 1990).

17. A trial work period of nine months is available to Social Security recipients. During this period, Social Security checks continue.

18. P. Arno, D. Shenson, N. Siegel, P. Franks & P. Lee, *Economic and Policy Implications of Early Intervention in HIV Disease*, 262 J. A.M.A. 1493 (1989).

19. This provision is included in the Medicaid AIDS and HIV Amendments Act of 1990 sponsored by Rep. Henry Waxman [hereinafter Waxman bill].

20. HIV and Medicaid, *supra* note 6, at 151.

21. The federal poverty line for 1990 is $522 per month for a single individual.

22. Authorization is not tantamount to being issued a card. Applicants must bring a letter proving presumptive SSI approval to the Medicaid office where they may be issued or mailed a temporary card. Advocates in several states report difficulties with this procedure. *See* text *infra*.

23. Payment of continuation premiums under Medicaid is authorized in only a few states. If enacted, the Waxman bill would give all states the option of paying continuation premiums for eligible HIV-infected people.

24. McCormack, *supra* note 7, at 52-53.

25. HIV and Medicaid, *supra* note 6, at 60.

26. *Id.* at 59. Baily reports that these restrictions vary from "very mild" to "so severe" as to render the service coverage virtually meaningless." *Id.*

27. People who have been disabled for twenty-nine months and still meet Medicaid's financial guidelines may be eligible for both Medicaid and Medicare simultaneously.

28. *See* Philip Lee, Testimony to the National Commission on AIDS, Nov. 3, 1989, at 26, 27-28.

29. HIV and Medicaid, *supra* note 6, at 64-66.

30. D. Andrulis, Testimony Before the National Commission on AIDS, Nov. 2, 1989, at 12-13.

31. These are covered by the "2176 Waiver," issued by the Department of Health and Human Services.

32. Report of the Presidential Commission on the Human Immunodeficiency Virus Epidemic 143 (1988) [hereinafter Watkins Commission Report].

33. *Id*. at 142.

34. *Id*. at 142-43.

35. New York City Mayor's Conference on AIDS, Proceedings (Feb. 1990).

36. *Id*.

37. For example, service providers report that no nursing home in the state of Georgia accepted patients with AIDS, even though that state's Medicaid program reimburses for nursing home services. The refusal of health care providers to treat HIV-infected patients is analyzed in chapter 4 ("The Very Fabric of Health Care").

38. Intergovernmental Health Policy Projuect (IHPP), Intergovernmental AIDS Rep., Mar.-Apr.1990, at 5 [hereinafter IHPP Rep.].

39. McCormack, *supra* note 7, at 222-25.

40. HIV and Medicaid, *supra* note 6, at 76.

41. *Id*. at 77.

42. A study of Medicaid procedures reported that application forms ranged from three to fifty-two pages in length. Not surprisingly, 60 percent of application denials in certain states were based on "failure to comply with procedural requirements." *Id*. at 39-40.

43. *Id*. at 39.

44. 135 Cong. Rec. E336 (daily ed. Feb. 22, 1990) (Remarks by Rep. Waxman).

45. Watkins Commission Report, *supra* note 32, at 143.

46. Rep. Waxman has introduced legislation to give states the option to offer such care without waiver to people with AIDS who are under the age of 18. This provision would substantially speed and improve care options for children with AIDS and their families.

47. *See* Green & Arno, *supra* note 1, at 1265.

48. HIV and Medicaid, *supra* note 6, at 108.

49. Currently only eighteen states link reimbursement through DRGs. IHPP Rep., *supra* note 38, at 3.

50. Baily cites New York's system, which bases reimbursements on cost variations within individual hospital environments. HIV and Medicaid, *supra* note 6, at 105.

51. The Waxman bill, *supra* note 19, would entitle hospitals to receive at least 25 percent of standard non-Medicaid charges for inpatient care of Medicaid-eligible persons with HIV disease.

52. HIV and Medicaid, *supra* note 6, at 106.

53. *Id*. at 109.

54. General Assistance programs, as well as state-run drug assistance programs and other programs, serve to fill the gaps in Medicaid and Medicare. The U.S.

Public Health Service has established a state-administered fund to pay for AZT, pentamidine, and alpha interferon. McCormack, *supra* note 7, at 49. In New York State, a program called the AIDS Drug Assistance Program (ADAP) makes approved AIDS drugs available at no cost to uninsured people with resources above the Medicaid limit through a special federal-state program. Advocates agree that this program has been of tremendous value to low- and middle-income working persons with HIV disease. Interestingly, lack of publicity about the program has led to both underutilization and very loose eligibility standards.

General Assistance programs, which serve very poor people, provide temporary cash benefits and Medicaid eligibility in certain states. These programs usually do not use disability criteria, and so do not serve SSI-eligible persons.

7

THE HIV EPIDEMIC IN PUERTO RICO

By Luis A. Lavin and William B. Rubenstein

Introduction

Puerto Rico, with a total of 4,956 cases, has one of the highest incidences of AIDS in the United States.[1] Based on Puerto Rico's officially reported AIDS cases, the Island has the nation's second-highest rate of AIDS, 56.4 cases per 100,000 population. The San Juan area alone has more than 2,500 known AIDS cases. San Juan has approximately 76 AIDS cases per 100,000 persons, ranking fourth in AIDS rates among large metropolitan areas; only San Francisco, New York City, and Ft. Lauderdale have higher incidence rates. In terms of per capita rate of new cases, however, Puerto Rico has the nation's highest rate, more than three times the national average.[2]

AIDS in Puerto Rico has been and remains a disease primarily of intravenous drug users, with gay and bisexual men making up a significant minority of the cases. Approximately 58 percent of all adults and adolescents with AIDS in Puerto Rico contracted HIV from intravenous drug use and 17 percent from gay or bisexual contact; 9.4 percent report both gay or bisexual contact and intravenous drug use; and 15.6 percent are attributed to heterosexual contact. Puerto Rico also has the highest percentage of women with AIDS, 18 percent, in the entire United States. Indeed, in Puerto Rico AIDS is the leading cause of death among all women ages 15 to 44.

But these grim statistics may tell only half the story. Dr. Johnny Rullan, Puerto Rico's epidemiologist and executive director of the Governor's Interagency AIDS Commission, acknowledges that the official count is underreported by as much as 40 percent. By this estimate, Puerto Rico's AIDS incidence would be 63 per 100,000, more than one and one-half times New York State's and almost five times that of Massachusetts. Nearly one in every twenty adults between the ages of 25 and 44 seen at San Juan Municipal Hospital for non-AIDS-related illnesses was found to be carrying HIV. Among San Juan residents of all ages an average of 2 percent are already infected. The Island's blood donors, considered a cross section of lower-risk Puerto Ricans, have HIV infection rates twenty-seven times the U.S. average. Dr. Rullan estimates that islandwide the number of HIV-infected people could be as high as 70,000.[3]

Puerto Rico has been stymied by the many public policy issues presented by the HIV crisis — education and prevention efforts are almost nonexistent, and discrimination is rampant. What's worse, the woefully underfunded public health care system has been overwhelmed by the epidemic: AZT remains available to only 315 adults out of the 20,000 adults currently enrolled in Medicaid who should be receiving the medication,[4] and the government is not funding any prophylaxis for *Pneumocystis carinii* pneumonia (PCP).

This chapter will examine and make recommendations on the Puerto Rican situation with respect to these three issues: education and prevention (in section I), discrimination (in section II), and access to health care (in section III). The third section focuses specifically on the legal issues presented by a state program that purports to ration health care due to limited resources. By examining the legal implications of different types of rationing strategies, the section sets forth the legal principles that can be employed to fight denials of care — and thus guarantee access to health care — in an era of shrinking government resources.

I. Background: Education and Prevention

Although the incidence of AIDS in Puerto Rico has reached a level that warrants immediate mobilization of all forces able to deal with the problem, attempts to educate the general populace and prevent the spread of HIV disease have barely been initiated: the issue has instead been transformed into a political and religious conflict. The sociocultural and political contexts of life in Puerto Rico have made the Island's response to the HIV epidemic more complex, with nearly every factor having a dual face.

First, as the statistics outlined above make clear, the epidemic on the Island is primarily one of intravenous drug use: the virus is spreading mainly through the sharing of needles. Prevention programs would therefore have to be geared towards educating addicts about — and providing them with — clean needles, and ultimately toward getting them into drug treatment programs. However, as is true throughout the United States, drug users in Puerto Rico and efforts to curb the spread of HIV disease among them are most difficult. While in the rest of the United States educational efforts geared toward informing men who have sex with men about safe sex practices have met with some success, clean needle programs always face political opposition and drug treatment programs are typically underfunded and undervalued. It is not surprising, then, that the centrality of drug use to Puerto Rico's HIV crisis has averted attention from the epidemic and that a basic program to address this primary route of HIV transmission has not taken hold.

The major secondary routes of transmission on the Island involve sexual activity — homosexual activity and/or sexual activity between an intravenous drug user and his or her partner. But calling public attention to these modes of HIV transmission is made exceedingly difficult by the near absolute ban placed upon public discussion of sexuality on the Island, as well as by strictly rigid gender roles and by strong societal opposition to homosexuality.[5] Women are constrained from speaking with their male partners about condom usage: "Suggesting to a husband or a partner that he use a condom may be a social taboo because it is perceived as an indication of insolence or defiance against the men... [or is] perceived as an indication of a woman's infidelity."[6]

Indeed, in Puerto Rican culture the primary expectation of women is that they will bear children.[7] Children are viewed as a positive measure of manhood and womanhood. So great is the affirmation associated with children that discussion of birth control is considered sacrilegious. Women's economic dependence on men is enormous and often overshadows issues of HIV prevention to the extent that many women will not leave men to reduce their exposure to HIV. While such cultural factors appear to make HIV education and prevention efforts exceedingly difficult, some commentators have noted that:

Social reality is considerably more complex than reified descriptions of these
cultural concepts might suggest. For example, many Latino families have been
torn apart by chronic underemployment, racism, health problems associated
with poverty, alcoholism, drug use, and domestic violence. Increasingly, Latino
women are heading households. Among Puerto Rican households in the U.S.,
for example, about 44 percent are currently headed by women. Another example of the frequent incongruity between the ideal and the real is the notable
number of unwed Latino adolescents, especially those born in the U.S., who
become pregnant.[8]

In observing "the diversity, complexity, changing nature, and struc-
tural causes of gender patterns in the Latino population," these commentators correctly note that "Latino culture can either contribute to or
help prevent the sexual transmission of HIV."[9]

If speaking to women about the importance of condom usage
challenges social norms, speech about homosexuality also defies tradition in Puerto Rican culture. "Homosexuality remains taboo in Puerto
Rico, as elsewhere in Latin America, and many gay people with AIDS
prefer to say they are IV drug users rather than risk the stigma of
homosexuality."[10] There is not a large, organized gay community in
Puerto Rico, and, in fact, "social hostility and homophobic violence in
Puerto Rico are reported as factors in the migration of some gay men
and lesbians to the U.S."[11] The lack of a visible gay community may put
men who have sex with men in Puerto Rico at increased risk of infection: if "these men do not define themselves as gay, they may tend to
ignore AIDS prevention messages targeted to the gay community....
Moreover, they probably do not benefit from the social reinforcement
for safe sex practices that has evolved in the wider gay community.
These men are also potential sources of infection for Latino women and
children."[12]

The Island's social mores are strictly reinforced by the central role
of the Catholic Church in the life of most Puerto Ricans (approximately
70 percent of Islanders are members of the Church). In particular, the
Church has stifled the expansion and acceptance of preventive measures such as safe sex education and condom distribution. In fact,
Archbishop Luís Cardenal Aponte Martínez of San Juan has warned
that it is a greater sin to use condoms than to get AIDS.[13] The lack of
condom use is particularly problematic since studies suggest that 30
percent of heterosexuals engage in anal intercourse, which is believed
to be a highly efficient means of transmitting the virus.[14] Although the
Catholic Church is well aware of the devastation caused by the disease

— it is at the forefront of providing care[15] — its stand on the issue has been uncompromising. The Church has prohibited sex instruction in Catholic schools and has opposed any education plan that promotes the use of condoms for the prevention of HIV transmission. The opposition has been so great that the Church threatened to cancel its contract with Triple S (its medical insurer) if the company proceeded with an educational program that included the use of condoms to check the spread of HIV. The company did not give in to the pressure.[16]

Despite these strong Church-enforced cultural traditions, which lead to condemnation of drug users and gay men, there exists a strong tradition of family among Puerto Ricans, which can provide valuable counterbalance in the midst of the epidemic. For instance, while one commentator noted that "homosexuality is detested culturally," she did so in the context of making the point that despite this hatred, "family ties are for the most part strong enough that many homosexuals and intravenous drug users maintain them, so no social isolation need occur during the disease."[17] Similarly, Puerto Rican drug addicts "are commonly not rejected by their families, at least not for IV drug use alone."[18] According to these commentators:

> These findings indicate that although family ties may be damaged or even broken among Puerto Rican IV drug users, they, like Mexican Americans, retain an emotional attachment to kin that may prove useful in AIDS prevention and drug abuse treatment. Family oriented approaches have been described as being especially appropriate for working with Puerto Rican substance users and are commonly employed by indigenous healers in the Puerto Rican community.[19]

While family might provide important support for people with HIV disease, the other major source of such support throughout the epidemic in the United States has come from community based organizations. Unfortunately, the concentration of drug users among the HIV-infected in Puerto Rico, combined with the lack of a visible gay community, has impeded the emergence of an active and effective AIDS community on the Island. Thus, unlike in the gay communities of most major U.S. cities, there has not been until recently a strong and visible affected group that organized to promulgate educational information and to care for the sick.[20]

Beyond the difficult task of addressing transmission among drug users, the social restrictions on sex education, the constraining role of the Catholic Church, and the lack of a visible AIDS community, the efforts to develop a sound public health response to the epidemic have also been impeded by partisan political controversy. Prior to 1985, one political party controlled both the Commonwealth and the San Juan City government. But in the 1984 elections, a different party obtained the governorship, with the consequence that the mayor of San Juan became the major elected opposition official.[21] This political division first moved into the HIV arena in the course of a public debate between the Island's Secretary of Health (who announced in 1986 that Puerto Rico was "the only place on earth where the incidence of AIDS was falling") and the Director of Health for San Juan (who announced in 1987 that the incidence of AIDS in the city was so high that San Juan "was probably the most contagious place in the world to live").

The controversy peaked in 1987 when the U.S. Health Resources and Service Administration (HRSA) rejected requests from both the Commonwealth and the municipality for millions of dollars of HIV funds because of their failure to cooperate with each other. HRSA stated that, "There's no sense of cooperation between the two," and told the warring factions to "work together in the future if you expect a grant from us, and put aside differences." San Juan's rejected proposal would have established an AIDS outreach center and a hotline and provided nursing care, a hospice, test sites, and AIDS education.[22]

This episode has come to typify the handling of the HIV crisis in Puerto Rico: it has consistently been framed by political debate — whether about the level of incidence, the source of funding, the means of transmission, or the encouragement or nonencouragement of condom usage.[23] Thus, one decade into this epidemic, the Commonwealth has not instituted a basic HIV information campaign, much less undertaken targeted educational initiatives dealing with clean needles or safe sex. "The Puerto Rico Department of Public Instruction does not introduce sex education at the elementary level, and the scope and content at the intermediate and superior levels varies from school to school. The department has received a grant to form a formal policy, but it has not been released yet."[24] Moreover, "[c]ondoms... are neither promoted nor distributed by the public health system despite the Commonwealth's own estimates that 40,000 people are walking around with the HIV virus."[25] As one commentator has summarized the problems:

> In Puerto Rico, AIDS appears to have been coopted by the party politicians, and
> its controversies turned into themes which can be bickered about. Whether it
> should be concluded that the local political structure is so strong that it is able
> to overcome the exigencies of a powerful and potentially widely fatal epidemic,

or that the people are unable to view phenomena, even as devastating as the AIDS epidemic, other than through political approaches is difficult to say. It can be concluded, without doubt, however, that unless a strong apolitical, socially organized assault is mounted on AIDS by the people, a society such as Puerto Rico will have difficulty surviving the epidemic.[26]

II. Discrimination Generally

The high incidence of HIV disease in Puerto Rico coupled with the absence of any educational efforts has caused a sense of panic. This panic, in turn, has been expressed in particularly virulent forms of intolerance and bigotry toward those infected with HIV. Persons with HIV disease are often treated in a hostile manner by family, friends, and health care professionals, resulting in their stigmatization and alienation. The human suffering and devastation caused by these acts of discrimination can rival the devastations of HIV itself. These forms of discrimination are not unique to Puerto Rico; however (as discussed more fully below) a number of critical factors make remedying them more difficult in Puerto Rico than elsewhere in the United States.

In 1988, Dr. Rullan, the Island's epidemiologist, conducted a poll that underscores the many misconceptions and fears that create the environment for discrimination.[27] The study revealed that many Puerto Ricans do not understand how HIV is transmitted.

- 32 percent of the persons questioned believed that children infected with the virus should not be allowed to attend school with other children
- 44 percent stated that persons with AIDS should be isolated from the rest of the population
- 50 percent believed that persons infected with AIDS had been infected through their own will

Moreover, because HIV disease is largely associated with specific groups, many people apparently believe that the disease can be contained through punitive actions against those groups:

- 44 percent considered AIDS to be a problem that affected only gay men, drug addicts, and hemophiliacs
- 43 percent wanted the government to keep a list of persons known to carry the virus

- 37 percent believed that AIDS patients should be forced to wear identifying bracelets to warn others

The level of intolerance and antipathy is illustrated by the following three anecdotal examples of HIV-related discrimination.

A. A Hospice in Luquillo

The controversy surrounding the opening of an AIDS hospice in the Sabana Ward section of Luquillo exemplifies the level of misinformation and prejudice in the Puerto Rican community with regard to the HIV epidemic.[28]

In 1989, Jorge Serrano, an HIV-infected man, and his wife, Mariana Rodríguez de Serrano, formed the Association of Relatives and Friends of AIDS Patients (known by its Spanish acronym AFAPS) to provide services for people with HIV disease on the Island. One of the group's first projects was to be a hospice for people with AIDS; at the time, there were only three hospices and a total of fewer than thirty beds for AIDS patients in Puerto Rico, although there were more than 4,000 confirmed cases of AIDS. The AFAPS hospice which was to be located in the Municipality of Luquillo, in the Sabana Ward, was to house ten patients with end-stage AIDS and was to "afford AIDS patients a place to 'die with dignity' in a home-like setting while providing necessary medical and counseling services to the patients and their families." In February of 1990, AFAPS leased a site for the project from the Evangelical Church of Puerto Rico. Money was donated to renovate the structure by the United Fund of Puerto Rico, and clients were solicited to come to Luquillo.

No sooner had the project been launched, however, than the residents of the Luquillo area voiced adamant opposition to it. The residents built a makeshift structure across from the hospice that they called "Dignity Plaza" and from which they "monitored" the hospice's activities around the clock. They harassed the residents of the facility by posting signs warning of the supposed dangers created by the operation of the hospice and threatened and intimidated the proponents of the facility. Opposition to the hospice relied upon familiar misconceptions and stereotypes about HIV:

> Among the reasons expressed for opposing the hospice are the possibility that mosquitoes might transmit the AIDS virus to the community; the undesirability of having former drug users and homosexuals living in Sabana Ward; the belief

that the hospice site is flood prone, thus giving rise to a risk of contamination through inundation; the risk of transmitting AIDS-related infections such as pneumonia; the risk that the hospice might decrease the value of surrounding property; the risk that hospice residents might pose a danger to students attending a nearby school.

As a consequence of the community's adamant opposition, the Permits and Regulation Administration (*Administración de Reglamentos y Permisos* — ARPE) in Luquillo refused to grant the permit needed to open the facility, stating that the area could be used only for agricultural purposes. The hospice's attorneys challenged the denial, filing a lawsuit in the U.S. District Court in Puerto Rico. Specifically, the attorneys claimed that the patients were discriminated against on the basis of a handicap (AIDS) in violation of the federal Fair Housing Act; the court agreed.[29] The court found that the presence of AIDS patients in the Loquilla area would not pose a health risk to the residents, writing:

> there is absolutely no evidence supporting the conclusion that the tenancy of ten terminal AIDS patients carries a significant threat to the safety of the community. To the contrary, the uncontested scientific and medical evidence establishes that HIV is not readily transmissible through food, mosquitoes or casual contact, and that the presence of the hospice poses no risk to the community at large. A.R.P.E.'s denial of the permit, therefore, cannot be justified on public health grounds.

The court issued an order saying that anyone who "willfully injured, intimidated or interfered" with the hospice would be held liable under the federal housing law. Judge Fuste concluded:

> no one can blame the residents of any town for making a priority of the health and safety of their families and community, but when legitimate concern is fanned by a profound misunderstanding of the causes of AIDS, the rush to panic can easily result in illegal and unjustifiable discrimination against not only the disease's victims but also against the laudable efforts of individuals working to contain the flames.

B. A School in Rio Piedras

The bias found in Luquillo is not isolated — it may be found all over the Island and is not limited to discriminatory acts against persons with HIV disease who are gay or intravenous drug users. Puerto Rican children face the same alienation and bias. Marisa Blay, the director of Proyecto Amor (Love Project), a home for children with AIDS in Caimito, Rio Piedras, states that discrimination against students with

HIV disease in Puerto Rico is prevalent throughout the public school system.[30]

For example, in 1990, the mother of two HIV-infected children who were living at Proyecto Amor attempted to enroll the children in the Colomban Rosario elementary school in Rio Piedras. After the mother informed the school that the children were infected, she was told there was no room for her children. The principal gave the mother a number of excuses for not allowing the children into the school (for example, that the children did not reside in the school district) and suggested that the children go to a school that was located in the Caimito area near the group home. However, the Caimito school also refused to accept the children based on their HIV infection. Blay, as director of Proyecto Amor, informed the press of the discriminatory practices against the two children. Several articles soon appeared about the case in the *San Juan Star*, after which the Rio Piedras school agreed to enroll the children.[31]

C. Rejected by Two Hospitals

Discrimination against people with HIV infection also takes place within the health care system itself. The ill treatment received by Pedro Rodríguez presents such an example.[32] The 31-year-old Rodríguez was diagnosed with AIDS in New York City in 1986 and began receiving treatment there. He traveled to Puerto Rico in January of 1988, suffering from Kaposi's sarcoma (KS). Once on the Island, Rodríguez required the attention of a doctor for the treatment of his KS tumors. He visited the Rio Piedras Medical Center, which twice refused to admit him because it claimed that without his medical records from New York, its doctors did not know how to treat him.

After being sent away without treatment, the pain caused by the infected tumors became so unbearable that Rodríguez was taken back to the emergency room at the Rio Piedras hospital. Once again, he received no medical attention for the cancerous tumors, but rather was given only a shot of a painkiller and sent home the next day. Unable to deal with the pain, Rodríguez again returned to the hospital. He was then told that there were no rooms available and that he would have to go to the Regional Hospital in Bayamón.

Upon his arrival at the Regional Hospital, Rodríguez was immediately placed in an isolated corner of the emergency room where he remained for three days, receiving only antibiotics and painkillers.

He was never provided with gauze to clean his tumors nor did anyone attempt to do it for him. His family brought him food because no hospital employee would feed him. Rodríguez was also subjected to the cruelties and ignorance of a group of medical students. The students, upon seeing the infected and bleeding tumors, made sounds of disgust and immediately left the area. The excruciating pain and the degradation tormented Rodríguez to the point where he twice attempted unsuccessfully to commit suicide: first he ripped an IV from his arm, hoping that he would bleed to death; later he attempted to suffocate himself with a plastic bag.

After six weeks in Puerto Rico, Rodríguez returned to New York City, where he was immediately taken to St. Clare's Hospital. Doctors there told him that the medication and antibiotics administered in Puerto Rico were too strong for cancer and AIDS patients and could have killed him.

Rodríguez's case, albeit a single example, highlights a number of critical deficiencies in the care of people with HIV disease in Puerto Rico. First, on a purely medical level, Rodríguez's doctors simply did not know how to treat HIV disease. Second, the hospital staff, including the doctors, were not aware of — or chose to ignore — how HIV is transmitted, and thus refused to properly care for and feed Rodríguez. Finally, the health care professionals' disgust for individuals infected with HIV rendered them unable to provide objective and adequate medical care. As one commentator has summarized the situation:

> Health workers have also been hesitant to care for AIDS victims due to fear of contagion, and the Union of Nurses and Health Workers has called for strict isolation of all AIDS patients to protect their members. One of the private hospitals announced a policy of refusing to accept AIDS patients, and although other hospitals quickly announced that they would treat any who came to them, editorial opinion was very critical of the refusal. The Puerto Rican Medical Association stated that all hospitals, private and public, "had the capacity" to care for AIDS patients, but did not publicly announce as policy that they should do so.[33]

There is, unfortunately, nothing stunningly unique about these three stories of discrimination. Each is typical of incidents across the United States since the start of the HIV crisis. A variety of collateral issues, however, make discrimination in Puerto Rico particularly intractable.

First, the absence of sound education and information means that these types of discriminatory incidences are still taking place ten years into the epidemic. While "hysterical reaction" cases have occurred throughout the country, the incidences of such cases diminished throughout the 1980s as most Americans learned more about the epidemic.[34] It remains true that when a community confronts its first case of AIDS, hysteria is apt to run wild. What distinguishes Puerto Rico is the level of hysteria that continues to dominate public discourse about the disease well into the early 1990s.

Second, Puerto Rican law provides a poor mechanism for combatting such irrational discrimination. Elsewhere in the United States, local laws have been critical for people with HIV disease. Prior to the Americans with Disabilities Act taking effect, federal laws protected persons from discrimination only in entities receiving federal funding (through the Rehabilitation Act) and, after 1988, in housing (following Congress's amendments to the Fair Housing Act). Local laws prohibiting discrimination against the disabled have therefore been important weapons in protecting the HIV-infected from discrimination, especially in private-sector employment and in places of public accommodation.[35]

Puerto Rican law, however, has not been such a weapon. While Puerto Rico does have a handicap discrimination law,[36] it did not become effective until mid-1985. The law covers only employers and entities that receive money from the Puerto Rican government, so it does not extend to discrimination by the private sector. The administrative agency charged with enforcing the law is a consumer protection agency that has not engaged in any HIV-related enforcement activities nor apparently handled any HIV-related complaints. Indeed, there has not been a definitive ruling on whether the law's definition of handicap includes HIV disease. Even if complaints were filed and handled by the administrative agency and the law interpreted to protect the HIV-infected, the law contains no "remedies" section setting forth what relief could be ordered against discriminating parties. In fact, then, the Puerto Rican handicap discrimination law is little more than a promise to the HIV-infected. The only law with potential teeth to protect the rights of people with HIV disease are federal laws, as in the hospice case.

A third and related problem exacerbating discrimination on the Island is the complete lack of legal services for people with HIV disease. A key aspect of overcoming discrimination is insuring that persons suffering prejudice have the practical resources necessary to obtain redress. Often, the single most important factor is whether a person has the advice and representation of an attorney. The ACLU's national survey of HIV discrimination found that an inadequate number of attorneys were available to represent persons facing the problems associated with HIV disease.[37] Nonprofit community groups, relying primarily on volunteer labor, have provided the bulk of legal services for persons with HIV disease. With rare exceptions, such as the lawyers who represented the hospice in the Luquillo case, these community efforts do not exist in Puerto Rico. Of course, this scarcity of legal resources is not unique to people with HIV — it is just one aspect of the unavailability of legal services for the poor and for civil rights cases in general on the Island.

Elsewhere in the United States where legal services are generally unavailable, individuals can often file complaints themselves with administrative agencies. (In reality, most do not, because typically they will not know about the availability of such a remedy without a lawyer!) These federal or state agencies will then, ideally, investigate the individual's complaint and pursue the case if discrimination is found. In Puerto Rico, though, this administrative system is not available. As noted above, the agency charged with enforcing the local law does not do so. What's worse, the administrative agencies charged with enforcing the federal laws do not have offices on the Island. Thus, an individual could file a complaint with the federal Department of Health and Human Services' Office of Civil Rights against a health care provider that denied her treatment. The HHS OCR regional office that covers Puerto Rico, however, is located in New York City. Filed complaints have to be sent to New York and are rarely investigated by the compliance officers on the mainland, who operate with limited budgetary resources.

In sum, discrimination against the HIV-infected in Puerto Rico may not be unique. It does appear, however, to be particularly virulent and durable. And it is not easily redressible, given the lack of HIV education and the absence of enforceable local law, the scarcity of legal resources, and the absence of a human rights commission to provide enforcement authority and moral leadership.

III. Access to Health Care

A. Background

The public health care system in Puerto Rico is abysmal. Visits to public hospitals and interviews with health care providers and recipients indicate that *all* indigent Puerto Ricans, not just those with HIV, must wait days for substandard medical care in dirty, understaffed, and overwhelmed public hospitals. As bad as the Puerto Rican health care system is for indigents, though, it is even worse for indigent Puerto Ricans with HIV disease.[38] Individuals with HIV infection are frequently turned away from hospitals because they are deemed "incurable."[39] And in contrast to indigent cancer patients who receive chemotherapy treatment under Medicaid, persons with HIV disease cannot get the most basic medical treatment: AZT.[40]

A major reason for this sad state of affairs is the high percentage of Puerto Ricans on Medicaid and the corresponding lack of funds. Laura Torres, of Puerto Rico's Department of Health, estimates that approximately 60 percent of Puerto Rico's population qualifies for Medicaid.[41] However, if the U.S. mainland's minimum economic qualifying standard were used, 80 percent of the Island's population would qualify for Medicaid.[42] Of Puerto Rico's approximate 3.3 million residents, 1.8 million are deemed indigent and approximately 900,000 are enrolled in the Medicaid program.[43] Yet, despite the huge number of medically indigent people, Puerto Rico receives only a block grant of $79 million under Medicaid. By contrast, the fifty states receive a fixed percentage of their total expenditures for medical services from the federal government.

Unlike in the rest of the United States, Puerto Rico's Medicaid program does not reimburse for private physicians who provide services to Medicaid recipients, nor for private pharmacies that dispense medication. Instead, Puerto Rico's Medicaid program requires that Medicaid recipients be treated in specially designated hospitals and that they acquire medication from so-called public pharmacies, usually located in the same public hospitals.[44]

In Puerto Rico, unlike the rest of the United States Medicaid does not cover AZT. Other critical drugs, such as pentamidine, are also not covered.[45]

Puerto Rican government officials blame limited financial resources — the so-called $79 million dollar Medicaid "cap" — for not doing more to combat HIV in general, and for not covering AZT in particular.[46] Indeed, public health officials estimate that if all persons eligible to receive AZT were given the treatment, AZT costs alone would exceed the $79 million in Medicaid funds that Puerto Rico receives each year from the federal government.[47] Puerto Rican government officials concede that HIV-infected individuals are treated differently than other indigent patients, such as cancer patients, who are provided with chemotherapy treatment under Medicaid.[48] But they claim that the reason for the different treatment is that HIV is a "new" disease.[49]

While Puerto Rico's Medicaid director admits that drugs such as AZT and pentamidine are not covered by Medicaid because of their high cost, the agency has not conducted a cost-benefit analysis to determine if it is cheaper, in the long run, to provide them.[50] In fact, "the local Medicaid agency is unable to identify the specific costs that are associated with persons with AIDS in Puerto Rico."[51]

Since Medicaid does not cover AZT in Puerto Rico, the only way for indigent individuals to obtain AZT is by enrolling in one of the extremely limited clinical trial programs. These programs provide free AZT to approximately 315 adults throughout the entire Island and are restricted by severe limitations.[52] For example, so-called active IV drug users, who are considered unreliable, are automatically excluded from participating in the CLETS clinical program.[53]

B. Legal Ramifications

The health care situation confronting individuals with HIV disease in Puerto Rico raises several issues, each with its own legal implications. First, there is Medicaid's refusal to reimburse for AZT; this is a legal issue addressed by Medicaid regulations. Second, there is the possibility that a hospital or program in Puerto Rico will simply not treat people with HIV disease — for any medical problem — deeming such persons either too infectious or "incurable." This stark refusal to treat individuals based on their diagnosis clearly violates federal disability law. Finally, there is the situation in which people with HIV disease receive limited health care because of limited availability of funds; in some instances, they may receive the same low level of health care as everyone else; in others, a rationing process may occur in which HIV-infected persons receive little or no health care on the grounds that they represent a poor use of scarce resources. The legal ramifications of these issues are discussed in the three subsections below.

1. Medicaid Refusals to Reimburse for Drug Treatments Based on Diagnosis

Puerto Rico's Medicaid program is not the first to refuse to reimburse for AZT: similar denials by Medicaid agencies were successfully challenged in Kansas and Alabama.[54] What makes Puerto Rico unique is its special, and complicated, relationship to the Medicaid program itself.

The Medicaid program, established by Title XIX of the Social Security Act,[55] is a cooperative federal-state program set up to enable states to furnish medical assistance to families and individuals unable to meet the costs of medical services. Costs of the program are shared by the federal and state governments. In Puerto Rico's case, the federal government gives the Commonwealth, as of 1990, a block grant of $79 million, which Puerto Rico matches.[56] Although states are not obligated to participate in the Medicaid program, if they do, they must operate their state programs in compliance with federal statutory and regulatory requirements.[57] This mandate applies also to Puerto Rico.[58]

Each state (including Puerto Rico) that participates in the federal Medicaid program must cover six mandatory services. The participating state may also elect to provide other optional medical services, such as prescription drugs.[59]

Once a state chooses to offer such optional services, it is bound to act in compliance with the Medicaid statute and the applicable regulations in the implementation of those services,[60] including the requirement that "each service must be sufficient in amount, duration and scope to reasonably achieve its purpose."[61] Although a state has considerable discretion in fashioning its Medicaid program, the discretion of the state is not unbridled: "[a state] may not arbitrarily deny or reduce the amount, duration, or scope of a required service... to an otherwise eligible recipient solely because of the diagnosis, type of illness or condition."[62] Moreover, the state's plan for determining eligibility for medical assistance must be "'reasonable' and 'consistent with the objectives' of the Act."[63] This provision has been interpreted to require that a state Medicaid plan provide treatment that is deemed "medically necessary" in order to comport with the objectives of the Medicaid Act.[64]

Since Puerto Rico is bound by the Supreme Court's "medical necessity" interpretation of 42 U.S.C. § 1396a(a)(17) and has chosen to provide prescription drugs as part of its optional medical services under Medicaid, its failure to provide AZT violates 42 C.F.R. § 440.230(b) and

§ 440.230(c) of the Medicaid regulations.[65] Puerto Rico might attempt to argue that the limited block grant received from the federal government prevents it from covering AZT. However, governing case law would appear to reject such an argument.[66] Additionally, the Island's special status as a Commonwealth does not preclude application of the Medicaid statute.[67]

Accordingly, although the question has not been litigated, it appears that the Puerto Rican Medicaid program *must* cover the costs of AZT and other medically necessary drugs, as the Kansas program was required to do in an earlier case.

Because Puerto Rico's failure to cover AZT violates Medicaid regulations, the Commonwealth could be ordered to provide the drug to the HIV-infected. It is important to note, however, that it is far from certain that Puerto Rico given the $79 million cap in the federal share of its Medicaid could pay for AZT without eliminating or radically reducing other medical services. Thus, the $79 million cap on Medicaid funds to Puerto Rico must be removed and replaced with the percentage reimbursement as used by the fifty states. Although HHS Secretary Louis Sullivan has stated that he would ask Congress to lift the $79 million ceiling on Medicaid funding to Puerto Rico,[68] no action has yet been taken by Sullivan or Congress. The Medicaid cap should not provide an excuse for Puerto Rico's discriminatory treatment of the HIV-infected — although financial reality cannot be ignored. Indeed, the financial reality lurks behind the general rationing of health care.

2. Refusals to Treat Persons with HIV Disease

Health care may be rationed on the Island in an openly discriminatory manner toward people with HIV disease — that is, to simply preclude treatment for the HIV-infected altogether, regardless of whether the individual is sick with a broken leg or end-stage AIDS. Again, such action would not be unique to Puerto Rico. Health care facilities on the mainland have often refused to treat the HIV-infected, as is discussed more fully above, in Chapter 4 ("The Very Fabric of Health Care").

This is the strongest sort of claim a person with HIV disease who has been refused hospital care can bring. She has been denied routine medical care because of her disability, at a hospital designed to provide such care. This sort of discrimination violates federal antidiscrimination statutes. A hospital could attempt to argue that people with HIV disease were not "otherwise qualified" for its services, but because the hospital provides health care, and the assumption is that the individual with HIV is going there for health care, this would not be a strong argument. Similarly, a contention that the hospital would not have infection control procedures sufficient to accommodate people with HIV disease must fail, as all health care institutions are required to have such procedures in place by the federal Occupational Safety and Health Administration.[69]

Beyond simply turning away people with HIV disease, a second manner in which a hospital might undertake discrimination against people with HIV disease would be to treat them for non-HIV-related illnesses (for example, a broken leg) or for some manifestations of HIV disease (for example, dermatitis) while refusing to treat central manifestations of HIV disease. To assess the legal implications of this type of refusal to treat HIV disease, it is necessary to have an understanding of the program's overall policies. The most discriminatory possibility is that the program might have facilities to accommodate people with pneumonia or cancer, but would refuse to accept people with HIV disease who have PCP or KS. If the program did treat cancer but not KS, pneumonia but not PCP, it could not attempt to justify its actions on the basis of economic rationing (see subsection 3, below). It would simply be discriminating against the HIV-infected, in violation of federal statutes for the same reasons stated above. On the other hand, if the program's refusal to treat PCP or KS was made pursuant to a policy that also refused to treat other similar illnesses (for example, end-stage cancer), such a decision would be more difficult to attack legally.

3. Rationing Certain Costs Associated with HIV Disease

A more prevalent, and legally more complicated, situation arises when a hospital or state program that is set up to provide a broad range of services makes triage decision not to give those services to certain classes of patients due to lack of resources. Hypothetically, at least, the program could elect not to provide services to people with non-HIV-related conditions, such as those in need of kidney dialysis or those with advanced diabetes, as well as those with HIV disease. These individuals are seen as being too expensive to treat or as having too short a life expectancy. With federal expenditures to Puerto Rico's Medicaid program capped at $79 million, such justifications are implicit in the Commonwealth's handling of the HIV crisis.

Again, however, Puerto Rico is not alone. An example of such a policy on a state level to cut medical costs is Oregon's proposed new Medicaid program. The Oregon legislature ranked 709 ailments, using a variety of factors, from quality of life to cost effectiveness. The final proposal suggests that Medicaid fund only the top 587 procedures on the list. This proposal was made in the context of efforts to increase Medicaid coverage of basic services and was meant to widen the base of health insurance among state residents while cutting overall costs. Although aggressive medical treatments for end-stage HIV disease is not covered by the proposed policy, early treatment of HIV (including AZT and other drugs) is among the twenty-five diseases given highest priority by the state.

Rationing decisions of this type when made by a state actor implicate the Constitution's equal protection clause and when made by an entity receiving federal funding (state actors or not) raise issues under the statutes prohibiting discrimination based on disability.

a. Equal Protection

A medical program's decision not to treat terminal illnesses for economic rationing reasons would be difficult, though not necessarily impossible, to attack under the Constitution's equal protection clause. Much would depend upon whether the decision were truly based upon economics (and not prejudice) and whether the economic analysis was both rational and fair.

As a preliminary matter, the equal protection clause calls on courts to scrutinize state action most closely where that action either implicates a fundamental right (such as the right to vote) or discriminates on the basis of race, alienage, or national origin. Health care is not, unfortunately, a fundamental right within our current constitutional jurisprudence, and thus a state's denial of health care would not in and of itself trigger heightened judicial scrutiny.[70] Moreover, it is unlikely that a court would closely scrutinize a program that discriminated against the class of terminally ill persons unless, perhaps, it could be shown that this discrimination was prejudicially motivated. Thus the state would need only to show that its rationing program had a "rational relationship to a legitimate governmental purpose."

In similar cases, the Supreme Court has upheld "saving money" as a legitimate goal properly served by excluding certain types of illnesses from insurance-type plans. For example, in *Geduldig v. Aiello*,[71] the Court upheld a California disability insurance program that excluded "pregnancy" from its definition of disability, finding the program to be constitutional. The Court held that the state's goals of keeping premiums down and the scheme solvent were rationally related to excluding pregnancy. Similarly, in a line of cases dating from the 1950s, the Court has ruled that the state can justifiably choose to address certain social problems rather than others, stating that the state "may take one step at a time, addressing itself to the phase of the problem that seems most acute to the legislative mind."[72] Thus, the state does not generally incur the obligation to assist people with terminal illnesses simply because it assists other sick people. Equal protection does not mandate this "all or nothing" reasoning. Finally, according to the reasoning of *Harris v. McRae*[73] — where the Court held that the government was not constitutionally bound to pay for therapeutic abortions under Medicaid — the Constitution does not hold the state responsible for conditions it does not actively create. Thus, if the state is not actively preventing HIV-infected individuals from getting health care, it would not be responsible for failing to provide it at state facilities.

The equal protection argument could be bolstered in several ways. First, the claim would trigger stricter judicial scrutiny if it could be shown that the exclusion of terminally ill persons has a disparate impact on a class entitled to greater constitutional protection — such as racial minorities. (Obviously, the latter claim would be of limited use in Puerto Rico.)[74] However, disparate impact claims generally require some showing of intent to discriminate against the class involved — the disparate impact is used as evidence of that intent. Since excluding people with terminal illnesses would in fact affect individuals across the board, it would be difficult to prevail upon this argument as well.

A second manner in which to bolster the equal protection argument would be to demonstrate that the exclusion is designed to punish the *class of people* with terminal illnesses rather than to advance a compelling governmental goal such as excluding high costs so as to maintain the financial solvency of the pool. Under governing case law, a state generally cannot argue that its goal (here, for example, to protect the fiscal viability of its health care program) justifies excluding a class of people from coverage. In *Shapiro v. Thompson*,[75] the Supreme Court invalidated a residential durational requirement for welfare eligibility stating:

> [w]e recognize that a State has a valid interest in preserving the fiscal integrity
> of its programs. It may legitimately attempt to limit its expenditures, whether
> for public assistance, public education, or any other program. But a State may

not accomplish such a purpose by invidious distinctions between classes of its citizens.... . The savings of welfare costs cannot justify an otherwise invidious classification.[76]

Similarly, in *Memorial Hospital v. Maricopa County*,[77] the Court held unconstitutional a law barring indigents who had not resided in the state for twelve months from free nonemergency medical care. Again the Court reasoned that there was no rational distinction between the group covered by the state's insurance and those excluded. While the plaintiffs' interest in adequate health care was large, the state interest in saving money by excluding certain classes of people was simply not compelling. The government "must do more than show that denying free medical care to new residents saves money" if the law is to survive an equal protection claim.[78]

These cases suggest that if there is evidence that the exclusion is intended to discriminate against people with terminal illnesses because the state dislikes them for some reason, a challenge could be successful. Such evidence could follow from the fact that terminal illnesses, although often the first excluded, may not necessarily be the most expensive. This argument goes to the lack of a "rational basis" for a program that excludes only terminal illnesses, or certain terminal illnesses, from coverage.[79]

Nonetheless, an equal protection challenge to a state program that excluded coverage of terminal illnesses for the purpose of rationing health care — particularly one that did so across the board — would probably fail. As one commentator has noted:

> May the government curb its own health care costs by reducing its benefits for the indigent or by rationing expensive lifesaving technologies? The consensus of the relatively sparse literature is that it may. Health care, like other welfare assistance, is not a fundamental right, except perhaps for prisoners who cannot secure health care for themselves. Barring discrimination on racial, ethnic, or religious grounds, the government is generally free to create such programs as it wishes, to serve whom it pleases, and to alter or reduce the distribution of benefits. Exercise of discretion will generally be upheld, even though the resulting programs may have a differential impact on particular racial groups or socioeconomic classes.[80]

b. Discrimination Statutes

All persons seeking medical care are essentially disabled.[81] By choosing to treat some and not others — for whatever reason — a program is choosing among people with disabilities. When it does so because it does not like one group of people, disability discrimination statutes could be useful tools, as outlined above. However, when a program makes such an interdisability choice for economic reasons — for example, when a program decides not to treat the terminally ill — the legal analysis is not so clear cut. Section 504's applicability to such a rationing program is not addressed explicitly in the law or its implementing regulations, nor has it ever been authoritatively decided by the U.S. Supreme Court.[82] The Americans with Disabilities Act also does not explicitly address this question; moreover it did not begin to take effect until 1992, and thus no cases of any kind have been litigated under it as of this writing. Accordingly, one can only lay out the principles by which such a claim would be adjudicated and speculate from related cases its probable outcome.

An important related case with which to begin consideration of the issue is *Alexander v. Choate*.[83] The case concerned a challenge to a rationing program designed by the Tennessee Medicaid agency. Faced with a $42 million budget shortage in 1980-1981, the state instituted a variety of cost-cutting measures, including a reduction from twenty to fourteen in the number of inpatient hospital days per year that the agency would pay on behalf of Medicaid recipients. The cutback was challenged on the grounds that it had a disparate impact on people with handicaps. The Court rejected this claim; it found that "the reduction, neutral on its face, does not distinguish between those whose coverage will be reduced and those whose coverage will not on the basis of any test, judgment, or trait that the handicapped as a class are less capable of meeting or less likely of having." The Court ruled that section 504 guarantees people with handicaps "meaningful access to the benefit that the grantee offers" but does not "guarantee the handicapped equal results."[84]

Alexander v. Choate can be distinguished from the rationing program posited here. First, in that case Tennessee adopted what appeared to be a facially neutral rule — fourteen days' inpatient care for everyone. Here we are positing that a program specifically chooses a particular group of persons with disabilities ("incurables") and denies them medical coverage on that basis. Moreover, the Tennessee program did provide some coverage for people with disabilities, albeit not enough for their needs as compared with nondisabled individuals. The rationing situation posited here concerns a *complete* denial of health care to a particular class of persons because of their prognosis. Nonetheless, *Alexander v. Choate* does evidence a frightening willingness on the part of the Supreme Court (which one would expect to find throughout the lower judiciary) to uphold as reasonable the rationing/cost-saving programs implemented by the state.

It may be important, then, to consider the differences between a state or federal rationing plan and a hospital's decision not to treat a certain group. Either may have a similar impact on the individual at issue. Theoretically, it should not matter whether one is analyzing the legality of a state program rationing health care (such as Oregon's plan, discussed above) or a hospital program turning away the terminally ill. Nonetheless, a second important principle in this area is that "Section 504 does not invalidate federal statutes or executive orders that provide benefits for only one group or only some groups of disabled people."[85] Indeed, federal regulations specifically state:

> *Programs limited by Federal law.* The exclusion of nonhandicapped persons from the benefits of a program limited by Federal statute or executive order to handicapped persons or the exclusion of a specific class of handicapped persons from a program limited by Federal statute or executive order to a different class of handicapped persons is not prohibited by this part.[86]

This principle has been enforced in federal case law to deny claims of interdisability discrimination brought against federal programs,[87] and has frequently been utilized to uphold Medicaid regulations that discriminate between different disabilities.[88] Unfortunately, other courts have misunderstood these cases to stand for the proposition that claims of interdisability discrimination are never cognizable under section 504.[89]

In fact, in the absence of specific federal statutes or regulations limiting programs by disability group, most courts have ruled that section 504 does extend to discrimination among people with different disabilities.[90] For example, in a New York case, a paraplegic law student sued the state, claiming that the higher rate of reimbursement funding for tuition and maintenance for blind students as compared to students with other disabilities violated section 504. The court found that the plaintiff had stated a cause of action under section 504 for discrimination vis-à-vis other disabled students, citing the section 504 regulations and explaining that section 504's application to such a claim was supported by "the bulk of the authority."[91]

Beyond a straightforward class-based discrimination claim, a rationing program could also be attacked on the basis that it denies individuals with disabilities their right to receive individualized assessments of their needs. By turning away all patients with AIDS, for example, a program would be making the determination that such persons were terminally ill and could not benefit from medical care. This generalized assumption is precisely what section 504 is designed to prevent. Recipients of federal funding are prohibited from making "placements and disburs[ing] services based not on an individual assessment of the abilities and potentials of each resident but on the generalized assumption that certain *groups* of people...are unable to benefit from certain activities and services."[92]

If the court did find that section 504 or, if, in the future, the ADA applies to discrimination between people with different disabilities, a program could be expected to claim several defenses, apart from reliance on Medicaid requirements or independent federal regulations. First, a defendant could argue that its discrimination was based not on the person's disability, but was rather a cost-saving device: legally this might be asserted as a claim that the individual was not being discriminated against "solely because of" his handicap, as required by section 504.[93] Even if accepted under section 504, however, such an argument would be unavailing under the ADA, which does not include the "solely because of" language. Second, a program might argue that its services are provided only to those whose lives it can meaningfully extend, and, therefore, persons with terminal illnesses are not "otherwise qualified" or eligible for the program. This argument, however, would seem to reflect little more than thinly veiled dislike for the disabled and could probably be refuted on factual grounds. It would also be a misreading of the concept of "otherwise qualified." Under the applicable regulations, a person is qualified if he or she "meets the essential eligibility requirements for the receipt of such service."[94] Most hospitals do not hold, as an eligibility requirement, that the person must get well.[95] Finally, a program could be expected to argue that its policy denying care to the terminally ill was "neutral," as was the argument in *Alexander v. Choate*, discussed above. However, a complete denial of services to a particular class of individuals because they are deemed "incurable" appears to be anything but "neutral." At the very least, section 504 should require a court to prohibit the program's decisions from being made "in an arbitrarily discriminatory manner."[96]

In sum, a health care rationing program that denied treatment to the terminally ill, including the HIV-infected, could be attacked under both section 504 and the ADA, as well as under the equal protection clause. While these legal questions have not yet been authoritatively resolved, interdisability discrimination claims should be cognizable under the Rehabilitation Act and the ADA and should bar rationing programs that have the effect of limiting treatments for a particular class of disabled persons, such as those with HIV. Even though HIV disease is presently incurable, HIV-infected persons are entitled to the treatments that are available and to the same level of care as any other member of society.

IV. Recommendations

The problems presented by HIV disease in Puerto Rico are receiving increasing attention. With funding from the federal government, the Resident Commissioner for Puerto Rico and the Puerto Rico Federal Affairs Commission, with the assistance of the National Council of La Raza (NCLR), have hosted a "Think Tank" AIDS Forum for the past several years. Additionally, community-based organizations and informal efforts on the Island are growing, and direct action groups like ACT-UP have sprung up in Puerto Rico. This elevated regard for the problems presented by HIV disease will be an important factor in addressing the issues outlined in this chapter. Each issue discussed requires attention.

First, the basic epidemiological facts concerning the incidence of the disease on the Island must be ascertained effectively to make planning more efficient.

Second, Puerto Rico must create immediately a comprehensive plan to provide accurate, nonjudgmental information about HIV disease to the populace. The plan must include frank information about "safe sex" practices, condom usage, and the danger of needle sharing. The information provided must be *created* in Spanish — not translated from English — and must be culturally relevant. Nonetheless, creative efforts must be undertaken to neutralize the opposition of the Catholic Church to these lifesaving endeavors. Women should be especially targeted for HIV-related education. Health care providers should also receive special education and support, not only about HIV disease itself and its manifestations but also about attitudes toward the HIV-infected.

Third, educational efforts must be undertaken to counter the rampant bias and prejudice experienced by people with HIV disease. If it does not already do so, Puerto Rican handicap discrimination law must be amended to protect the HIV-infected, and the administrative agency charged with its enforcement must be empowered to remedy discrimination against HIV-infected persons. This agency — as well as government leaders generally — must also provide moral leadership, speaking out against HIV-related bias on the Island. Legal services must be made more available to people with HIV disease, through the legal services program or through specific training programs. If necessary, financial incentives should be offered to lawyers to provide assistance to people with HIV disease.

Fourth, people with HIV disease must be given the same health care as others on the Island — and health care for all must be raised above its current abysmal level. The problem of scarce resources cannot legally be "solved" by denying care to the HIV-infected. Rather, a series of initiatives must combine to increase access to health care for all Puerto Ricans. Congress must remove the cap on federal Medicaid contributions in order to strengthen the provision of health care on the Island and in order to ensure that persons with HIV disease receive the same medical treatment and medicine available to others. Puerto Ricans, like all other American citizens, deserve and are entitled to basic health care, including potentially life-prolonging medication such as AZT. Puerto Rican officials must develop a comprehensive health care delivery system for the HIV-infected. Such a system must include the provision of primary health care, drug treatment, and care specifically targeted for women. It must provide anonymous HIV testing and T-cell monitoring, prophylactic drugs, and antivirals like AZT, as well as treatments for opportunistic infections. Outpatient ambulatory services, inpatient care, and hospice services must be ensured, particularly through the provision of a skilled case management system.

Individuals, organizations, government officials, foundations, corporations, and others who are combatting HIV disease on the mainland must begin to consider Puerto Rican issues as part of their mandate. The Island is part of the United States, with inextricable links to the mainland. The epidemic in Puerto Rico is an American epidemic.

NOTES

1.   Unless otherwise noted, the statistics in this section can be found in the testimony presented to the National Commission on AIDS during its November 27-28, 1990, hearings in Puerto Rico [hereinafter Commission].
2.   Lambert, *AIDS Travels New York-Puerto Rico "Air Bridge"*, N.Y. Times, June 15, 1990, at B-1, col. 1 [hereinafter Lambert].

3. The statistics in this paragraph are from *Puerto Rico's Burden Reaches Crisis Stage*, Boston Globe, June 18, 1990, at 8, col. 2.
4. The number of people who are medically eligible to receive AZT is subject to some debate. For example, Dr. Rullan estimates that around 20 to 25 percent of the people utilizing the public health care system are now receiving AZT, instead of 65 percent of the total who should be receiving it. Commission, *supra* note 1, at 56.
5. *See generally* Cunningham, *The Public Controversies of AIDS in Puerto Rico*, 29 Soc. Sci. Med. 545 (1989) [hereinafter Cunningham].
6. Commission, *supra* note 1, at 10-11.
7. The following characterization of Puerto Rican culture is from Commission, *supra* note 1, at 10-11.
8. Singer, et al., *SIDA: The Economic, Social, and Cultural Context of AIDS among Latinos*, 4 Med. Anthropology Q. 72, 93 (1990) [hereinafter Singer].
9. *Id*. at 101.
10. Howell, *AIDS in Puerto Rico*, N.Y. Newsday, Dec. 11, 1990, at 75.
11. Singer, *supra* note 8, at 102.
12. *Id*. at 104.
13. The Archbishop is quoted as having stating that "the harm caused by the use of condoms is more serious than the AIDS contamination." *Peor el profilacto que el SIDA*, El Nuevo Día, May 2, 1989.
14. *Id*.
15. Lambert, *supra* note 2.
16. *Ultimatum a Triple S*, El Nuevo Día, Nov. 22, 1987, at 7.
17. Cunningham, *supra* note 5, at 550. Nevertheless, as with most else about AIDS in Puerto Rico, this point is not without its counterpoint. Others have noted that "[p]hysicians in New York tell of Puerto Rican patients driven to the mainland by their families' rejection." Lambert, *supra* note 2.
18. Singer, *supra* note 8, at 89.
19. *Id*. at 89-90.
20. *See* Cunningham, *supra* note 5, at 550.
21. The analysis of the political situation that follows is drawn from Cunningham, *supra* note 5, unless otherwise noted.
22. The information in this paragraph can be found in, Olsen, *No Federal AIDS Funds: Local Health Agencies Told to End Rift*, San Juan Star, Sept. 29, 1987, at 1.
23. Cunningham, *supra* note 5, at 550.
24. *Id*. at 549.
25. Ramírez, *Our AIDS Epidemic*, San Juan Star, May 27, 1990, at 19.
26. Cunningham, *supra* note 5, at 551.
27. The results of the poll reported here are taken from Capo, *AIDS Patients Face Widespread Bias in P.R., Study Says*, San Juan Star, July 31, 1990, at 9.
28. This story is taken from the facts represented in Association of Friends and Relatives of AIDS Patients v. Regulations and Permits Admin., 740 F. Supp. 95 (D.P.R. 1990).
29. The plaintiffs also alleged a violation of their constitutional rights. However, as the court decided in the plaintiffs' favor on their statutory claim, it did not reach the constitutional argument, although it characterized it as "promising." *Id*. at 107.
30. This story is taken from Luquis, *Public School Finally Admits Two Children with AIDS*, San Juan Star, Aug. 7, 1990, and related news stories.

31. These discriminatory practices occur notwithstanding Department of Education memoranda prohibiting schools from denying entrance to the HIV-infected.

32. This story is taken from Brossy, *Patient's Woes Reveal AIDS Care*, San Juan Star, Mar. 7, 1988, at 17.

33. Cunningham, *supra* note 5, at 549.

34. *See* American Civil Liberties Union AIDS Project, Epidemic of Fear (1990) [hereinafter Epidemic of Fear].

35. For a fuller treatment of these issues, see *id.*

36. P.R. Laws Ann. tit. 1 § 505 (Supp. 1988).

37. Epidemic of Fear, *supra* note 34, 72-74.

38. It is estimated that 90 percent or more of persons with AIDS in Puerto Rico are medically indigent. Commission, *supra* note 1, at 32.

39. *Id.* at 32.

40. *Id.* at 57.

41. Interview by Luis A. Lavin with Laura Torres, Director of Administración de Facilidades y Servicios de Salud ("AFASS"), in San Juan, P.R. (April 27, 1990).

42. *Id.*

43. Commission, *supra* note 1, at 66, 73.

44. The information in these two paragraphs comes from interviews with Laura Torres, *supra* note 41.

45. Commission, *supra* note 1, at 74, 89, 93.

46. *Id.*

47. *Id.*

48. *Id.* at 57.

49. *Id.*

50. Interview by Luis A. Lavin with Angeris Duran Guzman, Director of Puerto Rico's Medicaid Program, in San Juan, P.R. (May 1, 1990).

51. Commission, *supra* note 1, at 73.

52. *Id.* at 100.

53. The information in this paragraph, except as otherwise noted, comes from an interview by Luis A. Lavin with Dr. Rivera Castano, Director of Puerto Rico's Latin American Center for Sexually Transmitted Diseases (CLETS), in San Juan, P.R. (May 1, 1990).

54. Mair v. Barton, No. 87-4206-R, 1988-1 Medicare & Medicaid Guide (CCH) 36, 692 (D.Kan.July 27, 1987).

55. 42 U.S.C. §§ 1396 *et seq.* (1988).

56. *Id.* §§ 1308 (a) (c) (1), 1396b(u) (4).

57. *Id.* § 1396a.

58. *See id.* § 1301(a) (1).

59. *Id.* § 1396d(a) (12).

60. Ellis v. Patterson, 859 F.2d 52, 56 (8th Cir. 1988).

61. 42 C.F.R. § 440.230(b) (1990).

62. *Id.* § 440.230(c).

63. Beal v. Doe, 432 U.S. 438, 444 (1977) (*quoting* 42 U.S.C. § 1396A(a)(17)).

64. *Id.* at 445-46.

65. *See Mair*, No. 87-4206-R, 1988-1 Medicare & Medicaid Guide (CCH) ¶ 36,692; *cf.* Weaver v. Reagan, 886 F.2d 194 (8th Cir. 1989) (state could not deny Medicaid coverage for off-label use of AZT).

66. *See, e.g.*, Montoya v. Johnston, 654 F. Supp. 511 (W.D. Tex. 1987) (holding that states could not arbitrarily limit coverage to otherwise eligible Medicaid recipients).

67. *See* United States v. Skandier, 785 F.2d 40, 43 (1st Cir. 1985).

68. L. Luquis, *Sullivan Will Ask Congress to Lift Ceiling on P.R. Medicaid Funding*, San Juan Star, July 31, 1990, at 1.

69. *See* 54 Fed. Reg. 23,134 (1989) (proposing amendments to 29 C.F.R. pts. 1910 *et seq.*, regarding occupational exposure to bloodborne pathogens).

70. *See* Harris v. McRae, 448 U.S. 297 (1980); Maher v. Roe, 432 U.S. 464 (1977).

71. 417 U.S. 484 (1974).

72. Williamson v. Lee Optical Co., 348 U.S. 483, 489 (1955).

73. 448 U.S. 297 (1980).

74. A form of this argument was made by the ACLU of Oregon in a nonconstitutional case challenging the exclusion of people with AIDS from a self-insurance program at a private company in that state. The plaintiff argued that exclusion of people with AIDS was gender-based discrimination because it had a disparate impact on men, as 90 percent of persons with AIDS in Oregon were male. After the state [equal employment opportunity commission] made a finding of probable cause that such an exclusion constituted illegal discrimination against men, the case was settled favorably for the plaintiffs. *See* Doe v. Beaverton Nissan, No. ST-EM-HP-870108-1353 (Or. Bur. Labor & Indus. 1986).

75. 394 U.S. 618 (1969).

76. *Id.* at 633.

77. 415 U.S. 250 (1974).

78. Another example of this principle is James v. Strange, 407 U.S. 128 (1972), in which the Supreme Court held that a statute designed to recover legal fees from indigent criminal defendants was unconstitutional because it denied these indigent defendants hardship exemptions allowed to civil debtors. "The statute before us embodies elements of punitiveness and discrimination which violate the rights of citizens to equal treatment under the law." Id. at 142. Similarly, in United States Dept. of Agric. v. Moreno, 413 U.S. 528 (1973), the Court held that a law altering the definition of "household" in order to exclude "hippie communes" from participation in the food stamp program was unconstitutional: "For if the constitutional conception of 'equal protections of the laws' means anything, it must at the very least mean that a bare congressional desire to harm a politically unpopular group cannot constitute a legitimate government interest." *Id.* at 535.

79. The rational basis is not an impossible barrier to overcome. In Doe v. Austin, 848 F.2d 1386 (6th Cir. 1988), *cert. denied sub nom.* Cowherd v. Doe, 488 U.S. 967 (1988), the court found that a Kentucky statute that provided judicial commitment hearings for the mentally ill but not for the mentally retarded violated the equal protection clause, since there was no rational basis for the distinction. Citing the Supreme Court holding in Cleburne v. Cleburne Living Center, Inc., 473 U.S. 432, 439 (1985), the Sixth Circuit stated that when "a state enacts legislation which treats different classes of people differently, the classification drawn by the statute must be rationally related to a legitimate state purpose." *Austin*, 848 F.2d at 1394. Kentucky's justifications for their civil commitment policy did not meet this standard.

80. Morreim, *Cost Containment and the Standard of Medical Care*, 75 Cal. L. Rev. 1719, 1742 (1987) (citations omitted).

81. Not all such persons would necessarily be "handicapped" or "disabled" as these terms are defined in section 504 and the Americans with Disabilities Act. Thus, a rationing program could raise two different types of claims: it could be framed as discrimination between legally disabled persons (as the terminally ill would undoubtedly meet the statutory definition of disability) and non-legally disabled persons; or it could be framed as a case of discrimination between persons with different types of disabilities (interdisability discrimination). The first would result from a claim that a program was turning away the terminally ill to care for persons without grave illnesses. The second would result from a claim that a program was turning away the terminally ill to care for other seriously ill persons. A true rationing program would in fact probably present both situations. This discussion considers rationing as an issue of interdisability discrimination unless otherwise noted.

82. Indeed, the closest case in point is a tentative opinion from a federal district court in Missouri from the late 1970s holding that the closure of acute inpatient facilities and some emergency room and outpatient facilities in one hospital and their merger into another hospital did not constitute discrimination against people with handicaps. Jackson v. Conway, 476 F. Supp. 896 (E.D. Mo. 1979), *aff'd*, 620 F.2d 680 (8th Cir. 1980).

83. 469 U.S. 287 (1985).

84. The regulations implementing Section 504 state in pertinent part:

> A [federal aid] recipient, in providing any aid, benefit, or service, may not... on the basis of handicap:

> Afford a qualified handicapped person the opportunity to participate in or benefit from the aid, benefit or service that is not equal to that afforded to others;...

> Provide different or separate aid, benefits, or services to handicapped persons or to any class of handicapped persons unless such action is necessary to provide qualified handicapped persons with aid, benefits or services that are as effective as those provided to others;...

> Otherwise limit a qualified handicapped person in the enjoyment of any right, privilege, advantage or opportunity enjoyed by others receiving an aid, benefit or service.

45 C.F.R. § 84.4(b) (1990). These regulations seem to indicate that people with a particular disability are not to be excluded from a program simply on the basis of that disability, whether other disabled people are served by the program or not.

85. Tucker & Goldstein, Legal Rights of Persons with Disabilities 7:25 n.133 (1991) [hereinafter Tucker & Goldstein].

86. 45 C.F.R. § 84.4(c) (1989).

87. *See, e.g.*, Traynor v. Turnage, 485 U.S. 535, 549 (1988) (section 504 does not prohibit "exclusion of a specific class of handicapped persons from a program limited by Federal statute or executive order to a different class of handicapped persons"); Knutzen v. Eben Ezer Lutheran Hous. Ctr., 815 F.2d at 1353 (10th Cir. 1987) (where HUD regulations provide for housing for a specific group of disabled people, section 504 cannot be used to expand the delivery of those benefits to other groups of disabled people).

Courts that are reluctant to use section 504 for anything other than discrimination between people with disabilities and nondisabled persons often cite *Traynor* to support this distinction. *See, e.g.,* P.C. v. McLaughlin, 913 F.2d 1033, 1041 (2d Cir. 1990) (denying disabled man's claim of discrimination under section 504 where he was not given education provided to other disabled students). Such a reading of *Traynor* misunderstands the context in which that case arose and thus misapplies its holding. *Traynor* arose in the context of a federal statute (Veterans' Administration regulations) that limited benefits to a certain group of disabled people. The claim in *Traynor* was therefore specifically limited by federal regulations, which thereby limited the applicability of section 504 as discussed above. *Traynor* does not, therefore, stand for the proposition that claims among disabilities are never recognized by section 504.

88. Thus, for example, in Doe v. Colautti, 592 F.2d 704 (3d Cir. 1979), the court upheld a state medical assistance program that limited inpatient reimbursement for psychiatric patients to sixty days though the program had no time limits for inpatient care for physical illness. The court wrote: "Because Congress so carefully drew these lines in the Medicaid statute, we do not believe, in the absence of any specific evidence supporting Doe's position, that Congress intended § 504 of the Rehabilitation Act to obliterate the distinctions between the medical care a state medical assistance program must cover and the care it need not include." *Id.* at 710.

Similarly, New Hampshire's provision of medical assistance to blind youth under eighteen, but not to any other disabled youth, withstood a section 504 challenge in Duquette v. Dupuis, 582 F. Supp. 1365 (D.N.H. 1984). Without reaching the issue of whether section 504 prohibits discrimination among people with different disabilities, the court held that the Medicaid Act funding provisions which required such assistance to blind youth took precedence over section 504. "Section 504 does not impose binding conditions on the use of federal Medicaid funds such that New Hampshire would be required to extend medical assistance benefit [sic] to all classes of disabled persons if it provides assistance to persons disabled by blindness." Duquette, 582 F. Supp. at 1369-70. *See also* Bernard B. v. Blue Cross and Blue Shield of Greater New York, 528 F.Supp. 125 (S.D.N.Y. 1981), *aff'd*, 679 F.2d 7 (2d Cir. 1982).

89. Colin K. v. Schmidt, 715 F.2d 1, 9 (1st Cir. 1983) ("[while] we have serious doubts whether Congress intended § 504 to provide plaintiffs with a claim for discrimination vis-a-vis other handicapped individuals, the argument is not without support"). *Colin K.*'s statement was merely dicta expressing doubt and acknowledging that other courts disagree.

90. *See, e.g.,* Clark v. Cohen, 613 F. Supp. 684, 692-93 & n.6 (E.D. Pa. 1985) (claims between classes of disabled people were cognizable under section 504), *aff'd* 794 F.2d 79 (3rd Cir.), *cert. denied* 479 U.S. 962 (1986); Gieseking v. Schafer, 672 F. Supp. 1249, 1263 (W.D. Mo. 1987) ("a section 504 cause of action may lie where plaintiffs assert discrimination between classes of handicapped persons"); Garrity v. Gallen, 522 F. Supp. 171, 213, 217 (D.C.N.H. 1981) (disparity in quality of facilities and programs provided to severely as opposed to mildly mentally disabled residents of state school for the retarded was discrimination under section 504); Schornstein v. New Jersey Div. of Vocational Rehabilitation, 519 F. Supp. 773, 778 (D.C.N.J. 1981), *aff'd* 688 F.2d 824 (2d Cir. 1982) (state Division of Vocational Rehabilitation decision not to provide interpreter

for deaf client in college, when D.V.R. provided adaptive services for clients with other disabilities, was cognizable discrimination under section 504).

91. McGuire v. Switzer, 734 F. Supp. 99, 114-15 & n.16 (S.D.N.Y. 1990). This bulk of authority is well supported by Congress's intent in enacting section 504. As two commentators have opined:

> Section 504 should be read as prohibiting discrimination against handicapped people vis-à-vis other handicapped people, as well as vis-à-vis non-handicapped people. Discrimination against particular classes or subclasses of handicapped people is just as invidious as any other form of discrimination and, as such, is within the scope of discriminatory conduct Congress sought to prohibit when enacting Section 504.

Tucker & Goldstein, *supra* note 85, at 7:24.

92. Garrity v. Gallen, 522 F. Supp. 171, 215 (D.N.H. 1981).
93. *See, e.g.,* Clark v. Cohen, 613 F. Supp. 684, 693 (E.D. Pa. 1985), *aff'd on other grounds,* 794 F.2d 79 (3d Cir. 1986), *cert. denied,* 479 U.S. 962 (1986).
94. 45 C.F.R. § 84.3(k)(4) (1990). The ADA refers only to eligibility.
95. As with the "solely because of" defense discussed in *supra* note 93, the ADA renders this question moot as well, as the term "qualified" is not even utilized in Title III of the ADA. Rather, the law says that services cannot be denied to a person with a disability, ADA § 302 (a), but that a provider can have an eligibility criterion that screens out a person with a disability only if that criterion is necessary for the provision of services, ADA § 302(b)(2)(A). Again, it would be impossible for a hospital to argue that having a criterion that the person must get well is necessary for the provision of hospital services.
96. *McGuire,* 734 F. Supp. at 114 n.17.

III

NEW ISSUES IN CIVIL RIGHTS

A substantial portion of what has been called the rights revolution — the expansion of individual liberties recognized by the law — occurred in the fields of criminal law and employment law. In the former, the emphasis lay in curbing the absolute power of governmental authorities, such as police and prosecutors, to interrogate and incarcerate persons accused of crimes. In the latter, civil rights laws were enacted to shield individual members of historically disadvantaged minority groups from discriminatory workplace practices.

These two areas have also been important in contests over the rights of persons with HIV disease. In the first years of the epidemic, as Chapter 8 describes, many observers feared that widespread isolation of persons with this disease would occur under often archaic quarantine statutes. That fear has not been realized, however, as public health professionals in charge of enforcing these laws realized that such actions would be not only ineffective but counterproductive in the efforts to stem the spread of HIV. Unfortunately, criminal prosecutors have undermined this public health consensus: there has been an upsurge in criminal prosecutions against persons with HIV, often for conduct (such as spitting or biting) which poses no risk of transmitting the virus. Chapter 8 analyzes the nature of these criminal cases and considers the disjuncture between the prosecutorial and public health approaches. It urges that all actions to deprive liberty be subject to the efficacy and necessity standards that apply in the public health context.

The workplace is an arena where many persons with HIV must contend daily with the possibility of discrimination. As treatments for the disease become more effective and patients live longer and more productive lives, there are more and more Americans with HIV on the job. In this area of law, perhaps more than any other, the extension of previously established principles of civil rights law has been the most important and the most successful. Congressional enactment of the Americans with Disabilities Act in 1990 included most private businesses among those covered by a federal law barring discrimination based on disability. Chapter 9 explains how that new law will settle some longstanding issues related to HIV in the workplace, and sharpen others that are likely to dominate future debates in this area.

HIV disease presents a critical new front in the continuing fight for the civil rights of all Americans. If society permits the rights of HIV-infected persons to be compromised because of hysteria or dislike of those with the disease, it will be weakening the premise at the heart of this country's civil rights revolution — that individuals should be judged according to their abilities, not according to the fears and prejudices of others. Sustenance of this basic American premise will require vigilance for the rights of the HIV-infected in the 1990s.

8

THE CRIMINALIZATION OF HIV

By Mark H. Jackson

Introduction: Public Health v. Criminalization

When the virus that causes AIDS was first identified more than eight years ago, legal commentators feared that in the resulting public hysteria public health officials would implement measures that would deprive people infected with, or suspected of being infected with HIV of their civil rights. At that time, commentators identified quarantine or isolation as the most serious threat to the civil liberties of people with AIDS.[1] There was good reason to fear that public health officials would implement quarantines to fight the AIDS epidemic. First, quarantine historically has been a popular method of controlling infectious diseases. In the past, various states have imposed quarantines to combat smallpox, tuberculosis, bubonic plague, venereal disease, and other diseases.[2] What is more, courts historically have upheld these measures on the ground that states should be provided broad latitude under their police powers to fight perceived health crises.[3]

Not surprisingly, then, several public officials and others began calling for the imposition of quarantines soon after the AIDS crisis was identified.[4] In fact, in response to the growing crisis, several states amended their quarantine statutes, many of which had been enacted in the nineteenth century. The amendments sought both to include AIDS as a disease that may warrant the imposition of quarantines and to make quarantine rules more consistent with the principles of procedural due process that had developed during the past fifty years. Other states enacted AIDS-specific legislation that, among other things, provided for the isolation or quarantine of people with AIDS.[5]

It is remarkable, in light of this history, that in the past decade there have, in fact, been very few attempts by states to quarantine or isolate people infected with HIV. It has become clear that many public health officials throughout the country have concluded that a public health response consisting of coercive measures, such as quarantines, would be inefficacious, as well as unconstitutional.

Public health officials have recognized that HIV infection is different from other known infections and sexually transmitted diseases in ways that render many of the traditional public health responses invalid. First, it has been firmly established that HIV cannot be transmitted through casual contact. Scientists have identified only three ways in which HIV can be transmitted: (1) by certain types of sexual contact; (2) by blood-to-mucous-membrane contact; and (3) perinatally. Moreover, a person can substantially reduce the risk of transmission by taking precautions while engaging in some high-risk activities; for example, by using condoms while engaging in sexual contact, and by sterilizing or bleaching needles before using drugs intravenously. Although the medical community has concluded that there is a theoretical risk of transmitting the virus through saliva (by biting or spitting), there has been no reported instance of HIV being transmitted in that manner.

Second, HIV is a disease for which there is no known cure. Although certain drugs, most notably AZT, have been identified as prophylaxes against the onset of opportunistic infections, no drug has been proven to forestall these ultimately fatal diseases indefinitely. In addition, there is no known way of eliminating a person's infectiousness (the ability to transmit the virus to others).

Although anyone engaging in activities that transmit the virus is theoretically at risk of contracting it, the HIV epidemic is largely associated with gay men, IV drug users and their sex partners, and hemophiliacs. Because of the fatal nature of the disease and the fact that HIV has hit groups that are already the subjects of public disfavor, people diagnosed as being seropositive have been subject to an alarming degree of harassment, discrimination, and social stigmatization.[6] Finally, the sheer volume of people infected with HIV (estimated to number one million within the United States) would render the imposition of any coercive measures unworkable.

These characteristics of HIV infection have convinced many public health officials that the use of coercive measures against people infected with the disease would be both impossible to implement and ineffective in fighting the spread of the disease, since the use of coercive measures would discourage people at risk from getting tested and seeking treatment. Instead, public health officials have almost universally recommended that states combat the disease through intensive efforts to educate people about the modes of transmission and the ways to reduce the risk of transmitting or contracting the virus. In order to encourage voluntary testing and subsequent diagnosis and treatment, states have legislated that information that would identify a person as HIV-positive be kept largely confidential.

In choosing to forgo coercive measures, public health officials have not only responded to what they perceive to be public health imperatives; they have, no doubt, also been affected by developing judicial precedent, which has mandated that public officials proposing public health measures that affect the fundamental rights of individuals demonstrate that such measures are medically justified. In the *Arline* case, the U.S. Supreme Court ruled that an elementary school teacher diagnosed with tuberculosis, and subsequently fired from her job, was considered "handicapped" under the Rehabilitation Act of 1973. The Court remanded the case to the trial court to determine whether the school could rehire the teacher and "reasonably accommodate" her needs. The Court determined that the Rehabilitation Act permits the dismissal of an employee on the basis of his or her being infected with a contagious disease only if there is "a significant risk of communicating [that] disease to others." Significantly, the Court directed that lower courts "should defer to the reasonable medical judgments of public health officials."[7] Although *Arline* was litigated under the provisions of the Rehabilitation Act, it and subsequent cases have clearly held that courts, when confronted with public health measures that limit certain people's constitutional rights, will conduct an independent review of the medical facts to determine whether these measures are necessary.[8]

By contrast to the public health system's determination not to institute sweeping coercive measures, the criminal justice system has forcibly tested, prosecuted, convicted, and sentenced people for committing certain crimes while infected with HIV. State prosecutors and criminal courts are, in effect, making AIDS policy — policy that largely contradicts and undermines current public health strategies. This chapter will demonstrate that it is inappropriate for the criminal justice system to apply criminal statutes to HIV-related crimes — both as a matter of law and as a matter of sound public policy. The chapter is divided into two sections: the first considers the HIV testing and prosecution of individuals charged with biting or spitting and demonstrates the legal and public policy problems with such prosecutions; the second section considers the HIV testing and prosecution of individuals charged with sexual offenses — crimes, unlike biting and spitting, that could pose more than a theoretical possibility of transmitting the virus — and, similarly, demonstrates the legal and policy difficulties with such prosecutions.

I. Mandatory Testing and Prosecution of Persons Charged with a Crime for Spitting and Biting

Since the mid-1980s, courts have been confronted with cases in which individuals with HIV disease, or suspected of having HIV disease, have been charged with serious crimes for biting or spitting or have been the subject of motions to compel HIV tests for the purpose of determining whether to charge them with additional crimes. Although not limited in their ability to bring such cases, prosecutors appear to do so only when a law enforcement official is bitten or spit upon, usually by an individual already in police custody. Defendants in these cases typically have been charged with crimes of attempted murder and/or assault in the first degree:

- In October 1989, a resident of Georgia was convicted by a jury of aggravated assault with the intent to commit murder after biting a police officer who was investigating a domestic dispute between the defendant and his roommate. The defendant was sentenced to ten years in prison.[9]

- In April 1990, a prison inmate with AIDS was convicted of attempted murder in New Jersey for biting a sheriff and exclaiming, "Die, you pig!"[10]

- In December 1989, a defendant infected with HIV and imprisoned in a Texas jail was sentenced to life in prison for attempted murder for spitting at a prison guard.[11]

- In Minnesota, an HIV-infected federal prisoner was convicted of assault with a deadly and dangerous weapon for use of his mouth and teeth in a prison fight.[12]

- In Alabama, a man was charged with assault in the first degree for biting a prison guard during an altercation. The Alabama court reached the opposite decision from the Minnesota case, reversing the lower court's conviction on the grounds that HIV could not be transmitted through a human bite, and, unlike in Minnesota, no expert medical testimony was introduced at trial to show that a human bite alone could cause "serious physical injury."[13]

- In New York, a prosecutor sought to compel a person arrested for prostitution (who had been convicted of that crime on two previous occasions) to submit to an HIV test after she bit a police officer during processing and told the officer she was "going to get him with her germs." According to reports, the prosecution intended to file additional charges against the defendant in the event the tests came back positive.[14]

As discussed below (in subsection B), there is no legal basis for charging people infected with HIV with serious crimes for biting or spitting; because of the lack of legal basis for such cases, HIV testing in these circumstances is unwarranted (as demonstrated immediately below in subsection A). Even if there were an arguable legal basis for bringing such charges, however, subsection C argues that a course that seeks to punish people for engaging in acts that cannot transmit the virus is unsound public policy.

A. Testing a Defendant's HIV Status[15]

A threshold question in HIV-related prosecutions is whether the defendant is, in fact, infected; to that end, many prosecutors seek forced testing of persons suspected of being HIV-infected following a biting or spitting incident.[16]

In most circumstances, forced testing of a person charged with biting or spitting at a law enforcement official for HIV would violate the Fourth Amendment to the Constitution. The Fourth Amendment protects "the right of the people to be secure in their persons, houses, papers, and effects, against unreasonable searches and seizures..." A person's Fourth Amendment rights are implicated if the conduct at issue infringes an expectation of privacy "based on societal expectations that have deep roots in the history of the Amendment."[17] A court-administered blood test, such as the one required to test for HIV, constitutes a "search" that implicates the Fourth Amendment,[18] both because of the physical invasion of the person's body and because individuals have a reasonable expectation of privacy in the personal information their bodily fluids contain.[19] In order for a search to be "reasonable" under the Fourth Amendment, (1) it must be accomplished pursuant to a warrant issued upon "probable cause" and (2) the government's interest in the results of the search must outweigh the invasion of privacy to the person being tested.[20]

"Probable cause" is usually understood in the criminal context — a search is unreasonable unless a law enforcement official has probable cause to believe that the person to be searched has violated the law. In a typical biting or spitting case, however, there is no probable cause that an HIV test will reveal material evidence that the crime of attempted murder or first-degree assault has been committed.

A determination whether probable cause exists in a given case cannot be made without regard to the elements of the particular crime charged. In order to make out a case for attempted murder, for example, a prosecutor would need to show that the defendant (1) had the intention of killing another person; and (2) committed an overt act "which except for the interference of some cause preventing the carrying out of the intent would have resulted in the commission of a homicide."[21] In prosecuting a person for attempted murder in a biting or spitting case, the prosecutor would need to show that the defendant either (1) was aware or believed that he or she was HIV-positive at the time of the alleged attack, and (2) believed that the disease could be transmitted by biting or spitting at the victim.

Given these requirements, in an attempted murder case an HIV test result is irrelevant to the prosecutor's case. The issue in the attempted murder case is not whether the defendant was HIV-infected, but whether the defendant *believed* he or she was HIV-infected and further believed that biting or spitting could kill another person. If a defendant wrongly believed that he or she was infected and bit a person intending to kill, that defendant would technically be guilty of attempted murder. A positive HIV test result unaccompanied by evidence that the defendant knew or believed he or she was HIV-positive would not be probative. On the other hand, if there was testimony that a defendant knew or believed he was HIV-positive, an HIV test result would be irrelevant. Even if a person's HIV status at the time of the attack were somehow relevant to the elements of the crime, a test administered *after* the event will not indicate that the defendant was HIV-positive at the time of the incident.[22] In fact, a positive test result several months after a defendant has been arrested will be more prejudicial than probative of the issue of whether the defendant was HIV-positive at the time of the alleged crime and therefore probably inadmissible as evidence.

In addition, the test results do not prove that the defendant believed (albeit wrongly) that HIV could be transmitted through a bite or in saliva. The state would have the almost impossible task of demonstrating that the defendant had been advised that such transmission was possible, and that he believed such advice. If a person with AIDS was aware that HIV could not be transmitted via a bite or saliva, he or she could not be convicted of attempted murder or first-degree assault even if that person threatened to kill an officer by engaging in that act.

HIV test results are even less meaningful in a first-degree assault case, and thus mandatory testing in such a case is clearly unjustifiable. In order to make out a case for first-degree assault, a prosecutor must show that the defendant (1) intended to cause serious physical injury, and (2) did cause serious physical injury (3) by means of a deadly or dangerous weapon.[23] In such a prosecution, the fact that a defendant was HIV-positive is irrelevant. If an HIV-infected person cannot cause death or serious physical injury by biting or spitting at another person, one of the elements of the offense, there can be no reason for seeking to determine the defendant's status in order to prosecute such a crime.

In sum, it is difficult to see how states can demonstrate probable cause to support the testing of people charged with attempted murder or first-degree assault for biting or spitting at law enforcement officials.

In addition to the absence of probable cause in this context, a prosecutor would also be hard pressed to satisfy the second prong of the Fourth Amendment standard — that the state's interest in the results of the test outweighs the defendant's interest in his or her privacy. Forcing a person to subject himself to an HIV test constitutes a substantial invasion of privacy to that individual. The privacy interests of a person being forced to submit to an HIV test go well beyond a person's interest in not having his body intruded upon for the purpose of finding evidence of a crime. A mandatory HIV test essentially forces a person to learn whether he or she has been infected with a disease that, in all likelihood, will be fatal in the next several years. A positive HIV test will almost certainly have a devastating impact on a person's emotional and physical well-being. But mandatory testing goes even further: it discloses these extremely sensitive results to other people, subjecting the person tested to possible harassment (which is especially likely to occur within the prison setting) and discrimination in almost all facets of life, including employment, housing, and family relationships.

At the same time, the government's interest is vague and indeterminate. The government can have only two possible reasons for seeking to test a person who bit or spit at an officer. First, the government seeks to punish the offender, or to deter the offender, and others, from such conduct, by bringing more serious charges against an HIV-positive defendant. Second, the government wishes to advise the officer of his or her exposure to HIV. Neither goal is sufficient to warrant testing the defendant involuntarily. As discussed above, HIV test results are irrelevant to the elements of attempted murder and assault in the first degree. Since the test would not aid the prosecution in obtaining a conviction, it cannot possibly outweigh the defendant's substantial privacy interest. More fundamentally, since a person with AIDS cannot transmit the virus by biting or spitting at another person, the defendants in these cases are not dangerous. Accordingly, the state's interest in testing defendants for the purpose of prosecuting them for crimes more serious than assault and battery cannot outweigh the individuals' interests in their privacy.

The government's second interest — to advise the victim of his or her exposure — also cannot overcome the individual's strong privacy interest. Although an officer would no doubt want to know whether he or she has been infected with the HIV, it is considered almost impossible to transmit the disease through a bite or saliva.[24] In any event, testing the defendant for the virus will not tell the officer whether he has been infected: it will only tell him whether he or she has been possibly exposed to the virus. The only way the officer can know whether he or she has been infected is to be tested periodically in the months following the incident. In fact, the defendant's test results can be misleading. Even if the defendant tests negative for the virus, it is still possible that the defendant is actually HIV-infected but has not yet developed antibodies to the virus. An officer cannot, therefore, on the basis of a defendant's negative test results, conclude that he or she has or has not been exposed to the virus. Again, the officer must be tested in order to be sure of the results. Since an HIV test performed on a defendant will be inconclusive regarding the officer's status, the purported need for a test does not override the defendant's privacy interests. (A more detailed consideration of this balance appears below, on pages 246-249, in the context of the discussion of testing sex offenders.)

Nothwithstanding this constitutional analysis, many states have enacted statutes permitting testing of defendants after a biting incident; one such statute, California's Proposition 96,[25] was upheld against a constitutional challenge by a California appellate court in the *Johnetta J.* case.[26]

In *Johnetta J.*, the petitioner allegedly became disruptive while attending a child dependency hearing in San Francisco Superior Court. When a sheriff's deputy attempted to remove her physically from the courtroom, she inflicted "a deep bite on the deputy's arm which penetrated the skin and drew blood." Petitioner was charged with felony assault with force likely to produce great bodily injury, felony assault on a police officer, and misdemeanor interference with an officer. Subsequently, the deputy sheriff invoked the provisions of Proposition 96 in order to compel the assailant to be tested for HIV.

In upholding the statute, the California Appellate Court ruled that the electorate, by adopting Proposition 96, had determined that there was a "special need" in cases such as this one to justify the relaxation of the normal Fourth Amendment probable cause requirements. Specifically, the court pointed to the compelling interest of local government in protecting "the health and safety of its employees faced with the possibility of becoming infected with HIV in the line of duty." According to the court, because officers would typically have no indication of whether there was probable cause to believe that an assailant was *infected* with HIV, it was a reasonable solution to "test those persons who assault peace officers if there is probable cause to believe the officer has been exposed to the assailant's bodily fluids."

In balancing the respective interests of the parties, the court made two critical findings. First, the court interpreted the expert medical testimony that there was only a theoretical risk of transmission of HIV through saliva to mean that it was possible that such a transmission could take place and that "the available evidence is insufficient to determine conclusively that HIV cannot be transferred through a bite." Second, the court agreed with the deputy sheriff's argument that the testing of the assailant was "medically useful." Although the court conceded that in order for an officer to be sure of his or her HIV status he or she would have to be tested, it nonetheless concluded that if the assailant's blood test were negative, the chances of infection would be smaller and the testing would, therefore, diminish the officer's anxiety. Moreover, the court concluded that if an assailant tested positive for

HIV, the physician treating the officer would monitor the officer's health more closely.

The court's decision in *Johnetta J.* is flawed in several respects. Most significantly, it places greater weight on the anxiety of the deputy sheriff than on the almost universally accepted medical knowledge regarding the possibility of transmitting HIV by means of saliva. The court improperly interpreted the testimony that there was only a "theoretical possibility" of such transmission to mean that there was some possibility. The clear meaning of the expert testimony was that there has been no reported case of transmission of HIV through saliva, but there was no scientific way to rule out entirely the possibility of such a transmission.[27] Second, the court places excessive weight on the degree to which the test results would relieve the anxiety of the peace officer and potentially aid in treatment. Based on the medical evidence presented, the police officer's fears (although perhaps understandable) are unjustified. They should certainly not form the basis for the court's decision. Moreover, as the court itself acknowledges, the test results are not only inconclusive, they can be misleading: if an officer could, in fact, contract HIV through a bite, it would be a mistake for an officer to become less anxious simply because the assailant tested negative. In addition, the fact that the police officer cannot reasonably rely on the tests of the assailant, but instead must himself be tested, strongly suggests that the police officer's interests do not outweigh the interests of the assailant.

The court did indicate in its opinion, however, that it did not believe that Proposition 96 was a prudent public policy. At the end of its opinion, the court writes:

> Although we uphold the statute's constitutionality, we cannot rule on its wisdom. Proposition 96 mandates costly hearings and testing procedures consuming the time and resources of the courts and public entities. Testing, if frequent, will undoubtedly amount to a measurable drain on the fiscal resources of local governments...[The medical experts who testified] opine that the only really effective means of determining HIV infection is for the concerned public safety employees to undergo their own tests.[28]

B. Convicting an HIV-Positive Person for Biting or Spitting

As the above analysis demonstrates, it would be nearly impossible for a prosecutor to prove beyond a reasonable doubt the elements of either first-degree assault or attempted murder in the context of a spitting or biting incident.

A first-degree assault requires proof that the defendant's actions have actually caused harm. Even if a prosecutor could prove beyond a reasonable doubt that a particular defendant intended to cause serious bodily harm to another, and that a defendant's mouth and/or teeth constituted a deadly weapon, it is highly unlikely that a defendant could truly cause serious bodily harm — due to HIV infection specifically — by biting or spitting at a police officer. As HIV cannot be transmitted by these acts, there would be no basis for the conviction. This was the precise basis upon which the Alabama Court of Criminal Appeals reversed the defendant's conviction of assault in the first degree in the *Brock* case.[29]

In *Brock*, the defendant, a prisoner with AIDS, was convicted of first-degree assault after biting a prison guard. The appelate court reversed the conviction on several grounds. First, the court ruled that the state had failed to prove that the defendant used his mouth and teeth under circumstances "highly capable of causing serious physical injury," because it failed to prove that HIV could be transmitted through a bite. (The court expressly refused to take judicial notice of that allegation.) Second, the court pointed out that there was no proof that the bite *caused* serious physical injury. Finally, the court ruled that there was no evidence that the defendant *intended* to cause physical injury since there was no proof that the defendant was aware, or had been informed, that HIV could be transmitted through a human bite.

The charge of attempted murder is more difficult to overcome because in most states a person can be convicted of that crime even if it is impossible to kill another person by biting or spitting.[30] The prosecutor merely needs to prove that the defendant believed he or she was infected, believed he or she could transmit the virus by spitting or biting, and did so intending to kill the other person. For instance, the Model Penal Code provides:

> (1) that a person is guilty of an attempt to commit a crime if, acting with the kind of culpability otherwise required for the commission of the offense, (2) he purposefully engages in conduct which would constitute the crime if the attendant circumstances were as he believes them to be....[31]

Based on this type of reasoning, an Indiana appellate court reinstated the jury's conviction of an individual for attempted murder, even though it had not been established that the defendant could have killed the alleged victim by his acts.[32] The defendant had apparently attempted to commit suicide by slashing his wrists. When paramedics arrived to administer aid, the defendant "stood up, ran toward [one of the paramedics], and screamed that he should be left to die because he had AIDS." When the paramedic told the defendant that they were there to help him, the defendant allegedly stated that "he wanted to f—— [the paramedic] and give it to him." The defendant allegedly began "jerking" his arms at the paramedic, causing blood to spray into the paramedic's mouth and eyes, began spitting at emergency medical technicians, "scratched, bit and spit" at one of them, and "grabbed a blood-soaked wig and struck [one of the paramedics] with it."

The trial court had vacated the three counts of attempted murder on the basis that the state did not prove that "the conduct of spitting, throwing blood and biting" can constitute a "substantial step" in causing the death of another person because the state did not introduce evidence that HIV could be transmitted in that fashion. The Court of Appeals reversed the trial court's ruling and reinstated the attempted murder counts, finding that under Indiana law the state was not required to prove that defendant's conduct could actually have killed another person. According to the court, "It was only necessary for the State to show that [the defendant] did all that he believed necessary to bring about an intended result, *regardless* of what was *actually possible*."

Quite apart from whether it is wise to prosecute people for serious crimes that are impossible to commit, a person infected with HIV who intends to kill another person by biting or spitting at that person, believing (wrongly) that it is possible, may be technically guilty of attempted murder. It would be extremely difficult, however, for the prosecution to prove its case. First, the prosecution would need to prove that the defendant was aware at the time of the alleged crime that he or she was HIV-positive. But even assuming the defendant was aware of his or her HIV status, it would be difficult for the prosecution to prove that the defendant intended to kill the victim. The prosecutor would need to show that the defendant believed that HIV could be transmitted through a bite or saliva. Because HIV *cannot* be transmitted by such acts, a prosecutor should not be able to rely merely on a defendant's threats to kill the other person to show that a defendant believed HIV could be transmitted that way. The prosecutor should be required to point to some other proof that the defendant held this mistaken belief. Even if the defendant made a threat while spitting or biting, it is unlikely that the person was doing anything more than trying to scare the officer — particularly when the incidents usually take place during a highly charged event, such as an arrest or prison fight (or, as in the Indiana case, when the defendant is on the verge of suicide). A court should treat such a threat in the same way it would treat the prosecution of a person who says, "I am going to kill you," and punches the victim in the face. The assailant there would be prosecuted, if at all, for simple assault, not for attempted murder.

C. Public Policy Reasons Against Prosecuting Cases of Biting or Spitting

By prosecuting people for serious crimes for committing what amount to less than dangerous acts, the criminal justice system is undermining sound public health strategies for combatting HIV infection.

First, prosecutors are going further than public health officials ever considered for measures to combat HIV. Prosecutors are even moving beyond the principles of behavior-based quarantines, which have been rejected by public health officials. Behavior-based quarantines call for the isolation of people infected with the virus who engage in certain conduct *which is known to transmit the virus* after being warned by health officials of the dangers of engaging in those acts. Most plans for quarantines contain built-in mechanisms by which people can prove that they no longer represent a threat of transmitting the virus to others. In contrast, the criminal prosecution of people involved in biting and spitting cases isolates them (in some cases for life) for acts that are not known to transmit the virus. Moreover, unlike many quarantine plans under which a defendant would have been previously warned about the dangers involved in his risky behavior (which would educate people about the ways the virus can be transmitted and make it clear before isolation that the defendant was acting with the requisite intent), criminal prosecutors seek to prove that the defendant had a *subjective misconception* regarding the ability to transmit the virus.

Second, states are spending scarce resources in prosecuting people who have not engaged in dangerous acts. Although some of these acts can technically meet the elements of a given crime, courts are already overburdened with cases involving people who have engaged in acts that violate the law and are actually harmful.[33]

Third, the criminal justice system's approach to prosecuting these cases will have no impact on the spread of HIV. The successful prosecution of people who have bitten or spat at law enforcement officials will result in the jailing of people who have not been shown to engage in truly risky behavior. The fact that a person bit a guard during a prison scuffle, for instance, does not mean that that same person will engage in behavior which *can* transmit the virus, such as sharing a contaminated hypodermic needle or engaging in unsafe sexual activities.

Indeed, fourth, prosecutions place a premium on an individual's ignorance of his HIV status and create a disincentive to be tested, because prosecutions for supposedly HIV-related crimes would be far more difficult where the defendant does not know whether he is HIV-positive. Furthermore, such prosecutions discourage testing in a more general way by raising the specter of severe punishment for even spontaneous and minor acts by HIV-positive individuals. Persons who may be at risk will want to avoid finding out whether they belong to a stigmatized and potentially punished class. These cases lead to the proposition that to avoid severe sanctions based solely upon HIV status, the safer course is to avoid being tested for HIV infection. Such a state-created disincentive would deprive some HIV-positive individuals of the chance to extend their lives through medical intervention and encourage avoidance of information about safe, preventive behavior.

Finally, the criminal justice system's approach undermines AIDS education efforts. Convicting people infected with HIV of attempted murder and first-degree assault for biting or spitting at another person (in what are usually highly publicized cases) sends the erroneous message to the community that they and their children are at risk of similar acts in their own lives. These types of prosecutions create an atmosphere of fear and ignorance which breeds further discrimination and harassment of people infected with the HIV. It is exactly the wrong message to send.

II. Mandatory Testing and Prosecution of People Charged with Crimes Involving Behavior Known to Transmit HIV

A. Mandatory Testing of People Charged with Sexual Assault

Prosecutors in several states are routinely requesting court orders directing that defendants *charged* with crimes of sexual assault and rape submit to HIV testing. Some prosecutors are requesting HIV testing pursuant to state statute,[34] while others are requesting mandatory testing without specific legislative authority. The Watkins Report recommended that states require that "sexual offender[s] submit to an HIV test at the earliest possible juncture in the criminal justice process.[35]

States have articulated a number of different rationales in support of motions to impose HIV tests on these defendants. In one case, a New York trial court imposed as a condition to a defendant's release on bail that the defendant, who was charged with rape, must undergo an HIV test and confirm that he was not infected with the virus. The New York Supreme Court granted the defendant's writ of *habeas corpus*, invalidating that requirement, but suggested that the legislature enact legislation mandating such testing.[36] In other cases, the state has moved for an HIV test in order to bring more serious charges against the defendant. In a Wisconsin case,[37] for example, the prosecution sought to learn the HIV status of the defendant who had been charged with two counts of sexual assault in order to determine whether to bring additional charges of "injury by conduct regardless of life," and "endangering safety by conduct regardless of life." Other prosecutors have sought to test defendants in order to justify requests for "enhanced" or "exceptional" sentences. In a Florida case,[38] the defendant was tested for HIV four days prior to his trial on charges of sexual battery. Although the jury was not notified of the results, the court, relying on defendant's positive test results, sentenced the defendant to concurrent thirty-year terms on each count, rather than the recommended guidelines for such an offense of twelve to seventeen years.[39]

Finally, certain prosecutors have requested that defendants submit to tests for public health reasons, either (1) to notify the victim of the alleged crime about potential exposure to the virus;[40] (2) to diagnose the defendant to form the predicate for treatment and/or quarantine;[41] or (3) to protect the prison population from possible transmission.[42]

It is not difficult to understand why mandatory testing of people charged with sex offenses would meet with widespread public approval. Individuals charged with committing heinous crimes do not garner society's empathy. Moreover, legislators and prosecutors have characterized forced HIV testing as a "victim's rights" measure, aimed at educating the victim of a rape about whether he or she has been exposed to the virus.[43] The Watkins Report states:

> Victims of sexual assault deserve consideration and must be given attention and support so that they will not be forgotten in the tragedy surrounding the HIV epidemic. The Commission believes that it is important to plan an ap-

proach which will take into consideration both the emotional impact of an assault and the possible exposure to HIV.[44]

When couched in those terms, people are certainly going to be more sympathetic to the health and safety concerns of, for example, the victim of a rape than to the rights of the person charged with such a crime. But if one examines the issue more closely and dispassionately, there appears to be no basis for mandatory testing of people charged with sexual offenses.

Prosecutors seeking mandatory HIV testing of persons charged with crimes involving sexual assaults must meet the same standards described above in connection with the biting and spitting cases. They must demonstrate that there is probable cause that the test will reveal evidence of a crime, and they must show that the state's interest in determining a particular defendant's HIV status outweighs the Fourth Amendment interests of the defendant.[45]

In order to meet the probable cause requirement in cases in which a defendant has been charged with a sexual offense, the state must demonstrate that the test will reveal evidence that the defendant committed a crime in addition to the underlying sexual offense (such as reckless endangerment or indifference to human life).[46] Specifically, the prosecution would need to show that it was likely that the test results would reveal that the defendant was HIV-infected at the time of the alleged incident and that such knowledge would form the basis of a separate offense. If a positive test result is obtained weeks or months after the incident, however, it could not prove the defendant's HIV status at the time of the crime as it might reflect seroconversion subsequent to the criminal act. Thus, the fact that a defendant tests positive for HIV after the commission of the alleged crime would usually be irrelevant.[47]

Similarly, a prosecutor seeking to impose an HIV test on a defendant for the purpose of including such information in a presentence report cannot demonstrate probable cause. The test can reveal only that the defendant was HIV-positive at the time of the test, not at the time of the crime. If a court were to impose a greater sentence on a defendant merely because of a positive test for HIV sometime after the alleged attack (without evidence that he or she was HIV-positive — and aware of that fact — at the time of the alleged crime) the court would be improperly punishing the defendant for being ill.[48]

Finally, there will usually be no valid legal basis upon which a defendant should be ordered to submit to an HIV test for the purpose of informing the victim of his or her possible exposure to the virus.[49] As discussed above, the constitutional analysis of this question requires a balancing of the state's interest in the information against the suspect's constitutionally protected right to privacy. The suspect's right to privacy is important in the context of HIV-related information, as has been recognized by federal constitutional opinions.[50] Given the impulse to punish the HIV-infected in the criminal justice system (as discussed throughout this chapter), any suspect's privacy interests with regard to forced testing should be keenly protected.

The state's interest in the information is presumably to give the information to the victim.[51] The victim's interest in receiving the information has been expressed as flowing from her need to make decisions about treatment options based upon the information and/or to make decisions about whether or not to engage in sexual practices that could transmit the virus to her partner. With regard to either rationale, however, the suspect's serostatus will not give the victim the information she needs to make these decisions — namely, whether she has seroconverted. What the victim really wants to know is whether she (or he) became infected during the rape, knowledge she can only gain through being tested herself several months following the sexual offense. The alleged perpetrator's HIV status will not answer that question. At best, if he is negative, it may calm her fears somewhat, although, because the negative test result could be a "false negative," she will still need to undergo testing to ensure she was not infected. On the other hand, if the suspect's test result is positive, it similarly will not tell the victim whether she has been infected. Indeed, given the highly unlikely odds of transmission from a single rape,[52] the suspect's test result might unnecessarily alarm the victim. Regardless, however, she will need to undergo her own HIV testing to ascertain her status.

Because the suspect's HIV status will not tell the victim whether she has been exposed to HIV, it should be recommended that she not engage in risky sexual activities following the sexual offense, regardless of the suspect's HIV status. (Of course, unless an individual knows for certain that neither she nor her partner is HIV-infected, she should never engage in unsafe sex.) The "treatment options" rationale is also a bit of a red herring, in that — except for two rare circumstances — there are no critical treatment decisions to be made for persons newly infected with HIV. Medical intervention would not be recommended until the immune system had begun to deteriorate, which typically takes years. The victim will know whether she seroconverted by being tested herself during the several months following the sexual offense and thus will have sufficient time to make treatment decisions.

One of the exceptions to this "no medical intervention" rule follows from recent research suggesting that AZT, if administered within hours of a person's being infected with HIV, could prevent the growth of the virus within that person's immune system.[53] Based on this development, medical workers at a number of hospitals, including the National Institutes of Health, are offered the option of taking AZT as prophylaxis after suffering a significant exposure (such as from a deep needle-stick) to the blood of an HIV-infected patient. There is no definitive evidence, however, one way or the other about the efficacy of AZT in this context.

This research has now been used as the basis for an argument that a rape victim should be allowed to require that his or her alleged attacker be tested for HIV so that if the attacker is positive, the victim can take the AZT treatment.[54] If the recent medical evidence is accurate, though, the suggested intervention should not depend upon the suspect's HIV status. After all, as discussed above, a person can test negative for HIV and actually be positive. If AZT really works as suggested, a person who is the victim of a rape should not rely on possibly false test results when she could guarantee not being infected by taking the treatment. With few serious side effects from the short-term use of the AZT, many victims would choose to err on the side of caution and take the drug regardless of the HIV test results of the person charged with the crime. Moreover, it is unlikely that this scenario will arise often, as it is rare that a suspect of a sexual offense will be apprehended within the extremely short time period apparently necessary for the AZT treatment to be effective.[55]

The more difficult exception to the "no medical intervention" rule involves the case of a pregnant woman who has been the victim of a sexual offense in which the suspect has been apprehended shortly after the crime. If this woman would make reproductive decisions based on the suspect's HIV status — in other words, if she would seriously consider abortion were there a possibility she had been exposed to HIV — and such decisions would not be possible for her were she to wait the three-to-six-month period for her own test results, she might well be able to articulate an interest in the suspect's test results even though they would not give her the definitive answer she sought. This extraordinarily exceptional case appears to be the only one in which a rape victim could truly utilize the limited information she would receive by knowing the suspect's status.

In all other cases, the defendant's substantial privacy interests will outweigh the victim's asserted interest in his test results.

B. Convicting Sex Offenders Who Are HIV-Positive

Once a court or jury has been advised that a defendant charged with a crime of sexual assault is HIV-positive, it is likely that that defendant will be convicted of a greater crime, or if already convicted, given an exceptional sentence.[56] Unfortunately, people continue to react to AIDS in emotional, often hysterical, ways. The short history of the epidemic is filled with cases of people mistreating and discriminating against people infected, or suspected of being infected, with HIV. Not only do many people maintain irrational fears about contracting HIV, they also harbor dislike for those portions of the population that have been affected most by the disease: gay men and intravenous drug users. Because of these factors, it is likely that a defendant whose positive HIV status is revealed in court will be treated more harshly simply because he or she is infected.[57]

In cases in which a person is convicted of a sexual assault (by an act that can transmit HIV) and in which it is further proven that he or she was aware of being HIV-positive at the time of the attack, a state may be justified in seeking to charge that defendant with a more serious crime. Stated simply, that person has committed an offense that is even more serious than the underlying offense and, therefore, could legitimately be punished more severely. In many current cases, however, a more stringent penalty is being sought against a person based not on previous behavior, but on *status* as an HIV-infected person. There is absolutely no justification, for example, in imposing a harsher sentence on a defendant convicted of a sexual offense who is HIV-positive without proof that he or she was aware of his or her status at the time of the offense.[58] The Florida case of *Cooper v. State*,[59] demonstrates that there is a real danger that courts will impose a greater punishment on a defendant simply because he or she is infected.

In *Cooper*, the defendant was convicted of sexual battery, solicitation, and aggravated assault. Defendant had been charged with sexually molesting a minor who had been released by a county jail into defendant's custody. Four days prior to trial, the defendant's test results indicated that he was HIV-positive. Although the jury was not informed of defendant's status, the court imposed concurrent terms of thirty years on each of the two sexual battery counts, five years on the solicitation count, followed by a consecutive ten-year term of probation on the aggravated battery count — a substantial departure from the recommended guideline sentence of twelve to seventeen years. The court imposed this heightened sentence despite the fact the there was no proof that the defendant was aware of his status at the time of the alleged attacks. In fact, the only testimony on that subject was defendant's testimony that he was not aware of his HIV status until the tests results were revealed to him. In an alarming decision, the court in *Cooper* held that the fact that the defendant was gay was sufficient reason to impose the harsher sentence. The court wrote:

> Because of his life-style, [defendant] knew or should have known that he had been exposed to the AIDS virus and that by sexual battery upon his victim there was a strong likelihood that the victim could be exposed to AIDS.

It is entirely improper for prosecutors to charge people with more serious crimes based solely on the fact that a person is a member of a high-risk population or ultimately tests positive for HIV. Such prosecutions open the door to abuse, harassment, and discrimination against already disfavored groups. The further prosecutors move away from crimes requiring proof that the defendant intended to cause harm and was actually aware that he was HIV-positive at the time of the alleged offense, the greater the risk that people will be convicted and imprisoned for who they are and not for what they did.

C. Mandatory Testing of People Charged with Prostitution

In addition, some states have enacted legislation permitting (or mandating) state agencies to test people charged with prostitution for HIV infection,[60] presumably in an effort to prevent the spread of HIV through acts of prostitution.[61] Although the statutes do not explain the precise purpose for testing prostitutes, the only conceivable purpose is punitive: to impose a greater sentence on a prostitute who knew he or she was HIV-positive when engaging in certain acts of prostitution, or to learn whether a prostitute is HIV-positive to impose more serious punishment (isolation, in particular) the next time there is a prostitution conviction. Regardless of the purpose, there is no legal basis for mandatory testing of prostitutes.

First, in situations in which the state has no reason to believe that a particular person charged with prostitution is HIV-positive, it cannot demonstrate probable cause to warrant the testing of that person. The mere fact that a person has been charged with the crime of prostitution does not, by itself, constitute the type of particularized suspicion necessary to demonstrate probable cause.[62] Even if particularized suspicion were not required, there is no evidence that prostitutes are infected with HIV, or infect others, at a rate that would warrant special treatment.[63]

Second, in a situation where the state seeks to test a person charged with prostitution in order to charge him or her with a more serious crime, the state will again be faced with the problem of proving that the prostitute was HIV-positive at the time of the alleged act of prostitution and was aware of that fact. In most situations, the state will be unable to make such a showing.

In *Illinois v. Madison*,[64] an Illinois state court declared unconstitutional an Illinois statute providing for the mandatory testing of people convicted of prostitution.[65] The court based the ruling on its determination that the state had no probable cause to believe that the defendants (people convicted of prostitution) may test positive for HIV. First, the court determined that the state had failed to show the "individualized suspicion" necessary for a finding of probable cause. Second, the court noted that the risk of contracting the virus from prostitutes is low and therefore there was no basis for the State's contention that the fact alone that the defendants were convicted of prostitution establishes a reasonable belief that they may test positive for HIV. The court in *Madison* also found that the statute did not foster any governmental interest that would outweigh the defendant's Fourth Amendment interests. The court noted that the legislative history indicated that the statute's primary function was to benefit victims of sexual offenses. It then noted that since there were no "victims" in the case of the two defendants before the court, the statute did not further its purported goal.

State statutes providing for the forced testing of prostitutes for HIV are unconstitutional for the reasons set forth in *Madison*. Such statutes represent extreme legislative cynicism. Politicians can point to these measures as proof that they are doing something about the AIDS problem. But these same politicians are, no doubt, aware that these measures, aimed at easy targets for coercive legislation, do very little to prevent the spread of HIV.

If, on the other hand, a prosecutor can demonstrate that a prostitute has engaged in acts that can transmit the virus[66] and was aware of being

HIV-positive at the time he or she performed such acts, there is a basis for charging the prostitute with a more serious crime. But attempts to charge prostitutes with such crimes based merely on the fact that they are prostitutes or because they ultimately test positive for HIV are misplaced. The more sound public health approach is to educate people sufficiently so that both prostitutes and their clients (as with all persons engaging in sex) engage in sexual acts that cannot transmit the virus, or use barriers to help prevent transmission when engaging in more risky behavior.

Conclusion

To the extent that the criminal justice system becomes involved in HIV-related cases, prosecutors should not prosecute people for acts for which there is no significant risk of transmission. It is particularly inappropriate to prosecute people for serious crimes for biting or spitting. These prosecutions, if successful, punish people who have engaged in harmless acts and will, therefore, do nothing to stop the spread of HIV disease. If states are going to prosecute people who have engaged in acts that can transmit the virus (such as certain sexual assaults and needle sharing), they should do so only when it can be demonstrated that these people knew they were HIV-infected at the time they committed the act and that they engaged in acts that can transmit the virus. A person should not be punished for an additional crime merely for being ill.

The criminal justice system, however, is an inappropriate mechanism through which to combat the AIDS crisis. Individual prosecutors scattered throughout the country, untrained in the medical intricacies of HIV, should not be employing coercive measures (such as forced testing and incarceration) — particularly when the public health system has largely ruled out such measures.

In attempting to "criminalize" certain behavior by people infected with HIV, the criminal justice system has largely ignored the conclusions of public health officials. The strategy of some prosecutors of charging people with serious crimes for committing certain acts while knowing they are infected, discourages people from learning their HIV status and seeking diagnosis and treatment. Further, by attempting to charge people with serious crimes for actions that cannot transmit the virus, prosecutors are undermining efforts to educate people about the *real* risks of transmission.

In addition, prosecutors are opening the door to further harassment and discrimination against gay men and IV drug users. There is a real risk that judges and juries will punish people not because they have committed dangerous acts, but because they are gay or use drugs. These prosecutions also permit judges and juries to punish people for being infected with HIV. In the cases brought under the Rehabilitation Act, the courts let it be known that they would not permit public health policies to be driven by unfounded public fear of HIV disease. The criminal prosecutions described above, on the other hand, are guided almost entirely by public hysteria. They allow judges and juries to act on their fears — even when such fears are contradicted by medical fact.

Finally, by seeking convictions of people infected with AIDS, prosecutors are using precious public funds that could be better spent educating people about the true risks of HIV and the ways such risks can be reduced.

NOTES

1. The threat of quarantine and isolation are discussed in W. Parmet, *AIDS and Quarantine: The Revival of an Archaic Doctrine*, 14 Hofstra L. Rev. 53 (1985); S. Burris, *Current Topics in Law and Policy: Fear Itself: AIDS, Herpes and Public Health Decisions*, 3 Yale L. & Pol'y Rev. 479 (1985) [hereinafter *Fear Itself*]; L. Gostin, *Traditional Public Health Strategies, in* AIDS and the Law: A Guide for the Public (Harlon L. Dalton et al., eds., 1987) [hereinafter *Health Strategies*]; D. Merritt, *Communicable Disease and Constitutional Law: Controlling AIDS*, 61 N.Y.U. L. Rev. 739 (1986) [hereinafter Merritt]; Sullivan & Field, *AIDS and the Coercive Power of the State*, 23 Harv. C.R.-C.L. L. Rev. 139, 142 (1988) [hereinafter Sullivan & Field]; Note, *The Constitutional Rights of AIDS Carriers*, 99 Harv. L. Rev. 1274 (1986).

   The terms "quarantine" and "isolation" refer to two distinct public health measures. *See Health Strategies, supra.* The two terms will be used interchangeably in this chapter to refer to public health measures that seek in some way to separate an infected person from the general population. Public officials and legal commentators typically discuss two types of quarantines: "disease-based" quarantines, which would isolate from the general population all people who have been infected with HIV, and "behavior-based" quarantines, which would isolate people who have knowingly engaged in behavior likely to transmit the virus to others. Since it is almost universally accepted that a disease-based quarantine would be unconstitutional or unworkable (Sullivan & Field, *supra*, at 146 n.28, *Health Strategies, supra*, at 1033), most calls for the imposition of quarantines refer to behavior-based quarantining of "recalcitrant" people with AIDS.

2. Sullivan & Field, *supra* note 1, at 142.

3. *See, e.g.,* People v. Strautz, 54 N.E.2d 441 (Ill. 1944) (upholding state's authority to commit to a clinic two persons charged with prostitution for treatment of their venereal disease); *Ex parte* Company, 139 N.E.2d 204 (Ohio 1922) (upholding state's authority to quarantine prostitutes who tested positive for syphilis and gonorrhea); *Ex parte* Johnston, 180 P. 644 (Cal. Dist. Ct. App. 1919) (upholding quarantine of women who tested positive for gonococcus infection); *see also* Jacobson v. Massachusetts, 25 S. Ct. 358 (1905) (affirming state's right under its police powers to require that its citizens be vaccinated against smallpox). *But see* Jew Ho v. Williamson, 103 F. 10 (C.C.N.D. Cal. 1900) (enjoining the City of San Francisco from imposing a quarantine around twelve blocks in Chinatown for the purpose of controlling the spread of bubonic plague where such quarantine was not reasonable); Greene v. Edwards, 263 S.E.2d 661 (W. Va. 1980) (granting petition for writ of *habeas corpus* brought by man involuntarily committed because he was infected with tuberculosis because he was not provided a lawyer until after the commitment proceedings had commenced).

4. These calls are discussed in Sullivan & Field, *supra* note 1, at 139 n.1; *Health Strategies, supra* note 1, at 1016 n. 1; Merritt, *supra* note 1, at 774-75.

5. Sullivan & Field, *supra* note 1, at 144.

6. Report of the Presidential Commission on the Human Immunodeficiency Virus Epidemic ("Watkins Report") 119-20 (June 24, 1988) [hereinafter Watkins Report]; *see also* American Civil Liberties Union AIDS Project, Epidemic of Fear (1990).

7. School Bd. of Nassau County v. Arline, 480 U.S. 273 (1987); *see also* Chalk v. United States Dist. Court, 840 F.2d 701 (9th Cir. 1988) (directing a school to reinstate teacher of hearing-impaired students who was diagnosed as seropositive because there was not a "significant risk" of transmission); Glover v. Eastern Neb. Community Office of Retardation, 686 F. Supp. 243 (D. Neb. 1988) (regulations calling for the mandatory HIV testing and reporting of employees of group homes for retarded people violated the Fourth Amendment because the undisputed medical evidence indicated that the risk of an employee infected with HIV transmitting it to a client is "approaching zero"), *aff'd*, 867 F.2d 461 (8th Cir. 1989).

8. One commentator has argued that the standards developed by the courts in Rehabilitation Act cases should be applied to a review of the constitutionality of any state health action. *Fear Itself, supra* note 1, at 479. Burris argues that a state health action that infringes on individual rights is justified only if:

    > (1) a medical risk assessment has defined the health threat and its dimensions; and (2) the chosen response is the least restrictive medically appropriate means of dealing with the risk.

    Id. Similarly, Gostin has concluded that compulsory public powers are justified only if they meet the following criteria:

    > There is a significant risk of transmission of the AIDS virus; the public health response is efficacious in preventing a primary mode of transmission of the virus; the economic, practical, or human rights burdens are not disproportionate to the public health benefits; and the public health power is the least restrictive alternative that would prevent viral transmission.

L. Gostin, *The Politics of AIDS: Compulsory State Powers, Public Health, and Civil Liberties*, 49 Ohio St. L.J. 1017, 1019 (1989) [hereinafter Gostin].

9. Scroggins v. State, 401 S.E.2d 13 (Ga. 1991); *see Jury Finds Man Guilty of Using AIDS as Weapon*, Atlanta Const., Oct. 21, 1989, at C-2.

10. *Inmate with AIDS Guilty of Trying to Kill by Biting*, N.Y. Times, Apr. 12, 1990, at B-4.

11. State v. Weeks, slip op., No. 15173-C (Tex. Dist. Ct. 1989).

12. United States v. Moore, 846 F.2d 1163 (8th Cir. 1988). The court in *Moore* acknowledged that the prosecution had failed to prove that HIV could be transmitted through a human bite, but held that a human bite, by itself, could constitute a "deadly and dangerous weapon." *Id.* at 1167.

13. Brock v. State, 555 So.2d 285 (Ala. Ct. App. 1989), *aff'd*, 580 So.2d 1390 (Ala. Ct. App. 1991); *see also* State v. Haines, 545 N.E.2d 834 (Ind. Ct. App. 1989). Cayuga County District Attorney Paul Carbonaro threatened to bring attempted murder charges against inmates at a New York prison who reportedly had "thrown feces, urine, semen and blood on guards and a nurse." *AIDS Notes*, The Weekly News (TWN), Dec. 6, 1989, at 38. According to a report in *TWN*, guards reported that in some cases, inmates screamed such things as, "If I have AIDS, I'm going to take you with me." *Id.*

14. *See* People v. Caldwell, No. 11595-89, AIDS Litig. Rep. (Andrews Pub.) 2716 (N.Y. Sup. Ct. 1989). The defendant ultimately agreed to submit to the test. *See also* People v. Richards, 87-1715 FG (Mich. Dist. Ct. 1987) (HIV-infected person in Flint, Michigan, charged with assault and intent to commit murder after he spat at four police officers).

15. Although this report only discusses those cases in which the propriety of testing has been challenged in court, there are certainly many more examples of forced testing that have gone unreported. It is not uncommon for police officers to request that hospitals test people they have arrested because the police officers have been bitten, spat at, or pricked with needles. Interview with Peter Laquer, Director of AIDS Programs at Woodhull Hospital, Brooklyn, New York. Although under many state laws a person cannot be tested without his or her consent, short of a court order, a police officer or hospital administrator is in a position to compel a person to be tested. Laquer has reported that over a period of a few months, he had been requested on five occasions by police officers to test a person that had been arrested. Laquer suggests that hospitals establish clear guidelines for treating such requests. First, the hospital should make certain that a person is not coerced into being tested. The hospital should have an administrator available to counsel the person outside the presence of the arresting officer. Second, if the hospital tests the alleged assailant, after receiving his or her consent, it should also encourage the police officer to be tested.

16. According to the Intergovernmental Health Policy Project, eleven states now have laws that require or permit such testing. They are: Colorado, Florida, Illinois, Iowa, Maine, New Hampshire, Ohio, Pennsylvania, Utah, Washington, and West Virginia. In other states, judges often order the testing even in the absence of a specific legislative mandate.

17. O'Connor v. Ortega, 480 U.S. 709, 716 (1987) (*citing* Oliver v. United States, 466 U.S. 170, 178 n. 8 (1984)) (government employee has a reasonable expectation of privacy in certain portions of his office).

18. Schmerber v. California, 384 U.S. 757 (1966) (blood test administered to a person charged with driving while intoxicated implicated the Fourth Amend-

ment); Skinner v. Railway Labor Executives' Association, 489 U.S. 602 (1989) (blood and urine testing of railroad employees implicated the Fourth Amendment, although Court ultimately upheld such testing); *Glover*, 867 F.2d at 463 (after determining that a regulation providing for the mandatory HIV testing of employees of a group home for the mentally retarded implicated the Fourth Amendment, the Eighth Circuit ruled that the tests were unreasonable because the risk of an infected employee transmitting HIV through casual contact was "approaching zero").

19. *Schmerber*, 384 U.S. at 757; *see also* National Treasury Employees Union v. Von Raab, 489 U.S. 656 (1989); *Skinner*, 489 U.S. at 617-18; Executives' Ass'n v. Burnley, 839 F.2d 575 (9th Cir. 1988).

20. *Skinner*, 489 U.S. at 603-04. The Supreme Court has delineated certain circumstances — beyond the "normal need for law enforcement" — when it will dispense with the warrant and probable cause requirements, based upon "special needs." *Id.* at 603. In *Skinner*, for example, the Supreme Court dispensed with the warrant and probable cause requirement in affirming regulations requiring the mandatory urine testing of certain railroad employees. The Court determined that the government's interest in ensuring the safety of railroad travel constituted a "special need." *Id.* Similarly, in *O'Connor*, the Court ruled that a workplace investigation of a federal employee by his employer went beyond the "normal need for law enforcement," and was, therefore, not governed by the probable cause requirement. *O'Connor*, 480 U.S. at 727.

 If the government compels a defendant to submit to an HIV test for the purpose of charging him or her with a more serious crime, the test would constitute "normal" law enforcement and there would be no basis for abandoning the probable cause requirement in those circumstances. A more difficult question is presented in a case in which a law enforcement official seeks to compel an assailant to be tested solely to learn if he had been exposed to the virus.

21. 40 Am. Jur. 2d *Homicide* § 566 (1964). *See also* Model Penal Code § 501 (1985).

22. Barlow v. Superior Court, 236 Cal. Rptr. 134 (Cal. Dist. Ct. 1987), *review denied* (Cal. App. Ct. 1987) (no probable cause to impose HIV test on defendant who had bitten a police officer and was charged with attempted murder and attempt to inflict great bodily injury because the results of tests administered months after the event would not be relevant to his knowledge on the date of the alleged act).

 In People v. Santana, Index No. 4419/83, slip op. (N.Y. Sup. Ct. 1983), the court declined to order a rape defendant to undergo an HIV antibody test four years after the rape occurred. The New York City Commissioner of Health filed an affidavit in the case demonstrating the futility of after-the-fact testing of the defendant. *See* Joint Subcommittee on AIDS in the Criminal Justice System of the Committee on Corrections and the Committee on Criminal Justice Operations and Budget of the Association of the Bar of the City of New York, AIDS and the Criminal Justice System: A Final Report and Recommendations 68 n. 83 (July 1989) [hereinafter New York Bar Report]; *see also* State v. Farmer, 805 P.2d 200 (Wash. 1991), *reconsideration denied*, 1991 W.L. 135984 (July 2, 1991) (test results at time of sentencing of sex offender not probative of HIV status at the time of the underlying sexual offense).

23. *See, e.g.*, Brock v. State, 550 So.2d 285 (Ala. Ct. App. 1989).

24. For a good discussion of the exceedingly low risk of transmitting the virus through saliva, see Gostin, *supra* note 8, at 1023-25.

25. Proposition 96 provides for the mandatory testing of, among others, persons charged with interfering with the official duties of public safety employees if "probable cause exists to believe that *a possible transfer* of blood, saliva, semen or other bodily fluid took place between the defendant and the peace officer...." Cal. Health & Safety Code § 199.951 (West Supp. 1991)(emphasis added). Proposition 96 also can be invoked by victims of a sex crime and by employees of a "custodial facility" in situations involving the transmission of bodily fluids. *Id.*

26. Johnetta J. v. Municipal Court, 267 Cal. Rptr. 666 (Cal. Ct. App. 1990).

27. One of the experts, Dr. Marcus Conant testified as follows:

> When I use the term "theoretically possible"...I do not mean that the possibility of transmission is in any way real or significant. Because it is impossible to prove or conclusively establish negative findings unless the finding in question violated established principles of science, scientists will always say a theoretical possibility exists, even if the possibility is so extremely remote as to be without real value.

Id. at 674.

The court's opinion conflicts with the Nebraska District Court's opinion in *Glover*, 686 F. Supp. 243. In *Glover*, the court did not allow the theoretical possibility that HIV could be transmitted through casual contact to justify a mandatory testing of employees of a health services agency. The court wrote:

> There was testimony in this case that there can be no guarantee that the [agency's] clients could not possibly contract the AIDS virus, and thus the policy is necessary because of the devastating consequences of the disease. This overly cautious, "better to be safe than sorry" approach, however, is impermissible as it infringes on the constitutional rights of the staff members to be free from unreasonable searches and seizures.

Id. at 251.

28. *Johnetta J.*, 267 Cal. Rptr. at 685; *see also* Gostin, *supra* note 8, case no. 927 (Rice v. Palo Alto Municipal Court) (police officer entitled to compel the testing of a person arrested for drunk driving when the officer and defendant were cut during the arrest and there were affidavits from the defendant's mother and roommate stating that the defendant was a homosexual).

29. Brock v. State, 550 So.2d 285 (Ala. Ct. App. 1989).

30. Some states have statutes that provide the courts with discretion to dismiss certain charges or reduce a sentence if the defendant's conduct was so inherently unlikely to result or culminate in the commission of a crime. *See* Minn. Stat. Ann. § 609.17 (*cited in* State v. Haines, 545 N.E.2d 834, 839 (Ind. Ct. App. 1989)). Courts in those states should routinely dismiss attempted murder charges brought against a person with AIDS who bit or spit at another person.

31. Model Penal Code art. 5, § 5 (1985). *See also* 21 Am. Jur. 2d 160:

> Whenever the law makes it a crime to take one step toward the accomplishment of an unlawful object with the intent or purpose of accomplishing it, a person taking that step, with that intent or purpose, and himself capable of closing every act on his part to accomplish that object cannot protect himself from responsibility by

showing that by reason of some fact unknown to him at the time of his criminal attempt, it could not be fully carried into effect in the particular instance.

And one who, believing a gun to be loaded, points it at another and pulls the trigger, may be convicted of attempted murder, though the gun was not loaded.

32. State v. Haines, 545 N.E.2d 834 (Ind. Ct. App. 1989).
33. Gostin points out that it is iniquitous to prosecute AIDS carriers for "low risk behavior," noting that society already tolerates other activities that pose equal or greater risks, such as dangerous driving. *See Health Strategies, supra* note 1, at 1020.
34. According to the Intergovernmental Health Policy Project, the following twenty-one states have statutes that permit a sex offender's HIV test results to be disclosed to victims:

> Ariz. H.B. 2173 (1990); Ark. H.B. 1496, Act 614 (1989); Cal.; Colo. S.B. 8 (1988); Fla. H.B. 1590, ch. 89-350 (1989); Ga. H.B. 1281, Act 1440 (1988), H.B. 554, Act 411 (1991); Idaho H.B. 351, ch. 220 (1989); Ill. H.B. 4005, Pub. Act 85-1399 (1988); Ind. S.B. 9, Pub. L. No. 88-123 (1988); Kan. H.B. 2659 (1988); La. S.B. 379, Act 419 (1991); Mich. H.B. 4008, Pub. Act 471 (1988); Miss. H.B. 592, ch. 425 (1991); Nev. S.B. 73 (1989); Ohio S.B. 2 (1989); Okla. H.B. 1012 (1991); Or. H.B. 2030, ch. 568 (1989); S.C. H.B. 2807, Ratification No. 547 (1988); Tenn. H.B. 52 (1991); Tex. S.B. 66-XX, ch. 55 (1987); Va. H.B. 815, ch. 957 (1990).

Eight states have laws permitting victims to specifically request that charged or convicted sex offenders be tested for HIV:

> Ariz. H.B. 2173 (1990); Cal. S.B. 2643, ch. 1088 (1988); Fla. H.B. 1590, ch. 89-350 (1989); Ga. H.B. 554, Act 411 (1991); Kan. H.B. 2659 (1988); Or. H.B. 2030, ch. 568 (1989); Tenn. H.B. 52 (1991); Tex. S.B. 66-XX, ch. 55 (1987).

35. Watkins Report, *supra* note 6, rec. 9-63.
36. People v. McGreevy, 514 N.Y.S.2d 622 (N.Y. Sup. Ct. 1987).
37. State v. Bullock, Case No. 88-CF-427, slip op. (Wis. Ct. App. 1988).
38. Cooper v. State, 539 So. 2d 508 (Fla. Ct. App. 1989).
39. *See also* State v. Guayante, 783 P.2d 1030 (Or. App. 1989) (defendant infected with HIV sentenced to thirty years, ten more than recommended for similar crimes, for repeated sexual encounters with an underage girl).

In People v. George, 524 N.Y.S.2d 557 (N.Y. App. Div. 1988), the defendant, who pleaded guilty to attempted sodomy, argued that the disclosure of his HIV status in the presentence report unfairly influenced his sentence. The court denied the appeal. In State v. Farmer, 805 P.2d 200 (Wash. 1991), *reconsideration denied*, 1991 WL 135984 (July 2, 1991), the Washington Supreme Court held that a trial court had unconstitutionally ordered the defendant to submit to HIV testing for purposes of sentencing, ruling that the results of his test at that point in time were not probative of his HIV status at the time of the underlying sexual offense. The Supreme Court did, however, permit the trial court to consider other evidence of defendant's HIV status for purposes of sentencing.

40. People v. Cook, 532 N.Y.S.2d 940 (1988) (defendant who had pleaded guilty to rape was not deprived of his constitutional rights when forced to undergo an HIV test upon the request of the victim, who was concerned for her health and safety); People v. Thomas, 529 N.Y.S.2d 429 (N.Y. Sup. Ct. 1988) (court granted People's motion to test defendant *after* guilty plea to charge of rape so that the victim could know if she has been exposed to the virus).

41. Commonwealth v. Mason, No. 2015 (Pa. Commw. Ct. 1987) (court ordered that defendant charged with rape and associated crimes be tested for HIV pursuant to state statute "designed to diagnose, treat and/or quarantine those likely to transmit venereal disease to unsuspecting and innocent persons," because it was only way victim will know if she has been exposed to the virus).

42. Shelvin v. Lykos, 741 S.W.2d 178 (Tex. Ct. App. 1987) (court of appeals granted defendant's writ of *mandamus* voiding trial court's order directing that defendant, charged with sexual assault, be tested for HIV, ruling that notification of victim and prison safety were insufficient grounds upon which to order the tests).

43. A Florida newspaper has reported that Florida Attorney General announced a 1990 "victim's rights legislative package" which would require any person indicted on charges of rape or sexual assault to be tested for exposure to HIV and provide that the victim of the alleged crime be given the results. *AIDS Notes*, The Weekly News (TWN), Dec. 6, 1989.

44. Watkins Report, *supra* note 6, at 131.

45. *Skinner*, 489 U.S. at 603.

46. A defendant's HIV status is irrelevant to whether the defendant committed a traditional sexual offense, whose elements normally include (1) the commission of a sexual act; (2) without the other person's consent. 65 Am. Jur. 2d *Rape* § 2; *see also* Model Penal Code § 213.1.

47. *See infra* note 48.

48. This was the holding of the Washington Supreme Court in State v. Farmer, 805 P.2d 200 (Wash. 1991), *reconsideration denied*, 1991 WL 135984 (July 2, 1991), as described *supra* at note 39.

49. Several commentators and courts have considered this question at length. *See, e.g.,* Bedward, *AIDS Testing of Rape Suspects: Have the Rights of the Accused Met Their Match?* 1990 U. Ill. L. Rev. 347 (1990); Note, *AIDS and Rape: The Constitutional Dimensions of Mandatory Testing of Sex Offenders*, 76 Cornell L. Rev. 238 (1990); Note, *Constitutional Questions: Mandatory Testing for AIDS under Washington's AIDS Legislation*, 24 Gonz. L. Rev. 433 (1988-89); Note, *AIDS, Rape and the Fourth Amendment: Schemes for Mandatory AIDS Testing of Sex Offenders*, 43 Vand. L. Rev. 1607 (1990); *see also* Virgin Islands v. Roberts, 756 F. Supp. 898 (D.V.I. 1991); People v. Durham, 533 N.Y.S.2d 944 (Sup. Ct. 1990); People v. Thomas, 529 N.Y.S.2d 429 (N.Y. Sup. Ct. 1988).

50. *See, e.g.,* Doe v. Borough of Barrington, 729 F. Supp. 376 (D.N.J. 1990) (constitution protects the family from governmental disclosure of one member's infection with HIV); Doe v. Coughlin, 697 F. Supp. 1234 (N.D.N.Y. 1988) (enjoining the involuntary transfer of HIV-infected prisoners to a segregated dorm because the transfer would result in the disclosure of HIV status); Woods v. White, 689 F. Supp. 874 (W.D. Wis. 1988) (holding that prisoners have a constitutionally protected right of privacy with regard to medical

records, and that HIV-infected prisoners have a strong interest in protecting themselves against the dissemination of HIV-related medical information).

51. One court has articulated the state as having it own independent interest — namely, maintaining the health of the victim because she will need to be a witness at the underlying criminal trial. Roberts, 756 F. Supp. at 903 (D.V.I. 1991). However, as discussed below, this reasoning is in error in that there are no special medical interventions that would follow even if the victim knew she had been exposed to HIV. *See infra* at 308. Another court, in sanctioning a pre-trial HIV test, stated that such a test was also in the *defendant's* own interest. Haywood County v. Hudson, 740 S.W.2d 718 (Tenn. 1987).

52. One commentator has emphasized that it is extremely unlikely that a person would contract HIV through a single sexual episode. Blumberg, *AIDS: Analyzing a New Dimension in Rape Victimization, in* AIDS — The Impact on the Criminal Justice System 82 (Merrill Publishing ed., 1990) [hereinafter Blumberg]. He estimates that of the approximately 45,640 rapes committed each year in the United States, we can expect less than one case of AIDS resulting from forced vaginal intercourse each year. Blumberg notes that there is no reported case of a person contracting HIV as a result of a rape involving forced vaginal intercourse.

Similarly, Dr. Robert Klein, a leading national expert on HIV transmission, states, "HIV transmission can occur through rape. The risk of this occurring when the rapist is infected is unknown, but has been estimated to be less than or equal to 0.2%. Genital ulcer and trauma would probably make transmission more likely than in their absence." Klein, *HIV and Rape: A Review of the Scientific Literature* (1990) (unpublished manuscript on file at the ACLU).

53. This information is summarzied in the *Roberts* case, 756 F. Supp. at 903-04. Despite the impressive list of string cites there, most scientists agree that this evidence is quite limited and drawn largely from an animal model. *See* Note, *AIDS and Rape: The Constitutional Dimensions of Mandatory Testing of Sex Offenders*, 76 Cornell L. Rev. 238, 243-44 (1990); *see also* Getlin, *AZT as a Prophylactic Agent for HIV Exposure: Biological, Clinical and Social Implications* (1991) (unpublished manuscript on file with the ACLU) ("there is [sic] no good data to support or refute the efficacy of AZT in this setting and none are likely in the near future"). Moreover, efforts to study the question have largely failed as an NIH study was "discontinued because of difficulty enrolling a sufficient number of patients... who were willing to be randomized to the placebo arm of the study." *Id.*

54. *See* New York Bar Report, *supra* note 22, at 70 n.84.

55. Dr. Klein states (after noting that in the animal model the effectiveness of the antiretroviral therapy is related to the speed with which it is administered after exposure):

There are no data bearing on the question of whether antiretroviral therapy (such as AZT) given after exposure to HIV in the human can actually prevent infection. Consequently there is no information on how quickly AZT need be given in such a setting. It is highly questionable whether a rapist with an unknown HIV status can be tested, and reliable results obtained, in time to determine whether action should be instituted in an attempt to prevent HIV infection in the victim. It is unknown whether preventive action could be timely and effective even if the rapist's HIV status were known at the time of the event. Furthermore, there are no data on the dose and duration of preventive therapy with AZT should it be instituted. Recent evidence that AZT has carcinogenic potential, and lack of information about any possible effect on the fetus, might also be important factors to weigh in considering the risk-benefit of giving a rape victim AZT to prevent HIV infection. There is no firm consensus in the medical community about the value of AZT prophylactically after a single heterosexual exposure to HIV, even when the rapist is known to be HIV positive.... In sum,... [p]rophylactic AZT after exposure may prevent or delay infection, but this is not proven. If effective at all, delay in instituting AZT would probably decrease effectiveness.

Klein, *HIV and Rape: A Review of the Scientific Literature* (1990) (unpublished manuscript on file at the ACLU).

56. In *Farmer*, the court imposed a harsher sentence on the defendant based on the defendant's positive HIV status and the testimony of his friends that he was aware of his HIV status at the time of the alleged crime. 805 P.2d 200.

57. *See, e.g.*, Wiggins v. Maryland, 554 A.2d 1989 (Md. Ct. App. 1989).

58. Several commentators have expressed the view that the traditional criminal statutes are difficult to apply to acts committed by people infected with HIV. *See* Sullivan & Field, *supra* note 1, at 162; *Health Strategies, supra* note 1, at 63-64. At the time they wrote their analyses, these commentators predicted that states would be tempted to use their traditional criminal statutes against people with HIV. Although they correctly identified prostitutes and IV drug users as likely targets of AIDS-related prosecutions, they were particularly fearful that states would seek to bring criminal charges against gay people who engaged in sexual activities which society would consider "risky," such as engaging in sexual acts without disclosing to their partners that they were infected, or without using barriers to reduce transmission. These commentators opposed such criminalization because it would involve the state in monitoring the private affairs of individuals.

Our research has revealed that very few criminal prosecutions have been brought against people who have engaged in consensual sex. (Idaho has attempted to prosecute two individuals under a state law making it a felony to expose another to HIV knowingly. Idaho Code § 39-609. In Idaho v. Lewis, Criminal No. 16217 (Idaho Dist. Ct. 1989), the state sought a conviction under that statute against a man alleged to have attempted to have sex with a 15-year-old. The state ultimately dropped those charges when the defendant was sentenced to life imprisonment for child molestation. B. Miller, *From Star Athlete to AIDS Defendant*, Idaho Statesman, Apr. 27, 1990, at 1-A. The State of Idaho recently commenced a criminal action against Kerry Stephen Thomas for allegedly having unprotected sex with a woman knowing he was infected with HIV. That action is pending. *Id*).

Rather than pursue the impossible task of monitoring the sexual conduct of all of the populations at risk, prosecutors have focused their attention on those people who have already been arrested for crimes involving acts that are perceived to be capable of transmitting the virus. *See, e.g.*, People v. Hawkrigg, 525 N.Y.S.2d 752 (Sup. Ct. 1988).

59. 539 So. 2d 508 (Fla. Ct. App. 1989).

60. According to the Intergovernmenal Health Policy Project, the following twenty-eight states now statutorily sanction such testing:

Ariz. H.B. 2173 (1990); Ark. H.B. 1496, Act 614 (1989); Cal. S.B. 1007 (1988); Colo. S.B. 8 (1988); Fla. S.B. 576, ch. 86-143 (1986); Ga. H.B. 1281, Act 1440 (1988); Idaho H.B. 432 (1988), H.B. 351, ch. 220 (1989), H.B. 638, ch. 310 (1990); Ill. H.B. 2044, Pub. Act 85-935 (1987); Ind. S.B. 9, Pub. L. 88-123 (1988); Iowa S.B. 2157 (1988); Kan. H.B. 2659 (1988); Ky. H.B. 425 (1990); La. H.B. 460, Act 666 (1988), S.B. 379, Act 419 (1991), S.B. 380, Act 316 (1991); Md. S.B. 719 (1990); Mich. H.B. 4008, Pub. Act 471 (1988); Miss. H.B. 592, ch. 425 (1991); Nev. A.B. 550, ch. 762 (1987), A.B. 273, ch. 423 (1989),S.B. 73, ch. 138 (1989); N.D. S.B. 2048 (1989); Ohio S.B. 2 (1989); Okla. H.B. 1012 (1991); Or. H.B. 2067, ch. 600 (1987), H.B. 2030 ch. 568 (1989); R.I. S.B. 3438, ch. 88-405 (1988), H.B. 9075 ch. 90-169 (1990); S.C. H.B. 2807, Ratification No. 547 (1988); Tenn. H.B. 52, ch. 25 (1991); Tex. S.B. 66-XX, ch. 55 (1987), S.B. 959(1989); Va. H.B. 815, ch. 957 (1990), S.B. 340, ch. 913 (1990); Wash. S.B. 6221, ch. 206 (1988); W. Va. H.B. 303 (1988).

61. *See* Complaint, Hooking Is Real Employment (HIRE) v. Ledbetter, No. C87-1767A (N.D. Ga. Aug. 6, 1987) (group is challenging the Department of Human Resources' regulations requiring HIV tests of convicted prostitutes); Nevada v. Kearns, No. C86584X, AIDS Litig. Rep. (Andrews Pub.) 2504 (Nev. Dist. Ct. Mar. 9, 1989) (Nevada prostitute was sentenced to twenty years' imprisonment pursuant to a Nevada statute providing for such sentences for persons engaged in prostitution while knowing they are HIV positive).

62. *Skinner,* 489 U.S. at 604. Although the Supreme Court in *Skinner* determined that "a showing of individualized suspicion is not a constitutional floor, below which a search must be presumed unreasonable," *id.*, the Court's statement that a showing of "some quantum of individualized suspicion" is usually required when the standard of probable cause is dispensed with assumes that the probable cause requirement must be based on individualized suspicion.

63. *See* J. Decker, *Prostitution as a Public Health Issue, in* AIDS and the Law 81, 82-84 (H. Dalton et al., eds., 1987) [hereinafter Decker]; Blumberg, *supra* note 52, at 98.

64. No. 88-123613, slip op. (Ill. Cir. Ct. 1989).

65. Ill. Rev. Stat. ch. 38, para. 1005-5-3(g).

66. It has been well documented that prostitutes are usually asked to perform acts which are not likely to transmit the virus. Decker, *supra* note 63, at 84. In addition, many prostitutes require that their clients use condoms. U.S. Centers for Disease Control [CDC], *Antibody to Human Immunodeficiency Virus in Female Prostitutes,* 257 J. A.M.A. 2011 (1987). In fact, it is more likely that a prostitute will *contract* the virus from a client than that she will *transmit* it to a client.

9

WORKPLACE ISSUES: HIV AND DISCRIMINATION

By Chai R. Feldblum

Introduction

A stable and consistent workplace environment is essential to the economic and emotional needs of most working-age individuals. People with HIV disease are no different. Most people with HIV disease want to be able to continue working, want to be able to interact with their coworkers without fear of stigma or humiliation, and, like others interested in mobility and advancement, they want to be able to secure promotions and obtain new jobs.

People with HIV disease, however, sometimes face enormous resistance from employers. Every study of AIDS-related discrimination to date has found that the largest category of complaints concerns employment.[1] Sometimes employers refuse to hire or retain HIV-infected workers because of ignorance and fear about how HIV is transmitted. Sometimes employers act out of fear regarding increased health insurance costs. And sometimes employers are simply responding to the fear and ignorance of the individual's coworkers.[2] Whatever the cause, the result is an unwarranted limitation on workplace opportunity: the person with HIV disease is fired from a job, or not hired for a job, or not promoted, or not given a raise, even though the person is qualified to work and able to keep working.

In 1990, Congress enacted a new law that constitutes a breakthrough in this area. The Americans with Disabilities Act (ADA) prohibits workplace discrimination based on disability, including HIV disease. One of its important features is that it will eventually cover all employers in the United States that are currently covered by the law prohibiting discrimination on the basis of race, sex, religion, and national origin.[3] This includes most private businesses in the country. Congress modeled the ADA on a prior law (the Rehabilitation Act of 1973) that also outlaws discrimination based on disability but that applies only to the federal government itself and to private and state employers that accept federal funds or have federal contracts or subcontracts.

The employment-related provisions of the ADA will take effect in stages. The law becomes effective on July 26, 1992, for employers with twenty-five or more employees, and on July 26, 1994, for employers with fifteen to twenty-four employees. Employers with fewer than fifteen workers are not covered by the ADA, as they are not covered by Title VII of the Civil Rights Act of 1964.

When the ADA is fully in effect, it will be by far the most comprehensive statute protecting persons with HIV disease from employment discrimination.[4] Thus, the most important issue for the 1990s with regard to job discrimination will be how to maximize the protections of the ADA. Because the groundwork for the ADA, and the key to understanding it, lie in the existing Rehabilitation Act of 1973, we begin with an analysis of that law.

The Rehabilition Act of 1973

A. Overview

Section 504 of the Rehabilitation Act of 1973 establishes that:

> No otherwise qualified individual with handicaps...shall, solely by reason of her or his handicap, be excluded from participation in, be denied the benefits of, or be subjected to discrimination under any program or activity receiving Federal financial assistance....[5]

Section 504 covers any program or activity that receives some form of financial assistance from the federal government, as well as programs and activities conducted by agencies of the federal government.[6] This provision typically applies to hospitals, clinics, public schools, most colleges and universities, and most public social service agencies.[7] Another section of the Rehabilitation Act, section 503, covers entities that have a contract of more than $2,500 with a federal department or agency for the provision of goods and services.[8]

All the provisions of the Rehabilitation Act cover persons with a "handicap."[9] The law defines "handicap" as a "physical or mental impairment" that "substantially limits one or more...major life activities."[10] This is a broad, generic definition of handicap. The regulations implementing section 504 make it clear that the term "handicap" is intended to include a wide range of impairments that substantially limit various life activities — for example, mobility impairments, vision and hearing impairments, epilepsy, cerebral palsy, heart disease, cancer, drug and alcohol addiction, and mental impairments.[11]

The statutory definition of a person with a "handicap" also includes someone with a record of such an impairment and someone who is perceived as having such an impairment. Thus, for example, a person who has recovered from a substantially limiting physical or mental impairment, but is discriminated against because of the record of that impairment, is protected. In addition, an individual who does not have an impairment that actually limits the person in a major life activity (for example, a person with a significant cosmetic disfigurement) or an individual who has no actual impairment at all (for example, a gay man who is believed to be HIV-infected but is not) is covered under Title V of the Rehabilitation Act if he or she is discriminated against in employment because a covered employer regards him or her as having a disability.[12]

The fact that an individual has a handicap, has a record of having a handicap, or is regarded as having a handicap, establishes the initial coverage for that person under the Rehabilitation Act. In each case, however, the law also requires that the person be an "otherwise qualified person with a handicap."[13] This means that the person, apart from his or her handicap, meets the requirements of the particular employment position, service or benefit in question.[14] The "otherwise qualified" requirement was added by Congress to address (often misplaced) fears that section 504's antidiscrimination provision would mandate the hiring or retention of a person with a disability, even when that person's disability made him or her actually unable to perform a particular job.

Unlike antidiscrimination protection extended to individuals on the basis of race, sex, or national origin, however, there is an additional, necessary component that is part of the antidiscrimination protection extended to individuals on the basis of disability. A person with a disability is often perfectly qualified to perform a job — if some adjustment is first made in the job structure, job schedule, physical layout of the job, or job equipment.[15] If these adjustments or modifications — which are called "reasonable accommodations" — are made, a person with a disability might then be qualified for the particular job he or she seeks.

The section 504 regulations, therefore, define a "qualified person with a handicap" as someone who is qualified to perform the essential functions of a job with "reasonable accommodation," if necessary.[16] If a reasonable accommodation would enable the person with a disability to be qualified for a job, the employer or other entity receiving federal funds has an affirmative duty to make that accommodation. There is a limit, however, to the employer's obligation. An accommodation need not be provided if it would impose an "undue hardship" on the employer.[17] Undue hardship has been interpreted by the courts as an action that would cause significant difficulty or expense for the employer, resulting in "undue financial and administrative burdens" or "fundamental alterations" of the employer's business.[18]

B. Application of the Rehabilitation Act to People with HIV Disease

The Rehabilitation Act does not set forth a defined list of impairments or medical conditions which are covered as handicaps. Rather, as explained above, the law sets forth a broad, generic definition of handicap that encompasses a range of physical and mental conditions. From the first notice of HIV disease in this country in 1981, and from the first notice of cases of discrimination based on AIDS and HIV infection, the Rehabilitation Act has been used to redress such instances of discrimination when a covered entity has been involved. These cases have established critically important principles of law for people with HIV disease.

One of the most important cases in the development of HIV-related discrimination law was a Supreme Court decision interpreting section 504 in a case involving a person with tuberculosis.[19] In that case, the U.S. Department of Justice argued (in a friend of the court brief) that if an employer discriminated against an individual because of a *fear* of the individual's *contagiousness*, and not because of the individual's actual disability, the actions of the employer were not prohibited by the Rehabilitation Act.[20]

The Supreme Court resoundingly rejected this argument. In a strong and sweeping opinion, the Court held that an employer covered under section 504 could not discriminate on the basis of fear of contagiousness. The Court explained that the contagious effects of a disease could not be "meaningfully distinguished" from the disease's physical effects on an individual and that "[i]t would be unfair to allow an employer to seize upon the distinction between the effects of a disease on others and the effects of a disease on a patient and use that distinction to justify discriminatory treatment."[21] In addition, the Court emphasized the harms caused by myths and stereotypes regarding people with disabilities and stressed that Congress sought to eliminate such discrimination through the broad definition of "handicap" in the Rehabilitation Act.[22]

The Court's ruling in *Arline* was particularly significant for people with HIV disease. Under the analysis put forward by the Department of Justice, an employer would have been allowed to discriminate against a person with HIV if the employer's action was based on the fear that the person could transmit HIV to others. Such discrimination would not have been prohibited, under the Department's analysis, regardless of how irrational or unreasonable the fear of contagion was.

The *Arline* decision effectively eliminated this approach. Under the Supreme Court's opinion, a person with a contagious disease could not be discriminated against under section 504 — neither because of the disabling effects of the disease itself *nor* because of a fear of contagiousness of the disease. Such an individual, of course, still had to be "qualified" for the job in question. As the Court explained, this meant that the person with a contagious disease could not pose a "significant risk" to others in the workplace, which risk could not be eliminated by reasonable accommodation.[23]

Prior and subsequent to the Court's decision in *Arline*, a series of lower courts interpreted section 504 to include both AIDS and asymptomatic HIV infection as "handicaps" covered under the act.[24] In turn, building on those cases, Congress noted that individuals who are HIV-infected, whether symptomatic or asymptomatic, are covered under the Rehabilitation Act and other disability antidiscrimination laws. For example, when Congress passed the Civil Rights Restoration Act of 1987, it added a new provision to section 504 stating that persons with "contagious diseases or infections" were not covered under section 504 if they posed a "direct threat to the health or safety of others."[25] This provision codified the standard in the *Arline* case, that individuals with contagious diseases who pose a significant health risk to others in the workplace, which cannot be eliminated by reasonable accommodation, are not qualified for the jobs they seek to hold.[26] At the same time, however, several members of Congress explained that the specific reference to contagious *infections* in the new provision was to reaffirm coverage of people with asymptomatic HIV infection under section 504 unless such individuals posed a direct threat to others.[27]

The analysis in cases involving employment discrimination because of AIDS or HIV infection has been relatively straightforward.[28] Plaintiffs must first establish that they have a "handicap" under the act — i.e., that they have AIDS, are HIV-infected, or are perceived as having AIDS or HIV infection. The individuals then put forward the case that they were fired, or otherwise discriminated against, because of these handicaps or perceptions of handicaps. In most published cases, these facts have not been contested by the employers.

As noted above, in order to prevail, an individual must also be "otherwise qualified" for the position in question. That is, the individual must be capable of performing the essential functions of the job without posing a significant risk of transmitting HIV to others (i.e., he or she may not pose a "direct threat to the health or safety of others"). Because the consensus of medical opinion is that HIV is not transmitted through casual contact in the workplace,[29] employers have generally not prevailed on the assertion that the person with AIDS or HIV infection is not qualified because of a health risk to others.[30]

II. The American with Disabilities Act

The Americans with Disabilities Act (ADA) was enacted in July 1990. The ADA will set the terms for how people with HIV disease can enforce their rights against discrimination in the areas of employment, public accommodations, transportation, public services, and telecommunications.[31]

The employment title of the ADA, Title I, can best be understood as deriving from two laws. The substantive provisions of the title, which prohibit employment discrimination on the basis of disability, stem from the regulations and case law implementing sections 501, 503, and 504 of the Rehabilitation Act. Thus, issues such as what constitutes "discrimination" on the basis of disability, or what is required as a "reasonable accommodation," are derived from requirements established under the Rehabilitation Act. The goal of the drafters of the ADA was to draw as much as possible from the fifteen years of experience under the Rehabilitation Act in order to create a workable and understandable law.

The procedural requirements of the employment title, by contrast, are drawn from Title VII of the Civil Rights Act of 1964. Title VII prohibits discrimination on the basis of race, color, sex, religion, or national origin on the part of employers with fifteen or more employees. One of the purposes of the ADA was to finally establish parity in the coverage of federal civil rights laws between people with disabilities and other protected categories. Thus, the procedural requirements of the ADA — such as, which employers are covered under the ADA and what remedies are provided by the law — are drawn from and are equivalent to those in Title VII.[32]

Because the ADA's substantive definitions and requirements are drawn from the Rehabilitation Act, people with AIDS and HIV infection are covered under the ADA, just as they are covered under the Rehabilitation Act. In addition, certain areas of particular importance for people with HIV disease were explicated in the statutory language and legislative history of the ADA.

A. Coverage of People with HIV Disease

The ADA uses the same three-prong definition of "disability" as is used in the Rehabilitation Act to define "handicap." A person with a disability is thus defined as:

1. someone with a physical or mental impairment that substantially limits the person in one or more major life activities;

2. someone with a record of such an impairment; or

3. someone regarded as having such an impairment.[33]

The legislative history to the ADA explicitly notes that people with AIDS and HIV infection are covered under the first prong of this definition of disability.[34] Indeed, the legislative history uses the appropriate term "HIV disease" rather than "AIDS," "ARC," or "HIV infection." This correctly reflects the current medical view that the traditional strict categories of AIDS, AIDS-Related Complex (ARC) and asymptomatic HIV infection do not accurately reflect the continuum of the disease. The term "HIV disease," by contrast, is a single term encompassing the spectrum of manifestations of HIV-related illness, from asymptomatic HIV infection through AIDS.[35]

Individuals who do not actually have HIV disease but are regarded as having HIV disease and are discriminated against on that basis are covered under the third prong of the definition.[36] In a lawsuit brought under the ADA, it will be the burden of the person bringing the lawsuit to prove that the employer has regarded him or her as having HIV disease and has acted in a discriminatory manner based on that perception.[37]

There are some differences between the ADA and the Rehabilitation Act regarding individuals who are covered under the statute, as well as some clarifications in the ADA regarding coverage, that have relevance for people with HIV disease.

First, an individual who currently engages in the illegal use of drugs is not covered as a person with a disability when the employer "acts on the basis of such [illegal drug] use."[38] In other words, an employer may fire, refuse to hire, or otherwise discriminate against an individual because of that individual's illegal drug use. However, if that illegal drug user also has HIV disease, and the employer discriminates against the individual because of the HIV disease and not because of the illegal drug use, that individual remains covered under the ADA.[39]

Second, the ADA states explicitly that "homosexuality and bisexuality are not impairments and as such are not disabilities under [the ADA]."[40] This has always been the case under the Rehabilitation Act as well. Because homosexuality and bisexuality are no longer classified as mental impairments by the American Psychiatric Association,[41] an individual who is discriminated against solely on the basis of sexual orientation has no cause of action under either the Rehabilitation Act or the ADA. However, if a gay man or a lesbian has HIV disease and is discriminated against because of the HIV disease, that person is protected in exactly the same way as anyone else with the disease.

In addition, if a person who is gay is regarded as having HIV disease and is discriminated against because of the perception of having that disability, that individual is covered under the third prong of the definition of disability as an individual who is "regarded as having such an impairment." It would be irrelevant that the cause for the perception is that the person is gay. The relevant point, for coverage under the statute, is that the employer has regarded the applicant or employee as having a disability and has discriminated against the person on that basis.

Third, the ADA includes an expansion of coverage from the Rehabilitation Act. Experience over the years has shown that people who are simply friends or relatives of people with disabilities are sometimes discriminated against because of their association with a person with a disability. When Congress passed the Fair Housing Amendments Act of 1988, in which protection against discrimination was extended to people with disabilities in the sale or rental of private housing, Congress added protection for people who associate with people with disabilities.[42] Congress added the same protection in the ADA, providing that employment discrimination includes "denying equal jobs or benefits to a qualified individual because of the known disability of an individual with whom the qualified individual is known to have a relationship or association."[43]

There were various efforts made, during the legislative process, to restrict this provision to individuals who associate with people with disabilities through marriage, blood, or care-giving relationships. All of these restrictive efforts failed.[44] The provision, therefore, extends broad protection to any individual who is a friend of, who lives with, who cares for, or who otherwise has an association with a person with HIV disease.[45] A person bringing a charge of discrimination, however, must prove that the discriminatory action occurred because of that person's association with a person with HIV disease.

B. Qualified Person with a Disability

Under the ADA, a person with HIV disease, just like a person with any other disability, must be a "qualified person with a disability."[46] This is defined in the ADA as a person who, "with or without reasonable accommodation, can perform the essential functions of the employment position that such individual holds or desires."[47]

This requirement consists of two basic components. The first component deals with "essential functions." Employers retain the prerogative under the ADA not to hire, or to refuse to retain, workers who cannot perform the essential functions of a job. "Essential functions" mean basically what they sound like: functions that are not marginal or tangential to the job in question. Thus, an employer is allowed to refuse to hire or retain a person with a disability who, because of the disability, truly cannot perform an essential function of the job. It is not legitimate, however, for the employer to refuse to hire or retain a person with a disability who, because of his or her disability, cannot perform some job task that is marginal to the job.[48]

The second component deals with reasonable accommodation. A person with a disability often can perform the essential functions of a job if some modification or adjustment is first made in some aspects of the job. Like the Rehabilitation Act, therefore, the ADA affirmatively requires that employers provide such reasonable accommodations to the known physical or mental disabilities of their applicants and employees.[49] Moreover, in determining whether an individual is able to perform the essential functions of a job, the law requires that an employer consider whether there are any reasonable accommodations that can be provided to the individual that would enable the individual to perform the job.[50]

The ADA lists as examples a number of modifications and adjustments that might fall within the framework of reasonable accommodations.[51] These are simply examples of types of accommodations that could be considered. The basic purpose is to identify aspects of the disability that make it difficult or impossible for a person with that disability to perform certain essential aspects of a job, and then to determine if there are modifications or adjustments to the job environment or structure that will enable the person with a disability to be qualified to perform the job.

There is a limitation to the employer's obligation to provide a reasonable accommodation. As under section 504 of the Rehabilitation Act, an employer need not provide an accommodation if doing so would impose an "undue hardship" on the employer. An accommodation is considered to rise to the level of an "undue hardship" if providing it would result in a "significant difficulty or expense" for the employer, taking into account such factors as the financial resources of the employer, the size and type of the employer's business, the number of employees and the nature and cost of the accommodation.[52]

Most people with HIV disease (like people with many other disabilities) are qualified to remain in their jobs, or to obtain new jobs, without the provision of any accommodations. Such individuals are protected simply by the basic prohibition against discrimination, including discrimination based on myths, stereotypes, and ungrounded fears.

Some people with HIV disease, however, do need various reasonable accommodations in order to perform the essential functions of their jobs. The most common type of accommodation needed is flexible work schedules and time off to accommodate treatment schedules or fatigue problems.[53] Some people with HIV disease develop other impairments, such as visual impairments or mobility impairments. In those situations, the reasonable accommodations designed for individuals with visual or mobility impairments would be available for the person with HIV disease.

As with all other reasonable accommodations, the obligation to provide accommodations to people with HIV disease is limited by the requirement that the accommodation not pose an undue hardship on the employer. Thus, larger employers can be expected to be required to provide more significant accommodations to people with HIV disease than smaller employers.[54]

There are several other elements to the requirement that a person with a disability must be "qualified" to perform a job that have relevance for people with HIV disease. First, the determination as to whether an individual is a "qualified person with a disability" must be made at the time of the employment decision and may not be based on speculation regarding an individual's future capabilities.[55] Thus, for example, a person with HIV disease who is qualified to do a job at the time a particular employment decision is made may not be disqualified based on the employer's assumption that the person may become so ill in the future as to be incapable of performing the job.[56]

The ADA's requirement that determinations regarding qualifications must be made at the time of the employment decision is an important and necessary one. Many people who have disabilities that are medical conditions face some possibility of becoming incapacitated in the future. If an employer could refuse to hire the person based on the fear that the person would end up not being qualified some time in the future, any statutory employment protection would end up being more words than reality. Of course, if the person *does* become unable to do the job at some point in the future because of his or her disability, and no reasonable accommodation will enable the person to perform the job, the employer may fire the person at that point.[57]

Second, the ADA sets forth, as an explicit qualification standard, that a person with a disability "shall not pose a direct threat to the health or safety of other individuals in the workplace."[58] "Direct threat" is defined in the ADA as "a significant risk to the health or safety of others which cannot be eliminated by reasonable accommodation."[59] This provision stems directly from section 504 and from *School Board of Nassau County v. Arline*, the Supreme Court decision interpreting section 504.[60]

In section 504 cases, people with HIV disease have almost consistently been held not to pose a direct threat to the health or safety of others.[61] Courts have concluded that a threat of transmission of HIV does not exist based, primarily on recommendations issued by the Centers for Disease Control of the U.S. Public Health Service.[62] Cases brought under the ADA will also, in all likelihood, conclude that people with HIV disease do not pose a direct threat to others.

The area where the possibility of "direct threat" based on a "significant risk" is likely to be most heavily contested is the employment of HIV-infected health care workers (HCWs). Intense publicity surrounding the transmission of HIV that occurred in one dental office in Florida led the Centers for Disease Control to publish new recommendations in July 1991 concerning this issue.[63] The new recommendations contain these statements:

- "Infected HCWs who adhere to universal precautions and who do not perform invasive procedures pose *no risk* for transmitting HIV or HBV [hepatitis virus] to patients." (emphasis added)

- "Currently available data provide no basis for recommendations to restrict the practice of HCWs infected with HIV or HBV who perform invasive procedures not identified as exposure-prone," provided that the workers comply with what are known as "universal precautions" for infection control (such as using gloves and masks and complying with standards for sterilization and disinfection).

- "HCWs who perform exposure-prone procedures should know their HIV antibody status... HCWs who are infected with HIV... should not perform exposure-prone procedures unless they have sought counsel from an expert review panel and been advised under what circumstances, if any, they may continue to perform these procedures. Such circumstances should include notifying prospective patients of the HCW's seropositivity before they undergo exposure-prone invasive procedures."

These new recommendations were attacked, by a range of groups, on several policy grounds. First, they appeared to be an overreaction to the sympathetic, but unique, case of the dental patients in Florida, and thus an example of public health policy-making driven by public emotion rather than by science. Indeed, there were few data offered by the CDC to support its proposed restrictions. In all instances involving actual follow-up studies of patients of HIV-infected HCWs, except for the dentist in Florida there had never been a reported case of doctor-to-patient HIV transmission. The CDC thus relied, instead, on a projected risk assessment model that suffered from numerous technical flaws. These flaws made the CDC's final projections of the possible risks of HIV transmission in the health care setting highly speculative.[64]

Second, setting forth suggested restrictions on HIV- and HBV-infected HCWs without having the sufficient appropriate data to justify the restrictions was regarded by many experts as irresponsible. These restrictions were seen as forcing a host of resultant sacrifices that were not justified by the virtually nonexistent risk involved: the loss of qualified health care professionals; the ruin of professional careers for no reason; the loss of the social resources invested in their training; and the likelihood of an increasing reluctance by noninfected HCWs to treat HIV patients, because of an increased unjustified fear regarding the risks of HIV transmission and because of the fear of not only acquiring the disease, but of losing their professions.[65]

Finally, at the time the CDC issued their recommendations, it did not set forth clearly which specific invasive procedures should be considered "exposure-prone." Instead, the CDC set forth a general definition of "exposure-prone procedures" and urged local medical and dental professional groups to decide which procedures met the definition. In early November 1991, the CDC convened a meeting of such groups to help establish a list of exposure-prone invasive procedures. Almost uniformly, the professional groups refused to establish such a list because data were lacking to indicate a real risk of exposure during invasive procedures.

In addition to these policy problems, the CDC's recommendations raised serious legal questions. First, how could such an extremely low, indeed minuscule, risk justify restrictions on employment when the legal standard mandated by federal law is a "significant risk"?[66] Previous cases have held that the standard of "significant risk" cannot be satisfied simply by any increment greater than zero risk,[67] by a "mere elevated risk,"[68] or by a risk which is "remote."[69] The EEOC regulations to the ADA take a similarly strict approach.[70] Moreover, state approaches may be contradictory. New York explicitly defines "significant risk" in such a way that the federal recommendations would violate state law.[71]

Second, the CDC proposals appeared to violate the principle that risk must be measured objectively. An objective approach would require placing the risk of HIV transmission in context and perspective by comparing it with other comparable risks — an approach that was not undertaken by the CDC. New and unfamiliar risks, or risks that in some way bear the weight of stigma, are frequently overestimated, while familiar ones tend to be underestimated.

Third, the law requires that any supposedly safety-driven policy may not be applied in an invidious manner. A risk related to one kind of disability may not be singled out for elimination if other comparable risks are completely ignored. This is so often the heart of AIDS discrimination — the singling out of people with this particular disease for adverse treatment on the flimsiest of evidence.[72]

All of these issues will have to be addressed and resolved as the courts tackle antidiscrimination cases brought by HIV-infected HCWs under the ADA. Although it is impossible to predict the outcome of those cases, it will be the duty of courts to fulfill their role of requiring rational policy-making based upon objective medical evidence rather than upon fear and prejudice.

People with HIV disease are also sometimes confronted with employers who argue that, "for their own good," people with HIV disease should not work in various job settings. The EEOC regulations to the ADA include a "risk to self" concept, although the statute itself explicitly deals only with individuals who pose a direct threat "to others."[73] The standard for an employer invoking "risk to self" under the regulations is very high. Employers must demonstrate that there is a high probability that the individual will cause himself or herself substantial harm.[74] This standard would not justify excluding people with HIV disease based on the speculative concern that they would cause some harm to themselves in a workplace setting.[75]

C. HIV Testing

The provisions in the ADA regarding medical examinations and inquiries of job applicants, including examinations to test for antibodies to HIV, basically follow the regulations issued under section 504.[76] There are certain additional clarifications made in the ADA, however, regarding restrictions on testing employees.

1. Preemployment Testing of Job Applicants

Under the ADA, an employer may not require an applicant for a job to submit to a medical examination or answer medical inquiries before a conditional job offer has been made to the applicant.[77] At any point in the application process, however, an employer may ask the applicant whether the applicant has the knowledge, skill, and ability to perform the essential functions of the job. Thus, for example, an employer may ask, in the initial application stage, whether the person has the educational and professional qualifications necessary for the job. The employer may also ask whether the applicant can do certain job functions, such as drive a car, lift fifty pounds, or answer the telephone, if these are functions of the job.[78]

After an employer has determined that an applicant possesses the necessary qualifications for a particular job, and has decided to offer the applicant the job, the employer may choose to extend to the applicant a conditional job offer. Once that conditional job offer has been extended, the employer may then require that the applicant undergo a medical examination or answer medical inquiries and may condition the offer of employment to the applicant on the results of that medical test or inquiry.[79]

There are, however, certain conditions placed on the use of such examinations and inquiries. First, if an employer wishes to require a medical examination or inquiry, the examination or inquiry must be required of *all* applicants for a particular job category, not simply of selected applicants. For example, an employer may not require that only certain applicants for a job take an HIV test. Rather, the requirement of the HIV test must be a routine one requested of all applicants for a particular job category.[80] Second, the information obtained as a result of the medical examinations must be kept strictly confidential. This information must be maintained on forms separate from the general application forms, must be maintained in separate medical files, and must be treated as confidential medical records.[81] Only a limited number of individuals may gain access to these records.[82]

This confidentiality requirement represents an important protection for applicants who undergo HIV testing. There is currently no general federal confidentiality law protecting HIV test results.[83] The ADA, however, creates a federal cause of action for breaches of confidentiality of medical records obtained by the employer through testing of job applicants. This protection supplements whatever other causes of action an individual may have under state laws for breaches of confidentiality (e.g., through medical records, privacy laws, or HIV testing laws).

Third, and of key importance, the results of the medical examination may not be used to withdraw the conditional job offer from an applicant unless the results indicate that the applicant is not qualified to perform the essential functions of the job.[84] As one legislative report explains: "The results of the medical examination cannot be used to discriminate against a person with a disability if the person is still qualified for the job."[85]

This two-step process in preemployment testing (first a conditional job offer, then the permitted testing) is designed to protect applicants with disabilities by allowing them to isolate if and when a discriminatory hiring practice has been influenced by their disability. Assume, for example, that an applicant was judged sufficiently qualified for a job so as to receive a conditional job offer, and assume further that the only medical information of interest revealed by the examination was that the person was infected with HIV. If the conditional job offer was withdrawn after the medical exam, the applicant could assert that his or her HIV status was the determining factor in the employment decision, and the burden would then fall on the employer to show otherwise.

At the same time, the two-step process protects employers by allowing them to discover disabilities that will, in fact, limit an applicant's ability to perform a job prior to the applicant receiving a final job offer. For example, assume that the medical examination reveals that an applicant has a degenerative eye condition that makes the applicant, even with reasonable accommodation, incapable of performing the essential functions of a particular job. In that case, the conditional job offer could legitimately be withdrawn under the ADA framework.[86]

As this description indicates, the protections of the ADA are obviously not absolute, because employers may require that all applicants for a job undergo HIV antibody tests without first proving that such tests are directly related to the job.[87] Nevertheless, because employers are restricted from using the results of HIV antibody tests to withdraw conditional job offers unless the HIV status is relevant to the job, and because employers face liability if any HIV test results that they have required are inadvertently disclosed, it is likely that most employers will generally not require applicants to undergo HIV antibody tests. An area where litigation with regard to preemployment testing may still be expected is in the area of applicants for health care positions.[88]

2. Testing of On-the Job Employees

An employer may require a medical examination of an employee only if the employer proves that the test is "job-related and consistent with business necessity."[89] As explained by the legislative reports: "Once an employee is on the job, the actual performance on the job is...the best measure of the employee's ability to do the job. When a need arises to question the continued ability of a person to do the job, the employer may...require medical exams that are job-related and consistent with business necessity."[90]

The standard of "job-related and consistent with business necessity" is derived from regulations issued by the Department of Labor to implement section 504.[91] According to the legislative reports, this standard is to be interpreted consistently with cases decided under section 504 prior to the decision by the Supreme Court in *Wards Cove Packing Co. v. Atonio.*[92] In practice, this means that the employer must demonstrate that the medical examination is necessary to measure the employee's actual performance of essential job functions.

The ADA makes clear that employers may continue to offer voluntary medical examinations to their employees — for example, as part of "corporate wellness" programs. Results of such examinations, however, are subject to the same requirements governing preemployment exams with regard to confidentiality and, similarly, may not be used to discriminate against an individual who remains qualified for a job.[93]

D. Health Benefits

The protections provided by the ADA with regard to health benefits for people with HIV disease are less than clear. The final regulations promulgated by the EEOC have not addressed this issue in depth, and final resolution will probably come only in court decisions. However, some parameters of the discussion can be drawn at this point.

The ADA provides that a covered entity may not discriminate against an employee in the "terms or conditions of employment."[94] The legislative reports note that these terms and conditions include "fringe benefits available by virtue of employment, whether or not administered by the covered entity."[95] A covered entity may also not participate in a contractual relationship that has the effect of subjecting the employees of the covered entity to discrimination, including a contractual relationship with "an organization providing fringe benefits to an employee of the covered entity."[96]

The ADA, therefore, does seem to contemplate that certain practices with regard to the provision of fringe benefits, including, presumably, health coverage, would be illegal under the act. The ADA, however, also includes a general provision with regard to insurance. This provision states that nothing in the ADA shall be construed to prohibit or restrict:

1. an insurer (or other entity administering benefit plans) from underwriting risks, classifying risks, or administering risks that are based on or not inconsistent with state law;

2. a covered entity from establishing or administering a bona fide benefit plan that is based on underwriting risks, classifying risks, or administering risks that are based on or not inconsistent with state law; or

3. a covered entity from establishing or administering a bona fide benefit plan that is not subject to state laws that regulate insurance.[97]

This provision, however, also has its own exception built into it. According to the provision, the three outlined insurance exceptions may not be used as a "subterfuge" to evade the purposes of the ADA.[98]

The various legislative reports, and some members of Congress, attempted to provide some guidance in this area.[99] There are various principles that may be derived from this legislative guidance:

(1) Employers may not refuse to hire an individual because the individual will cost the employer more in terms of insurance premiums (or, in the case of self-insured plans, in terms of health care costs). Thus, an employer could not refuse to hire a person with HIV disease because such individuals are likely to cost more in terms of health insurance coverage.[100]

(2) Employers and insurance companies may continue to include preexisting condition clauses in their health plans, even though such clauses eliminate benefits for a specified time period, for people with disabilities.[101]

(3) Employers and insurance companies may limit coverage for certain *procedures* or *treatments*. For example, a health plan presumably

may place a limit on the number of blood transfusions for which it will reimburse participants.

(4) An employer may not, however, have a health plan that denies coverage "completely" to an individual based on diagnosis. For example, while a plan may include certain limitations for people with kidney disease (e.g., a limit on the amount of kidney dialysis), the plan may not deny coverage to the employee with kidney disease for conditions not connected to the permissible procedure limitations (e.g., coverage for treatment of a broken leg).[102] Moreover, the plan could also not deny coverage to that individual for other procedures or treatments connected with the kidney disease itself.[103]

The overall thrust of the ADA's legislative history appears to be that insurance companies, and employers maintaining insurance plans, should be allowed to continue offering such plans as long as exclusions or limitations in the plan are based on sound actuarial principles. Of course, some employers may think that it makes sense, as an actuarial matter, to try to deny coverage completely for people with kidney disease or people with HIV disease. Such an attempt, however, may well be seen as a "subterfuge" for evading the purposes of the law, if in practice it will mean that people with HIV disease or kidney disease will not be able to become employed. Thus, it is quite possible that it would not be permissible to select out one disability, such as kidney disease or HIV, for differential treatment without actuarial data justifying the distinction.[104]

E. Remedies

Title I of the ADA adopts the same administrative and judicial remedies provided by Title VII of the Civil Rights Act of 1964. As under Title VII, therefore, a plaintiff must first go through the administrative process established under the Equal Employment Opportunity Commission. Plaintiffs then have a private right of action in court and have the right to get injunctive relief, including reinstatement in a job, orders for back pay, and, in some cases, front pay.[105]

In the past, under Title VII, plaintiffs were not entitled to receive compensatory or punitive damages. In 1991, Congress amended the remedies provision of Title VII to allow for compensatory damages in cases of intentional discrimination and for punitive damages in cases of malice or reckless indifference to the rights of others.[106] Those damages will be available for violations of the employment title of the ADA as well. The ADA also provides payment for attorneys' fees and other litigation expenses (including expert witness fees) for parties who prevail in ADA claims.[107] Such reimbursement would apply for expenses incurred in both administrative and judicial proceedings.[108]

Section 501(b) of the ADA further provides that the ADA may not be construed to invalidate or limit the remedies or rights established by any federal law or state law that provides greater or equal protection to people with disabilities. This "anti-preemption" provision is designed to ensure explicitly that other federal laws (such as the Rehabilitation Act) and state laws will continue to provide protection to people with disabilities. This also includes the remedies, such as compensatory and punitive damages, that may be available under state laws.[109]

Conclusion

The early years of the HIV epidemic were marked by a high level of ignorance, fear, and hysteria regarding both HIV and people who had any form of HIV disease. This fear and hysteria caused some employers and coworkers to shun people with HIV disease and to discriminate against them in the workplace. Public education regarding HIV disease has helped to quell many of these fears and concerns, but, unfortunately, not everyone has received the message. People with HIV disease are still being subjected to unjustified workplace discrimination.

The Rehabilitation Act of 1973 provides that applicants and employers who are unfairly discriminated against on the basis of HIV disease — by the federal government, by federal contractors, or by recipients of federal funds — have some recourse under the law. The recently enacted Americans with Disabilities Act will finally extend that protection to most American workers.

NOTES

1. *See* American Civil Liberties Union AIDS Project, Epidemic of Fear 22-23 (1990) [hereinafter Epidemic of Fear]; Gostin, *The AIDS Litigation Project: A National Review of Court and Human Rights Decisions, Part I: The Social Impact of AIDS*, 263 J. A.M.A. 1961 (1990).
2. *See* Epidemic of Fear, *supra* note 1, at 1-3, 19-24.
3. *See* Title VII of the Civil Rights Act of 1964, 42 U.S.C. § 2000e *et seq.* (1988 & Supp.).

4. The employment protections of the ADA are found in Title I of the law. Title III of the ADA also prohibits discrimination against customers and clients with disabilities in a wide range of privately owned businesses and service providers. This protection will be particularly important for people with HIV disease who have often faced discrimination by health care providers. Epidemic of Fear, *supra* note 1; *see also* chapter 4 ("The Very Fabric of Health Care") on the duty to treat. Discrimination in the rental or sale of residential buildings is already prohibited under a law passed by Congress in 1988, amending the Fair Housing Act of 1968. *See* 42 U.S.C. § 3600 *et seq.* (1988).

5. 29 U.S.C. § 794 (1985 & Supp.).

6. Federal agencies are also subject to an antidiscrimination and affirmative action requirement in employment with regard to their own employees under section 501 of the Rehabilitation Act. *See* 29 U.S.C. § 791 (1988); 29 U.S.C.A. § 791 (Supp. 1991).

7. In Grove City College v. Bell, 465 U.S. 555 (1984), the Supreme Court held that if one part of an institution receives federal funds, only *that* part was bound by the requirements of any federal law that covers a "program or activity" receiving federal financial assistance. In response to the *Grove City* decision, Congress passed the Civil Rights Restoration Act of 1988, Pub. L. No. 100-259. That law restored the broad definition of "program or activity" that had existed prior to the *Grove City* ruling and established that a "program or activity" includes an entire institution that is engaged primarily in providing education, health care, housing, social services, or recreation whenever any part of the institution receives federal funds. 29 U.S.C.A. § 794(b) (Supp. 1991). Thus, currently, if any part of such an institution receives federal funds, the entire institution is covered under section 504 of the Rehabilitation Act.

8. 29 U.S.C. § 793 (1988). Section 503 requires that federal contractors use affirmative action to employ and advance people with disabilities. The federal agencies and courts have interpreted this provision to include an anti-discrimination component. *See, e.g.,* Moon v. Department of Labor, 747 F.2d 599 (11th Cir. 1984).

9. Reflecting the terminology popular at that time, the Act refers to people with "handicaps." People with disabilities and their advocates prefer to use the term "disability" rather than "handicap." Except where necessary to convey accurately the legal requirements of the Rehabilitation Act, this chapter will use the term "disability" rather than "handicap."

10. 29 U.S.C. § 706(7)(A) (1988).

11. 45 C.F.R. § 84.3(j)(2)(i); Appendix A, No. 3 (1990). Major life activities include activities such as walking, talking, breathing, and working. Most physical or mental impairments do result in such limitations. For a detailed discussion of the definition of "disability," see Feldblum, *The Americans with Disabilities Act: Definition of Disability,* 7 Labor Lawyer 11 (1991).

12. 29 U.S.C.A. § 706(8)(B) (1990); *see also* S. Rep. No. 1297, 93rd Cong., 2nd Sess. 16, 37-38, 50 (1974).

13. 29 U.S.C. § 794 (1988 & Supp. 1990).

14. *See* School Bd. of Nassau County v. Arline, 480 U.S. 273, 287 n.17 (1987); Pushkin v. Regents of Univ. of Colo., 658 F.2d 1372, 1385-87 (10th Cir. 1981).

15. For example, a person who uses a wheelchair may need a table adjusted for height or may need a ramp built to allow access. Persons with varying degrees of a hearing impairment may need a telephone amplifier or an interpreter.

Someone with a chronic physical condition may need some time off each week for medical treatments.

16.   45 C.F.R. § 84.3(k)(1) (1990).

17.   45 C.F.R. § 84.12(a) (1990).

18.   *See Arline,* 480 U.S. at 287 n.17 (citing Southeastern Community College v. Davis, 442 U.S. 397 (1979); Alexander v. Choate, 469 U.S. 287 (1985); Strathie v. Department of Transp., 716 F.2d 227 (3rd Cir. 1983)). The standard of "undue hardship" under the Rehabilitation Act is thus significantly greater than the *de minimis* standard that the Supreme Court has established for purposes of religion under Title VII of the Civil Rights Act of 1964. *See* TWA v. Hardison, 432 U.S. 63 (1977).

19.   *Arline,* 480 U.S. 273 (1987).

20.   *Id.* at 282 & n.7 (summarizing Department of Justice argument).

21.   *Id.* at 282. The Court also rejected the contention that the Rehabilitation Act was not intended to apply to contagious diseases.

22.   *Id.* at 282-86.

23.   *Arline,* 480 U.S. at 287 n.16.

24.   *See* Local 1812, AFGE v. Department of State, 662 F. Supp. 50, 54 (D.D.C. 1987); *see also,* Chalk v. United States Dist. Court, 840 F.2d 701 (9th Cir. 1988); Doe v. Centinela Hosp., No. CV-87-2514-PAR (C.D. Cal. 1988); Ray v. School Dist. of DeSoto County, 666 F. Supp. 1524 (M.D. Fla. 1987); Thomas v. Atascadero Unified School Dist., 662 F. Supp. 376 (C.D. Cal. 1986).

25.   Pub. L. No. 100-259, § 9; 29 U.S.C. § 706(8)(D) (1988).

26.   *See id.; see also,* 134 Cong. Rec. S1738-40 (daily ed. Mar. 2, 1988) (colloquy among Senators Edward Kennedy, Lowell Weicker, and Tom Harkin).

27.   *See, e.g.,* 134 Cong. Rec. H574 (daily ed. Mar. 2, 1988) (statement of Rep. Owens); 134 Cong. Rec. H572-73 (Mar. 2, 1988) (statement of Rep. Weiss); 134 Cong. Rec. E487 (Mar. 2, 1988) (statement of Rep. Hoyer). In addition, when Congress passed the Fair Housing Amendments Act of 1988 it noted that both AIDS and HIV infection were covered under the new law. The regulations of the Department of Housing and Urban Development, implementing the Fair Housing Amendments Act, included "HIV infection" as a physical impairment covered under the law. 54 Fed. Reg. 3245 (1989). In September 1988, the U.S. Department of Justice released a legal memorandum concluding that people with AIDS and people with asymptomatic HIV infection were covered under section 504. *See* Memorandum of Douglas W. Kmiec, Acting Assistant Attorney General, Office of Legal Counsel, Dept. of Justice (Sept. 27, 1988).

28.   *See, e.g., Chalk,* 840 F.2d 701; Shuttleworth v. Broward County, 639 F. Supp. 654 (S.D. Fla. 1986).

29.   *See* U.S. Centers for Disease Control [CDC], *Update: Universal Precautions for Prevention of Transmission of HIV, HBV and other Bloodborne Pathogens in Health Care Settings,* 37 Morbidity & Mortality Wkly. Rep. [MMWR] 377 (1988); CDC, *Recommendations for Prevention of HIV Transmission in Health-Care Settings,* 36 MMWR Supp. 2S (1987); CDC, *Recommendations for Preventing Transmission of Infection with HTLV III/LAV During Invasive Procedures,* 35 MMWR 221 (1986); CDC, *Recommendations for Preventing Transmission of Infection with HTLV III/LAV in the Workplace,* 34 MMWR 45 (1985).

30.   While plaintiffs with HIV disease have prevailed in most employment discrimination cases, there have been cases in which courts have found such individuals not to be "otherwise qualified" for positions they sought. For example, in one case a district court upheld an HIV testing program instituted

by the State Department for foreign service employees, concluding that people with HIV infection would not be qualified to serve as foreign service officers because of inadequate medical facilities in certain countries. *Local 1812, AFGE,* 662 F. Supp. 50. The result in that case was probably dictated significantly by the district court's reluctance to interfere with the inner workings of the State Department. Reluctance to interfere with certain governmental institutions, such as the military, prisons, and the foreign service, has been apparent in many other cases. A second category of cases in which some plaintiffs with HIV infection have not prevailed, and where further litigation may be expected, is that relating to HIV-infected health care workers.

31. Much of the following general description of the ADA has also appeared in Feldblum, *Employment Protections, in* The Americans with Disabilities Act: From Policy to Practice (Milbank Memorial Fund, 1991). This article explicates those general provisions with regard to people with HIV disease.

32. For the sake of brevity, this chapter will use the term "employer" to designate an entity covered under Title I of the ADA. In practice, however, Title I covers the same entities that are covered under Title VII: employers, employment agencies, labor organizations, and joint labor-management committees. In any place where the term "employer" is used in this chapter, therefore, the range of covered entities is intended.

33. ADA, § 3(2).

34. *See, e.g.,* Report of the House Committee on Education and Labor, H.R. Rep. No. 101-485, 101st Cong., 2nd Sess., Part 2 at 52 ("[A] person infected with the Human Immunodeficiency Virus is covered under the first prong of the definition of the term 'disability' because of a substantial limitation to procreation and intimate sexual relations.") [hereinafter Education and Labor Report]; Report of the House Committee on the Judiciary, 101st Cong., H.R. Rep. No. 101-485, 101st Cong., 2nd Sess., Part 3 at 28 n.18 [hereinafter Judiciary Report]; Report of the Senate Committee on Labor and Human Resources, S. Rep. No. 101-116, 101st Cong., 1st Sess. 22 [hereinafter Senate Report]; *see also* statement of Rep. Owens, 136 Cong. Rec. H4623 (daily ed. July 12, 1990); statement of Rep. Edwards, 136 Cong. Rec. H4624 (daily ed. July 12, 1990).

35. For legislative statements regarding use of term "HIV disease," *see* statement of Rep. Edwards, 136 Cong. Rec. H4624 (daily ed. July 12, 1990): "[U]nder the ADA, people with *HIV disease* will finally be protected in private employment situations." (emphasis added); statement of Rep. Owens, 136 Cong. Rec. H4623 (daily ed. July 12, 1990): "[T]he ADA will offer critical protection to people with HIV disease in a range of areas. People with *HIV disease* are individuals who have any condition along the full spectrum of HIV infection — asymptomatic HIV infection, symptomatic HIV infection or full-blown AIDS." (emphasis added). *See also* statement of Sen. Kennedy, 136 Cong. Rec. S9697 (daily ed. July 13, 1990); statement of Rep. Waxman, 136 Cong. Rec. H4626 (daily ed. July 12, 1990).

The final regulations issued by the Equal Employment Opportunity Commission (EEOC) to implement Title I of the ADA, and by the Department of Justice (DOJ) to implement Title III of the ADA, also recognize that people with HIV disease, including people with asymptomatic HIV infection, are covered under the first prong of the definition. In its discussion of the first prong of the definition, the EEOC's guidance notes that some impairments, "such as HIV infection, are inherently substantially limiting" and thus covered under the ADA's definition of disability. *See* 56 Fed. Reg. 53,741 (1991).

Similarly, the DOJ's regulations provide that "HIV disease (symptomatic or asymptomatic)" is included in the list of covered physical impairments. *See* 28 C.F.R. § 36.104(1)(iii); 56 Fed. Reg. 35,593, 35,548 (1991).

36. *See* EEOC Regulations, 56 Fed. Reg. 35,742 (1991).

37. *See, e.g., Pushkin*, 658 F.2d at 1385-87 (general burden of proof requirements).

38. ADA, § 104(a).

39. *See* Education and Labor Report, *supra* note 34, at 77.

40. ADA, § 511(a).

41. Homosexuality was removed from the list of mental disorders by the American Psychiatric Association in 1974. *See* American Psychiatric Association, Diagnostic and Statistical Manual III (1974).

42. Section 804(f)(1)-(2) of Fair Housing Act of 1968 as amended, 42 U.S.C. § 3604(f)(1)-(2) (1988).

43. ADA, § 102(b)(4). There are some differences between the language of the "association provision" in the ADA and in the Fair Housing Act. During consideration of the ADA, representatives of the business community raised the concern that an employer might fire an employee without knowing that the employee had an association with a person with a disability and then be faced with a charge of discrimination because the employee, in fact, had some relationship with a person with a disability. It was never the intent of the drafters of the ADA to cover that type of situation. The language of the provision was therefore modified to clarify that the law covered a person who was "known" to associate with a person with a "known" disability.

   A similar prohibition on discriminating against a person or an entity based on that person's or entity's association with a person with a disability appears in Title III of the ADA as well. *See* ADA, § 302(b)(1)(E).

44. *See, e.g.,* Judiciary Report, *supra* note 34, at 38.

45. Both the EEOC and DOJ, in their guidance to the ADA regulations, note the broad scope of the association provision. *See* 56 Fed. Reg. 35,747 (1991) (EEOC); *Id.* at 35,558-59 (DOJ).

46. *See* ADA, § 101(8) (defining a "qualified person with a disability"); ADA, § 102(a) (prohibiting discrimination against a "qualified person with a disability").

47. ADA, § 101(8).

48. The concept of "essential functions" comes directly from the 1977 regulations issued to implement section 504. *See* 45 C.F.R. § 84.3(k) and Appendix A (1990). The concept is further explicated in the EEOC regulations to the ADA. *See* 56 Fed. Reg. 37,743-44 (1991).

49. As noted, the reasonable accommodation requirement applies to the *known* limitations of an applicant or employee. Thus, the employer's obligation is triggered by a *request* from an applicant or employee for a reasonable accommodation. Employers are not required to have a "crystal ball" to divine what disability an applicant or employee may have that would necessitate a particular reasonable accommodation.

50. ADA, § 102(b)(5)(A)-(B); *see also* Education and Labor Report, *supra* note 34 at 62-67.

51. ADA, § 101(9). These include: making modifications to the physical layout of a job facility so as to make it accessible to individuals who use wheelchairs or who have other impairments that make access difficult; restructuring a job so as to enable the person with a disability to perform the restructured job; establishing a part-time or modified work schedule (these would be useful to

accommodate people with disabilities who have treatment needs or fatigue problems); reassigning a person with a disability to a vacant job; acquiring or modifying equipment or devices (such as buying a telephone amplifier for a person with a hearing impairment); adjusting or modifying exams, training materials or policies (such as giving an application examination orally to a person with dyslexia or modifying a policy against dogs in the workplace for a person with a service dog); and providing qualified readers or interpreters for people with vision or hearing impairments.

52. ADA, § 101(10) (definition of undue hardship); ADA, § 102(b)(5)(A) (requirement to provide a reasonable accommodation unless it imposes an undue hardship); *see also* EEOC Regulations, 56 Fed. Reg. 35,744-45, 35,747-49 (1991).

53. Such needs were explicitly recognized by several members of Congress. *See, e.g.*, statement of Rep. Owens, 136 Cong. Rec. H4623 (daily ed. July 12, 1990): "The reasonable accommodation provision of the bill will be particularly important in ensuring that people with HIV disease have the right to flexible work schedules and to time off to accommodate the treatment needs of their various disease-related conditions." *See also* statement of Rep. Edwards, 136 Cong. Rec., H4624 (daily ed. July 12, 1990); statement of Rep. Waxman, 136 Cong. Rec. H4626 (daily ed. July 12, 1990); statement of Sen. Kennedy, 136 Cong. Rec. S9607 (daily ed. July 13, 1990).

54. Reasonable accommodations includes modifying procedures and making purchases of assistive equipment. It is useful to note, however, that the adoption of "universal precautions" to prevent the transmission of HIV is probably not accurately termed a reasonable accommodation in most situations. "Universal precautions" refer to the procedures recommended by the Centers for Disease Control (CDC) for prevention of transmission of HIV. These procedures consist primarily of use of gloves and masks. *See* Department of Labor, Occupational Safety and Health Administration (OSHA), 29 C.F.R. § 1910.1030(b) (1989) ("'Universal precautions' is a method of infection control in which all human blood and certain human body fluids are treated as if known to be infectious for HIV, HBV and other bloodborne pathogens.")

Universal precautions are recommended by the CDC and by OSHA for use in any settings in which there is a possibility of transmission of blood. The guidelines require that the recommended precautions be used as a general, universal matter. They are not designed to be adopted solely when a person who is known to be HIV infected is known to be in the particular setting.

The adoption of universal precautions, therefore, is different from the provision of a reasonable accommodation. By its very nature, a reasonable accommodation is individualized: it is requested by, and designed to respond to, a particular person with a disability to enable that individual to perform the essential functions of the job. In addition, there is an undue hardship limitation on the provision of a reasonable accommodation. By contrast, the adoption of universal precautions is a mandate regardless of the presence of an individual known to have HIV disease in the setting.

55. *See, e.g.*, Judiciary Report, *supra* note 34, at 34 ("The determination of whether a person is qualified should be made at the time of the employment decision, e.g., hiring or promotion, and should not be based on the possibility that the employee or applicant will become incapacitated or unqualified in the future."); EEOC Regulations, 56 Fed. Reg. 35, 743 (1991); *see also* statement of Rep. Hoyer, 136 Cong. Rec. E1914 (daily ed. June 13, 1990) (same); statement

of Rep. Owens, 136 Cong. Rec. H4623 (daily ed. July 12, 1990) (same, regarding genetic testing).

56. This point was noted several times with regard to individuals who are identified, through advances in genetic testing, as carrying a disease-associated gene. *See, e.g.*, statement of Rep. Edwards, 136 Cong. Rec. H4625 ("Under the ADA,... such individuals [who are carriers of a disease-associated gene] may not be discriminated against based on the assumption that they will become sick in the future and will not be qualified to do their jobs."); statement of Rep. Waxman, 136 Cong. Rec. H.4627 (July 12, 1990) (same).

While the EEOC's interpretive guidance appears inappropriately to cast some doubt on the coverage of genetic carriers under the definition of disability, *see* 56 Fed. Reg. 35,741 (1991), the EEOC clearly provides that the determination as to whether a person with a covered disability (such as HIV infection) is qualified may not be based on speculation regarding an individual's future capabilities. *Id*. at 35,743.

57. Some employers have voiced concerns regarding the requirement to hire individuals who may be unable to work two or three years in the future. However, no employer is ever assured of complete certainty with regard to his or her workforce: any employee (with or without a disability) may have an accident, may move to another city, or may choose to change jobs. The ADA thus seeks to strike an appropriate balance in social policy. It does not allow employers to refuse to hire people with disabilities on the basis that such individuals might become unqualified in the future, because that would create a huge loophole in the law's antidiscrimination protection. However, employers are allowed to discharge employees with disabilities once they are no longer qualified to work, thus protecting the employer's interest in maintaining a capable and efficient workforce.

58. ADA, § 103(b).

59. ADA, § 101(3).

60. 480 U.S. 273 (1987).

61. *See, e.g.*, *Chalk*, 840 F.2d 701; Martinez v. School Bd. of Hillsborough County, 861 F.2d 1502 (11th Cir. 1988); Thomas v. Atascadero Unified School Dist., 662 F. Supp. 376 (C.D.Cal. 1987). *See also* Baxter v. City of Belleville, 720 F. Supp. 720 (S.D. Ill. 1989) (case brought under the Fair Housing Act, which includes identical "direct threat" language in the statute); Glover v. ENCOR, 867 F.2d 461 (8th Cir. 1989) (case arising under Fourth Amendment, concluding absence of threat from residential mental health care workers).

62. *See supra* note 29 for citations of CDC guidelines.

63. CDC, *Recommendations for Preventing Transmission of Human Immunodeficiency Virus and Hepatitis-B Virus to Patients During Exposure-Prone Invasive Procedures*, 40 Morbidity & Mortality Weekly Rep. RR-8 (July 12, 1991).

64. *See* Barnes, Rango, Burke & Chiarello, *The HIV-Infected Health Care Professional: Employment Policies and Public Health*, 18 Law Med. & Health Care 311 (1990). U.S. Congress, Office of Technology Assessment, *HIV in the Workplace*, 4-10 (November 1991) (hereinafter OTA Study).

65. *Id*. at 320-22; Feldblum, *A Response to Gostin: The HIV-Infected Health Care Professional*, 19 Law Med. & Health Care 128-33 (1991). OTA Study, *supra* n.64, at 14.

66. *See* Feldblum, *Disability Anti-Discrimination Laws and HIV Testing of Health Care Providers*, 2 Courts Health Sci. & L. ___ (1991) (in press) [hereinafter *Disability Anti-Discrimination Laws*]. *See also* OTA Study, *supra* n. 64, at 15 (noting that

it is "questionable whether the courts should use the CDC conclusions if such conclusions have not been accurately based on 'public health' risks.)

67. *Strathie*, 716 F.2d 227.

68. Mantolete v. Bolger, 767 F.2d 1416 (9th Cir. 1985).

69. *Thomas*, 662 F. Supp. 376; *Martinez*, 861 F.2d 1502.

70. *See* 56 Fed. Reg. 35,745 (1991).

71. N.Y. Com. Codes R. & Regs., tit. 10, § 63.9.

72. In two cases not involving AIDS, federal courts noted that the singling out of mentally retarded children with HBV, while nonretarded children were not tested and singled out for HBV, New York State Ass'n for Retarded Children v. Carey, 612 F.2d 644 (2nd Cir. 1979), and the refusal to allow hearing-impaired persons to use equipment that could be dislodged or broken while vision-impaired persons were routinely allowed to use eyeglasses, Strathie, 716 F.2d 227, severely undercut the safety rationales argued by the defendants.

73. ADA, § 103(b); EEOC Regulations, 56 Fed. Reg. 35,745 (1991).

74. EEOC Regulations, 56 Fed. Reg. 35,745 (1991).

75. The regulations and case law under the Rehabilitation Act allow an employer to consider the potential risk of an applicant or employee to himself or herself as part of the determination as to whether the individual is qualified. The standard to be met by the employer, however, is also high in that context. An employer must demonstrate that there is a real probability of substantial harm to the individual. *See* Bentivegna v. United States Dept. of Labor, 694 F.2d 619, 622 (9th Cir. 1982); *Mantolete*, 767 F.2d at 1422.

An employer would not be able to meet this standard with regard to people with HIV disease in most cases. The type of opportunistic diseases that a person with HIV disease may be exposed to exists in every setting; the sources for these diseases exist in the air all the time, and people without depressed immune systems ward them off without difficulty. Thus, the possibility that a person with HIV disease would be more significantly exposed to opportunistic diseases in a particular work setting, as compared to the general outdoors, has no solid basis.

76. 45 C.F.R. § 84.11 (1990).

77. ADA, § 102(c)(2)(A).

78. *Id*. § 102(c)(2)(B).

79. *Id*. § 102(c)(2)(B).

80. *Id*. § 102(c)(3)(A).

81. *Id*. § 102(c)(3)(B).

82. Individuals who may obtain access to the records are: (1) supervisors and managers who need to be informed regarding necessary restrictions on the duties of the employee or regarding necessary accommodations; (2) first aid and safety personnel, if appropriate in the individual case, who may be informed if the disability would require emergency treatment; and (3) government officials investigating compliance with the ADA who may be provided the information. *Id*. § 102(c)(3)(B). The EEOC regulations and accompanying guidance set forth clearly the restrictions and requirements regarding medical examinations and inquiries. *See* 56 Fed. Reg. 35,750-51 (1991).

83. The Ryan White Comprehensive AIDS Resources Emergency Act of 1990 (CARE Act), Pub. L. No. 101-381, does provide some confidentiality protections.

84. ADA, § 102(c)(3)(C).

85. Judiciary Report, *supra* note 34, at 43; *see also* EEOC Regulations, 56 Fed. Reg. 35,751 (1991).

86. Testing for the illegal use of drugs is not considered a medical examination for purposes of the ADA and is, therefore, not subject to the ADA's restrictions on medical examinations. ADA, § 104(b)(d)(1). An employer's allowance under the ADA to test for the illegal use of drugs, however, is qualified by the employer's obligation not to identify (even inadvertently), through a medical examination, the existence of a disability prior to a conditional job offer. For example, persons with HIV disease take specific drugs that may be identified through a drug test. In order to assure compliance with the ADA's preemployment medical provisions, therefore, the legislative reports suggest that employers either assure that the required drug tests identify strictly the illegal use of drugs, or give the drug tests only to applicants who have received a conditional job offer. *See* Judiciary Report, *supra* note 34, at 47; Education and Labor Report, *supra* note 34, at 79-80.

87. *See* Feldblum, *Medical Exams and Inquiries under the Americans with Disabilities Act: A View from the Inside,* ____ Temp. L.Q. _____ (1991) (in press), for analysis of the political realities necessitating this provision of the ADA.

88. *See supra* pp. 274-276 for a discussion of HIV-infected health care workers; *see also Disability Anti-Discrimination Laws, supra* note 66.

89. ADA, § 102(c)(4)(A).

90. Education and Labor Report, *supra* note 34, at 75; *see also* Senate Report, *supra* note 34, at 39; EEOC Regulations, 56 Fed. Reg. 35,751 (1991).

91. *See* 29 C.F.R. § 32.14 (1990).

92. 109 S. Ct. 2115 (1989). The *Wards Cove* decision changed the burden of proof allocation and the "business necissity" standard for cases brought under Title VII of the Civil Rights Act of 1964 in a manner that made it harder for plaintiffs to prevail. By contrast, under the ADA, both the standard for what constitutes "business necessity," as well as the allocation of the burden of proof, is derived from section 504 cases decided prior to *Wards Cove. See* Senate Report, *supra* note 34, at 38; Education and Labor Report, *supra* note 34, at 72. The EEOC Regulations follow this approach, adopting the section 504 standard and burden of proof allocation. *See* 56 Fed. Reg. 35,751 (1991).

93. ADA, § 102(c)(4)(B)-(C).

94. *Id.* § 102(a).

95. *See* Judiciary Report, *supra* note 34, at 35 (*citing* Section 504 regulations, 45 C.F.R. § 84.11(b) (1990)); Education and Labor Report, *supra* note 34, at 55 (same).

96. ADA, § 102(b)(2). The EEOC regulations incorporate these same restrictions. 29 C.F.R. §§ 1630.4(f), 1630.6(b) (1990); 56 Fed. Reg. 35,736-37 (1991).

97. ADA, § 501(c). The EEOC regulations repeat the same exception. 29 C.F.R. § 1630.16(f); 56 Fed. Reg. 35,739 (1991).

98. *Id.* There is no extensive legislative history on the meaning of the term "subterfuge." Two of the main sponsors of the ADA, however, did address this issue briefly. Those statements focus primarily on the fact that "subterfuge" is not to be interpreted as it was by the Supreme Court did in the case of Public Employment Retirement Sys. of Ohio v. Betts, 109 S. Ct. 256 (1989); *see* Statement of Rep. Edwards, 136 Cong. Rec. H4624 (daily ed. July 12, 1990) ("The term 'subterfuge' is used in the ADA simply to denote a means of evading the purposes of the ADA. It does not mean that there must be some malicious intent to evade the ADA on the part of the insurance company or

other organization, nor does it mean that a plan is automatically shielded just because it was put into place before the ADA was passed. Indeed, there is currently a bill moving through Congress to overturn the *Betts* decision and we have no intention of repeating a decision with which we do not agree."); Statement of Rep. Owens, 136 Cong. Rec. H4623 (daily ed. July 12, 1990) ("Questions have been raised to me recently as to whether the term "subterfuge" should be interpreted consistent with the Supreme Court's decision in *Betts*, (1989) in connection with the Age Discrimination in Employment Act of 1967. The answer is no. We use the term "subterfuge" to denote a means of evading the purposes of the ADA. It does not mean that there must be some malicious or purposeful intent to evade the ADA on the part of the insurance company or other organization. It also does not mean, as was the case in *Betts*, that a plan is automatically shielded just because it was put into place before the ADA was passed.... The provision regarding subterfuge...should not... be undermined by a restrictive reading of the term "subterfuge," as the Supreme Court did in *Betts*.").

99. *See* Senate Report, *supra* note 34, at 29 and 84-86; Education and Labor Report, *supra* note 34, at 59 and 136-38; Judiciary Report, *supra* note 34, at 37-38 and 70-71. *See also* Statement of Rep. Owens, 136 Cong. Rec. H4623 (daily ed. July 12, 1990); Statement of Rep. Edwards, 136 Cong. Rec. H4624 (daily ed. July 12, 1990); Statement of Rep. Waxman, 136 Cong. Rec. H4626 (daily ed. July 12, 1990); Statement of Sen. Kennedy, 136 Cong. Rec. S9697 (daily ed. July 13, 1990). The EEOC also provides some guidance, derived from the legislative history and the statutory language. *See* 56 Fed. Reg. 35,746, 35,753 (1991).

100. *See, e.g.,* Education and Labor Report, *supra* note 34, at 136; Statement of Rep. Owens, *supra* note 99, at 4623; Statement of Rep. Edwards, *supra* note 99, at 4624; EEOC Regulations, 56 Fed. Reg. 35,743, 35,751 (1991).

101. *See, e.g.,* Education and Labor Report, *supra* note 34, at 59; Judiciary Report, *supra* note 34, at 38; EEOC Regulations, 56 Fed. Reg. 35,746 (1991).

102. *See* Education and Labor Report, *supra* note 34, at 59; Judiciary Report, *supra* note 34, at 38; EEOC Regulations, 56 Fed. Reg. 35,746 (1991).

103. *See* Judiciary Report, *supra* note 34, at 38. *See also* Statement of Rep. Waxman, *supra* note 99, at 4626; Statement of Rep. Edwards, *supra* note 99, at 4624. This last example seems to indicate that it would not be legitimate to have a blanket exclusion of one particular disability.

104. One possible way of reconciling the ambiguous legislative history, therefore, is to understand the ADA as allowing employers and insurance companies to deny coverage for diseases that have similar actuarial and financial risks. Thus, for example, a company could perhaps deny coverage completely for a particular disease, if it similarly denied coverage for other diseases with similar actuarial and financial risks. Likewise, an employer could place an identical dollar amount cap on all disabilities posing equal financial risks. This would ensure that people with certain diseases that carry social stigma, such as HIV disease, were not unfairly singled out and discriminated against. The EEOC regulations seem to adopt this approach. *See* 56 Fed. Reg. 35,753 (1991) ("[A]n employer...cannot deny a qualified individual with a disability equal access to insurance or subject a qualified individual with a disability to different terms or conditions of insurance based on disability alone, if the disability does not pose increased risks. Part 1630 requires that decisions not based on risk classifications be made in conformity with non-discrimination requirements.").

105. "Front pay" is an amount usually equal to one or two years salary awarded when the victim of discrimination cannot be hired or reinstated and has been unable to secure a job with equivalent pay.

106. S. 1409, 102nd Cong., 1st Sess. (1991).

107. *Id.* § 505.

108. *Id.*

109. *See* Education and Labor Report, *supra* note 34, at 135; Judiciary Report, *supra* note 34, at 69-70; Statement of Rep. Hoyer, 136 Cong. Rec. E1920-21 (daily ed. June 13, 1990).

AUTHORS

PHYLLIS ARNOLD is a Research Instructor in Law at the New York University School of Law. Prior to joining the faculty at NYU, Ms. Arnold was an Assistant Corporation Counsel of the City of New York.

ELIZABETH B. COOPER is Staff Counsel to the ACLU's AIDS Project. Her work at the ACLU is funded by the Skadden Fellowship Foundation.

CHAI R. FELDBLUM is a Visiting Professor of Law at Georgetown University Law Center and the Legislative Counsel to the ACLU's AIDS Project (on leave). Her work was instrumental in Congress's passage of the landmark Americans with Disabilities Act in 1990.

NAN D. HUNTER, an Associate Professor of Law at Brooklyn Law School, was Director of the ACLU's AIDS Project from 1986-1990.

MARK H. JACKSON, a lawyer in New York City, was the Coordinator of the ACLU AIDS Project's Public Policy Program from 1989-1990.

LUIS A. LAVIN is a lawyer in the Government Bureau of the Massachusetts Attorney General's Office.

WILLIAM B. RUBENSTEIN is Director of the ACLU's AIDS Project and a Lecturer in Law at Harvard Law School.

DANIEL SHACKNAI, now a student at Cornell University Law School, was the Research Assistant to the ACLU AIDS Project's Public Policy Program from 1989-1990.